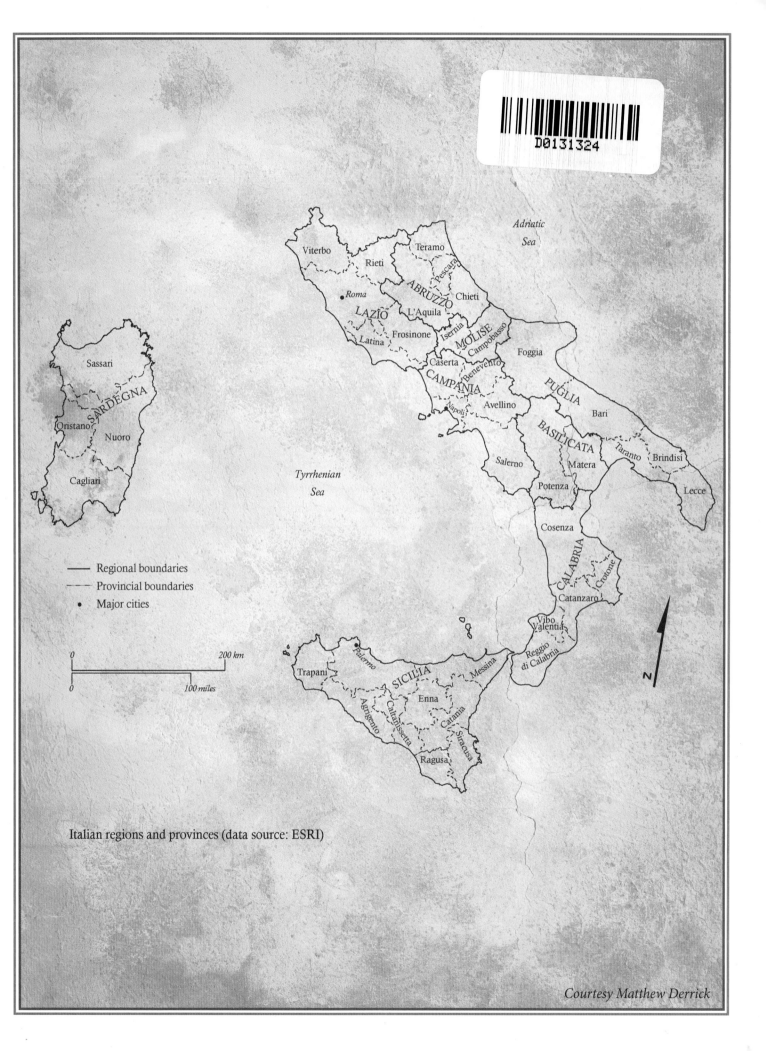

Adriatic
Sea

Viterbo

Teramo

Rieti

Pescara

ABRUZZO

Chieti

Roma

LAZIO

L'Aquila

Isernia

MOLISE

Campobasso

Frosinone

Foggia

Latina

Caserta

Benevento

CAMPANIA

PUGLIA

Napoli

Avellino

Bari

BASILICATA

SARDEGNA

Sassari

Oristano

Nuoro

Salerno

Matera

Taranto

Brindisi

Cagliari

Potenza

Lecce

Tyrrhenian
Sea

Cosenza

— Regional boundaries
- - - Provincial boundaries
• Major cities

CALABRIA

Crotone

Catanzaro

Vibo
Valentia

Reggio
di Calabria

N

0 _____ 200 km

0 _____ 100 miles

Palermo

Trapani

SICILIA

Messina

Agrigento

Enna

Caltanissetta

Catania

Ragusa

Siracusa

Italian regions and provinces (data source: ESRI)

The
Journey
of the
ITALIANS IN
AMERICA

Vincenza Scarpaci

The
Journey
of the
ITALIANS IN
AMERICA

VINCENZA SCARPACI

FOREWORD BY GARY R. MORMINO

PELICAN PUBLISHING COMPANY
2009

*The word "Pelican" and the depiction of a pelican
are trademarks of Pelican Publishing Company, Inc.,
and are registered in the U.S. Patent and Trademark Office.*

Library of Congress Cataloging-in-Publication Data

Scarpaci, Vincenza.
  The journey of the Italians in America / Vincenza Scarpaci ; foreword by
Gary R. Mormino.
     p. cm.
  Includes index.
  ISBN-13: 978-1-58980-245-2 (hardcover : alk. paper) 1. Italian Americans—
History. 2. Italian Americans—Social life and customs. 3. Italian Americans—
Ethnic identity. 4. Immigrants—United States—History. 5. United States—
Civilization—Italian influences. 6. United States—Emigration and immigration.
7. Italy—Emigration and immigration. I. Title.
  E184.I8S26 2008
  973'.0451--dc22
                                       2008018199

Front-jacket photograph:
A Brooklyn Wedding. The author's parents, Antonina Gerardi and Francesco
Scarpaci, celebrated their wedding on April 15, 1928, at Our Lady of Loreto
Church in Brooklyn, New York. The couple met on a blind date, but their
courtship was allowed to continue only with family supervision. Antonina was
born in Brooklyn to parents from Calatafimi, Trapani, and Francesco's parents
brought him to America from Barcellona, Messina, in 1902. Both fathers shared
the cost of the reception, and Francesco's cousin, Bessie Cali, designed and
made the wedding gown. The wedding party, mostly Italian-American family
members and friends, included two non-Italians who Antonina befriended at
work. This Italian national parish church featured the work of architectural
designer Adriano Armezzani, who used builder Antonio Federici's cast-stone
variation of concrete block to create the sculptural decoration for this and other
buildings. Antonio's son, Gaetano Federici, carved statues of Saint Peter and
Saint Paul to embellish the façade of the church. (*Author's collection*)

Frontispiece:
Dedication of Service Flag. Neighborhood residents in Newark, New Jersey's
predominantly Italian-American Fourteenth Ward display a flag honoring the boys
leaving for the service, August 23, 1942. The flag had been blessed at Saint Rocco
Catholic Church, whose bell tower can be seen at the right of the flag. Some estimates
indicate that twelve percent of all those serving in the armed forces were Italian
American, the largest ethnic group in the military. (*Courtesy* Italian Tribune)

Printed in Singapore
Published by Pelican Publishing Company, Inc.
1000 Burmaster Street, Gretna, Louisiana 70053

Contents

Foreword 6
Preface 7
Acknowledgments 8
Introduction 10

Chapter 1. ORIGINS 27
    Life in Italy 29
    The Trip 40

Chapter 2. SPANNING THE MILES 45
    Maintaining Ties 47
    Bringing Italy to America 55

Chapter 3. FINDING A HOME 65

Chapter 4. ITALIANS AT WORK 79
    Civilizing America 82
    Supplying Ethnic Needs 93
    Providing for America 103
    Enriching America 114

Chapter 5. ITALIANS AND THE LAND 132
    On the Land 134
    Attachment to the Land 144
    Agricultural Entrepreneurs 150

Chapter 6. RELIGION AND THE RITES OF PASSAGE 157

Chapter 7. BECOMING AMERICAN 172
    Celebrating America 176
    Responses to Events Here and Abroad 186
    Wartime 192
    Seeking Justice 209
    Tragic Loss 215
    American Life 220
    Socialized Needs 233
    Political Involvement 239
    Interaction 246

Chapter 8. ITALIAN-AMERICAN ISSUES 257
    The Symbol of Columbus 262
    Crime and Discrimination 267

Chapter 9. WHERE IS OUR HERITAGE? 273
    Little Italies 279
    Italian Americans Visit Italy 285
    Italianization of America 291
    Preserving Our Heritage 296

Index 309

FOREWORD

The publication of *The Journey of the Italians in America* represents a joyous event in Italian-American studies. For five decades, Vincenza Scarpaci has kept the faith. As the daughter of Italian immigrants, as a scholar and activist, friend and colleague, she has nurtured the dream of recording and understanding the buoyancy of Italian Americana.

In *The Journey of the Italians in America*, she has brought together hundreds of images of Italian immigrants at work and play. From the quarries of Barre, Vermont, to the cigar factories of Tampa, Florida, from the fruit orchards of Washington to the artichoke farms of Castroville, California, Italians have left their imprint. Hands that once dug coal and shoveled dirt now hold positions of power and influence. But *The Journey of the Italians in America* is not a study of triumphalism and Horatio Alger mobility. It is a study of who we were and why we must never forget.

Vincenza Scarpaci brings to the writers' craft a lifetime of rich experiences and varied vantage points. Born in the Oceanhill section of Brooklyn, New York, the daughter of Frank and Lena Scarpaci, she moved to the south shore of Long Island as a teenager. Educated at Hofstra University, she earned her graduate degrees at Rutgers University, where she studied under the tutelage of one of the great mentors of immigration history, Rudolph Vecoli.

Her doctoral dissertation dealt with Italian immigrants in Louisiana's sugar parishes, 1880-1910. It sparked a lifetime interest in the extraordinarily diverse experience of Italian immigrants.

From 1968 to 1980, Scarpaci taught at Towson State University (now known as Towson University) in Baltimore, Maryland, where she befriended Barbara Mikulski and was exposed to rich varieties of the American ethnic experience. She played a seminal role in the embryonic American Italian Historical Association and helped many young scholars in the new field of ethnic studies. In 1981, she coedited with Robert Harney *Little Italies in North America*.

In the 1980s, Scarpaci encountered the West Coast, where she has since lived. In San Francisco, she discovered SS Peter and Paul Church, and later co-authored a history of the institution. In the 1990s, she and her gentle husband, Peter Rodda, moved to Eugene, Oregon, where she encountered still more chapters of the Italian experience. She has also become a student of the Italian-American odyssey to Florida. Her parents moved to Clearwater, Florida, where her beloved mother Lena turned one hundred in March 2008. *"Cent anni!"*

In *The Journey of the Italians in America*, a lifetime of scholarship and observation are brought together in tender and vivid images. One is reminded of the story of young Oscar Handlin, who wrote in the book *The Uprooted* that he set out to write a history of immigrants in America, only to discover that immigrants *were* American history. So, too, Scarpaci has shown us that Italian immigrants are ingrained in the American experience.

Gary R. Mormino
Frank E. Duckwall Professor of History
University of South Florida, St. Petersburg

PREFACE

How does one begin to illustrate the breadth and depth of Italian lives in America? When I embarked upon this venture, I believed that a book could embrace the fullness and the variety of that experience. I underestimated the complexity and the richness of *la storia*. So I decided to establish priorities. I knew I could not explore every area of Italian settlement, nor could I illustrate every aspect of the story. I included some Canadian images to show the interrelations of the flow to North America. (United States ethnocentric terminology often overlooks the reality that the entire Western Hemisphere is America.) I selected the major themes of the immigrant process, such as life in Italy, the journey, finding a home, work, religion, daily life, and becoming American. But when I examined these themes more closely, I discovered many nuances as they evolved in a setting, which constantly tested how immigrant traditions and expectations would relate to a new environment and social system.

In addition, I chose to explore areas often overlooked in the kaleidoscope of nostalgia that characterizes most picture books. Most accounts focus on the areas of greatest settlement—the northeastern United States. However, the Italian presence touched every corner of America. While most settled in urban, industrial centers, some *contadini* worked and prospered on the land.

Also, the record is incomplete without acknowledging major issues within contemporary Italian America—specifically the role of Columbus in a society that recognizes accountability for past injustice, the issues of group pride, anti-defamation, the discomfort of claiming the less-than-perfect record of individuals, and segments of the immigrant and later generations.

I trusted to my interpretative belief that an account that viewed material or artistic achievement as the greatest good for the greatest number undervalued the millions of Italian Americans whose ordinary lives provided the strength of character and courage to face adversity and uncertainty in a strange environment. Some of the Italian experience in America is not heroic or triumphant—a view of the shadow side of betrayals, domestic abuse, and indecent behavior, which characterized the lives of many immigrants and their descendants, does not dishonor the past. Instead, it is the acceptance of the full array of failings as well as successes that enables a group to understand its past and use these insights to influence the present and plan for the future.

While I was predisposed to predict that my search would uncover a panorama of vivid and provocative stories, I was not prepared for the wealth of material I gathered, which touches the heart of the Italian experience of America. Paul Paolicelli captures the essence of this truth when he wrote, "As for the Italian Americans, our story is as essential to American history as any. Can you imagine an America without Italians? I, for one, would not even want to try. If there is such a thing as 'italicity,' then we have proven it by our American actions. Italian Americans have not only succeeded in this culture, they have often defined the culture itself. . . . Our adventures in this land have enriched both us and it." My hope is that readers will recognize their past and present in these pages and will learn more about the richness of their heritage as it unfolded in America.

*To Rudolph J. Vecoli whose scholarship sparked my curiosity about the
Italian-American experience and whose encouragement and example inspired
a generation of research in immigration history.*

*And to my husband, Peter U. Rodda, whose gentle presence, unwavering support,
and active participation helped to bring this book to fruition.*

ACKNOWLEDGMENTS

Acts of kindness and generosity cannot be measured by a line in a book. If I was to list all the individuals and institutions that have paved my way towards completion of this long labor of love, this section would require countless pages of text. First of all, each credit line not only assigns the source, but also identifies each individual, family, and institution that made my dream a reality. Some contributors spent hours gathering the detail necessary to transform a standard picture caption into a dynamic, informative description. Some granted hospitality or arranged opportunities for me to talk to groups or to meet people who had stories and pictures to share. Some donors opened their door to a stranger in town for a day who sent them scurrying to retrieve items stored away. I cannot begin to describe the kindness, generosity, and good will each donor provided. I especially thank: Rocchina Rusitano, Cookie Curci, Catherine Tripalin Murray, Bobby Tanzilo, Francis Ianni, Justine Mataleno, Andrea Mistretta Quaranta, Barbara DiNucci Hendrickson, Joan Calcaterra Filpula, Norma Webb, Joe Rossi, Al DeCesaris, Catherine Chippari Paige, Loretta Martin, Carmy Buttice, Roger Nincheri, Eleanor Ficele, Nicholas and Andrew Granitto, Laura Sabatino, Dolores Di Rienzo Michalczyk, Gene Fioretti, Maurice Perillo, Dorothy and Virgil Criscola, Lorraine Toye, Marilyn McCann, Sharon Emanuelli, Virginia Bugni, Philip and Romana Antonelli, Steve Montecucco, Vincenza Iannuzzi Cerrato, Ray Martire, Carlo Piccolo, Don Geusaldi, Ray Culos, Sal Vacca, Pierina and Jim Miller, Robert Naccarato, Pauline Regali Kuehnel, Daniel Niemiec, John Panepinto, John Perri, Mike Salardino, Charles Latuda, Tony Castro, Jeff Caracci, Mary Carol Orizotti, Steve Zulpo, Betty Rupanis, Lou Phillips, Paul Morebito, Richard Vannucci, Count Guido Deiro, Ron De Poma, Luigi Charini, Cathie Lucca, Norma Barbieri, Joe Amendola, Lucia Galizia, Remo Minato, Nancy Calinger, Fred Granata, Kerry-Lynne Demarinis Brown, Diane Amato Partain, Barbara Larson, Jim Michelotti, Tina Fostad, Sam Patti, David Venneri, Anne Graziano Piazza, David Ferraro, Jo Saunders, and Greg Chaupette. Everyone extended patience, tolerance, and understanding to an author who found herself sifting through a mountain of images that expanded the standard categories of the immigrant experience into an astounding variety and intricacy of family history.

The richness of the materials included in my book speaks to the depth of the Italian experience in America. In the last thirty years, families have documented their stories as a tribute to their ancestors and as a gift to their descendants. Each of these stories reinforces the wider context of the immigrant experience. The dedication and perseverance of family historians has created a reservoir of perspectives from the heart of the ethnic group. I applaud the efforts of these family history researchers who may be the last people to gather the few remnants of the immigrant experience.

The National Italian American Foundation provided a grant to help cover a portion of the expenses incurred in completing this project. Courtesies of kind came from the Immigration History Research Center; the Utah State Historical Society; The Priest River Museum; The World Museum of Mining; Museo Storico Civico Cuggionese; The Maryland Historical Society; Museo Regionale Dell'Emigrazione "Pietro Conti," Gualdo Tadino, Italia; the Senator John Heinz History Center of Western Pennsylvania; the Oregon Historical Society; and the University of South Florida Tampa Library Special Collections.

Museum and archival staff walked the extra mile in providing supporting information to accompany the photos from their collections. Special mention is due to the following: Don Veasey, Alisa Zahler, Joel Wurl, Daniel Necas, Lucy Berkley, Roberta Arminino, Gianluigi Garavaglia, Maria Sakovitch, Catia Monacelli, Marylyn Cork, Joyce Finnerty, Susan Sherwood, Gabe Donio, Paul Basile, Joan Alagna, Pal Di Julio, Aaron Schmidt, Eric Frazier, Dona DeSanctis, Lucy Bacon, Patricia Bakunas, and Lillian Petroff.

While families and individuals shared their treasured

possessions, colleagues in the field of Italian immigration, such as Nicolas Ciotola, Stephanie Longo, Dominic Candeloro, Ernesto Milani, Andrew Canepa, Joan Saverino, Lou Iorizzo, Frank Cavioli, Jerome Krase, Gary Mormino, Celeste Morello, Al Baccari, Larry DiStasi, and Paul Paolicelli offered to share the materials they've collected for their own research. Without a conceptual framework, even a treasure trove of material lacks direction. My friend and fellow historian Louise Wade challenged me to clarify my efforts to educate and provoke readers to consider each picture on its own and as part of a particular theme. Robert Immordino not only shared his diverse collection of Italian influences in America, but also provided important insights for consideration. I owe a huge debt of gratitude to Gary Mormino who served as a sounding board and reviewed parts of the manuscript. When in the darkest night, Pelican required me to reduce my overly long manuscript, Susan Caperna Lloyd's heroic gift of time and energy made an important difference in expediting the painful cutting process. Louise Westling, George Wickes, and Steven Smith helped me to streamline further the oversize manuscript.

My husband, and best friend, Peter Rodda, served as my fellow traveler—literally into the depths of Montana, Colorado, and New Jersey—but also as a proofreader, record manager, fact checker, and kind critic. So many good friends, Liz Nelson, Priscilla Aronin, Ruth Mordhorst, Fred Kinsman, Denise Segnor, and Alex Kelly offered their skills and willingness to manage spreadsheets, file, and check for errors and other essential requirements for such a wide-ranging project. Sylvia Giustina offered her Italian language skills and fine-tuned proofreading. Annette Pfautz, Bill Reinken, and Don Siemens shared their expertise with this newcomer to the world of applying computer technology to process historical images. The patience and flexibility of Tiffany Mitchell; Aimee Yogi, for the long haul; and, early-on, Schyuler Roche and Laura Berryhill helped to provide structure to the process of tracking donor information and editing and formatting text.

Pelican Publishing Company's faith in my project and especially the efforts of Terry Callaway, Heather Green, and Katie Szadziewicz in transforming my manuscript into this attractive package merits praise.

While I trust that the benefits of the assistance I received are evident in the final product, which consumed my full attention for three years, my hope in "birthing" this book is best articulated in Bartolomeo Vanzetti's parting words, "That last moment belongs to us—that agony is our triumph."

The Italian imprint on North America began with the voyages of Cristoforo Colombo, John Caboto, Amerigo Vespucci, and Giovanni da Verrazzano and continued through the European exploration and settlement, when Italian Jesuits and itinerant craftsmen traveled to the New World for God, adventure, freedom, and economic necessity.

Sailing under the Spanish flag, Columbus established a European outpost in the Western Hemisphere. In 1499, Italian navigator Vespucci and Alonso de Ojeda named the land they saw along the northern end of South America "Venezuela," or "little Venice" in Florentine dialect. Vespucci's accounts of his voyages prompted a German cartographer, Martin Waldseemüller, in 1507, to name the landmass to the south of the Caribbean "America." (A 1511 map by Gerhardus Mercator, a Flemish geographer, extended this name to the northern continent.) The Venetian John Cabot (born Giovanni Caboto) sighted Newfoundland in 1524 and claimed it for King Henry VII of England. In 1524, Verrazzano, sailing for Francis I of France, was the first European to sail up the east coast from North Carolina past Cape Cod to Newfoundland. His descriptions of New York harbor, his account of the Native American population, and encouraging reports about the agricultural potential of the land along the coast whetted the appetite of those seeking colonial riches.

During the sixteenth and seventeenth centuries, European expeditions and settlement projects included Italian priests and attracted immigrants with special skills. Italians in the Spanish Jesuit order traveled across North America (including Mexico), establishing missions. In 1539, Marcos de Niza, a Franciscan missionary, explored Arizona and New Mexico for Spain, and communicated with the Zuni and Pima. Between 1687 and 1711, an Italian Jesuit, Eusebio Kino, traveled extensively in Mexico, Arizona, and California, mapping the land, establishing missions, and introducing European crops and the practice of raising cattle.

Another Italian Jesuit, Gregorio Mengarini, worked in 1841 with the Indians in part of the northwestern territory, what is now Montana. He not only ministered to the Indians, but also rendered their language, Salish, into a Salish or Flathead grammar in 1861.

Henry de Tonti, a soldier born in Gaeta, Latina, accompanied the French Canadian government's expedition in 1679. He braved the dangers of the wilderness to travel westward across the Great Lakes region and then journeyed with Robert Cavelier, sieur de LaSalle, down the length of the mighty Mississippi. (Tonti and LaSalle erected a column at the mouth of the Mississippi River in 1682, claiming the territory for France.)

A sprinkling of Italian craftsmen also crossed the Atlantic in the seventeenth century to take advantage of the demand for skilled workers. Many were invited, such as the Italian glassblowers who settled in Jamestown. Early Italian arrivals paralleled the story of the Pilgrims. In 1657, a group of Italian Protestants, the Waldenses, left the Piedmont region and arrived in New Amsterdam. They sought refuge from religious persecution in the settlement they established at New Castle, Delaware. One hundred Italian indentured servants were brought in 1768 to raise indigo plants in New Smyrna, Florida. In 1701, William Alburtus (Alberti) settled in Maidenhead (now Lawrence), New Jersey, where he purchased five hundred acres of land. Six years later, he moved to Amwell, where he served as constable from 1722 to 1726. In the years before the American Revolution, Philip Mazzei, a friend of Thomas Jefferson and Benjamin Franklin, offered his political ideas and European plants and agriculture to the nation's founders.

In the early records of the English colonies, there are traces of Italian musicians, figure carvers, language teachers, wine merchants, and distinguished visitors. For example, Giovanni Gualdo, a wine merchant, as well as a composer and conductor, arrived in Philadelphia via London in 1767. These Italian encounters increased with the establishment of the United States. The Milanese botanist Count Luigi Castiglioni traveled through the new nation between 1785 and 1787, and his observations on the thirteen states, the national government, the Constitution, and, of course, the interesting plants he saw, were published in 1790. Lorenzo DaPonte, Mozart's librettist, came to New York from Venice in 1805 and taught Italian and Italian literature at Columbia University. Pietro Bacchi, a Sicilian scholar exiled for his revolutionary political activities, accepted a teaching position in Spanish and Italian at Harvard College.

In 1822, Giacomo Constantino Beltrami explored Minnesota, looking for the headwaters of the Mississippi River. Businessmen, such as Francesco Grossi, were selling ice cream in Toronto, Canada, in the 1830s. And in 1862, John Owen Dominis, the son of an Italian-American sea captain from Boston who had settled in Hawaii in 1819, married Queen Liliuokalani, the last reigning monarch of that nation before it was annexed to the United States.

Early Italians included artists and musicians. Italian

sculptors, such as Giuseppe Ceracchi, traveled and worked in the new nation during the 1790s. Ceracchi executed portrait busts of George Washington and John Adams, and, while in Philadelphia, tutored American-sculptor William Rush. Other Italian sculptors who came to America were Giovanni Andrei and Giuseppe Franzoni. They came at the invitation of Thomas Jefferson to do work on the Capitol. Earlier, Jefferson had employed Italian marble cutters to build the University of Virginia, and he was responsible for recruiting fourteen Italian musicians to form the first marine band. Italian operas, opera houses built especially for Italian opera, and Italian singers became part of the early cultural life of urban America.

In education, Giovanni Grassi, an Italian Jesuit, became president of Georgetown University; Giovanni Nobili and Michael Accolti established Santa Clara College in California; and Joseph Cataldo, after an active life spent in Montana, Idaho, Wyoming, Oregon, Alaska, and Washington (1867-1928), founded Gonzaga University in Spokane, Washington.

Records from the colonial period are scanty, and each state government handled its own immigration records. It was not until 1820 that the federal government began recording its own statistics, but even then, it was difficult to maintain accuracy because of the multipolitical units of a disunited, diverse Italy. Between 1820 and 1865, approximately seventeen thousand Italians entered North America. They settled mainly along the East Coast but some went west, literally opening the way for future generations. Italian seamen reached the West Coast in the 1830s, and the lure of gold attracted a larger number in 1849. Most were from Genoa, and their government, the Kingdom of Sardinia, sent consul Colonel Leonetto Cipriani to San Francisco in 1850.

These early pioneers established a link to Italy that reflected the economic culture of Italy and the political turmoil of a divided nation. As North American cities flourished, the tastes of the citizenry dwelt on the fashions, designs, architecture, and art forms of Europe. A look at the census of most early nineteenth-century North American cities shows Italian hairdressers, figure makers, language and music teachers, marble carvers, ship chandlers, and purveyors of fancy imported goods. Their major motivation for emigrating was the lure of economic opportunity, but some were political fugitives exiled because of their participation in organizations outlawed by the reigning princes or because of the failed revolutions of 1830 and 1848.

Yet, even this early outpouring of Italian migration loses significance against the larger pageant of population movement. For centuries, Italian seamen, explorers, merchants, and workers had traveled as far as China and as close as North Africa. When Columbus set forth on his voyages, colonies of Italians were living in Lisbon, Seville, Marseilles, and Constantinople. Even the early explorers labored for foreign monarchs as did the Italian craftsmen who traveled to the swamplands along the Baltic and transformed the area into the glittering St. Petersburg during the reign of Peter the Great.

It was the combination of the Risorgimento (unification), the mid-nineteenth-century transformation of Italian industry and agriculture, and overpopulation that sent thousands of Italians away from their homes. Outside Italy the availability of cheap transportation, recruitment, and incentives offered by foreign governments and the invisible hand of capitalism combined to match those in search of work with those in need of workers.

Large-scale emigration from Italy began in the early nineteenth century from the north. Emigrants traveled from Lombardia, Emilia-Romagna, and Veneto to South America, Argentina, and Brazil especially, but also to Uruguay. These countries gave government subsidies to encourage settlement, mainly for agricultural colonies. Italian workers from northern Italy had traveled seasonally to jobs in France, Switzerland, Germany, and even Tunis, but some later switched from this seasonal movement to take advantage of the inverted climate of South America—picking crops there during the Italian winter. Italian involvement in Latin-American life ran the gamut from Giuseppe Garibaldi fighting for the liberation of Uruguay to the predominantly Italian cosmopolitan cities of Sao Paolo and Buenos Aires. Italian immigrants made up nearly half of all arrivals in Brazil, and they were the largest group of foreigners in Argentina. Compared to this, the over four million in North America who arrived between 1820 and 1920 takes on a different perspective. In North America, the immigrant population remained a small percentage of the native born. Unlike Argentina, where a public election was held to determine whether the official language of the country should be Spanish or Italian, North America maintained the customs and traditions of the Anglo-Saxon language. Of course, during times of economic uncertainty and social unrest, the establishment believed itself in a state of siege as thousands of foreigners entered. Their numbers, however, did not translate into the power needed to challenge the social order; in fact, most wished to join that order, not to change it.

The unification of Italy, in 1861, tipped the emigrant flow from north to south. Laws prohibiting emigration had been strictly enforced in the Kingdom of the Two

Sicilies. The easing of restrictions, coupled with such factors as population growth, insufficient and ill-used land resources, and inadequate economic development, as well as individual motives, accelerated the exodus.

While unification had accompanied industrial development in the north, the Piedmontese rulers did not extend their economic program into the south. The freeing of Italians from foreign domination and local oppression did not signal the end of inequities or injustice. The large latifundia owned by the church and foreign nobility merely changed hands. Italy's entry into the world of industrial manufacture led to competition with other European countries. Tariffs acted as barriers to reduce outside competition, and yet they were not limited to manufactured goods, but also placed on agricultural exports—a mainstay of the south's economy. Unification also introduced a more efficient internal tax system that exacted revenues from all regions but did not share these revenues on an equitable basis. Therefore, the tax system further drained the resources of the south.

As conditions in the south contributed to an outward population flow, again the destinations varied. While the majority of emigrants headed across the Atlantic Ocean to North America, some settled in South America. Others traveled to Australia, North Africa, and other parts of Europe. This southern explosion did not signal an end to emigration from northern Italy. Emigrants still left but in smaller numbers.

As the momentum for migration increased, other factors were at work directing Italians to North America. Technological improvements in transatlantic transportation and the growth of trade between North America and Europe also played important roles. By the 1870s, steamships crossed the Atlantic in ten days. Trade routes that linked American ports with Europe became conduits for human traffic.

The Italian ports of Genoa, Naples, and later Trieste and Palermo, featured dramatic departure scenes daily. The emigration business employed more than ten thousand people in Italy. Ticket agents, boardinghouses, dockside hucksters, draymen, recruitment agents, manifesto printers, as well as stevedores, food and ship suppliers, seamen, government inspectors, and port officials represented an expanding industry.

The turning point for Italian immigration to America was 1880. While some seventy thousand came to North America between 1866 and 1879, close to four million arrived between 1880 and 1914. The high point of Italian immigration to America occurred between 1900 and 1910, when more than two million entered. Most entered through the port of New York—ninety-seven percent of those arriving in 1900 entered via Ellis Island, and of those Italians who arrived in Boston, Philadelphia, and New Orleans, fifty-four percent gave New York as their destination. Of course, not all immigrants remained in New York City. At least two-thirds of the Italians bound for Canada also arrived in New York. New York, like Naples, developed an industry designed to provide the accommodations and services necessary to expedite this human traffic. Men, women, and children paused there en route to the hinterlands to join family or work crews in mines and factories. In 1907 alone, as many as 285,000 Italians arrived in America.

Official statistics can do no more than suggest the implications of such a population movement. They paint a broad stroke across the canvas of history without acknowledging the variety it encompasses. For example, the official count was inaccurate. Before the unification of Italy, many Italians lived under foreign governments. Some immigrated first to other European countries, then to America and were listed under those jurisdictions. Some entered illegally. Many returned to Italy either on a seasonal basis or permanently—estimates range as high as one-half.

Migration chains developed in many ways. Men between the ages of fourteen and forty-five made up the bulk of the late nineteenth-century migration. They were recruited to work in mines, on railroads, in factories, and they were directed to locales by steamship agents and by *paesani* who wished to enlarge their commercial investments. Many towns in North America were so much alike that newcomers, with a limited knowledge of geography, had a hazy view of the nation in which they would eventually build their homes. Yet, they were somehow able to find a neighborhood in Chicago or a mining camp in New Mexico.

The majority of immigrants were agrarian. In America, they transferred *la zappa*, or "the hoe," to the pick-and-shovel work required to build the communication infrastructure. The Italian contribution to the refining of America also derives from the immigrant labor used to build reservoirs, streetcar lines, subways, railroads, and buildings, to pave streets, and to install and repair sewage lines.

While the unskilled immigrant contributed his strength and his labor, the skilled artisans—stone-cutters, masons, bricklayers, tailors, carpenters—and horticulturists provided experience and skill. When expert building craftsmen were required, North America looked to Italian artisans to do the ornate marble decorations on its public buildings, such as the South Carolina State House, and the mosaic tile grandeur of the indoor Roman pool at William Randolph Hearst's castle at San Simeon, California.

The immigrant population clustered in the industrial Northeast, where the combination of jobs and established colonies offered a semblance of *ambiente*. However, across the continent smaller circles of settlement developed, many by chance, such as the people from Carunchio, Chieti, who settled the community of White Cloud in northeastern Kansas. Robert Severo described the settlement in America of his ancestors as follows: "Always, I was told, they went because they had a friend, but surely there was somebody at one point who went and who had no friend."

However small in number, Italian immigrants established their presence. Wherever they settled in cities or towns, the Italians' custom of intensive agriculture to provide for their own family and for local markets expanded the truck-farming industry and introduced new vegetables to the American table. *Contadini* skills at raising and marketing fruits and vegetables created a renaissance in the wholesale and retail trades. Produce market areas from Baltimore and New Orleans to Detroit, Kansas City, and Seattle were dominated by the immigrant entrepreneur. In most communities, Italian peddlers sold vegetables and fruit door-to-door.

Italian immigrants in search of work or adventure fanned out across this country. Throughout the world, Italian seamen transported goods from one port to another. They shipped coal from Wales, marble to Baltimore, and wine from France. Each American port city experienced this transient Italian traffic. Over time, some Italian immigrants who read or heard about opportunities in the American West traveled directly to places like Albuquerque, New Mexico. Most of this fanning-out resulted from the location of work. Labor agents, operating in Italy, New York, Chicago, and Montreal, and in small mining, railroad, and factory towns across North America, channeled this human stream to work sites. Agents linked job seekers with employers. Federal and state governments and private entrepreneurs advertised, encouraged, and even paid fees to acquire a labor force. Many men from Italy arrived in port cities with tags attached to their clothes, indicating their North American destination, the place where they would work.

For example, the story of the Picatti family reflects a combination of chance and choice in migration. Gabriel Picatti and his family traveled from Rocca Canavese, Torino, to mining sites in Africa and Turkey where he worked in the early 1890s. Terrified by the violent conflicts then endemic in the Ottoman Empire, his wife, Maria, took their children and returned to Rocca Canavese. When Gabriel rejoined his family, his children speculate "that he pulled out a mining map of America and decided to go so far that Grandma could never run home again." And Roslyn, Washington, filled the bill.

For some immigrants, the work experience resulted in settlement. It was usually the combination of work location, living costs, and the need to be among *paesani*, and a response to the indifference or hostility of the American population, that fostered the growth of Little Italies. Concentrations of Italian population enabled the development and growth of ethnic business: butchers kept goats for Easter; grocers imported olive oil from the region favored by clientele; saloons sold beer and wine and provided tables for Italian card games; and boardinghouses often expanded into simple *casalingo* (homemade) restaurants, offering Italian dishes.

In some locales, *paese* (village) or family identification was reflected in housing patterns. *Calabresi* lived on one street, *Napolitani* on the next. In some cases, all the apartments in a building were rented out to relatives and their friends. Many boarding arrangements developed in a similar fashion. Apartments and houses were reconfigured to permit socioeconomic activities transported from Italy and adapted to America. While social aspects of immigrant life began at the basic level of food and shelter, it then moved into the areas of religion, business, work, and recreation.

Although the Italians brought with them an attachment to the *paese* world they left behind, they were able to adjust to the different forms it took in America. Grocery store owners, insurance salesmen, and barbers learned the dialects of their patrons; membership in recreational clubs and church organizations crossed *paese* lines; inter-*paese* and regional ties grew as children attended the same schools; women shopped at the same stores; and adults worked together and enjoyed each other's company as they spent warm summer evenings together. The larger world of the Italian immigrants did not erase their primary *paese* identity, but rather expanded it to include the new world in which they found themselves.

For most immigrants, life *oltremare,* or beyond the sea, was harsh and unpredictable. The predominantly male sojourners traveled to America to earn money, then return home. Those with skills could choose a locale and turn their talents into a comfortable living. But many artisans found that the American industrial system placed them in a restrictive economic setting. For example, a shoemaker from Bari ran a machine in a Lynn, Massachusetts, factory and his skill earned him more than the untrained workers, but he had little claim to the social status he had enjoyed in Italy. The tailor joined the ranks of the garment industry, where clothes were mass-produced. Only a few could seek the quality custom tailoring that catered to the upper classes. Produce merchants, food importers, and truck farmers began in modest, marginal ways, going from door-to-door, selling goods at prices their American competitors disdained, seeking new products, and facing the challenge of marginality. For some, success echoed that of Horatio Alger. Immigrants who owned produce stores went into wholesale merchandising; those who were hucksters opened freight-hauling businesses; and those involved in marginal truck farming developed agricultural cooperatives. The majority of the immigrants earned modest incomes with long hours and family assistance. Pushcart peddlers ripened bananas in their cellars, and the children of the iceman rose at five in the morning to help load their father's wagon.

Pick-and-shovel men traveled to shape-ups at construction sites in Baltimore the same way day laborers congregated in the town piazza in Italy. Others sought the help of fellow townsmen or *padroni* (labor bosses) who supplied railroad companies, mine companies, and factories with workers. The difficulty of not knowing English made the *padrone* a middleman (sometimes also banker, letter writer, ticket agent, or saloon or boardinghouse keeper), an important link in the immigrant chain.

Immigrants laboring in the slate quarries of eastern Pennsylvania; the smelting industries at Butte, Montana; Trail, British Columbia; and Pueblo, Colorado; the mines in southern Illinois; Kellogg, Idaho; and Jerome, Arizona; lumber camps in McCloud, California, and Blairmore, Alberta; and railroad construction work in distant outposts like Stampede Pass, Washington, and Terry, Montana, also suffered from loneliness, exploitation, and bone-tiring, dangerous work.

The women who emigrated with their families or to join husbands found employment near their homes. Depending on the location and the availability of work, Italian women contributed to their family income. In Italy, work for women was restricted to the home, to the immediate family, or *paese*-supervised occupations,

such as the silk workers of Lombardy and the women farm laborers in Apulia. However, in North America, the economy based on cash forced many to enter the work force. In Buffalo, New York, women worked in the canneries outside the city; throughout the truck-farming areas across America they helped harvest crops; in Providence, Rhode Island, they worked in factories or at home making jewelry; in Chicago, women shelled and sorted nuts, made candy, and worked in the men's clothing industry; in New York City, women made artificial flowers and children's toys and finished clothing at home or in factory lofts; and in Tampa, Florida, Italian women worked in the cigar industry. Most often they helped their entrepreneur husband, many shouldering the same workload as their husbands in family-run grocery stores, butcher shops, bakeries, and restaurants; some of these women ran the family business while their husbands worked elsewhere.

Children, too, were part of this economic enterprise. In Italy, compulsory education, when established and enforced, provided three years of rudimentary instruction. Many immigrants were semiliterate. The rate of illiteracy for women was higher, since education was considered an unnecessary luxury for most. In America, much of this traditional attitude continued. Most children left school as early as the law allowed so that they could begin work. Parents were caught between the lure of free education and the economic necessities of life. Some chose the former, making many sacrifices to help their children to further their education. Some took advantage of evening schools; others helped in their family business while they attended high school and college. Others, instead "graduated" into ownership of the family business.

This harsh life, far removed from a familiar landscape and family surroundings, heightened the tensions of daily work. The emerging industrial giants treated labor as another cost in production. They paid the lowest wages they could and usually preferred quantity to quality, which allowed them to dismiss workers who questioned long hours, low pay, and unsafe working conditions. However, mutual-assistance organizations developed at many work sites, such as the mining camp at Dawson, New Mexico. They provided benefits for widows and orphans, funeral arrangements, and some aid for those who became sick or injured. Some of these societies reflected the occupations of their members. For example, San Francisco, California, and Gloucester, Massachusetts, each had a society for fishermen, and Baltimore, Maryland, had one for tailors. Others reflected the *paese* or region of Italy, such as the Contessa Entellina Society of New Orleans, the Matrice Club of Cleveland, or the Lega Toscana of New York. Some combined region and type of work, as in the Società Lombarda di MS Bracciante (laborers) in Murphysboro, and later, Herrin, Illinois. These groups offered social activities for their members, ranging from shore parties along the Chesapeake Bay, favored by Baltimore's Italians, to the annual August picnic of the Dante Alighieri Society in the Sunrise Hartville area of Wyoming. These societies helped to make the transition to life in America much easier for the Italian immigrant.

One of the characteristics most noted about Italian immigration was the predominance of males. Essentially, the movement to North America simply extended the seasonal economic pattern long established by workers traveling all over Europe. Those men, who left alone, with a relative, or in a group of *paesani*, sought employment as a way to maintain their families' well being. The wages they earned were sent back or brought back to the *paese*. Their voyage, however far, still bound them to the community they left behind. The transition from sojourner to settler was a subtle one. The choice to move to America was not always a conscious decision, merely the acceptance that the wages earned in North America shored up the dependent family in the *paese*. Sojourners traveled back and forth fully expecting to return permanently to the *paese*. The process varied. Some fathers introduced their sons to the commuting arrangement; brothers, cousins, uncles, *paesani* did the same. In this way, the American experience was shared and assumed a communal aspect. The process extended to sisters, wives, and mothers when the family reassembled in North America. Some immigrants acknowledged that they felt more than an economic tie to North America. They responded to the variety of work opportunities and the promise of future advancement for their children.

But the decision to leave Italy was never simple. Many families never reunited. Some families were abandoned or forgotten. Individual immigrants, who experienced difficulties adjusting to the cultural crossing, were unable to reconcile the differences and feelings of discomfort and insecurity. They longed for the familiar that was lost and were repelled by the strangeness of their new environment. Most accounts of immigration, however, stress the positive aspects: the valiant struggle, the brief reverses, and then the long-sought-after victory—the purchase of a house, the economic security of steady work, and the achievements of the children. The stories brush past the reality of daily marginality, the sense of loss, the uncertainty of one's choice, the fear of discrimination and hostility, the frustration of not having the choice to go back, the alienation from other family members (usually American-born children), and *paesani* who appeared to repudiate all attachment to the language and customs in order to gain acceptance as Americans. Selective family memories filter out the immigrants who returned to Italy indigent, without hope, defeated by the system.

Some immigrants cushioned the adjustment cycle by encapsulating themselves within their re-created *paese* environment. In the large Italian-American settlements, entire sections seemed to resemble Naples more than the New World. The Little Italies of North America provided for some a cultural continuity, and within these locales, the concentration of immigrants supported a way of life that maintained a cultural, economic, and social identity. Spoken Italian and dialects filled the streets; familiar smells of cheese, salami, and garlic wafted on the breeze; street music was provided by the hurdy-gurdy and the organ grinder; women compared produce purchased from a huckster's cart; and posters announced Italian theater and opera performances or proclaimed the street entertainment of puppet shows. While the majority of the citizens in the Little Italies of North America lived in the crowded substandard housing abandoned by native-born Americans—usually in the oldest sections of the cities—their social structure reflected a cross-section of the immigrant population. The successful professional might not actually live there, but he maintained his office in the area; the businessmen, bankers, merchants, skilled craftsmen, and day laborers re-created a holistic community. Large numbers of people sometimes led to the establishment and maintenance of Italian churches served by Italian clergy.

Even in some rural areas and small towns, such as St. Helena, North Carolina; Tontitown, Arkansas; Newburgh, New York; and Wood River, Illinois, an Italian population introduced the character of *italianità*, the expression of Italianness, in a limited but spirited way, from the celebration of a patron saint's day to the introduction of new crops, intensive agriculture, and *paesani* fraternity. While to some native-born Americans, Little Italies appeared to be recreations of the Old World towns, this was not true. First, some non-Italians lived in every Little Italy; second, each immigrant concentration contained people from a different *paese, città, provincia,* and *regione;* and third, distinctions were made within the community according to how long one had been in North America. (Those who had arrived earlier often appeared American to the newly arrived immigrants.) Therefore, the multifaceted nature of Italian-American life prevented homogeneity. Institutionalized ethnicity promoted by fraternal organizations, religious activities, and the establishment of social agencies, such as hospitals, orphanages, schools, sports clubs, and immigrant aid societies, provided a veneer to cover the layered composite underneath.

Most important, not everything Italian that distinguished the immigrant from the native—language, food, dress, traditions, religion, and values—could remain immune to the surrounding culture. North America's mass-produced and inexpensive clothing, furniture, and household items influenced individuals, but, while the pots and pans in every home might be standard items, the ever-present cheese grater, ravioli cutter, *pizzelle* (cookies) iron, or *chitarra* (pasta cutter) reflected Old World continuity.

The Italian immigrant who attended mass and participated in church activities discovered that Roman Catholicism in America reflected the religious traditions of the Irish Catholics, who dominated the hierarchy. The religious expression and form of worship followed by the Italian immigrant appeared flamboyant, excessive, and pagan to other Roman Catholics. Street parades, in which a particular saint's statue was carried on the shoulders of the crowd and money offerings pinned to the statue's garments, where bands played stirring dramatic music, and vendors cooked and sold food and drink, shocked the sensibilities of a clergy who believed that dignity and respect required restrained and orderly devotion, with the priest guiding the faithful in demeanor as well as worship.

Naturally, Italian immigrants did not feel welcome in this atmosphere. The newcomers could hear their masses in Italian, but they were often forced to attend them in church basements. Even those American-born clergymen sensitive to the problems of the newcomers had mixed feelings about separate services conducted in foreign languages by foreign priests. They preferred to encourage rapid assimilation through the process of religion. Their reluctant acceptance of national (nationality-oriented) parish churches was based on the assumption that the Americanization of the second and third generations would soon end the linguistic and cultural differences between Catholics. Outside the national parishes, some neighborhood parishes requested the assignment of an assistant pastor of Italian background to conduct special services on the days of their favorite saints. Special orders of Italian religious men and women were formed to

minister to the spiritual needs of the immigrants. The Salesians, Scalabrinians, Sisters of the Sacred Heart, and the Filippini were the most prominent.

For many Italian men, particularly for the southern Italians, the church, both in Italy and America, filled few worldly needs. Most men attended church only on special occasions, such as to serve as a godparent or to get married. In southern Italy, the church had controlled vast estates on which the *contadini* labored, and even though the local clergy dispensed little charity, they expected donations or in-kind payment for every service rendered. The resentment against this situation in Italy did not lessen in America, where the clergy also expected the congregation to support the expenses of the parish. Men who sacrificed simple comforts to send money to families in Italy rejected the notion of weekly contributions to the church.

The hostility toward the organized church and a low rate of church attendance did not mean that the immigrant lacked religious devotion. Individually, the majority of men, as well as women, considered themselves Christians. They expressed their faith in their own manner, especially during feast-day celebrations, by fasting or by lighting devotional candles in church or at home.

In America, Protestant missionaries interpreted Italian religious behavior as a sign of disinterest in Catholicism. Believing the immigrant sections ripe for proselytizing efforts, they established missions, day schools, and health services in the Little Italies. Their staffs of volunteers reflected the middle class—sincerely religious and dedicated native-born American women who wished to bring both orderliness and spiritual comfort to the immigrant. The missions served milk and cookies, and sometimes meals, to the children who attended. They offered classes in childcare, sewing, English, music, and the Bible. Whether Methodist, Presbyterian, Baptist, or Episcopal, the missions attempted to obtain Italian pastors, or men who spoke Italian, for this work. Italian-immigrant pastors joined their North American brethren in ministering to the immigrant population, offering social services as well as spiritual guidance. For the most part, they seemed to teach by example—to dispense Christian charity and help without exacting payment or the promise of conversion. In each of the major cities, small Protestant congregations were formed, consisting of immigrants grateful for the personal care provided by the missions and interested in a religion that stressed the participation and understanding of the laity. Although many second-generation Italians remember receiving financial aid (clothes or shoes), attending play school, or enjoying cookies and milk in the Protestant mission, they accepted the aid without adopting the religion. Those few immigrants who did convert formed loyal and dedicated congregations.

Although Roman Catholicism was the established faith of the Italian nation, and most immigrants felt some allegiance toward it, not every Italian identified with its teachings. A small group of political radicals, anarchists, communists, and many socialists condemned organized religion as a form of exploitation. In North America, these anti-clerics would speak out against church activity when it seemed to dull political consciousness. A priest who counseled his flock not to strike or join a union would set the political critics into action.

Until the late 1930s, when Benito Mussolini extended Hitler's anti-Semitism into Italy, few Italian Jews had immigrated to North America. Prominent Italians and anti-Fascists, such as Enrico Fermi and Arturo Toscanini, whose wives were Jewish, exiles Emilio Segré and Salvador E. Luria, and others such as Max Ascoli, found refuge in the United States.

Wherever Italians settled, but especially in the Little Italies of North America, Old World traits were transplanted onto the new soil. The maintenance of these customs varied according to the different environments and adaptations and mutations resulted. Italian street vendors sold chestnuts and clams and produce from boxes strapped to their shoulders or pushcarts or wagons. Open-air markets operated daily in crowded immigrant sections. Women shopped every day, seeking bargains and arguing about the prices of items in a way reminiscent of the Old World, but in North America, they would buy items missing from *paese* markets, such as bananas and inexpensive, mass-produced clothing and shoes. And their preference for cheeses, olive oil, canned tomatoes, and macaroni, in turn, created opportunities for Italian importers and distributors. Salesmen representing import houses traveled to Italian communities where they supplied family-owned groceries with the products desired by customers. *Padroni* or individual entrepreneurs often followed work crews to railroad construction sites, where they established commissaries. A Baltimore man operated such a business for Italian miners in Keyser, West Virginia; an immigrant in Donaldsonville, Louisiana, drove his wagon from sugar plantation to sugar plantation selling Italian products to the immigrant cane workers.

Whenever possible, immigrants continued to raise or make the foodstuffs they preferred. In urban backyards and open lots and along railroad tracks, Italians raised whatever fruit and vegetables the climate would

support. In rural areas or in the outskirts of cities, some immigrants purchased land to grow vegetables to sell. Some built brick ovens in their backyards to bake bread, or took their homemade dough to the ovens of the local bakers. Many women made their macaroni at home. Before the holidays, merchants might order special items to be shipped directly from Naples or Genoa or via New York, Philadelphia, or Boston. Some immigrants asked relatives or *paesani* still in Italy to send crates of lemons, cheeses, olive oil, and figs. At holiday time, Italian and non-Italian farmers not only found buyers for their goats and lambs, but also customers interested in purchasing a pig to make sausage and cured meats in their homes.

Daily life for the typical immigrant family centered around the home, whether it was a tenement apartment or a modest one-family house. Coffee and milk with hard bread or toasted bread were served for breakfast to children and adults. Since the workingmen left early, their wives awakened at five o'clock to purchase cold cuts for the sandwiches their men would eat at work. Children also rose early to help with chores, such as lighting the furnace, loading their father's wagon, or delivering the bread he baked. Those women, who stayed up late every night finishing clothes, making paper flowers, decorating hats, making lace, and so on, faced a full day of routine household duties. Washing clothes and sheets for a family of five by hand could take an entire day. Many tasks were interrupted as the day progressed, such as when the children returned from school for lunch, for a trip to shop for dinner, or for the preparation of dinner.

Many children worked after school, helping merchants load carts, collecting rags and newspapers for sale, or helping in the family business. One second-generation man, whose father ran a butcher shop, said that at age sixteen, his father would leave the entire operation of the shop in his hands. Some families depended strongly on the few pennies their children earned, and one immigrant son remembers how his mother waited each night for him to bring the pennies he earned from his paper route so she could shop for the family dinner. Children also helped their mothers with work at home—finishing clothes, making flowers, and so on. They threaded needles, removed bastings, sewed buttons, and picked up and delivered bundles of clothing to the contract shops in the neighborhood.

Recreational choices were governed by income and work schedules. Most North-American workers labored six days a week, usually ten hours a day. Most evenings were spent resting from the day's toil. In the summer, visiting with neighbors on stoops, steps, porches, or park benches was the basic form of socialization. Relatives and *paesani* visited each other on Sundays or dropped in for a glass of wine or coffee during the week. Also on Sundays families often took streetcars to the nearest park or recreational area to eat outdoors. Urban families also went on excursions to the country to pick *cardone, cicoria* (respectively wild artichoke stalks and chicory or dandelion leaves), and blackberries. Men played cards and drank wine, and some immigrants joined their friends in the neighborhood saloon. Women often mended clothes, crocheted, and chatted. At the immigrant theaters, Italians could hear Shakespeare in Italian or a variety show featuring the character comedian Farfariello, whose sketches reflected immigrant life. In the large cities, Italian opera was part of the cultural life, and Italian immigrants purchased the least expensive opera tickets to cheer their favorite singers. Many Italian opera stars, conductors, and musicians toured North America.

Those immigrants who belonged to mutual benefit, *paese*, or fraternal associations attended monthly meetings and social events. The death of an association's member meant attendance by all at the funeral. These groups also joined in the celebration of Columbus Day, religious *feste* or, in some areas, Pioneer Days. They wore their organizational regalia—usually sashes in green, white, and red with the emblem of their society—as they marched behind the bands, made up of professional and amateur musicians, including Italian immigrants, which played operatic airs and marches.

Throughout the nineteenth century, the predominant social theory in America focused on the melting pot, and institutions such as churches and schools hoped to hasten the transition from Italian immigrant to American. Starting at Ellis Island (or Castle Garden, New York's immigration reception station before Ellis Island), the immigrant began to incorporate American ideals, customs, clothes, and language, which led to a unique culture, one that used the contributions of the immigrants to create a new system. Hidden somewhere in the American culture were the bits and pieces taken from the European immigrants. The American culture homogenized these components so that no one of its parts could be identified as foreign. In public schools, Italian children, like their Czech, German, Greek, or Finnish schoolmates, were encouraged by word as well as example to give up the traditions of their parents. It was stressed that American ways, from hygiene to history, were better, and native-born American classmates, unaccustomed to the ways of other groups, expressed their ignorance through ridicule. Immigrant children

were embarrassed by the differences, and most came to believe that their parents were backward and ignorant because they did not follow American customs. The pressure to conform gained momentum because the official policy of the school system coincided with that of native-born American schoolteachers.

Most second-generation Italian children used English to hide their teenage secrets from their parents. Many understood the Italian spoken by their parents but spoke only English. Author Mario Puzo wrote about the conflict he experienced in his New York City childhood when he discovered a separate world in the New England countryside during his summer Fresh Air Fund vacations. Wearing pajamas, eating American food, and observing the orderliness and quiet demeanor of the non-Italian American farm family he visited impressed him as superior to the way of life in his mother's tenement apartment. Puzo's afternoons spent at the library in the local settlement house took him away from his Italian-immigrant surroundings into a world peopled by the characters of James Fenimore Cooper, Nathaniel Hawthorne, and Herman Melville. The people around him in New York's Hell's Kitchen seemed crude and backward. As a child, he never saw Italians appreciating the beauty of the "American dream." He saw desperate men and women struggling on a mean level for existence. It was the example of another more valuable world that undermined the ways of second-generation Italian children and their respect for elders. The old ways seemed both quaint and inferior, and it was not until middle age, after his own success and security, that Puzo could view these lives differently.

For many Italian-American children the free public-school system served as the first step up the ladder of broader opportunity. In Puzo's experience, it was "choosing a dream." He wanted to be a writer, but his mother opposed the idea because she believed it out of his reach. (In Italy, only the nobility could aspire to such things.) But for the Puzo family, life in America did in fact change, since Mrs. Puzo attained her goal of owning a home on Long Island and her son became a very successful writer.

Other institutions, such as the public health service, visiting nurses, hospital clinics, and charity workers brought into the Little Italies other aspects of American culture. Often the communication between the social service worker and the Italian immigrant was through a middle person—a relative or neighbor who was bilingual or a school-age child serving as interpreter. Some agencies employed interpreters to assist in their work.

In settlement houses, such as Addams' Hull House in Chicago, Europeans were encouraged to practice or exhibit their Old World crafts, literature, and music. Social reformers hoped to instill a respect for the Old World customs by singling them out for praise in an American setting, where they were appreciated for their beauty. In New York City, an Italian lace-making school founded by socially prominent native-born women sought to combine the preservation of an Old World skill with profitable employment for immigrant women. (Although these skills were admired by the native American, they were seen as quaint vestiges of a time long past, and immigrant children preferred to see their parents move into modern times and act like modern Americans.)

Nevertheless, these American-oriented institutions did provide a support system for the immigrants. They organized to provide services to improve the quality of life even if the context was American. In school, the nurse taught children about personal hygiene and the teacher lectured on nutrition. Mothers learned modern methods of childcare and home economics at the community centers. Women formed clubs where they combined sociability with sewing and other needlework, preserved cultural traditions, and more.

City, town, and county governments offered many employment opportunities—street repair, streetcar track maintenance, sanitation work, and sewer and drain construction and repair. Male laborers assigned to work for the city came into contact with native-born Americans and immigrants from other countries. In his home and on the street, the immigrant encountered politicians and party representatives who encouraged him to become a naturalized citizen and to take part in the elective system. The local committeeman also mediated between the immigrant community and the government bureaucracy. Securing a peddler's license, repairing the aftermath of a child's petty crime, obtaining municipal jobs, and smoothing over rent difficulties were some of the issues that fell into his realm of action. Thus, the American political process, organized on the precinct level, brought the immigrant into the public arena. Individual businessmen, lawyers, and employment agents discovered the benefits of political influence, which enabled them to obtain favors for their conationals. The ambitious, active men in the immigrant community joined the party ranks, recruited followers, and guided them on Election Day. In some towns and cities, Italian-American politicians earned elective office. Constantine Lauretta served as mayor of Mobile, Alabama, in 1846; and Francis Spinola (a Union army general) was the first Italian-American in Congress, representing New York City from 1887 to 1891. Much of political success derived from multiethnic coalitions—a trade-off of support for candidates from different ethnic groups. Exposure to the American process of pressure politics intruded into the life of Little Italies and paved the way for a more involved interaction.

Problems of adjustment were not a simple matter of learning to dress, talk, and act like Americans. For the first generation, those Italian-born adults who immigrated to the United States, there was a wider contrast between the two cultures. Primary identity for most remained Italian. Even those who left their homeland because of *la miseria*, the frustrations of a life bound by legal traditions, did not repudiate their attachment to the familial practices of family ties, interdependence through godparenthood, social deference established along lines of property ownership, skills, and education, and pride in the local history and folklore of their *paese*. Their dialects, food, values, and common experience sustained them along the barren stretches of railroad construction sites in South Dakota, British Columbia, and in the bunkhouses of mining communities sprinkled among the farmlands of Oklahoma, Nebraska, Illinois, the small mill towns in Maine, and the fishing coasts of Pass Christian, Mississippi; Brownsville, Texas; Morgan City, Louisiana; and San Diego, California. For the majority of immigrants, the institutions they developed in North America extended their ties to *italianità* as they knew it. Immigrant institutions, such as the Italian-language press, the national parishes, the *paese* club, and the mutual-benefit association, established new forms of identity. Those immigrants who decided to stay in America began to mix the two cultures. Even those who returned to Italy discovered that time spent abroad had altered their attitudes and expectations about life.

Although the immigrant anticipated many hardships, he could not know the specific forms they would take. Throughout the nineteenth century and into the twentieth century, immigrants faced problems of nativism, xenophobia, and discrimination. The floodtide of Italian immigration occurred at a time when the North American socioeconomic system was adjusting to the forces of industrialism and urbanization. Development and exploitation of the vast resources available required capital, technological expertise, a domestic market, and a cheap labor force. The waves of immigrants crossing the Atlantic or Pacific responded to the opportunities offered by industry and state, local, and national governments. These workers fit into a system that viewed them as economic pawns—hands to dig the trenches, lay the railroad ties, and operate the mill equipment. Wages for labor were determined by the laws of supply and demand; employers sought to keep all costs, especially labor, at a minimum and felt little responsibility toward the workers.

The Italians were only one of the many immigrant groups who suffered the disdain of the native-born population. In the 1850s, native-born Americans had displayed signs in Boston reading, "Irish Need Not Apply." In 1856, the Know-Nothing Party (also known as the American Party) drafted a platform that proposed the end of immigration and made it difficult for foreigners to become naturalized citizens. In the 1870s, groups of workers on the West Coast attacked Chinese laborers, whom they accused of displacing native-born Americans by accepting lower wages and unsafe working conditions.

Before the 1880s, Italian immigrants did not attract specific condemnation. Nativism or xenophobia occurred in North America during times of domestic crises and was usually aimed at a large, visible group of strangers who appeared to threaten time-honored traditions. The Catholicism of Irish and German immigrants and their custom of sociable drinking frightened both those natives who believed that Romanism would undermine Protestant values and those who believed that alcoholic consumption was an evil leading to the corruption of society.

Before 1880, Italian colonies had grown gradually in such cities as New York, New Orleans, and San Francisco. These foreigners were pioneers who planned to settle permanently in America. Since many earned their living by providing goods and services to the English-speaking population, the emphasis for them was on acculturation—acquiring the language and customs of the host society, while perhaps maintaining some *italianità*. The leaders of these communities supported the appreciation of Italian opera, art, and architecture. Like their American counterparts, they lived near their place of work and their occupations dispersed them throughout each community.

After 1880, the situation changed both for Italians and for Americans. That year marks the turning point for immigration. Previously the bulk of immigrants originated in the northern and western nations of Europe (England, Scandinavia, the Low Countries, France, and Germany); after 1880, individuals from the countries of southern and eastern Europe (the Balkans, the Baltic countries, the Russian and Austrian empires, Italy, and the Ottoman Empire) predominated. Post-

1880 immigrants represented ethnocultures that differed dramatically from those who had come before.

Italians, Greeks, Jews, Poles, Serbs, and Finns concentrated in areas where there were available jobs. They crowded into mining, mill, and railroad towns and settled in the industrial/commercial sections of cities where they found work. The combination of numbers and concentration of settlement made the newcomers more visible and underscored their differentness. Many of these immigrants came to North America without resources and were forced to live cheaply and in substandard housing; they saved money to send back to Europe or to pay for the passage of relatives. Some came without skills and earned a meager wage in the street trades—peddler, bootblack, and street entertainer.

As the newcomers arrived, the American system appeared to be faltering. The expanding industrial capitalist system grew at an uneven pace. Cycles of prosperity, recession, and depression created anxiety for workers and management. The rapid growth of industrial centers placed a burden on housing, schools, law enforcement, and other institutions. A combination of factors, the most visible being the juxtaposition of dissimilar cultures, increased pressures and tensions caused by the social and economic uncertainties. While the immigrants did not create the economic situation they entered, their presence contributed to its growth for good and for ill. The same workers whose strong backs and willing hands enlarged the labor force also allowed the employers to manipulate them economically. The immigrants seemed eager to work for inadequate wages and to endure the discomforts of substandard housing and unsafe working conditions. Therefore, native-born Americans took advantage of the immigrants' desperation to meet financial obligations in their native country, their disposition to consider life in America as a temporary phenomenon, their dependence on the middleman *padrone* for jobs, and their interdependence on *paesani* for personal support and comfort.

Both native-born American capitalists and workers believed the immigrants were responsible for the problems to which they contributed. They believed that the immigrants tolerated, as some variety of Mediterranean fatalism, the unsanitary housing and dangerous, low-paying jobs; endorsed the truancy and even delinquency of their children; endured the exploitation of those conationals who overcharged *paesani* for food; stole their earnings through fraudulent banking; and engaged in extortion, kidnapping, and vendetta. They reasoned that the immigrants were accustomed to these low standards and perhaps even believed that these conditions in America were superior to those they left behind. Native-born Americans also suspected that all the attendant evils were part of the immigrants' baggage brought across the ocean. They accepted little responsibility for the domestic conditions that were in fact products of the system. Newspapers and magazines printed lurid accounts of the unsavory side of immigration. Most often, their criticism exposed a double standard. They allowed immigrants the free choice of earning low wages, except when they feared this created unfair competition for native-born Americans. They ignored the problems of unsanitary and inadequate housing until the epidemics of the ethnic ghetto threatened the health of the native-born population. They resigned themselves to vendetta crime as long as the victims were immigrants. If, however, the victims were natives, the authorities rounded up anyone remotely suspected of the crime. The vigilante mentality of Americans hastened to punish those believed guilty. The sensational lynchings of Italians in the 1890s and the early decades of the twentieth century were condoned by the general public. A disregard for the human dignity of the immigrants occurred each day, as they were denied jobs and housing and ridiculed and slandered. A direct form of discrimination was the ethnic slurs—wop, dago, guinea, and mafiosi—while a more subtle form was the reinforcement of the stereotype of lower educational aspirations among immigrants, as school officials counseled their children to take vocational and commercial courses.

When the immigrants seemed disinterested in organizing against oppressive conditions, their native-born coworkers felt betrayed. Yet, when some of these immigrant workers attempted to use the class-consciousness of European-worker ideology, many natives believed them too militant. In fact, whenever foreigners were involved in contentious labor disputes, they were called radicals and un-American. Natives ignored the domestic origins of these conditions, forgot their own pioneer heritage of revolution against tyrannical conditions, and their own history to take justice into their own hands and lash out against official and social oppression (such as the New York Draft Riots of 1863 and the Populist protests of the 1890s).

Italian immigrants were also criticized for focusing their attention on events and conditions in Italy, their readiness to return to Italy to fight for *la patria* in 1915, and their support for Italian national interests during the Versailles Conference of 1919. Italian immigrants were further criticized for sending money to their families in Italy rather than spending their earnings in America, for being slow to apply for citizenship, and for "selling" their votes to the local party boss.

But, by the 1920s, the nationality quotas of the immigration laws had drastically cut the flow from Italy as well as from other countries of southeastern Europe. Modest violations of Prohibition—such as making wine and selling it to *paesani* within the Little Italies—aroused almost the same indignation as that directed against organized crime syndicates. Gangland wars depicted in such films as *Little Caesar* and *The St. Valentine's Day Massacre* became the "measure" of the entire community. Bugs Moran and Dutch Schultz notwithstanding, somehow crime became an "Italian thing." The arrest in 1920 of Nicola Sacco and Bartolomeo Vanzetti for a payroll holdup and murder, their conviction in 1921, and their execution in 1927, highlighted this negative combination. These immigrant men were admitted anarchists and were charged and convicted of a crime.

While many well-known American-born writers, educators, and politicians admired and praised the emergence of premier Benito Mussolini in the 1920s, most began to question his imperial goals for Italy and his friendly relations with Adolf Hitler in the 1930s. Many Italian Americans basked in the initial glory and success of Mussolini because the economic achievement of his regime impressed other nations. Italy's sons and daughters abroad felt proud to be an indirect part of that achievement. If Americans respected the nation of Italy, they would presumably respect those who had emigrated from Italy.

The infatuation of some Italian Americans with Fascism in turn contributed to conflict and violence in America. Within the Italian-American community, some opposed the regime in Italy and its propaganda efforts. This opposition drew its strength from the small pockets of political radicals who fought all forms of Fascism. They were joined by individuals who questioned the loss of liberty in the Italian state and opposed Mussolini's imperialist policies. Dissension ranged from arguments and debates to written diatribes, public meetings, rallies, and sometimes open fighting. Americans disdained both extremes. But, when the Axis powers formed an alliance that threatened world peace, Americans suspected Italian Americans of split loyalties. Anti-Italian sentiment grew with the outbreak of war in Europe and Italy's invasion of France in 1940. President Roosevelt's description of this action as a "dagger" in the back angered many Italian Americans, who then voted for the Republican candidate for president, Wendell L.

Wilkie, in 1940. In Canada, Italian immigrants suffered more directly. Men lost their jobs, Italian-Canadian shops were vandalized, civil liberties were suspended under the War Measures Act, and hundreds were interned in camps.

On the eve of World War II, many Americans questioned the loyalty of Italian Americans to the United States. Once Italy declared war against America, Italian immigrants became enemy aliens. Midnight raids led by the FBI rounded up those who had spoken or written in favor of Fascism, those who had shortwave radios, and those who resided in military security areas (along the West Coast). Ten thousand Italian noncitizens in California had to move out of coastal military-zone areas. A few hundred were interned throughout the war.

Most Italian Americans and Canadians did not falter in their immediate commitment to the war cause. Sons of immigrants enlisted or reported to draft boards with the blessings of their parents. The fine line between hostility and acceptance was crossed as Italian-immigrant organizations held bond drives and did their part to help win the war for America.

During the 1930s and 1940s, children of immigrants faced subtle socioeconomic discrimination. Firms that did not hire Jews often also felt similar disdain in hiring Catholics whose names ended in vowels. Promotion on the basis of merit somehow seemed tied to having an American surname. The second generation straddled the barrier to acceptance. The choice seemed for some to be as simple as changing their name, moving away from the old neighborhood, or marrying a non-Italian. Certainly, their interaction with American institutions, organizations, government, politics, the armed forces, the church, and unions broadened their new self-concept.

Battered and bruised, misused and exploited, the majority of the immigrants faced each moment with hardened determination. They endured without abandoning all the amenities of life. They created support within the *paese* boardinghouse over a game of cards; they re-created the extended family that welcomed friends as well as relatives; they found companionship at work and at the street markets where the world became a town piazza; they sought out *paesani* and fellow Italians to join sports clubs, dramatic groups, and social and religious associations.

All non-Anglo-Saxon American groups have experienced some measure of suspicion and prejudice. Each group has sought ways of coping with it. Italian Americans developed a varied approach. In San Francisco, Sicilian fishermen protested against an increase in their license tax; in 1916, Italian Americans helped elect Fiorello LaGuardia to represent New York in the U.S. Congress; and in Lawrence, Massachusetts, in 1912, Italians initiated and were prominent organizers in the strike against the injustices of the mill operators.

On the job, they began to develop tactics of cooperation. Many joined craft unions. Some immigrants led the efforts for unions in the workplace and, in the 1930s, helped to form the industrial unions. Italian-American entrepreneurs also sought to ease the burden of risky working conditions. Barbers, shoemakers, and other artisans formed social groups that offered some health benefits; Italian fruit merchants, fishermen, and farmers formed cooperatives and associations to share the risk of uncertain markets and natural disasters.

Instead of perpetuating separateness from the American mainstream, the efforts to order and direct their lives brought them further into American society. Parallel forms of life strategies developed for each ethnic group. Italians found themselves a social mirror as the American technique of linking interest groups brought them into contact with all peoples. Italians supported the tributes to Columbus, such as Chicago's 1893 Columbian Exposition. The naming of the District of Columbia; Columbus, Ohio; and Columbia, South Carolina, and the Columbia River all predated mass Italian settlement.

To some extent, Italian immigrants benefiting from U.S. refugee and war-brides legislation, coupled with the 1965 repeal of the discriminatory immigration laws of the 1920s that had established nationality quotas, added some new life into Italian-American communities. But this influx paled in comparison with the Canadian experience.

In Canada, in 1950, a major influx of immigrants from postwar Italy reestablished vibrant communities. A booming economy, plus Canada's participation in NATO (North Atlantic Treaty Organization), helped to fuel the call for immigration. Both the Canadian government and private firms recruited workers. Early in this process, newcomers arrived with one-year contracts to work in the industrial sector, as domestics, or on the land. The majority came as permanent settlers, later sponsoring wives, children, and other relatives. Family "chain migration" from Italy was so intensive that, in 1958, Italy surpassed Britain as a source of immigrants in Canada. Ultimately, the more than half-a-million newly arrived Italians represented almost seventy percent of the entire Italian-Canadian population. The newcomers were products of a modern Italian society familiar with pressure politics and determined to maintain their

Italian heritage. They rallied to protest unfair working conditions and ineffective government systems and promoted the concept of bilingualism.

Italy's economic miracle of the 1970s reduced the impetus for immigration abroad. Within the U.S., the second and especially the third generation continued to infiltrate into the American mainstream. They shared their birthright, their education, and their future with all Americans. What remained as Italian was a modification, a dilution of the culture taken from the *paese* in the 1870s. By the 1950s, intermarriage, educational achievement and higher income, and the movement of Italians to the suburbs seemed to signal the end of ethnicity. What remained was nostalgia, a caricature of things remembered. What lay ahead appeared to be amalgamation and homogenization, the culmination of the melting pot.

Italian Americans had made it. In politics, business, the arts, education, they had come into their own. A cavalcade of well-known individuals whose identity was acknowledged by all Americans meant acceptance by the larger group. Such open recognition of Americans with ethnic names emerged at a time when the country was more aware of past guilt in the treatment of minorities. During the 1960s, the Civil Rights Act reaffirmed America's commitment to equality, and affirmative-action legislation enabled many individuals to aspire to top positions. Within the United States, the civil rights movement and the demand for black studies and bilingualism for Hispanics raised the awareness of other ethnic groups. Cultural pluralism rather than the melting pot now dominated the philosophy of the politicians and the educators. In Canada, the concept of multiculturalism paved the way for province-supported programs to collect materials and preserve the heritage of all groups from the native peoples to the latest arrivals. Millions of Americans began to seek their roots and found that their shared cultural traditions did not contradict their American identity.

Influenced by the example of minority advocacy, a group of Italian-American faculty and students at the City University of New York system petitioned CUNY's chancellor Robert Kibbee to address their academic needs and learning styles. Once Kibbee designated Italian Americans as an affirmative-action group, the way was clear for Italian-American legislators to create, in 1979, the Italian American Institute to Foster Higher Education. A long struggle ensued, which included a civil rights lawsuit in federal court to accord Italian Americans parity within the system, ultimately creating

The John D. Calandra Italian American Institute.

Although every ethnic group in American history had protested against mistreatment, the pattern of the 1950s and 1960s encouraged more formal, organized national campaigns. Ethnic organizations employed the media, organized rallies, picketed government offices, and bombarded politicians with petitions. They asked for a greater share in the American dream. Surveys were made of the "executive suite" to see if all Americans enjoyed their "fair" (potential) piece of the sources of power. Antidefamation became a conscious part of each group's policy. Asians picketed against the Charlie Chan image; Hispanics protested against the Frito Bandito; Poles rebelled against the Polish Joke Book.

In this ferment of seeking justice and recognition, some European Americans viewed efforts to level the playing field in equal access to jobs, decent housing, and adequate schools as a threat to undermine their status quo. In many urban areas of America, fears of how the personal costs of affirmative action, school busing, and neighborhood integration would change the world of the working-class urbanite increased ethnic hostility. Since many Italian-American urban enclaves survived the move to the suburbs, many of the people who remained held the line against change and expressed their frustrations in negative ways. In Cleveland, Detroit, New York City, Chicago, and elsewhere, turf wars between high-school students, picketing by parents opposed to school busing plans, and violence in the streets made headlines. While most Italian Americans had lived and interacted in harmony with other ethnic groups, including African Americans, the incidents of the Howard Beach, Bensonhurst, and Canarsie sections of New York; the Bridgeport section of Chicago; South Boston; and Newark, in which some Italians (sometimes exclusively) violently reacted, cast a shadow upon the entire group.

Individuals, such as James Groppi in Milwaukee and Geno Baroni as a member of President Jimmy Carter's administration, attempted to enlist all working-class ethnics to work together for equal benefits. Joseph Sciorra described his reaction to the Yusuf Hawkins killing in Bensonhurst, in 1989, as he marched along with the mainly African-American demonstrators. He carried a sign reading, "Italians Against Racism," which he used as a title of an essay he wrote for a collection entitled *Are Italians White?* Part of his triumph is that by the end of the march at least ten people had stepped away from the jeering, epithet-yelling bystanders to march along with him.

Sciorra and others, such as Libero Della Piana, editor of *Race Wire,* remind us about the "handful of Italian Americans [who] marched with Blacks in Harlem against Mussolini's invasion of Ethiopia in 1935; the Italian and Black sharecroppers in Louisiana [who] united against the common enemies: plantation owners and lynch law; [and] U.S. Congressman Vito Marcantonio (1935-1950) of East Harlem [who] defended the rights not only of Italian Americans but of Blacks and Puerto Ricans as well." They suggest that Italian Americans redirect their opposition to negative stereotypes to a higher level of standing up against all racism. Some Italian-American organizations responded, but they did so in defensive journalistic essays that refocused the debate from Italian-American racism to media defamation of Italians with portrayals of criminality.

Preparation for the bicentennial of the U.S. provided a way to celebrate the nation's multicultural heritage. Ironically, this resurgence of Italian-American ethnicity came to the surface as Italians increasingly became integrated into the larger society. Federal legislation provided funds to support preservation of the immigrant/ethnic past. Groups accelerated their cultural, archival, and educational activities. Ethnic historical societies blossomed, ethnic journals flourished, and scholars in all disciplines, from language to history to anthropology, turned full attention toward the immigrant/ethnic experience in America. For the Italians, these new associations included the American Italian Historical Association; the Italian American Anti-Defamation League; the National Italian American Foundation; the journal, *Italian Americana;* and The John D. Calandra Italian American Institute. Older organizations, such as the Order Sons of Italy in America, acknowledged support for preservation efforts.

This outbreak of activity among the ranks of ethnic leaders filtered down to the general public. As scholars researched the lives of the immigrants, they began to collect documents, letters, photos, and printed materials. Many immigrants were interviewed and asked to describe the events of the past, ones they had either experienced or learned about from others. The process of collecting, gathering, interpreting, and publicizing often expanded into a community effort, as members of families became amateur historians. To the surprise of many people, they discovered that instead of being completely assimilated, the majority of Italian Americans maintained a connection with their cultural heritage. They began to demonstrate their curiosity by subscribing to popular magazines, such as *I AM,*

Identity, and *Accenti,* and Italian-American newspapers. They attended historical conferences, began to ask for books on Italian subjects at their libraries, and retraced the steps of their immigrant ancestors to Italy. While Italian Americans felt this sense of continuity, it was mostly emotional and psychological; often a third- or fourth-generation person could not explain why he or she felt part of both cultures.

Marcus Lee Hansen, a famous historian of ethnicity, once suggested that the third generation would record the experience of their grandparents. He believed that the awkward self-consciousness that haunted many of the second generation made objective self-examination painful and difficult, if not impossible. He thought that the third-generation's confidence in belonging to America would allow them to venture bravely into their past. They would question their parents about the family's history. Most often, the parents could not answer these questions because they had been too busy making their way into American society or had felt the need to forget traditions in order to adopt the new. The third-generation's frustration would serve as a stimulus for them to visit great aunts, check through family trunks, take courses in family history, or decide to pursue graduate training in the humanities and social sciences to learn the tools of professional research. Others wrote memoirs and fictional accounts based on the immigrant experience. Many of the studies now in the libraries come from the pens of these descendents of immigrants.

The desire of people to know about their past in an effort to better understand their present lives is as old as human society. The true coming of age of any group is the moment when it can look at its past, the glories and successes, as well as the warts and the blemishes, with an open mind. For the Italian American this has meant the maturity to appreciate the contributions of the "little people," the inarticulate laborers who dug the New York City subways or who toiled in the canneries of California and Massachusetts. This has meant the ability to accept the wide range of Italian influence in American life, from the anarchists and the labor organizers to the pro-fascists and the bootleggers. With the bittersweetness of maturity comes the gratification over the hard-earned achievement of having built huge family businesses from storefronts or pushcarts, and the pride that results from the success of contemporary Italian Americans who bring their sensitivity of ethnic identity into their politics, their professions, their literature, their cinematography, and their art.

The process of self-appreciation remains alive and

positive as it builds on the present and plans for the future. Italian Americans today are charting their recent and personal past and present in much the same way that Cabot, Verrazzano, Malaspina, and Columbus charted the sea lanes and coasts of America. The joy of self-discovery and self-celebration has brought a new dimension to the lives of Italian Americans that reflects the uniqueness of American society.

What is an Italian American? Who are they? Since World War II, the majority of people in the United States who claim Italian heritage are third generation. Many have memories of grandparents who spoke little or no English, yet they see little in their daily lives that connects with those memories. The Canadian experience differs because of that nation's immigration policy, which enabled thousands to enter in the 1950s. Canadian Italians, therefore, have a new immigrant generation that assumed leadership roles in preserving the Italian language and culture. Even so, as the generational distance between first arrival and contemporary assimilated lifestyles increases, will the immigrant culture disappear?

In the 2000 census, over 15.7 million people identified themselves as Italian American, a seven percent increase (one million) over the 1990 census. The census bureau estimates there are twenty-six million Americans of Italian descent. A Canadian census of 2001 showed 726,275 individuals listing Italian as their single ethnic origin. An additional 544,090 listed Italian as part of their ethnic origin (multiple response) for a total of over 1.2 million Italian Canadians.

The heritage of a people can continue in a variety of ways. There are the obvious visual elements of customs, dress, life choices (endogamy), and retention of language; the less obvious ones are culture, attitudes and beliefs, and preferences in lifestyles.

Since most people do not analyze why they do things or think about things in certain ways, it is difficult for the majority of Italians to pinpoint any continuity in heritage. It is also difficult for the scholar—the social scientist who observes and measures behavior. Are Italian-American family attitudes different in degree from those of Polish Americans? Is the fact that many Italian Americans continue in blue-collar occupations, rather than in the professions, a statement of lack of upward mobility, prejudice, and discrimination, or perhaps a preference for the craft traditions that the third generation inherited from their fathers and grandfathers? The issue of the meaning of Italian-American identity and the persistence of their ethnicity is fraught with the dangers of overgeneralization, vagueness in interpretation, and definition of terms.

In postwar America, Italian Americans shared in the hopes and dreams for a peaceful world in which their children would prosper. They felt a special simpatico for the problems of Italy. Committees set up relief funds to aid those in Italy who suffered from the devastation of war. Italians contributed as individuals and as groups. They also influenced the activities of American organizations, such as the International Ladies Garment Workers Union, which established a trade school at Montebello outside Palermo. Natural disasters, such as floods and earthquakes, bring the Italian-American community forward to offer help. Across North America, great efforts were made to aid those who suffered in the 1980 earthquakes in southern Italy.

A review of Italian American involvement in and contribution to North America reads like a cavalcade of stars. The children and grandchildren of immigrants have achieved success in many areas, ranging from politics to the arts. Whether achievement in certain fields, such as the arts and drama, reflects a cultural preference on the part of Italian Americans is again a difficult issue. Rosa Ponselle and Giancarlo Menotti may have been more inclined to follow their careers in opera and music because this tradition is a favored one for Italians. In other areas such as sports, some suggest that the combination of streetwise gamesmanship and the attraction of professional careers intertwine so that talented Italian-American boxers, football players, and baseball players moved from their boyhood games into the major leagues.

Although each ethnic group is proud of those who achieve the acclaim of the larger society, continuity of ethnicity is measured more by the daily lives of Italian Americans. As the population scatters and intermarries, what happens to the Italian-American identity? Some traditions disappear, others continue in an altered fashion. No longer do the immigrants from the Sicilian provinces of Messina and Catania gather on Thirteenth Street between Avenue A and First Avenue in Manhattan to celebrate the feast of the Black Saint (the Madonna of Tindari), but it seems that a large cross-section of the population of metropolitan New York attends an expanded and extended Feast of San Gennaro each September in Little Italy. Population moves often result in the regrouping of Italians. Many Italians from North Denver moved to suburban communities of Wheat Ridge or Arvada, Colorado. In Canada, the movement out of immigrant neighborhoods to more prosperous residential areas has been significant, but even in the suburbs it is still common to find concentrations of

Italian Canadians who have chosen to live near one another because of kinship or village ties. In the Sunbelt areas, new lodges of the Sons of Italy still form. In the 1980s, a move to Fort Lauderdale, Florida, or Scottsdale, Arizona, need not signal the end to family dinners of lasagne and ravioli and tasty Italian bread. Ethnic family businesses follow the population trends. More recent Italian immigrants often settle in these diaspora-settlements where they add a taste of contemporary Italy. In a limited way, internal migration follows some of the patterns of the transatlantic crossing. In older neighborhoods, ethnic federation occurs as the Italian community expands to include newer immigrants. An Italian bakery sells Portuguese bread, an Italian national parish includes the newer Chinese communicants in its Columbus Day celebrations, and Italian cultural centers welcome all comers to attend language and dance classes.

Rites of passage still retain elements of the Italian heritage. The third generation presses the second generation for recipes of traditional holiday dishes. The choice of godparents still implies a special relation and obligation. Intermarriage often means a dualism (both traditions coexisting), rather than a fusion or loss of tradition. Third- and fourth-generation Italian Americans form organizations, such as FIERI (eighteen to thirty-nine year olds wishing to promote pride in their heritage) and POINT (genealogists Pursuing Our Italian Names Together) to achieve specific goals.

American society seems to guarantee some ethnic continuity. As "foreign" (non-European) ways become part of a more sophisticated, tolerant, and curious native-born population, each ethnic group finds encouragement in the interest taken in its festivals, cuisine, and language. With this endorsement of things Italian and Italian American, the children of the immigrants can choose to declare themselves the special beneficiaries of the simple as well as the grand legacy that belongs to all Americans.

The Mercato in Cittanova, Calabria, 1930s. This postcard image sent to relatives in the United States illustrated to them that little had changed in the small villages throughout Italy. Life for most people in these agricultural towns, surrounded by fields on the periphery, followed seasonal patterns. Village artisans provided products for sale and services to those able to pay or barter. Approximately eighty-five percent of Italians who immigrated to North America came from southern Italy, and many estimates indicate that Calabresi constituted the largest regional group. (*Courtesy Joseph J. Curulla*)

CHAPTER 1

ORIGINS

Migration was a way of life for Italians throughout the nineteenth century. They traveled within the Italian peninsula, to other areas of Europe, and to North Africa in search of work. Laboring in the mines and factories of industrial areas, they provided the artisan skills needed to construct and embellish the expanding cities.

Since the political, social, and economic divisions within the Italian peninsula prevented cooperative development, each area had its own problems and separate history, customs, and dialect. Even so, Italian nationalists fought and schemed to unite the nation. Efforts for unification precipitated political action, culminating in demonstrations and revolutions. The civil authorities, as we see in Puccini's opera *Tosca,* relentlessly pursued organizers as common criminals. Italy's political refugees sought safety in Europe. Some fled to the Americas.

Emigration from Italy increased in proportion to internal conditions and external opportunities. In the 1860s and 1870s, thousands of *contadini* (peasants) left the regions of Lombardia, Veneto, and Emilia-Romagna. Overpopulation, changes in agricultural tenure and cultivation, plus increased industrialization acted as a stimulus to their departure. In both northern and southern Italy, most families worked as sharecroppers and had few opportunities to move out of a subsistence barter system. Skilled craftsmen also could not make a living in locales where their customer base lacked sufficient income to pay for their services. Many artisans found work in European cities, returning home in the winter. Industrialization in the north, such as the silk industry and shoemaking, while more efficient than the small workshops, added another level of deprivation. Women and children worked in the silk mills for ten to fifteen hours a day for inadequate pay. In the 1880s and 1890s, conditions in southern Italy deteriorated as natural disasters, such as phylloxera (a disease attacking grape vines), spread. Recurrent, devastating earthquakes also spurred emigration from the south, especially notable was the Messina earthquake of 1908. The population suffered from the trade wars with European nations that cut off foreign markets for agricultural produce.

Increases in taxation also weighed heavily on a region in which exchange was often in kind or services rather than cash and earnings were low. Emigrants from the south headed to the Western Hemisphere, but mainly to North America, where rapid industrialization created opportunities for employment.

Although the majority of Italians viewed their departure with some level of trepidation, some individuals did not "want to leave" at all. They may have been sent by their family to shore up their security; with family migration, not every member left Italia with equal determination. For some, their fears, anguish, and misgivings were not banished with their arrival in America. They longed for the life they left behind and suffered a sense of loss that did not diminish over time.

Preparations for departure included obtaining a passport and a certificate listing a male's military status. Emigrants traveled to the nearest port of departure, and trade routes from these ports channeled traffic to American destinations. Although transatlantic transportation was relatively inexpensive (approximately thirty dollars), travel accommodations in steerage were far from adequate. Below deck, three hundred to six hundred people occupied communal open sleeping quarters. Each bunk averaged thirty cubic feet of space, and primitive sanitary conditions, seasickness, and overcrowding transformed steerage into a horrid place. Weather permitting, passengers spent most of their time above deck.

Arrival in America held many fears for newcomers. Most emigrants from Italy arrived in New York and entered through Castle Garden and later Ellis Island, which opened in 1891. There the men were separated from the women and children, but all were subjected to medical examinations and interrogation. Between 1897 and 1913, thousands of Italians arrived at Ellis Island. If they passed examinations and gained admission, they were ferried to the Battery section of New York City or to New Jersey train terminals to continue their journey to places across the continent.

Enterprising Italian Americans offered services to their arriving conationals. They could exchange money, provide transportation, recommend boardinghouses and hotels, or offer employment. Some of these individuals were unscrupulous and cheated the unwary. Authorities attempted to circumvent this problem by providing some of these services at ports of entry or by referring immigrants to charitable agencies. Organized by the local Italian-American community and subsidized by the Italian government, these agencies dealt with the personal difficulties of each newcomer.

North American industrialization, railroad building, urban development, mining, and manufacturing demands for workers opened avenues of opportunities for Italians to advance themselves economically through emigration. Once started, entire communities in Italy learned about and planned to follow their compatriots. These connections illustrate how migration chains funneled immigrants from one place in Italy to one place in America.

Social and economic disruptions in Italy after World War I, complemented by migration chains between Italy and America, extended the push and pull factors into the 1920s. Family members seeking to join relatives in America and political dissidents fleeing Mussolini's Fascist policies continued the flow of immigrants.

Following World War II's devastation, Italians again sought to leave the deprivation of limited opportunity behind them. More than seven million did so between 1945 and 1975, most leaving for Canada, Australia, and northern Europe rather than the United States because immigration laws (until 1965) limited entry to only a few thousand applicants from southern and eastern Europe. The Italian migration to Canada ultimately added approximately half-a-million Italians to the population.

Even after Italy's economy improved and blossomed in the 1970s and 1980s, Italian entrepreneurs recognized how the new romance of Americans, with things Italian, created a golden opportunity to export Italian products, food and wine, and travel packages.

Representatives of these companies, such as Benetton, established outposts in American cities. They also formed partnerships with Italian-American companies to whom they granted American distribution rights to their products. These more recent arrivals brought with them the lifestyles and socioeconomic system of contemporary Italy.

Throughout the twentieth century, a variety of motivations sparked the wish to emigrate. For some the choice to leave Italy was not a necessity, but a calculated decision to enjoy American lifestyles, provide children with wider educational and occupational opportunities, and to reunite families long separated. While the flood of emigration from Italy has lessened, there remain individuals and families whose Italian dreams respond to America's attractions. Each family has its own story that fits into the large and varied presence of Italians in America.

Daily Life. Life on Corso Vittorio Emanuele in Lonate Pozzolo, Varese, 1910 spilled outdoors with artisans and vendors displaying their wares and residents completing their errands on foot. *Paese* life included a rich variety of occupations and reflected an urban class structure. Many townspeople worked as sharecroppers tending fields, where they raised grass, corn, wheat, and rice in scattered small plots outside of town. Some *contadini* who left this community emigrated to Walla Walla, Washington, where they continued to work on the land. *(Courtesy Museo Storico Civico Cuggionese, Milano, Italia)*

Holding Tools of Their Trade. Young men in Trevignano, Veneto, pose for the camera, displaying carpenter tools. Many young men apprenticed to learn skills, such as stonemasonry, carpentry, barbering, blacksmithing, and tailoring. However, the customer base in these small towns could not provide enough income to support a family. So many of these men would "commute" part of the year to locales in Europe or emigrate to North or South America to seek their fortunes. Although Albano Andrighetti holds a guitar that he doesn't know how to play, he had studied carpentry. In the 1920s, Albano joined his older brother, Julio Andrighetti, who was already at work in a gold mine in Timmins, Ontario. In that cold climate, Albano could only work outdoors as a carpenter for five months of the year, so he too ended up working in the mine. Albano settled permanently in Timmins. Julio returned to Italy. *(Courtesy Traci L. Andrighetti)*

Harvesting Hay. The Giustina family's land spread in patchwork fashion on the mountain behind their house in San Vito di Cadore, Veneto. Life for the *contadini* required the involvement of the entire family. Children worked at an early age, and women, local customs permitting, labored in the fields, especially during harvesting. The farmers drank goat's milk and used cows' milk for cheese. The family raised hay that was carted to the barn by oxen to feed the livestock. Selling the meat was their major source of income. They grew root and green vegetables, barley, wheat, corn, turnips, potatoes, and beans and some flax to blend with wool for their clothing. *(Courtesy the Giustina family)*

Weighing sulfur in the mines at Porto Empedocle, Agrigento, c. 1905. Laboring long hours at difficult work for low wages seasoned these workers to view equally demanding jobs at higher wages in American coal mines, steel mills, or smelters, or building roads or railroads, as a chance to better their status. Emigrants from sulfur mining regions (located in north central as well as southeastern Sicily) found their way to Buffalo, New York (from Porto Empedocle), Birmingham, Alabama (from Campofranco, Caltanissetta), and Trenton, New Jersey (from Casteltermini, Agrigento). Emigrants from these regions continued to venerate San Calogero who performed miracles and cured the sick with the vapors of the caves of Sciacca, Agrigento, which he believed had therapeutic values. (*From* Porto Empedocle al Tempo dei Savoia: 1860-1946, *by Giovanni Gibilaro*)

Canning Factory, Nocera Inferiore, Salerno. This factory processed products for domestic consumption as well as for export. Italians in America imported tomatoes, olive oil, cheeses, and fish from Italy. Some entrepreneurs made contracts with companies that imported Italian foodstuffs under their own labels, such as Sole D'Italia, which was registered by a Philadelphia company before World War I. In the 1940s, the name was transferred to a distributor in Baltimore, Maryland. *(Courtesy The Maryland Historical Society, Baltimore, Maryland)*

Widening horizons for soldiers of the Italian Twenty-sixth Artillery Regiment, 1899. While in the military, Davide Ranieri (first row standing, second from left) and his comrades met men from other areas of Italy, who related tales of how emigrants could make a fortune in America. When most of these soldiers returned to their homes, they found few jobs available. In June 1892, Davide's oldest brother, Theodore, left Santa Maria del Giudice, Lucca, for America. He traveled to Iron Mountain, a Michigan Upper Peninsula mining community, where the miners were on strike and prospects for employment looked dim. He left for Kalispell, Montana, a logging community that supplied wood for the Great Northern Railway. Four months later, he left for Great Falls, Montana, where a new copper refinery was opening up offering lots of jobs. He wrote to his three brothers still in Italy and soon they joined him in Montana. *(Courtesy Larry Ranieri)*

R. C. LEWIS,
Frankfort, N. Y.

Banking on America. The entire Chippari family emigrated from Oriolo, Cosenza, c. 1890, and settled for two years in Frankfort, New York (near Utica). Giuseppe Chippari (age forty-one) and his son, Giambattista (age seventeen), posed in a photographer's studio before the family returned to Oriolo and purchased a parcel of land, on which they planted a vineyard and also olive, fig, and other fruit trees. Still unable to earn much money, Giuseppe returned alone to Frankfort, worked another couple of years and then returned to Italy. Giambattista married in 1896 and farmed one-third of the land his family now owned. Still dissatisfied, Giuseppe ceded his land to Giambattista and left, with his wife, Maria, and two of their sons, Francis and Salvatore, for Argentina in 1908. In 1920, Giambattista's son, Giuseppe, left alone for Frankfort, New York, also intending to make some money and return to Oriolo, but within two years, he had decided to marry and settle permanently after getting a job as a janitor at Remington Arms. *(Courtesy Catherine Chippari Paige and Dominick Frank)*

Women detaching cocoons spun on mulberry branches by silk worms in northern Italy, 1870s. Many young women traveled from home to work in factories spinning these fibers into silk. Wearing traditional costumes, which include an unusual hair ornament found only in Cuggiono, Milano, the women rolled their hair onto a metal bar with two bulbs at each end to form a braid. Rosa Cassettari, who emigrated in 1884, described this fashion in stories she related in Chicago's Commons Settlement House, published in *Rosa: The Life of an Italian Immigrant as told to Marie Hall Ets.* *(Courtesy Museo Storico Civico Cuggionese, Milano, Italia)*

Life as Work. Rosa Ligato (left) and her sister, Caterina Ligato Sorrenti, carry the family clothes to the river outside the town of Cittanova, Reggio Calabria. The Ligato family owned an olive orchard located outside of Cittanova. It had come to the family from Concetta Fonti Ligato, Rosa's mother. Working the orchard, picking and processing olives, occupied their time for six months of the year and from 7:00 A.M. to 5:00 P.M., six days a week. While Rosa was growing up, she went with her father to nearby mountains and hired laborers to make lime. They broke up quarried limestone and built fires to heat it to produce the lime. Rosa thought herself lucky on days when all she had to do was cook for the workers. The lime was brought back to town in a wagon to sell to builders for mortar for brick and stonework. Rosa was expected to help unload the wagon. *(Courtesy Joseph J. Curulla)*

The Streets of Naples, Italy, c. 1901. These streets bustle with life as women, children, and men pursue everyday activities. Children with peddler's baskets and families sitting outside, enjoying the sunshine after hanging out the family wash, illustrate the communal nature of Italian society, both in the larger cities as well as the urban villages throughout the nation. *(Courtesy Library of Congress, Prints and Photographs Division; reproduction # LC-USZ62-73452)*

Internal Migration for Work. Peasants, both women and men, often migrated to other regions of Italy to earn money to support their families because of limited opportunities in their own village. Here migrant workers from Umbria weed the fields, performing *la mondarella* in neighboring Lazio about 1905. The principal of "where there is work, there is bread," guided peasants to venture beyond their familiar surroundings and to seek information about employment. Landless workers' lives resembled scenes reminiscent of the film *The Tree of Wooden Clogs.* *(Courtesy Museo Regionale dell'Emigrazione "Pietro Conti," Gualdo Tadino, Italy)*

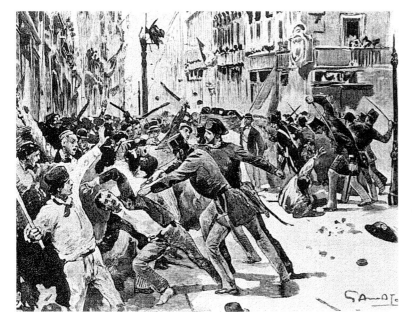

Carabinieri Subdue a Rebellious Group in Naples, Italy, 1893. Strikes and demonstrations did not only occur among industrial workers. In the early 1890s, peasants in central Sicily protested against landholding policies and taxes by storming municipal buildings and burning records. As the price of bread increased, peasants in the south raided bakeries and pillaged local shops and grain elevators. The riots spread northward, and in industrial cities like Milan, workers joined the demonstrations. The government retaliated by sending out troops to suppress the reactionaries. In such confrontations in Italy, many people were arrested and some were killed. Rather than face more oppression, some dissidents decided to emigrate. *(From* L'Illustrazione Italiana*)*

Family Unification. Benilda Albina Victoria Frazzini, age ten, poses with her schoolmates and teacher, Giacomo Scocchera, in San Pietro Avellana, Molise. (From top right corner, and down one row, she is third from the right, just in front of the flag.) During this period in Italy, school-age children were tutored to support the Fascist regime of Mussolini. (Notice the soldier and the cannon to the left.) Benilda's father, Emiliano Frazzini, had become a naturalized U.S. citizen in 1904, even before he married Lucrezia Carlini. Emiliano, like many immigrants, worked in the United States at mines in Minnesota and Colorado, going back to Italy only to father children. At this point in her life, 1922, Benilda had seen her father only two or three times for short periods. Once enough money had been saved and the proper paperwork completed, the entire family was reunited in the United States, in 1926, and settled in New Galilee, Pennsylvania, where Emiliano worked at the brickyard. *(Courtesy Mark Camillo DiVecchio)*

Sacrifices for War. In May 1943, the Italian government requisitioned the church bells of every town to be melted down for ammunition. Here the residents of San Massimo, Molise, are lining up the town's bells to be taken to the foundry in Agnone. Fortunately, when the armistice was signed, on September 8, 1943, the town's bells had not yet been melted down, and they were returned. John Hersey's novel *A Bell for Adano* describes a town that lost its church bell to Mussolini's war effort. In the book, the American Major Joppolo replaces the bell with one from the British navy. Soon after the war's conclusion, Vincenzo Laurella (circled in the photo) immigrated with his father to Toronto, Canada, to join his mother, who, as a Canadian citizen, had gone ahead to gain admission for her family. *(Courtesy Carmela Destito Buttice)*

Wall markings record political turmoil in towns such as Pedace, Cosenza. Notice Stalin's name on the door behind this group. During the 1920s and '30s, many Pedacesi were anti-Fascists and were jailed by Mussolini's government. Later the combination of World War II's devastation and food shortages resulted in widespread suffering, and Pedacesi voted their dissatisfaction with eighty to one hundred percent support for Communist mayors who addressed the immediate needs of the population. In 1944, Dora deLuca stands at left with her aunt's family (Cinnante). *(Courtesy Ray Martire)*

Family rituals connect generations as the Grosso family of Perosa Canavese, Torino, celebrate the christening of *piccola* (little) Marina's baptism, May 28, 1934. Marina's godmother, Rosi, who is also her grandmother, holds the infant on her lap as the baby's great grandfather, sitting proudly, faces the camera. Marina's great uncle looks over his sister Rosi's shoulder. A variety of agricultural implements frames the family and establishes the family's occupation and substantial land ownership. *(Courtesy Catherine Baccari)*

Making Bread. Widowed in 1946, Onelia Baggio DeGrandis was left with a young family. Her husband, who died of tuberculosis, had earned a good living as a commercial buyer and seller of livestock in Campigo, Treviso. The family only had one hectare of land—not enough to feed a family of eight—so she started to make bread, which she sold. Neighbors, who brought their dough to bake in DeGrandis' backyard brick oven, would give Onelia a loaf of bread as a courtesy payment. Here we see (left to right) Onelia's grandson, Antonio, held by his young aunt, Evelina; Onelia's daughter, Giovanna; Onelia; Gina, Antonio's mother; daughter Lavinia; and son Vito. Onelia's mother and siblings had emigrated from Campigo to settle in Trail, British Columbia, Canada before World War II. *(Courtesy Carlo Piccolo)*

World War II's deprivations challenged Italian ingenuity. Carlo Chiarani looks debonair in a coat made from a German blanket left behind as the army retreated from Torbole sul Garda, Trento. Carlo's wife, Natalia, dyed the white woolen blanket brown, then took it to a tailor who made the coat. Carlo wore it to meet his Italian-American friend, Davide Bonapace, in Madonna di Campiglio, in upper Val Rendena, Trento, in spring 1950. After this visit, Carlo, a *mezzadri* (a sharecropper who owes half of the yield to the landowner and receives the use of a farmhouse rent-free), decided to emigrate. Finally, after waiting almost five years for visas, his family left for Detroit, Michigan, in 1954, where relatives sponsored their admission. *(Courtesy Luigi Chiarani)*

Young Girls Trained to Sew. This c. 1951 picture comes from an orphanage near Campobasso, Molise, where the young girls learned to use sewing needles like artists. They produced magnificent linens with the encouragement of Sister Barbarina (Ambrosina Iannidinardo). Traditionally, young girls were taught to sew even during the years when they did not receive any formal school education from the state. Many women immigrants in America transferred these skills into dressmaking and fine embroidery, working in tailor shops, in garment factories, and hand finishing clothing at home. *(Courtesy the Iannidinardo family)*

Youngsters play in Bovino, Puglia, in 1952. Angelo and Renato dePompa (left to right) romp in the shadow of the Norman Castle Guevara, while their mother, Marta, looks on. The boys' father, Attilio, orphaned at fourteen, had struggled to become an accountant and was admired and respected by his *paesani* for his ability to work through the maze of Italian law. By 1957, Attilio had built his *palazzo,* an impressive three-story house with marble floors from Carrara. Attilio could have become mayor of Bovino. But his son recalled, "There was an uneasiness about my father which must have come from the pain of the early years. He had achieved more than any other person . . . but it was not enough. He wanted more for the children. He wanted to distance himself from a country he believed would one day go Communist. So we . . . ended up in East Orange, New Jersey." In 1961, unable to speak English, Attilio could not find commensurate work. He struggled for years but would not return to Bovino defeated. After the 1968 riots following the assassination of Dr. Martin Luther King, Jr., the family left for Florida. Attilio's dream ended there. *(Courtesy Ron DePompa)*

Family Connections. The Pinti family farms in Tocca Casauria, Pescara, c. 1955. The Pintis married in 1937 and had five children. Annetta Smarrelli Pinti's mother and brother had left for Syracuse, New York, in 1939 to reunite with her father who had worked in the United States from the early part of the 1900s. Hoping to provide a better life for their children, the Pintis decided to emigrate. Arriving in Syracuse in 1955, they lived with Annetta's parents until they were settled. Eustacchio Pinti found work laying tiles and prospered. Soon after, they purchased a home. *(Courtesy the Guardiani and Sticca families)*

Starting the Trip. The first step for many immigrants was to take a train, perhaps for the first time, from their hometowns to the port of departure, usually Genoa, Naples, or Palermo. Then they stayed overnight in a hotel. One young boy emigrating from Maschito, Potenza, in 1915, remembered that he and his sister were fascinated to find out that by turning a faucet water would pour into the hotel sink. The next morning, after passing a medical exam, which checked for diseases, immigrants boarded their ships to sail for American ports. (*Courtesy Museo Regionale dell'Emigrazione "Pietro Conti," Gualdo Tadino, Italy*)

Imploring Heavenly Protection. This prayer card was given to people departing the former Kingdom of the Two Sicilies (Italy south of Rome) to America. The card reads, "I am leaving my homeland, St. Joseph protect me!" The prayer on the back, translated to English, reads, "To you, O blessed St. Joseph, we the descendants of the great people who formed the Kingdom of the Two Sicilies, placed in a time of great tribulation, faithfully run to you and your blessed wife, the Virgin Mary, to seek your aid . . . for the fatherly love that you gave to the child Jesus, we beg you . . . to look with your loving eye and give your power and help, to us and our brethren who have been forced to emigrate from our country." These sentiments reveal an undercurrent of apprehension and regret that accompanied most immigrants heading to America. (*Courtesy Stephanie Longo*)

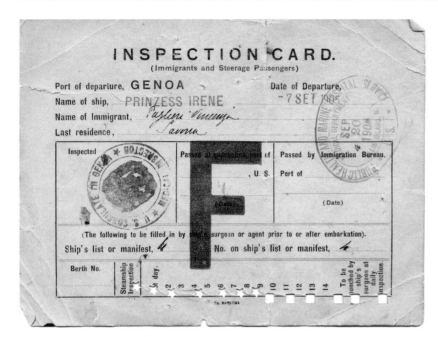

Health Inspection Card. Vincenza (Rosetta) Paglieri from Savona, Liguria, sailed on the *Princess Irene* with her husband and their three-year-old daughter to New York in September 1905. The United States Consulate's medical inspector stamped the card in Genoa, and at Ellis Island, the Public Health Medical Department stamped the card again. Rosetta's husband, Giacomo, became a partner in Stella Restaurant on Washington Street in Seattle, Washington's skid row, (date unknown). Open for breakfast and lunch, the restaurant offered a mostly meat and potatoes menu to the longshoremen, stevedores, and the down-and-out residents of this waterfront area. Giacomo's grandson remembers, "Giacomo would return home with squab [young pigeons] that people caught under the docks to barter for a warm meal." *(Courtesy Reginald E. Morgan)*

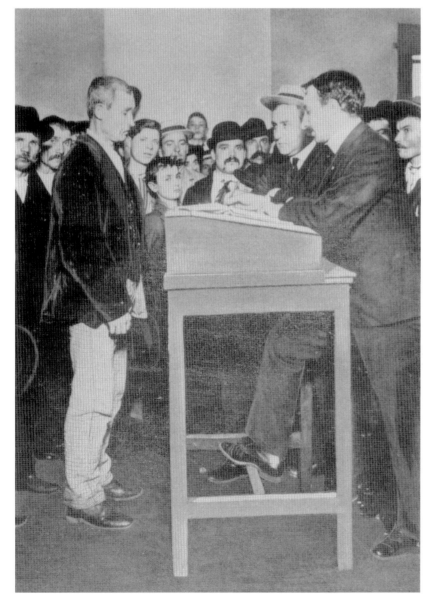

Help for Newly Arrived Immigrants, c. 1905. The Society for Italian Immigrants helped newcomers with a variety of matters, e.g. contacting their relatives who were already in the United States, locating lost baggage, helping to obtain railroad tickets for continuing inland, and at times interceding for immigrants facing deportation because they failed to meet the strict legal requirements for admission. For example, immigrants needed to demonstrate that they had some money so they would not become a public burden. The society acted as guarantors for many of these individuals and conducted appeals for those unjustly selected for repatriation. In 1908, Italy's *Commissariato dell' Emigrazione* published and distributed a pamphlet listing organizations in Boston, New York, San Francisco, and Montreal that assisted immigrants with information, the purchasing of tickets, and temporary en-route housing. (*From* Gli Italiani negli Stati Uniti d'America, *1906*)

Italians Arriving on Mulberry Street. Finding one's way through the crowded streets of lower Manhattan could be a problem for immigrants who were semiliterate or illiterate and spoke a dialect rather than standard Italian. Agents from the Society for Italian Immigrants offered to accompany new arrivals to their destination for a nominal fee of thirty-two cents rather than the outrageous sum of three or four dollars charged by freelance entrepreneurs. During years of heavy flow, between October 1902 and 1906, the society helped over forty-nine thousand immigrants. (*From* Gli Italiani negli Stati Uniti d'America, *1906*)

Changing Countries. Rose Maglione was born in Canada when her parents visited relatives there in 1909. The family returned to Foggia when she was a few months old. While prejudicial American immigration quotas prevented many Italians and southern and eastern Europeans from entering the United States in 1927, Rose entered the country on her British passport. Her father sent her to live with an uncle in Essex County, New Jersey, because he believed that since she was the smartest in the family and a skilled dressmaker, she would do well. She got a job sewing American flags. Her boss did not speak Italian, and she did not speak English, but he liked her work. (*Courtesy Michelle Vitale Loughlin and family, www.woolpunkstudios.com*)

International Clientele. The flow of traffic across the ocean provided a good source of income for agents of shipping lines. Many immigrants returned to Italy each year or every few years to visit family. Established immigrants sent prepaid tickets to relatives desiring to emigrate from Italy. Located at 17 Decatur Street in New Orleans, Louisiana, in 1900, the Del Orto Arturo Italian Bank served as the agent for shipping lines, whose ports of call included Palermo, Messina, Naples, and Genoa, in addition to its banking services, which included sending immigrant remittances back to relatives in Italy. New Orleans was a port of entry for many Italians heading to the sugar plantations of Louisiana, the cotton fields of the Mississippi Delta, and Brazos County, Texas, and other Southern cities. *(Courtesy Sidney J. Mazerat III)*

Detention Room for Women at Ellis Island, c. 1905. Known as the Isle of Tears, this inspection station was the first American encounter for thousands of Italian immigrants arriving after 1892. Newcomers were examined for contagious diseases and infirmities. The entire process was intimidating to Maria Carmela Mazzoni and her siblings, who left an orphanage in Tricarico, Matera, where they had been placed after the death of their parents. For Maria, the processing examination/interrogation went smoothly, but not for her youngest sister, Rose, who had been born with a slight limp. Weakened by the long, arduous journey, Rose seemed unfit for entry. Maria Carmela appealed the decision, begging the inspectors to reconsider. While Rose remained in the infirmary, her brother and sisters stayed by her side. Although impressed by this devotion, port authorities stood by their decision and ordered Rose to return to the Italian orphanage where she would reside until years later when she was finally able to return to America and join her family in San Jose, California. (*From* Gli Italiani negli Stati Uniti d'America, *1906*)

Family Chain Migration. The DeGrandis family in 1949. *Back row, left to right:* Giovanna, Gina, Onelia, Lavinia, and Angelo. *Front row, left to right:* Annamaria, Evelina, Vito. This photo was taken in their garden in Campigo, Treviso, before Angelo departed for Canada in July, 1949. Most of his mother's, Onelia Baggio DeGrandis, siblings already had preceded him to Trail, British Columbia, before World War II. Angelo traveled on an open emigration contract that waived the requirement for sponsorship for specific occupations, including farming. However, six months later, he was released from his contract, and he started work with Cominco (Consolidated Mining and Smelting Company of Canada), which processed zinc and lead, in Trail. Two years later, in 1951, his sister Lavinia joined Angelo in Trail. In 1953, it was sister Giovanna's turn, followed shortly by her other brother, Vito, in 1956. Angelo's mother and his youngest sister, Evelina, arrived in 1957. Gina, the remaining sibling, had married Anacleto Milani in 1949, and their children, Tony, Natalino, and Luciana, completed the family circle when they immigrated to Trail later in 1957. *(Courtesy Carlo Piccolo)*

Selective Recruitment of Professionals. Marcello Miceli from Latina, Lazio, responded to a radio advertisement. It requested any persons with a background in medicine (such as doctors or veterinarians) and engineers interested in working abroad to apply at Rome's city hall. As a trained engineer, Miceli built bridges in Italy. He was accepted for a position in the United States and took this picture from the ship's railing before it left the port of Naples in April 1958. Working for Myers Snow Plow, he eventually designed hydraulic units for snowplows. Later he started his own company, which his sons still operate. Marcello's wife, Esther, and their two sons joined him in Cleveland later that year. He told Esther that they would only stay in the United States for five years. Almost every summer she and their children spent two to three months visiting her family in Cisterna di Latina. Finally, in 1989, Esther decided to leave her husband and now grown children and return to Italy permanently. *(Courtesy Bianca M. Miceli Stone)*

Chapter 2

Spanning the Miles

Ties between Italy and America continued to link immigrants with their families and *paesani* at home. Immigrant husbands returned to visit their families or to escort them to America. Single male immigrants either traveled back to Italy to select a wife or sent letters to their families asking them to choose a suitable wife to send to America. Some individuals or families decided to repatriate.

Often the transition from sojourner to permanent resident in America depended upon the establishment of family life. The majority of migrants were men without women, alone in a strange land, seeking work to earn money needed for families still in Italy. The decision to reunite the family by sending for mothers, sisters, wives, and fiancées, and the decision to start a family by having relatives in Italy choose a bride to send to America or by returning to Italy to choose a wife, were the basic motivations for developing a fuller life in America.

Immigrants brought part of their homeland with them to America, and letters and exchange of photos enabled transatlantic communication. Sometimes a letter was entrusted to a friend returning to the home village rather than sent via mail. These letters provide intimate accounts of life in Italy and in America and are important historical documents.

Sometimes international events, such as wars, made family reunification impossible. During World War I, Italy was an ally of the United States, but Italians could not travel safely to America. Immigrants who had returned for a visit were "stranded" until the end of the conflict. World War II kept families separated for a different reason; since Italy was an enemy, allied with the Axis Powers, Italians could not be admitted. However, once Italy surrendered to the Allies in 1943, Italians in America sent packages of food and clothing back to their relatives in war-devastated Italy. During these difficult times, many Italians attempted to join relatives in the United States, South America, and Canada. Until 1965, the United States' strict quota system limited the flow of emigrants from Italy to the United States. Instead, large numbers of Italian immigrants answered the calls for workers in the oil fields of Australia and on construction crews in Canada; other Italians became guest workers of industrialized Europe in Switzerland, Germany, and Sweden.

Immigrant travel agents helped to secure tickets to send to wives and relatives for their passage to America. They also expedited leisure travel to Italy for Italian immigrants prosperous enough to tour the sights of Italy as well as visit their hometowns. This aspect of travel to and from Italy continues to connect Italian Americans to their relatives and the nation of their ancestry.

Newcomers created a customer base for imported products from Italy. Immigrants also brought implements with them, such as tools, *pizzelle* irons, ravioli cutters, or reconstructed them in America. They created affiliations with Italian organizations, such as sporting clubs. Language newspapers, purchased at a store, sent by mail, or lent hand-to-hand, informed sojourners of the news of home. They sent aid during times of need, such as the Messina earthquake in 1908; they celebrated events, such as the annexation of South Tyrol into Italy as part of the 1919 Versailles Treaty; and welcomed Italian government officials when they toured settlements in America. The mission of these officials was to report to the authorities in Rome on the status of *italiani all'estero* (Italians abroad).

For the most part, immigrants continued the practices they had followed in Italy, keeping traditions of growing and eating foods associated with seasons of the year and maintaining much of their religious and family rituals. In post-1960 America, some immigrants used their language, cooking, or designing skills to bring Italy to all Americans.

Keeping in Touch. Professional letter writers were common during the nineteenth and early twentieth centuries. This scrivener offers to write in Italian or French. Many people in Italy were semiliterate or illiterate and required the skill of a letter writer to communicate information to family members abroad. Of course, upon receipt of a letter, some recipients would ask a *paesani* to read the contents aloud. In 1917, the United States Congress passed a literacy requirement for immigrants. Every adult needed to be able to read in some language. *(Author's collection)*

First Son Born in America. Francesco Rosario Sacco and Calogera Piscitello sent this picture of their first child—a boy, Michele Giuseppe (Michael Joseph) Sacco, born in Milwaukee, Wisconsin, November 11, 1911—to their families in Italy. Francesco came from Casabona, Crotone, and Calogera was born in Santo Stefano di Camastra, Messina. They met and married in Wisconsin. In the photo, Michele Giuseppe's clothing is intentionally arranged to provide absolute proof of his masculinity. *(Courtesy Russell [Rosario] Sacco)*

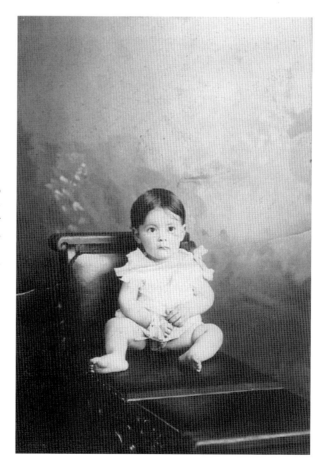

Birds of Passage. Vincenzo Arnone sits surrounded by his family, 1917. Pictured left to right are Tony, Joe, Rachela, Vincenzo holding Immaculata, Miliella, and Carmelina. Starting in 1881, Vincenzo, a peasant farmer, tending goats and raising chestnuts, traveled back and forth from Celico, Cosenza, to the United States. Returning to Celico, he married Rachela in 1887, and their first child was born in 1888. He re-entered the United States in 1890, after the birth of his second child, but was back in Celico to father a third child in 1894. Before the baby was born, he and his brother Carmine obtained naturalization papers in Chicago, Illinois. By late 1895, Vincenzo was back in Italy but quickly returned to the United States in March 1896. He returned to Celico, perhaps (we cannot be certain), for the birth of his next three children. By 1899, he was back in the United States and was listed in the 1900 Illinois census as living with his two brothers and his twelve-year-old son, Michele. They all worked on the railroad in Montgomery County, Illinois. Vincenzo returned to Celico for the last time in 1903. By 1917, he had fathered four more children and operated his own store and a tavern. *(Courtesy Rose Marie Sicoli-Ostler)*

Bringing America to Italy. Emigrating from Uzzano, Pistoia, Ettore Franchini, together with his brother, Ovidio Franchini, opened Franchini Bros., a wholesale/retail general merchandise store located at 300-302 North First Street in Albuquerque, New Mexico, c. 1913. The prosperous business specialized in groceries, olive oil, tobacco products, and imported Italian specialties. Immigrants wishing to visit Italy often purchased their steamship tickets from Franchini Bros. Ettore Franchini eventually sold his interest in the family grocery business to concentrate on travel services. With the help of his children and grandchildren, Franchini went on to establish one of Albuquerque's largest family-owned travel agencies. *(Courtesy Nicholas Ciotola collection)*

Recruiting Family Labor. Giuseppe Montecucco sent this picture of his new truck, which he used to transport his garden crops to market from Portland, Oregon's Reed College area, with a letter to his brother, Angelo, in Italy. Giuseppe's description (translated), written on the back of the photo, noted, "The large truckload of vegetables, in the front, all spinach; in the middle, lettuce; in the back, peas, carrots and lots of other stuff. In the front is Gimmi [Damonte], the husband of Mary [Montecucco]. Behind you can see where we stack the *barrelas* [wooden stands to stack harvested vegetables]." The accompanying letter asked Angelo to send his son, Paolo, to Portland, where he would join Angelo's brothers, Luigi and Giuseppe, already working on their land. *(Courtesy Stephen Montecucco and the Montecucco family)*

An Ocean Away. Luigi Fioretti came to America in 1914 from Carbonara di Bari and was hired to work in the coal mines near Cle Elum/Roslyn, Washington, as a "powder monkey," the guy who sets explosive charges. Three years later, after a major mine explosion that killed several miners, he decided to seek employment with the Northern Pacific Railway. Upon retiring, he returned to Italy in 1949. During his period in the United States, he made only two trips back to Italy, once in 1919 when he and his wife, Stella Milela, had a son and again in 1933 when Luigi brought his son, Matteo, back to Washington State. Stella remained in Italy because the American Consul in Naples would not issue her a visa due to a hiatal hernia. Over the years, she turned this rejection into proof of her independence as she would declare to her customers in the cantina she operated, "America, geed oudda here you som ba bitch! Non gooood, non goood, mang a na ting [not worth a thing]!" She saw her son again when he served in Italy as a soldier for the United States Army during World War II. *(Courtesy Matt and Antonetta Fioretti)*

The Grass Is Greener. A photo of Concetto Stagnitti (Connie), age eleven, and his mother, Paola, and father, Giuseppe Stagnitti, prior to their return to Linguaglossa, Catania, in 1921. Connie's parents and his four older siblings immigrated to Canastota, New York, in 1908. After a few years, Connie and his parents decided to return to Linguaglossa in order to reunite with family and because of Giuseppe's displeasure with the prejudice he experienced and his difficulty with the English language. After three years, in 1924, the family returned to America, when Paola missed her older, married children who had settled in Canastota. She also decided that her life in the United States was much better and easier than her life in Sicily. Back in Canastota, all of Paola's sons worked the farm with her husband, and in New York, she no longer had to work in the fields. In addition, she had access to a greater variety of material goods. Paola's youngest son, Connie, was happy to leave behind the poverty that he had witnessed in Sicily, where he worked in the fields to contribute to the support of his family. *(Courtesy Lynne Stagnitti Ahnert)*

Left Behind, 1930s. Angelo Bertucci and his wife, Maria Basile Bertucci, on their farm in Ustica, Palermo (an island off the north coast), sent this picture to their son and his family in San Francisco, California, and wrote on the back of the photo (translation): "Your dear parents, see how old they got? I will write in the future. I wait for your letters. Why don't you write? Dear kisses for everybody." Immigration provided opportunities for change, but change also separated families and transferred a limited social support system to America. *(Courtesy Angelo Bertucci)*

Planning to Return to Tocco da Casauria, Pescara. In 1932, Cesidia Sticca Guardiani sent this photo of her eight-year-old son, Gianni (fifth from right), posing in his Mussolini Youth uniform, to his father, Eustacchio, who had left in 1927 for work in the United States. Eustacchio dug sewers in Port Jervis, New Jersey, to earn enough money to purchase land in Italy. By 1929, Cesidia had purchased a house and land with the remittances she received. Perhaps this image of his son's future influenced Eustacchio to give up his Italian dream and instead bring his family to Staten Island, New York, in 1934. *(Courtesy the Guardiani and Sticca Families)*

Ambassador of Fortune, 1932. Pietro "Pete" DePasquale returns triumphantly for a visit to his hometown, Gamberale, Chieti. He achieved success as a contractor, owning a company in Pittsburgh, Pennsylvania. He gained respect as a prominent leader in Pittsburgh, especially for his role as one of the founders of the San Lorenzo Society. The organization sponsored and cared for newly arrived *paesani* from Gamberale. DePasquale's obvious success in America served to reinforce the belief of Gamberale's residents that emigration would improve their circumstances. *(Courtesy the Paolicelli and DePasquale families)*

Maintaining United States Citizenship. In 1928, Anselmo Minato recorded the arrival of his wife, Maria, and their children to the United States. Anselmo left Pagnano di Asolo, Treviso, for San Francisco, California, in 1912. He worked at various jobs in northern California, along with other immigrants from the province of Treviso. After fighting in the United States Army during World War I, Anselmo got a job with Pelican Bay Lumber Company in Klamath Falls, Oregon. He returned to Italy for a visit and married Maria Forato in 1922. His three-year visa required that he return to the United States to maintain his citizenship. When the local fascists tried to talk him into staying, he beat them up and had to leave town fast. His fourth child, Narciso, was born after Anselmo left Italy in 1926. He got a job with Chiloquin Lumber Company, located on the Klamath Indian Reservation in Chiloquin, Oregon. Maria and the children arrived in America in 1928, and she became pregnant in 1929. She had a difficult pregnancy, and the family decided to go to San Francisco for delivery assistance by an experienced Italian midwife. Maria's son, Remo, was born in the San Remo Hotel in San Francisco on February 12, 1930. *(Courtesy Alfeo E. Minato)*

Giustizia e Libertà! Holding a copy of the well-known anti-fascist underground newspaper, founded by intellectual/political exile Carlo Rosselli and printed in Paris, France, Frank (Francesco) Forges, born Antonio De Sanguine in Trani, Bari, sits in his New York apartment. De Sanguine/Forges had worked as a secret agent in opposition to Mussolini's Fascist government. He left Italy in 1926 when Mussolini issued specific orders to have him hunted down and killed. In New York, he continued his anti-Fascist activities, expressing his opposition toward Mussolini's regime. The Italian consulate in New York monitored his movements and reported to Rome. In 1937, Forges tried to arrange a lecture tour for his comrade, Rosselli, in the United States. Forges' plan ended abruptly when Italian Fascists murdered Rosselli on a country road in Normandy. *(Courtesy Sylvia Forges Ryan)*

Losing His Country. Leonard De Luca escorted his sister from Pedace, Cosenza, in 1912 for her marriage to Angelo Scarcello, a farmer in Rathdrum, Idaho. He worked on Angelo's farm to earn his fare back to Italy. When World War I started, he ended up in the United States Army and was gassed fighting in France. De Luca received a forty percent disability award. In 1926, he went to Italy and married Francesca Grande, and they had a daughter. Afterwards, he returned to the United States as a railroad worker in Spokane, Washington, to earn money to buy a farm in Pedace, which he did in 1932. He continued to send money to the Italian postal savings, which issued him bonds, but by the end of World War II, these bonds were worth very little. De Luca decided instead to bring his wife and daughter to the United States in 1947. He died from lung complications in 1972. *(Courtesy Ray Martire)*

Greetings from Italy. In 1949, in Campigo, Treviso, the DeGrandis family designed this "trick" shot to send to the children's aunts and uncles in Trail, British Columbia, Canada. The photo shows a stack of straw *(pagliaio)* turned on its side with the family standing on a step ladder. Most hay stacks were twenty feet or more high and about fifteen feet in diameter, built around a pole (dead tree). Pictured from the top are Vito, age fourteen; Evelina, age twelve; Giovanna, age sixteen; Lavinia, age twenty-four; Gina, age twenty-two; and their mother, Onelia Baggio DeGrandis, age forty-five. Onelia's son, Angelo, age twenty, left Campigo for Trail in July 1949. He emigrated through a contract program the government established to obtain farm labor. *(Courtesy Carlo Piccolo)*

Ties That Bind. In 1977, Ron DePompa returned to his birthplace in Bovino, Puglia, to introduce his American wife to his grandparents, Giustina Montecalvo and Raffaele Bonassisa. On the last day of his visit, Ron's *nonna* (grandmother) said they were going for a walk. First, they stopped at the market, where she bought some very large Spanish onions. From there Nonna led the way, "swinging the onions and clicking her shiny black shoes on the hot asphalt." They entered the *camposanto* (cemetery). She proceeded with her grandson to the graves of uncles and relatives, and after about the sixth round, she must have noticed his impatient look. "She pulled me closer to her and in a whisper [said,] "Ti ho portato qui così puoi sapere chi sei" ("I brought you here so you might know who you are"). On the walk back to the car to depart, Ron remembers thinking, "I knew I would never see her alive again and I would never go back. . . . I smelled the wild oregano on the side of the road and remembered happy days. . . . Nonna Giustina put down her onions, hugged me and whispered, "Ti voglio bene assai; ti voglio tanto tanto bene" ("I love you quite a bit; I love you very, very much"). *(Courtesy Ron DePompa)*

Bringing a Wife to America, 1968. Nunziata Pisani, age sixteen, marries Felice D'Elia in Contursi Terme, Salerno. Eleven years older than his bride, Felice had lived and worked in Brooklyn, New York, for seven years before visiting his hometown, greeting his friends, including the Pisani family. Nunziata's parents and her nine siblings lived in a farmhouse without electricity or running water. They made their own olive oil, pasta, bread, and wine, and they ate fruits and vegetables they grew themselves. Their animals, including cows, pigs, sheep, and chickens, provided both their food and income. Nunziata and her brothers and sisters would deliver milk to other families in the town. They would have to wake up at five in the morning, gather all the bottles of milk, walk two miles into town to deliver all the milk, and then go to school. Felice returned to Brooklyn with "Nancy" and resumed his work at the A&S Italian Pork Store on Avenue X. Frank Alfino from Milwaukee, Wisconsin, married his Italian pen-pal Lidia Fasi in Vicenza, Italy, in 1960. The location of their wedding reception, which was in the castle, near Verona, associated with Shakespeare's character "Juliet," gave a fairy tale quality to the occasion. *(Courtesy Nunziata Pisani)*

Italian Ambassador Visits Tontitown Settlement, c. 1905. Edmondo Mayor desPlanches traveled through the southern states to report on the condition of Italian immigrants who had settled in rural areas. At Tontitown, Arkansas, he was welcomed by Father Pietro Bandini (sitting in the carriage with his head bowed). Bandini led a group of immigrants disillusioned by the poor living and working conditions at Sunnyside Plantation in Arkansas in 1898 to found a new settlement named Tontitown in honor of the Italian explorer Enrico Tonti, who accompanied Robert Cavalier DeLaSalle during his exploration of the Mississippi Valley in 1682. DesPlanches spoke glowingly of the success enjoyed by the immigrant farmers who cultivated their own land. (*From* Gli Italiani negli Stati Uniti d'America, *1906*)

"King of Olive Oil." G. B. Levaggi arrived in California from his hometown of Lucca in 1865. For eight years, he mined for gold. In 1873, he established a fruit commission company, Levaggi and Barbieri. After a visit to Lucca in 1894, Levaggi returned to San Francisco and launched the Levaggi Import Company, which featured olive oil from Lucca. He supplied most firms on the Pacific Coast with this well-known product. Many Italian groceries across the United States stocked Lucca brand olive oil. (*From* Gli Italiani negli Stati Uniti d'America, *1906*)

Venice in America. Pietro Cipolato delivered one of the gondolas he had crafted from his workshop in Venice, Italy, to Venice, California, in 1907. After spending some time in San Francisco, he returned to Italy. The caption on the picture reads, "Shriners' day at Venice of America, Cal." Abbott Kinney, the developer of Venice, California, envisioned creating a "Venice on the Pacific," but the promotion fell far short of its goal and Venice was later annexed to Los Angeles. *(Courtesy Alfredo Cipolato)*

Mascagni's Tribute. The famous opera composer Pietro Mascagni *(Cavalleria Rusticana, 1890)* toured across the United States from 1902 to 1903 but was plagued by financial and other reversals as far as Chicago, Illinois. With the help of the Italian Consul, Antonio Ladislao Rozwadowski, and others in the Chicago Italian community, the Theodore Thomas Orchestra, which later became the Chicago Symphony, was retained for a series of concerts beginning in January. Both critical and popular successes, the Chicago concerts lifted the composer's spirits and raised enough money for Mascagni to travel to San Francisco, California, where he received an overwhelming welcome. Audiences there acclaimed his performances; appreciative patrons honored him with banquets and receptions. When the Italian Chamber of Commerce presented him with a gold-inlaid ivory baton, the composer responded, "This is the first time that I have been honored so warmly, so thoroughly, so spontaneously, [in America] and seen my own compatriots mixing with American citizens." He expressed his gratitude by composing a short lyrical piece (thirteen bars long) for the piano, entitled *Un pensiero a San Franciso* (A Thought for San Francisco) as a gift to the city. The *San Francisco Chronicle* printed a copy of the manuscript, reproduced here, on February 21, 1903, and the entire city celebrated Mascagni's gesture. *(Courtesy Library of Congress, Music Division)*

Pane e Lavoro. In lonely stretches along America's railroad lines Italian immigrants constructed ovens to bake the bread their families had eaten in Italy. Here a section gang working on the Chicago, Milwaukee, and Saint Paul Railroad near Terry, Montana, c. 1908, pose for photographer Evelyn Cameron. Section gangs of five or six men would live together in a boxcar (note the car in the background with a man standing in the doorway). They did their own cooking and constructed their ovens by digging in the hard ground and lining the bottom with bricks or rocks. The oven was filled with wood and when the bricks turned white from the heat, the ashes were removed and the bread baked on the hot bricks. Unlike some of her neighbors, Cameron spoke Italian, and she treated the immigrants with respect. She would take the pictures they requested to send back to their families, and when they moved down the line, she corresponded with them. *(Courtesy Montana Historical Society)*

Campanilismo: **Traditions Linger.** Immigrant gardeners, mostly from Lombardy and Calabria, settled in Walla Walla, Washington. Each group concentrated (not exclusively) in different sections of town. When the Italians, helped by financial contributions from the Irish parishioners of Saint Patrick's, constructed Saint Francis Church in 1915, just two city blocks away, Milanese immigrants gravitated to the pews on the west side of the aisle and Calabrese immigrants to the pews on the right. Stained glass windows donated by Italian families were also relegated to their "proper" side in the church. Separation did not signify hostility but an age-old tradition of feeling comfortable with those whose regional customs and dialect were similar. In Bryan, Texas, this pattern was more refined as Sicilians from Poggioreale, Trapani, farmed mainly on land along the Brazos River, while Sicilians from Corleone, Palermo, farmed the hilly land called Cameron Ranch. *(Courtesy Dorothy Fazzari)*

Carrying the Torch. In this 1918 picture, these youthful members of the Garibaldi Guards in Milwaukee, Wisconsin, hold a banner that reads, "The Socialists—The Sons of The Future." For many Italians Giuseppe Garibaldi represented the spirit of reform as well as national unification. Emigrants from the former Kingdom of Two Sicilies rallied to the cause of freedom when Garibaldi's Red Shirts landed in Marsala, Trapani, and won the battle against the Bourbon army at Calatafimi, Trapani. *(Courtesy Italian Community Center of Milwaukee, Wisconsin)*

Royal Consular Agent for Oklahoma. Giovanni Battista Tua was officially appointed the royal consular agent for the state of Oklahoma in 1910. Giovanni was born in Marseilles to parents from Foglizzo, Torino. He came to the United States in 1891 and worked in the mines of Osage, Kansas, and Hartshorne, Indian Territory, until 1897, when he moved to McAlester, Indian Territory. Many of the miners Tua met also came from the Piemonte region. In McAlester, he first worked for the Fassino brothers, who owned a buggy and wagon agency and a macaroni factory. Then Tua established his own business, a confectionary/cigar store and later the Owl Café. Tua became a naturalized citizen in 1902, five years before Oklahoma became a state. He gave up his business when he became consular agent and moved into a new office, establishing a steamship agency and a foreign exchange agency, and he issued visas and passports in connection with his consular duties. He often assisted Italian immigrants in their business transactions, in writing wills and recording land transactions, and he facilitated sending remittances of Italians to deposit in the Postal Savings Banks of Italy. (During World War I, and for a few years after, one day's total remittances could exceed ten thousand dollars). The office closed down during World War II, and after the war ended, Giovanni continued to serve his countrymen and his community in the McAlester area as a travel agent for steamship, rail, and, later, air travel. *(Courtesy Jane Tua Smith and Judy Tua Brown)*

Italy Triumphant. Albuquerque, New Mexico's Colombo Society celebrates Armistice Day in 1918 with a float honoring Italy's General Armando Diaz. Diaz led his troops across the Piave River in October 1918 to defeat the Austrian army in a crucial battle that helped to end World War I. Many Italian immigrants had returned to Italy in 1915 when Italy entered the war against Germany and Austria. In November of 1918, Italy's October triumph became part of the larger celebration. *(Courtesy Nicholas P. Ciotola / University of New Mexico, Center for Southwest Research, and Paul and Patti Marianetti)*

Transferable Skills. Pasquale Petosa, a stone cutter from Loranzana, Campobasso, built this stone cellar to store produce and smoked meat next to his family's log home on their Stillwater river farm near Columbus, Montana. Mike Jacobs (née Jacobucci) recruited Petosa, along with other Italian stonemasons living in Chicago, to work in Columbus. (Mike Jacobs had done most of the carving of the stone lions in front of Chicago's Art Institute.) The recruited workers cut Montana sandstone in the Columbus quarry to construct the Montana State Capitol in Helena, federal buildings in Butte and Helena, and the Masonic Temple in Missoula. Ultimately, Petosa and his son, Chris, established a monument business and carved grave markers. *(Courtesy Sharon Meredith)*

Bocce after Sunday Dinner. Italian workers at Colonial Gardens located in Fife, Washington, c. 1920, play the ancient game of bocce. Italian immigrants, mostly from the area near Genoa started this partnership in 1886 with each person owning one share. The gardeners grew table vegetables on approximately three hundred acres and peddled them through the streets of Tacoma. The partners hired newly arrived Italian immigrants to help cultivate and harvest the crops. Like others, Giuseppe Garré from Sant'Olcese, Liguria, first worked as a garbage collector in Tacoma before becoming a partner, c. 1915. *(Courtesy the Ed Garré Family)*

Conditions in America. Italian officials investigated the treatment of immigrants in America and condemned violence, exploitation, and discrimination. Reports warned prospective immigrants about these problems. Here a delegation headed by Fortunato Anselmo, the Italian vice-consul for Utah, visits Castle Gate, Utah, after a mine explosion in 1924. *(Used by permission, Utah Historical Society, all rights reserved)*

Church and State. Parishioners of Our Lady of Pompeii Church, in Chicago, Illinois, display Italian, papal, and U.S. flags to celebrate the concordat between Prime Minister Benito Mussolini and Pope Pius XI, June 9, 1929. This agreement ended a half-century of discord and strife between church and state in Italy, which began when Giuseppe Garibaldi entered Rome on September 20, 1870, and made it the capital of Italy. Until that time, the Pope had reigned as secular ruler of Rome. Under the terms of the Lateran Pacts of 1929, the Pope recognized Rome as the capital of the state of Italy and he was given sovereignty over Vatican City and complete independence. The Lateran Treaty also established Roman Catholicism as the state religion of Italy and provided for religious instruction in the public schools. *(Courtesy Dominic Candeloro)*

Concerns for Italians Abroad. In 1908, a group of six Italian organizations in Stamford, Connecticut, responded to an initiative of the Colonial Institute of Rome and the Italian Consul of New York to establish a permanent organization in Rome to represent Italian immigrant groups abroad—the *Congresso degl'Italiani all'estero* (Congress of Italians Abroad). Italian newspapers in New York and Rome published a report listing immigrants' major concerns—military draft abroad, understanding of district courts operation, protection of the jobs and earnings of workers, and the teaching of the Italian language. The United States Department of Labor also requested copies in order to acquaint itself with the situation of immigrants in Connecticut. Many felt that acquiring American citizenship and the consolidation of authority in Benito Mussolini's government would mitigate some of these issues. Finally, the group advocated a *Casa Italiana* to promote the educational advancement of immigrants, which would dispel some of the negative attitudes towards newcomers from Italy. *(Courtesy Stamford Historical Society)*

Italian Musicians. In 1939, St. Anthony's Band formed in New Castle, Delaware, under the baton of Don Domenico from Naples, Italy. The band committee provided Don Domenico a job and housing so he could direct the group. The band lasted only a few years, but it had thirty members who practiced each week at St. Anthony's club. Italian artists, composers, and musicians brought their talents and knowledge to America early in the life of the new nation. President Thomas Jefferson initiated the United States Marine Band when he recruited fourteen Italian musicians to form this group. (*Courtesy Francis A. Ianni*)

***Pomodori al fresco*, 1920s.** In August, the Italian immigrant women of Madison, Wisconsin, began the process of making tomato paste. *Left to right:* Rose Maltese, Angela La Bella, and Giacoma Oliva work in the open field on Desmond (Bowen) Court. St. Joseph's Church can be seen in the background. The women would take their tomato boards, usually 4-x-8, 1-inch-thick sheets of plywood, out of storage. They would cook down the tomatoes and then strain the pulp to remove the skin and seeds. Next, they spread the pulp on the boards, which were slightly tilted to drain off the excess juice, and set the boards in the sun to dry. (This process is replicated in the film *Cinema Paradiso.*) They turned the sauce repeatedly with a spatula to dry it out until it reduced to a thick paste. The thickened paste was rolled into two-pound balls and packed into crocks, covered with a layer of olive oil, and sealed with cheesecloth. In densely populated cities, Italian women set the boards out on their fire escapes or tenement house roofs to dry the tomato pulp. (*Courtesy Anthony [LaBella] Fiore*)

Stranded in America. Alfredo Cipolato was working in a hotel in Tripoli, Libya, when the Italian Line offered him an opportunity to work for six months at the Italian Pavilion restaurant at the World's Fair in New York City. He arrived around July 4, 1940. Shortly after, a bomb was discovered in the alley between the French, Italian, and British Pavilions. The police threw the bomb in a pond, and it exploded. Many speculated that the culprits were anti-fascists. Soon the Italian government closed its Pavilion, and Cipolato found work at New York's Waldorf Astoria and then, in Miami, at the Fontainebleau Hotel. On July 10, 1941, the United States broke off diplomatic relations with Italy, and Cipolato was arrested and placed in the Dade County jail before being sent to Ellis Island, where he and fifteen hundred Italian seamen were held until they were interned at Fort Missoula, Montana, for the war's duration. *(Courtesy Alfredo Cipolato)*

Rituals of Life and Death. When Italian immigrant midwife Mary Baldini died in 1950, the entire community attended her funeral, following the tradition of carrying the casket to the church for a final blessing. Mary had delivered virtually every Italian-American child born in New Castle, Delaware, until after World War II. Midwives trained in their profession knew their boundaries and would summon doctors if they expected a difficult and complicated birth. *(Courtesy Francis A. Ianni)*

Home Cooking in Spokane, Washington, c. 2000. Tullia Barbanti, who emigrated from Fossombrone, Pesaro, uses mostly recipes from her home region in her cooking classes. She wrote and published *Al Dente: Italian Cooking Done Just Right* in 1987, and the book is now in its second printing. She also prepares and bottles her sauce for sale at the farmers' markets and some retail outlets. Individuals who attend her cooking classes are customers from the market or students who met her in the Italian language class at Spokane Falls Community College. Most of them are of Italian-American heritage. *(Courtesy Tullia Barbanti)*

Finding *Zunchi* in America. *Left to right:* Paul Montecucco, Paul S. Montecucco, Frances Montecucco, and Janice Montecucco pick *zunchi* (bulrush) in Vancouver, Washington, in the early 1950s, continuing the tradition they followed in Vignole Borbera, Alessandria, where *zunchi* were used to tie a bunch of vegetables. After the *zunchi* were picked, they were soaked for three hours, then dried, and finally cut to size before being used. The bunches were tied, and the excess was cut off with the thumbnail. Picking *zunchi* for their farm was always a family outing that included a picnic lunch. *Zunchi* users, including the Genovese, in Portland, Oregon, Milanese (who called it *giunchi*), and Calabrese gardeners in Walla Walla, Washington, claimed that it was a fast and efficient way to tie the bunches, equal to or better than plastic ties. *(Courtesy Stephen Montecucco and the Montecucco family)*

CHAPTER 3

FINDING A HOME

Both chance and strategy determined the final destination of Italian immigrants. Men seeking work traveled to areas where opportunities beckoned. Immigrants mined iron and copper in the upper Midwest and constructed and maintained railroads in every region in North America. They fished the Gulf Coasts from Texas to Louisiana, the California coast from Monterey to San Francisco, and along the Atlantic. Their families farmed in Oregon, California, Illinois, New Jersey, and Louisiana. Some of these skills were learned in Italy, while others were acquired in America. Once a small nucleus of Italians settled in a community, others followed. Letters written to family and friends back home described this "America" of Pittston, Pennsylvania; Donaldsonville, Louisiana; Hibbing, Minnesota; and North Bay, Ontario, to prospective emigrants. As these communities increased in size, they, in turn, created business opportunities for Italian Americans who specialized in such ethnic enterprises as importing and retailing Italian products.

Concentrations of immigrants grew where jobs and Italian Americans intersected and established an *ambiente*. Italian-American communities reflected much of the regional culture that the immigrants brought with them, but their exposure to America also influenced the ways in which they responded to the conditions of daily life. Any attempt to recreate the Old World existence met the challenge of New World circumstances. What emerged was a structure tempered by selective accommodation.

Immigrants tended to cluster together on the same street, the same section of town or rural area. They filled their homes with the objects they used to work, cook, and recreate. They planted gardens and dug wine cellars to provide the amenities they valued in daily life. In the early 1900s, Italian immigrants to California discovered that the black-and-white-striped European land snails they had enjoyed eating in Italy were easily found in their new environment. This and other nonnative European snails had already been introduced (probably by Spanish and Mexican settlers), prospered, and spread, much to the dismay of nonsnail eating gardeners.

In many ethnic groups, the family is the unit through which the past is preserved and the values and customs that govern society are continued. The Italian family in America remained a source of this conservation, but individual members also encountered the larger American society.

Men found jobs that exposed them to non-Italians; their language expanded by incorporating English words, such as "job" (*giobba*) and "boss" (*bossa*). Even the women, who stayed home and seldom ventured beyond the geographic boundaries of *paesani* stores and the neighborhood, had to deal with non-Italians. No neighborhood remained the exclusive territory of any one group. The Little Italies of North America also housed Irish, Jewish, and Polish Americans, and most immigrant women communicated, in however limited fashion, with their next-door neighbors, their landlords, and the non-Italian dry-goods store proprietors. Both mother and father had to adjust to children who spoke to each other in English at home—sometimes in defiance of parents who could not understand them. Parents faced a school system that encouraged children to regard non-American tradition as obsolete and a society that simultaneously respected

Italian opera but often discriminated against the immigrant artisan barber, shoemaker, or baker who hummed arias from *Rigoletto*.

Within the context of family and community, Italian immigrants developed a social and cultural life that provided opportunities to enjoy the comfort of familiar sights, sounds, and smells and that fostered the cultural expression of the people. Most immigrants entertained relatives and close friends at home. Women would sit outside their houses and chat while children played in the crowded streets. Men would stop at a friend's home or a saloon and spend a few hours playing cards and drinking wine. The growing, preparation, and sharing of food dominated the lives of most Italians, who made each meal a social event.

Organ grinders, hurdy-gurdy players, and local musicians filled the streets with music. As a livelihood, street entertainment was common in southern Italian cities. Puppet shows in the tradition of *La Commedia dell' Arte* delighted the viewer. Italian musicians, among the earliest immigrants to America, played in the municipal and military bands and taught their skills to others. Musicians also formed bands to play at christenings, weddings, and public celebrations. Most families had at least one member who played the mandolin, the accordion, or the violin.

Local amateur groups scheduled performances of Italian opera and plays, and professional entertainers catered to the immigrant community. Comedians, notably Farfariello, characterized familiar American types, such as the city policeman.

Post-World War II immigrants often settled near their relatives who still lived in Italian enclaves or in newer suburban areas of the 1950s and 1960s. Mario R. Capecchi, winner of the 2007 Nobel Prize in medicine, immigrated with his mother to the United States in 1947 to join her brother in Bucks County, Pennsylvania. When his mother was arrested at their home in Verona by the Gestapo and imprisoned in Dachau because of her anti-fascist activities, four-year-old Capecchi lived on the streets and hid in the Italian Alps. Capecchi received a Ph.D. in biophysics from Harvard University and later developed the technique of gene targeting in embryonic-derived stem cells.

As Italy's economy prospered, some immigrants, professionals from the fields of engineering, medical research, and business, chose to settle in America. Their choice of location would depend more on their skill rather than a conscious decision to live near other Italians.

Despite the contrasts between old and new, Italians chose the American customs they found useful and ignored the suggestions that threatened to undermine their basic values of family and tradition. Out of this interaction grew the culture of the Italian Americans.

Italians in New Orleans. The 1850 census noted that the city of New Orleans, Louisiana, had the largest Italian population of any American city. Although the cities of New York, Boston, Philadelphia, and Chicago soon claimed higher numbers of immigrants, in New Orleans, Italian enterprise in fruit importation, produce marketing, groceries, bars, and other services added a distinct Italian presence. Many immigrants lived in the French Quarter; the intersection of Madison and Decatur streets is pictured here in 1906. During periods of Yellow Fever epidemics—serious outbreaks occurred in 1902 and 1905—Italians who lived in this crowded, rundown area were often blamed for spreading the disease. (*Courtesy Library of Congress, Prints and Photographs Division; reproduction # LC-D4-19309*)

Planned Communities. In the early 1890s, Alessandro Mastro Valerio founded the colonies of Daphne and Lambert in Alabama with settlers from the Tirolese area of northern Italy. Many prominent Italians believed that the immigrants should continue to apply their traditional agricultural skills in America's rural areas rather than struggle for existence in the harsh environment and work conditions they experienced in large cities. Mastro Valerio worked with state and federal agricultural agents to develop European vines on American rootstock suited for the climate. These vines produced early-ripening grapes that netted good prices in northern markets. Each family owned from ten to twenty-five acres of land acquired for $1.50 to $5.00 per acre. The settlers used the pinewood on their land to build their own houses. This prosperous farm family in Lambert, Alabama, c.1905, enjoys the bounty of their land, dining al fresco in what appears to be a bocce court. (*From* Gli Italiani negli Stati Uniti d'America, *1906*)

Crowded Streets in Lower Manhattan, New York. This row of tenements, numbers 260 to 268 Elizabeth Street, referred to by the photographer, Lewis Hine, as the "garment district," was typical of the housing environment of the immigrant workers who finished clothes at home. *(Courtesy Library of Congress, Prints and Photographs Division; reproduction # LC-USZ62-29125)*

Homesteading in America. Although most Italians arrived in the United States in the 1890s after the best lands were claimed for homesteading, some immigrants did claim land offered by the government. Giuseppe Garbarino and his wife, Katherine, from Denton, Texas, were married in Prescott, Arizona, in 1879. In 1864, Guiseppe, age fourteen, and his father left Versi, Lorsica, for Humboldt County, California. They lived with other Italian men and worked on a vegetable farm and prospected for gold. Giuseppe's father soon returned to Italy, and after ten years, Giuseppe moved to Arizona to prospect for gold. He settled in Willow Creek, Yavapai County, Arizona, where he ranched and continued to look for gold. This picture was taken at the homestead in 1916. *(Courtesy Georgia Garbarino Biller)*

Joint Households. During their first year in Parkersburg, West Virginia, the DiNucci, Carnevale, Borrelli, and Liberatore families (a total of twenty-five people) lived together in a large house of twelve to fifteen rooms. All came from the province of Campobasso. Each family had two bedrooms, but all the families used the same living room, and the cooking and eating were done on a cooperative basis. Each mother did her share of chores, such as cooking, washing dishes and clothes, and cleaning the house. On payday, based on how many there were in the family, each family contributed to the food kitty, and from that amount, they purchased food for all. They would also pay their share of the rent and gas. The two-acre yard provided playing space for the children and room for a vegetable garden and chicken coops. In this photograph, c. 1908, Catarina DiNucci (left) holds her third child of nine, Lena, her first American-born baby. The other two women are Peppina Carnevale and Catarina's cousin, Vincenza DiNucci Borrelli (far right). Vincenza is holding Virginia, her fifth child of ten, born in 1907, the same year as Lena. Standing in front of Caterina is her oldest child, Maria. Next to Maria are Rose and Stella Borrelli. *(Courtesy Barbara DiNucci Hendrickson for the Vellani and DiNucci families)*

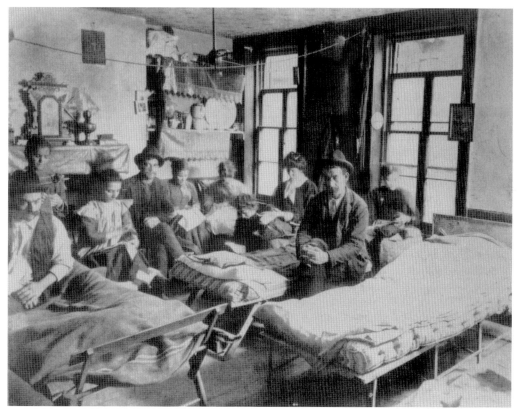

Cramped Quarters, New York City. Many Italian peasants found life in crowded lower-class sections of large cities overwhelming and debilitating. Immigrant families often took in boarders to help pay the rent, or offered space for relatives. In their son's documentary, *Italianamerican,* Catherine and Charlie Scorsese, parents of filmmaker Martin Scorsese, give a personal account of the number of relatives who shared their respective families' apartments. However, not all living arrangements were cofamilial and supportive, and many immigrants could not tolerate the daily drudgery of long hours at hard low-paid work or the "dormitory" space that merely provided a place to sleep. While personal ingenuity and strong determination might have helped maintain balance in this makeshift situation, many Italians returned to their home villages disillusioned and bitter. (*From* Gli Italiani negli Stati Uniti d'America, *1906*)

Upscale Life. The Pugliano family, in Carbondale, Pennsylvania, represents those Italian immigrants who found wealth and success in America. *From left to right:* Gabriel Pugliano Jr.; his sister, Violet Pugliano (Mussari); and their mother, Theresa Pugliano, relax in their well-appointed living room. Born in Calabria, Gabriel Sr. and his brother, Santo, had arrived in Carbondale, c. 1894, and opened a grocery store on Electric Alley, a busy area where produce was delivered and miners congregated. They prospered, and by 1901, they built the impressive brick Pugliano building, which still stands. Gabriel ran a bar/restaurant in one part of the lower level, and Santo sold groceries in the other section. Gabriel's family lived on the second and third floor of the building. The luxurious setting included a ballroom. Gabriel was highly regarded by the city's prominent leaders as well as by the Italian community. *(Courtesy the Anthony Talarico family)*

Family Ranch, Elk Park, Montana. Matteo Bugni emigrated from Locano, Torino, at the turn of the twentieth century. He traveled to Dewey, Idaho, c. 1901, where he worked in the mines and married Marietta Pajarola. In 1910, he moved his young family to Elk Park and with his brother, Domenico Bugni, purchased a ranch John Patritti had homesteaded in 1885. Matteo and Domenico sponsored the emigration of the rest of the family from Italy to Elk Park, and they raised cows for milk to sell to the Crystal Creamery in nearby Butte. The family ranched until 1935 when they sold the property to the Cerise family, owners of the Rock Springs Dairy. *(Courtesy Virginia M. Bugni)*

Home as a Workplace. With tags being tied at one end of the kitchen table and homemade macaroni drying on the other, the family of Desiderio Cella combine work and home life at their Framingham, Massachusetts, residence. Families lived in crowded, often dilapidated housing in the older sections of the cities. Three rooms often housed eleven people, and the kitchen, with its coal stove, served as the central area for most activities. The Cella children, whose parents came from the area of Piacenza, Emilia-Romagna, were named after countries: Afra for Africa, Francesca for France, Germano for Germany, Egytio for Egypt, Italina for Italy, and Irma for India. (*Courtesy Library of Congress, Prints and Photographs Division; reproduction # LC-DIG-NCLC-04287*)

Buried Under, 1916. Located about forty miles from Trinidad, Colorado, the Dawson Coal Mine in New Mexico suffered the second-largest mine accident in United States history. In the disaster, 265 men, many of them Italian, perished. Francesco Latuda from Magnago, Milano, ran the company bar and mercantile. In a letter to his mother in Italy in 1913, he described seeing the bodies of the men, many his friends, as they were taken from the mine. In the wake of this tragedy, Francesco decided to leave his position and settle in Trinidad. He financed the purchase of a ranch/farm near Trinidad for Mike Cantoria, his friend and former employee in Dawson. Mike, a Piemontesi, had three sons whom he did not want to sacrifice to the mines. The family became self-sufficient by raising milk cows, cattle, and sheep and by growing alfalfa, barley, wheat, and corn. They eventually repaid the loan given to them by Francesco. The largest mine tragedy in the United States occurred December 1907 in Monangah, West Virginia, claiming over 350 lives. Most of the miners were Italian immigrants from Molise and Calabria. (*Courtesy Charles D. Latuda*)

Relatively Close. Italian gardener families in Walla Walla, Washington, 1915, pose in front of Frank and Josephine Venneri's place on South Ninth (now Plaza Way). Frank's partner, Domenick Loiacano, and his wife, Concetta, lived in the house behind the Venneri's. Later Loiacano purchased land across the road. *From left:* Concetta Loiacano, Maria Ciarlo, Frank Venneri, Raffaela, Joe Barca (little boy), Vincenza Barca, Josephina Venneri, and Domenick Loiacano with the team of horses. Vincenza Barca was the sister of Peppina (Josephine) Venneri and Maria Ciarlo's husband Vincenzo. Josephine and her sister, Vincenza, had helped to introduce Concetta to Domenick. Vincenza escorted Concetta and Maria from Pedace, Cosenza, to Walla Walla early in 1915. These four families farmed in close proximity during the 1920s until the 1950s. *(Courtesy David A. Ferraro; courtesy Domenick and Concetta Morrone Loiacono)*

A Peaceful Haven in Columbus, Ohio, 1925. Helen and Emma Vellani stand in front of their home on South Eighth Street. Their parents, Virginia and Leonida Vellani, had farmed for a while in Cavriago, Reggio Calabria, but that life did not appeal to Leonida. In 1913, a family friend returned from America and described its possibilities. Leonida saw World War I on the horizon, and he did not want to be "cannon fodder" for the capitalists. (At age fourteen, his cousin, a priest, had taught Leonida socialist principles. The priest had gotten into trouble for starting a young people's socialist club in Cavriago.) Therefore, Leonida left for America, and his wife and four children joined him in Columbus in 1915. Leonida worked at the Bonney Floyd Steel Mill, and by 1918, the Vellani family had purchased this home. Virginia maintained her farming tradition by planting the garden with vegetables and the sides of the yard with grape vines. *(Courtesy Barbara DiNucci Hendrickson for the Vellani and DiNucci families)*

Little Italy, Ossining, New York. Children of Italian immigrants enjoy the first playground in this Hudson River Valley, New York, village, c. 1924. The "Hollow" playground on Aqueduct Street, directly off North Highland Avenue, was the area of town settled by Italians. Many of them were skilled stonemasons recruited from Italy to work on the Croton Dam, which was completed in 1906. Fellow *paesani* supplied the needs of these workers, offering services such as boarding houses, shoe repair, Italian groceries, and other essential items. *(Courtesy Ossining Historical Society Museum)*

A Home for His Bride. Andrew Gulotta from Campobello di Mazzara, Trapani, built this house on 609 Central Avenue in Yakima, Washington, for his wife, Leonarda, in the 1920s. Hardened by harsh life experiences, he left Sicily. After serving in the Italian army, Andrew departed for America in 1906. He worked for Northern Pacific Railway and was shipped to Tacoma, Washington, with a railroad gang. He worked through Yakima, where he discovered a land and climate that reminded him of Sicily. So he transferred to Yakima and worked on the Yakima Valley Transportation Company's streetcars. After that, he found work with the Cascade Lumber Company, and in 1919, he returned to Sicily and married Leonarda. He purchased the lumber he used to build the house from his employer. He continued to work for the company while also planting orchards and selling the fruit his trees produced. *(Courtesy Vincenzo A. Gulotta)*

Work Makes Home. The smokestack of the Anaconda smelter stands as a sentinel framing the small community of Black Eagle, developed across the river from Great Falls, Montana, c. 1928. Romeo Ranieri is centering the ball to his cousin Elondro (Ollie). In 1894, the first workers at the smelter consisted mostly of Italians from Tuscany, with some Croatians, and several other nationalities. Some immigrants in Black Eagle worked for Great Northern Railway. All of these settlers squatted on company land to be close to their work. They built scrap-lumber tarpaper houses/shacks, or took old railroad boxcars to fashion into homes. When Anaconda expanded in 1902, it reclaimed its land and the squatters moved about two miles to "Little Chicago," which had been established a year before by Montana Power Company (also owned by Anaconda). Lots sold for seventy-five dollars each. People built their own houses or moved their shacks or boxcars onto the lots they purchased, using them as the basis to add on. One of Ranieri's uncles (from Santa Maria del Giudice, Lucca) stuccoed the sides of his boxcar and added on rooms. Until the early 1940s, most homes had wood/coal stoves and outside toilets. *(Courtesy Larry Ranieri)*

Inviting Boarders. The New Roma Hotel in Point Richmond, California, provided living quarters for approximately thirty single Italian men and others who worked at Standard Oil and other nearby businesses. Stenciled on one of the windows is "Ravioli and Chicken Dinners Every Sunday." Owner Joseph Matteucci (b. Lucca); his wife, Nelli Quirolleo Matteucci; and daughters, Josephine and Rose, stand in front of their establishment, c. 1927. Known as the "mayor of Point Richmond," Joseph tended bar and managed the business, Nelli cooked, their three sons did whatever was needed, and daughter Josephine waited on tables. Joseph had worked in the gold mines in Jackson before moving to Richmond. *(Courtesy The Richmond Museum of History Collection)*

Combination Home and Business. Antonio and Raffaela Esposito and their son, Anthony, stand proudly in front of their combination grocery store and home at 257 Forbes Avenue in New Haven, Connecticut, c. 1931. Antonio came from Atrani, Salerno, and Raffaela from Minori, Salerno (both towns on the Amalfi Coast). They married in New Haven in 1914. Raffaela, who could not read or write, started the Italian American Grocery in their home on Wooster Street while Antonio worked at different jobs. By 1930, in addition to their Forbes Avenue building, the Espositos had acquired and rented out a two-family home on South Fulton Street. Many Italian-American proprietors used part of their homes for their businesses, which served the local area. By 1950, Antonio had taken a more active role in the store, making hot and cold Italian sandwiches for their customers. Raffaela prepared all the items for the hot sandwiches, such as sausage and peppers, eggplant and cheese, and meatballs, which she made fresh every morning. *(Courtesy Anthony N. Esposito)*

Clustered Together in Welby, Colorado. Italian families from Castiglione de Carovilli, Isernia, and Torricella Peligna, Chieti, about fifty miles north of Castiglione, pose in 1929 with the hog each farmer raised to slaughter for their family's annual sausage, salami, and prosciutto supply. The men, having been farmers in Italy, immigrated to work in the coal mines of Lafayette, Colorado, before moving to Welby, located a couple of miles north of Denver. They grew mostly lettuce, tomatoes, peppers, cauliflower, and onions on the land they purchased. Re-creating the land patterns in Italy, they built their homes close together and set them back from the road. Each family farmed from ten to twenty acres of long narrow fields, which extended from the back of their houses to the banks of the Platte River. The men would celebrate a job well done with a drink of homemade wine. *(Courtesy Barbara Nuoci Dahlberg)*

Services for *Paesani*. Angelina DeBortoli feeds her chickens in Chiloquin, Oregon, where jobs at the lumber mill located on the Klamath Indian Reservation attracted workers from many countries. Guglielmo, Angelina's husband, built their home in the '30s without indoor plumbing. Guglielmo had emigrated from Cornuda, Treviso, in 1914, carrying with him his share (approximately ten thousand dollars) of his family-owned quarry. After their marriage in 1921, Angelina deposited the money in the Bank of America (previously the Bank of Italy), and they used the interest as income. They supplemented their income by selling wine Guglielmo made with a large press in the garage, storing the wine in barrels in an earthen cellar under the house. Friends and neighbors, mostly from the Treviso, Veneto, region, gathered in their home to play cards, drink wine, and sing Italian songs. Angelina (Angoina in the dialect) charged for the wine that the guests consumed. She also earned money by providing meals and laundry services for the young, single Italian immigrants who worked at the Chiloquin Lumber & Box Company. *(Courtesy Tina M. DeBortoli-Frostad)*

Making a Home in the Wilderness. Nina Di Vito serves her husband, Joe, coffee to keep him warm before he "walks" the track along the Northern Pacific Railway at Humphrey, Washington, in 1934. This "settlement" had two section houses, one for the Di Vitos and the other for section hand employee, Johnny Rossi. Nina and their three daughters arrived in Humphrey from Carbonara, Bari, in 1932 to join Joe. In order to "prove" to the immigration officials that he was able to support his wife and children, Joe's cousin, Luigi Fioretti, signed over the deed to his homestead in Lester (ten miles down the track), which made Joe a "landowner." One immigrant daughter remembers the transfer of her father's one thousand-dollar bank account to various Italians in the Pacific Northwest to use as "proof" of solvency to obtain permission for their families to reunite in America. The bank account passed through many hands before it returned intact to its rightful owner. *(Courtesy Matt and Antonetta Fioretti)*

An American Estate, c. 1960. Luigi Totta from San Giovanni Rotondo, Foggia, designed and nurtured this one-acre vegetable and flower garden at his Waldwick, New Jersey, home. In the summers, he did landscape work for wealthy families in towns such as Upper Saddle River and Ridgewood. In the winter, he and his other Italian stonemason friends built retaining walls, houses, etc. Luigi combined information from *Barbanera,* an eighteenth-century astronomic and astrologic Italian almanac, with his personal gardening experience to calculate phases of the moon for the proper planting dates. His Italian-immigrant neighbors admired his efforts, and they aspired to meet or exceed Luigi's bounty in their own gardens. *(Courtesy Andrea Mistretta Quaranta)*

Company Homes, c. 1958. Rosaria and Giorgio Savarino taste their newly tapped wine outside their company-owned house in the coal camp of Carolina, West Virginia. Giorgio had returned to Modica, Ragusa, where his family had farmed, to find a wife and returned with Rosaria in 1921. Rosaria never really adjusted to America. Her life in Sicily, in her home with her father, the town blacksmith, had provided more comforts than the rough and tumble coal camps of America. Frequent strikes meant moving out of the company house into barracks. During one strike Giorgio was injured in a fight with "yellow dogs" (strikebreakers), and the police arrested him because of his union activities. *(Courtesy Joan L. Saverino)*

Reconstructing a Mansion. Francesco Moscia, an Italian immigrant left Torricella Sicura, Teramo, at the age of seventeen, in 1918 and headed alone to the United States for adventure. His father, Andrea Moscia, the postmaster, and his mother, Marsiglia Populini Moscia, a schoolteacher, and the rest of the family remained in Italy. First, Francesco worked in Pennsylvania's coal mines, and he later settled in Wayne, Pennsylvania (on Philadelphia's Main Line), where he worked as a stonemason. Other Italians from Teramo had also settled on Highland Avenue in Wayne, the city in which he met and married Rose Filipone in 1928. In the 1950s, Francesco reconstructed this mansion for his family on South Devon Avenue in Wayne, using materials from a house on the Harrison Estate that had been torn down in the 1940s. He reused everything—stone, windows, doors, and the terracotta roof. A family member still occupies the house. *(Courtesy Bonnie Moscia Dolce, Bernard Moscia, and the Moscia family)*

Building for Family in Toronto, Canada. Domenico Valle from Lago, Cosenza, built his first house in 1972 with the help of family and *paesani*. Until then his extended family, consisting of twelve people—Domenico; his wife, Giuseppina; their two children; his mother, Luigina; his two brothers and two sisters; and Giuseppina's brother and sister—lived in the first house he bought in 1963. Nonna Luigina cared for her grandchildren, cleaned and cooked for all twelve family members while the adult males worked mostly in construction and the women worked at a variety of jobs. By 1971, Domenico had become an insurance agent, but he was still dabbling in house construction on the side, using subcontractors to do specialized things like installing the windows. He would rent or sell the homes he constructed. *(Courtesy Domenico and Giuseppa Valle)*

CHAPTER 4

ITALIANS AT WORK

Most Italians came to America seeking work as a means to improve their family's condition in Italy. These migrants, overwhelmingly male, fanned out across America, taking jobs on railroad construction gangs, as street cleaners, rag-pickers, miners, ditch-diggers, brick makers, stonemasons, peddlers, street musicians, and as workers in shops and factories. Many lived in boardinghouses or in bachelor quarters where expenses were kept to a minimum. These men expected to move either when work was to scarce or the weather too severe. American immigration authorities labeled these impermanent workers "birds of passage" *(gondolieri)*. This practice created a distance between the immigrants and the communities in which they worked. Eventually these wayfarers chose either to return to their families in Italy or to remain in America. Many, who stayed, moved out of the laboring class into enterprise. Peddlers opened produce stores; tailors set up their own custom shops; lodging houses became restaurants; and stonecutters fashioned monuments and statues.

At the same time, the existence of the Italian community itself provided a market for ethnic business. Food importers, grocery stores, butchers, bakers, travel agents, and bankers catered to the particular needs and tastes of people who liked olive oil, goat's milk, and cannoli or those who needed help buying steamship tickets and sending money to relatives in Italy. A decision to remain in America encouraged economic expansion, such as real-estate investments and business ventures like selling musical instruments. Women and young children began to emigrate to reunite with their families in America. They earned money at a variety of jobs, ranging from crop harvesting to making artificial flowers. They also sold merchandise, cared for boarders, and helped their husbands and brothers operate retail businesses and service industries. Although most Italian women did not work away from home, some Italian immigrant women became entrepreneurs, owning and operating retail stores. For example, Fanny Franchini worked her way up from maid to manager in the hotel business in Albuquerque, New Mexico. She later partnered with her sister, Lena, and Ciro Chiordi to operate the Santa Fe Grocery and Sanitary Bakery at 901 South Second Street. The store stocked traditional items as well as imported Italian products.

Some immigrants arrived in America with specific skills and capital that attracted the patronage of Americans. These men offered the fancy goods and services desired by middle- and upper-class Americans, such as notions, cameos, decorative ironwork, stone carving, voice and music lessons, and hairdressing. They came to America either to advance their standard of living, for adventure, or in response to Italian political conditions or family disagreements. The very nature of their occupations and their small numbers in the Italian community contributed to their marginality as Italians. They might relate more to Americans than to the growing number of sojourners and settlers who worked and lived among conationals.

Italian immigrants' choice of work reflected a combination of availability, *paesani* connections, and preference for types of work. In the steel industry, Italians dominated the carpentry, repair, and rail shops. When the city of Pittsburgh constructed its filtration plant in 1905, most of the diggers and hod carriers were Italians. By the turn of the twentieth century, Italians dominated railroad-track section crews throughout America. Work on the railroad often influenced permanent settlement in areas far removed from immigrant enclaves. Italian section crews working near Priest River, Idaho, and Lester, Washington, decided to settle permanently. Italian immigrants built the infrastructure of sewers, paved streets, tunnels, trolley, subway and elevated lines in many communities. Italian hands tended the plantings in public parks, swept the streets and carted away garbage.

Contemporaries noted how much America relied on immigrants to fuel the economy. Mary Antin wrote, in *They Who Knock at Our Gates: A Complete Gospel of Immigration* (1914), "The Wall Street magnate would be about as effective as a puppet were it not for the army of foreigners who execute his schemes. The magic of stocks and bonds lies in railroad ties and in quarried stone and in axle grease applied at the right time. A. Harriman [owner of the New York Central Railroad] might sit till doomsday gibbering at the telephone and the stock exchange would take no notice of him if a band of nameless "Dagos" a thousand miles away failed to repair a telegraph pole. New York City is building an aqueduct [the Croton Dam] that will surpass the works of the Romans, and the average New Yorker will know nothing about it until he reads in the newspapers the mayor's speech at the inauguration of the new water supply."

Italian shoemakers, tailors, and restaurateurs, who offered hamburgers, waffles and other "American" food, reached out to the general public as customers. Other immigrants opened nonethnic businesses, such as bottling plants, laundries, auto repair shops, taxi companies, trucking companies, and construction materials supplies, which served the entire community.

Immigrant ingenuity discovered opportunities in "new" enterprises. While Amedeo Obici from Oderzo, Treviso, earned fame and fortune developing the processing and distribution for his successful Planters Peanut Company in Wilkes-Barre, Pennsylvania, and later in Suffolk, Virginia, Casimiro Spera, from Palermo, was developing an ice cream novelty, called the Hokey Pokey, which he began selling from a truck in New Jersey's Hamilton Township. With the proceeds from the ice cream, he and his wife opened a small grocery store. Joseph D. Carrier (Giuseppe Domenic Carriero), who in 1912, at age two, emigrated with his family from Pisticci, Matera, to Toronto, Canada, learned to make shoes at age fourteen. And in 1937, with an investment of ninety-two dollars, he started Joseph D. Carrier Shoes, which grew into a company of 1800 employees across Canada.

In the late 1890s, the Vaccaro brothers, Joseph, Felix, and Lucca, along with Salvatore D'Antoni, initiated a banana trade business between New Orleans and Honduras, creating the Standard Fruit & Steamship Company. John Riccardi, born in Bassiano, Latina, in 1882, came to this country in 1903, with little money to his name. In 1919, he founded the Roman Cleanser Company in Detroit, the first to introduce household bleach to the United States. Sebastiani Poli began to earn pennies as an organ grinder with a dancing monkey; this endeavor enabled him to eventually start a chain of movie theaters, which he eventually sold for thirty million dollars. Louis R. Perini, born in Massachusetts in 1903, of northern-Italian immigrant parents, would preside over the Perini Construction Company, one of the largest building firms in the country.

Italian-American achievement in the arts and performing arts, as well as in sports, has made an indelible mark on American society. It is impossible to gauge the full extent of this creative and innovative influence. The list of stage and movie actors, producers and directors, opera and cabaret singers, musicians, conductors, dancers, and comedians, who have gained international fame, seems endless. Perhaps the role of Italian Americans in the performing arts has received the highest acclaim from the public. In the early nineteenth century, Italian musicians played in the United States armed services bands, and Italian opera singers, such as Adelina Patti, toured American cities. Their musical contribution continued in the twentieth century with the spectacular careers of Enrico Caruso, Rosa Ponselle, Anna Moffo, Frank Lopardo, and Catherine Malfitano. Gian Carlo Menotti's *The Saint of Bleeker Street* and John Corigliano's compositions represent one form of artistic contribution while the work of James Dominick "Nick" La Rocca, Louis Prima, Rudolph Valentino, Henry Mancini, Liza Minelli, Madonna (née Louise Ciccone), Tony Bennett, Frankie Valli, Connie Francis, and Bruce Springsteen illustrate another.

There is a long list of American artists of Italian heritage who deserve acclaim. While many know the names of Constantino Brumidi, whose frescoes decorated the Capitol, and Luigi Palma di Cesnola, who served as the director of the Metropolitan Museum of Art, few have acknowledged the larger context of "the Italian shaping hand." Regina Soria, author of *American Artists of Italian Heritage, 1776-1945: A Biographical Dictionary*, wrote, "Italian immigrants imported not only their skills, but their need for the satisfaction of making beautiful objects . . . [which they brought] to the American scene in the most unexpected places: theaters, public buildings, churches, cemeteries, household objects, statuettes, and monuments. They would not accept ugliness in their everyday tools, household appliances, and decoration of their homes." She especially noted the "stonemasons . . . appreciated as craftsmen, but never given a special place in American culture and their names were hardly ever recorded." In fact, few nineteenth-century native-born American sculptors knew how to carve marble. Usually, they produced a model in plaster that had to be taken to Italy to be copied in marble by professional stone carvers. Italian sculptors and carvers embellished and enhanced many state capitol buildings across the United States; those in Madison, Wisconsin; Columbia, South Carolina; and Sacramento, California, are a few examples. Giuseppe Piccirilli and his six sons, who left Massa Carrara, Toscana, for New York city in 1888, were stone and marble cutters and carvers who executed Daniel Chester French's design for the heroic statue in the Lincoln Memorial.

Also notable are the contributions of Italian Americans to the film industry, including producer Albert R. "Cubby" Broccoli and directors Frank Capra and Vincent Minelli.

The Coppola family represents a performing arts dynasty with wide-ranging influence on the film industry. Francis Ford Coppola; his father, Carmine Coppola; and his sister, Talia Shire, received Academy Awards for the movie *The Godfather* (1972), based on Mario Puzo's novel. Carmine wrote the musical score, Francis directed, and Talia played

a member of the Corleone family. In 2003, Francis' daughter, Sophia Coppola, a successful film screenwriter and director, won an Academy Award for best original screenplay for her film, *Lost in Translation* (2003). Francis' films have helped to launch the careers of other Italian-American actors, such as Robert DeNiro, Al Pacino, and Nicolas Cage, his nephew.

Prominent Italian names in sports fill several museums, like the National Italian-American Sports Hall of Fame, in Chicago, and the Boxing Hall of Fame in Canastota, New York. Vince Lombardi, considered the most outstanding pro-football coach, led the Green Bay Packers to five national championships in the '60s. In 1983, Joe Paterno, coach of Pennsylvania State University's football team, was second only (among active coaches) to Florida State's Bobby Bowden.

For Italian immigrants, the phrase "bread and roses" expresses their determination to achieve success through hard work, a progression from pick-and-shovel men to entrepreneurs and descendants who have distinguished the world of law, medicine, letters, politics, finance, and business. Pride in producing the best as a reflection of self-esteem continues.

Climbing the Heights. Italian stonecutters completed the southwest clerestory arch of the Library of Congress, Washington, D.C., on June 28, 1892. The clerestory is a windowed wall rising above the flanking roofs to light or ventilate the interior of the structure. Italian artisans found work building and creating the ornamental and interior designs on major buildings in Baltimore, Maryland; Portland, Oregon; and Denver, Colorado, and in many other American cities. Of course, Italian artist Constantino Brumidi's ceiling and wall frescoes in the nation's Capitol in Washington, D.C., still fascinate visitors. *(Courtesy Library of Congress, Prints and Photographs Division; reproduction # LC-USZ62-51462)*

Contract Laborers. This 1888 scene shows contract laborers entering New York City's "Mulberry Bend" en route to jobs in coal mines. The artist shows the crowded street in that immigrant quarter, which Jacob Riis would later capture in photos on film. Although the Foran Act of 1885 made it illegal to import foreign labor into the United States, many companies continued to recruit workers, both skilled and unskilled, to fill their employment needs. Companies often paid Italian immigrants to recruit workers either in Italy or at port entries. Sometimes the person who recruited the workers accompanied them to the job site, where they continued to provide services (at a cost) to the workers. Not all of these recruiters exploited the men they recruited. Most *padroni* (bosses) acted as go-betweens for newcomers ignorant of the language and the work process. One Italian immigrant who got a job with the West Canadian Mine (coal) was fired because he could not understand instructions given in English. *(Courtesy Library of Congress, Prints and Photographs Division,* Frank Leslie's Illustrated Newspaper, *1888; reproduction # LC-USZ62-12265)*

Collecting Rags. In Erie, Pennsylvania, the Santone cousins and their relatives earned $1.50 for a ten-hour day as rag collectors in 1906. The first chapter of the novel *The Grand Gennaro,* by Garibaldi M. Lapolla, tells the story of one Calabrese, Gennaro Accuci, who "makes" America as a rag and junk collector in New York's East Harlem in the 1890s. *(Courtesy Joseph Santone)*

Stones into Wine. Samuele Sebastiani worked with his family on their farm in Tuscany where they grew grapes and made wine. He arrived penniless in San Francisco, California, at age eighteen, in 1893. His work in the vegetable gardens in the city did not provide enough money to purchase a vineyard; so in 1896, at age twenty-two, he bought a wagon and four horses to supply cobblestones for the streets of San Francisco. He went to Sonoma, California, and worked in the quarries cutting cobblestones and loading them onto his wagon to haul them to the city. He purchased a quarry, and his stones were used for some Sonoma buildings, including City Hall. The quarry in the picture was owned and operated by Samuele. By 1904, Samuele had saved enough money to buy land to grow grapes. The rest is wine history. *(Courtesy Sebastiani Vineyards, Sonoma, California)*

Water for New York City. Primarily Italian men work atop the spillway, c. 1900, of the New Croton Dam near Croton-on-Hudson, New York, and Ossining, New York. Notice the huge numbered granite stones waiting to be set. Italian stonemasons were recruited, c. 1893, for the monumental job of excavating the site and then quarrying local stone to be transported to the work site. The laborers built seventeen miles of small-gauge railroad track around the dam site and to the quarry and back to move the stone. Next to the pyramids of Egypt, Croton Dam was considered to be the largest hand-hewn stone structure in the world at that time. The men, some with families, lived in two settlements near the dam. Larkintown or Little Italy was at the top of a hill overlooking the site. The Bowery, with boarding houses operated by *paesani,* was at the bottom of the hill. Completed in 1906, the Croton Dam, for many years, supplied most of the drinking water for the New York metropolis, and it is still a significant source. (Courtesy Ossining Historical Society Museum)

Sweeping the Streets in Brooklyn, New York, c. early 1900s. Pietro DiGirolamo from Santa Maria, Benevento, started his career as a street cleaner. During the age of horse-powered transportation, Pietro used the big broom and shovel he carried to sweep up horse droppings and deposit them in the large pail on wheels he pushed along the streets he maintained. According to family memory, Pietro once "found a one hundred-dollar bill and was elated that he got to keep it. That was like manna from heaven to a man with eight children to feed." He taught himself to read and write in English and worked his way up to the position of inspector in the sanitation department. He worked and lived with his wife, Anna Marie, in the Bedford-Stuyvesant area of Brooklyn at 103 Utica Avenue. After he retired, he would sit on his front stoop, greeting all who passed by. They dubbed him, "mayor of Utica Avenue." *(Courtesy Mary Rubbo Dori)*

Out of the Mine. Angelo Merlino, from the Abruzzo region of Italy, worked in coal mines on his way westward across the United States in the 1890s. From 1896 to 1900, he worked at Black Diamond Mine (he is on the far left in this photo) in Washington State. By then his English was fairly good and his Italian coworkers encouraged him to go by wagon into Seattle, Washington, to buy their favorite Italian cheeses and wines. Soon Angelo had a good business hauling imported items from the Italian-owned Metropolitan Grocery Company to Black Diamond and Ravensdale. In 1900, Angelo got a chance to buy out one of the four partners of Metropolitan Grocery and moved his family to Seattle. Caesar Mondavi is another Italian who moved out of the mines in Minnesota's Iron Range and started a grocery store. Later he moved to Lodi, California, and became successful as the proprietor of Charles Krug Winery. *(Courtesy the Batali family)*

Bringing Music to the Streets. The hurdy-gurdy, used by Antonio Vivaldi in one of his compositions, brought music into the streets of America. Typically, a man pushed the heavy machine, balanced on two wheels, but these Italian women in Toronto, Ontario, cooperated in this enterprise. Charles Cirelli's wife helped him pull and push a hurdy-gurdy from Baltimore, Maryland, to York, Pennsylvania, for a carnival. His grandson recalls that Cirelli would "put a strap on [his wife's] arm and they would hook it to them, and him and her would go. And she would help him . . . They would have their sleeping gear, and they would just sleep alongside the road. The next morning get up and start pulling again. He didn't say how much, but they were making a lot of money at the carnival. . . . He would come home with a lot of money. Well, whether it was four dollars a day or five dollars a day, it was a lot of money." *(Courtesy City of Toronto Archives, Fonds 1244, Item 7285)*

Railroad Construction. A group of Italians from Williamsport, Pennsylvania, cut lumber for the railroad ties and trestles in Stonestown and Kettle Creek. The rail industry was the second-largest employer of immigrants in northeastern Pennsylvania after the coal mines. In fact, the derogatory song, "Where Do You Work-a John, On the Delawar Lackawan," written c. 1920, parodied Italian workers' broken English. In the northwest, near Bonners Ferry, Idaho, Italian workers made ties for Mike Lungo, a "veteran" contractor. Lungo had contracted Italian crews from Mexico to British Columbia. He also ran a camp with a hotel, store, and stable—charging boarders twenty-five cents a meal. America's dependence on the railroad to deliver raw materials and goods across the country necessitated an "army" of workers to maintain and repair the rails to handle heavy traffic. In the first half of the twentieth century, Italian immigrants and their children provided a large percentage of these workers. *(Courtesy the Daniele family)*

"Civilizing" America. A crew of nine Italian immigrant stonemasons build the dry-masonry retaining walls for the Columbia River Highway in Oregon, c. 1915: Gene Piro (right), Raffaele Curilo (second from right), and Mr. Camelleo (boss, far left). These men were imported from Italy to apply their skills for this visionary highway project. The stretch of road from the Sandy River to Hood River (along the Columbia River Gorge) was the showpiece of the highway. Seventeen bridges built along this stretch of highway combined utilitarian and aesthetic principles, with each bridge unique to its site situation. Italian stonemasons excavated native stone to blend the walls and bridges into the rocky hillsides surrounding the Gorge. These craftsmen also laid the foundation for Vista House at Crown Point, 725 feet above the river, without the use of cement or mortar. The highway extended from Hood River to Astoria by the summer of 1915. *(Courtesy Oregon Historical Society, image # 022216)*

Sewage Infrastructure. Antonio Guardiani from Tocca Casauria, Abruzzo, found a job installing sewers in Port Jervis, New York, when he arrived in the United States in 1929. During the Depression, he worked on similar jobs for the Works Progress Administration. Interestingly another Italian immigrant, Thomas Marnell, from the area of Naples, who progressed from railroad laborer to foreman in Syracuse, New York, and became a general contractor, obtained a patent in 1895 for a sewer excavator hoisting apparatus. This equipment improved the basic sewer construction process. *(Courtesy the Guardiani and Sticca families)*

Logging in Canada. Peter Bodio from Cadrezzate, Varese, uses a team of horses to pull logs from the woods in Blairmore, Alberta, c. 1930s. Born in 1903, the eldest of nine children, Peter, at thirteen, became sole family supporter, farming their own property. Making little progress, Peter left his brothers in charge and immigrated to Canada in 1920 to work for his uncle, Charles Sartoris. Returning to Italy in 1932, Peter married Lena Marrette, and they returned together to Canada. He continued working for his uncle until 1941 when he left to work in the local mine owned by the Canadian-American Coal and Coke Company. In 1946, the West Canadian Collieries offered him a contract hauling mine timbers. He and his cousin, Peter Sartoris, became partners in this endeavor. In 1949, they started a sawmill in South Fork and later moved the mill to Blairmore, and by 1952, Peter had organized his own lumber company, which he sold in 1964 to Crow's Nest Pass Coal Company. In "retirement," Peter continued to maintain his team of horses, which he drove in parades and used in pulling contests or just driving down the street. *(Courtesy Ernesto Milani collection)*

Garbage as Business. In some western communities, especially in the San Francisco Bay Area, enterprising Italian immigrants established scavenger companies. Owner/workers purchased shares in the business to provide the community with a systematic, dependable system. As private contractors, shareholders could attain a secure, steady income. Here Dominic "Mingo" Parodi (right) drives the wagon for the Richmond (California) Scavenger Company, c. 1920. Most of the men were from Liguria, but there were also Lombardi and Piemontesi. In 1944, at age eighteen, Richard Granzella, whose father was from Lombardia and mother from Liguria, paid six thousand dollars for a share in the now-named Richmond Sanitary Company. He put two hundred dollars down, and the remainder was deducted from his paychecks. *(Courtesy The Richmond Museum of History Collection)*

Work Dictates. Anselmo Minato sits with his son, Narciso (Ciso), in 1930, outside the sawmill in Chiloquin, Oregon, where Anselmo worked with a Swedish partner on the "green" chain—pulling boards off the conveyor according to size prior to their being stacked in the lumberyard for drying. In 1935, after Anselmo was injured at work, the resulting pain in his ankle and hip caused him to limp, and he could not cover the entire length of the conveyor to pull off all the boards. He worked the night shift, 6:00 P.M. to 1:30 A.M., and to protect his job, Anselmo allowed his sons, Ciso, age eleven, and Alfeo (Feo), age twelve, to assist him on alternate nights, pulling out the smaller boards on the far end of the green chain. The boys would be sleepy in school the next day. By 1939, Anselmo's pain was so severe he could not work. He went to the Veterans' Administration Hospital, where the doctors confirmed that his on-the-job accident had caused a fracture. The family received no compensation from the company. *(Courtesy Remo Minato)*

Preferred Jobs. When, in 1930, Olie (Elondo) Ranieri and his cousin, Romeo Ranieri, left their jobs at the Anaconda Company smelter for "cleaner" jobs with Great Northern Railway in Great Falls, Montana, they celebrated. Their immigrant fathers had worked at the smelter when they arrived in Great Falls. Olie and Romeo viewed their new jobs as a "step up" the occupational ladder. Here Olie works in the roundhouse. He remained with the railroad for over fifty-five years. *(Courtesy Larry Ranieri)*

Coal for Railroads. Coal-fueled engines powered the railroads well into the 1950s. Matt Fioretti shovels coal for Northern Pacific Railway at its Lester, Washington, coal supply point. In the late 1930s, he worked part-time while he was attending school. His father, Luigi, had returned to Carbonara, Bari, in 1933, to bring Matteo to live with him in Lester. Luigi had worked for Northern Pacific since 1918. *(Courtesy Matt and Antonetta Fioretti)*

From Water Boy to Cement Finisher, 1938. Leonardo Lipari's family came from Gibellina, Trapani, where he was born in 1896. They joined his father, Giacomo, in Louisiana, following him from job to job in Luddington, Patterson, Morgan City, and Bayou Boeuf before settling in Lake Charles. When his father died in 1915, Leonardo became the sole support of his mother and four younger siblings. He left home to avoid the draft because his family depended on his income. He found work as a water boy in Tomball, Texas, and later moved to Orange, Texas (near Louisiana), where he worked for the Gengo family (from Partanna, Trapani), who owned a soda bottling company there. He sent enough money home to enable his mother to purchase a house. He married the boss's daughter, Vincenza, and they moved to Lake Charles. In 1929, she died in childbirth, leaving him with four children. Later he married Domenica Giametta and had three more children. About 1935, Leonardo (now called Leon) earned $13.50 a week working for the Works Progress Administration; therefore, he was happy when Chris Di Carlo, president of the Italian American Club, helped him get a job as a ditch digger with the city. Leon worked his way up to foreman and then cement finisher, maintaining and repairing city streets. Counting from the right, Leon Lipari, wearing a black jacket, is the third person standing on the ground. Jack Di Bartolo, a family friend, is standing in the truck holding a shovel. *(Courtesy Mary Lipari "Liprie" Rivere)*

Grim Rewards. Around the age of eight, Vincenzo Vallucci immigrated to the United States with his parents, Loreto and Pasqualina (Ranaldi), from Arpino, Frosinone, c. 1915. His father worked in Brilliant #1 and then the Swastika Mine near Raton, New Mexico. The company owned the store and the houses in the area, and it sometimes paid the miners in script, redeemable only at the store. Before the union gained recognition by the company, miners had to provide their own tools, which they purchased at the company store. Vincenzo married Adelina (Rea), who had also emigrated from Italy with her family and found work in the mine. He died on February 3, 1945, when a coal car jumped the track and pinned him to the wall or rib, crushing him. (The "rib" in the mining industry is also the side or wall.) Adelina and her eight children moved to the town of Trinidad, Colorado, where her eldest daughters, Bertha and Loretta, found jobs to help support the family. In 1942, the coal company changed the name Swastika to Brilliant #2 to avoid any association with the ancient symbol co-opted by Germany's dictator, Adolf Hitler. *(Courtesy Thomas Sciacca)*

Millman at Bunker Hill, Kellogg, Idaho, 1955. Natale Truant, a millman at Bunker Hill Mill, emigrated from San Martino al Tagliamento, Udine, in 1921. After initially settling in Trail, British Columbia, Natale moved to Harrison, Idaho, in 1923, where he worked in the sawmill. Since jobs at the mining complex paid better than the sawmill, Natale, along with other Harrison men, applied for work. At first, the Harrison men walked the Union Pacific tracks to Kellogg on Sunday night and then walked back to Harrison on Friday nights, but gradually, they moved their families to the Kellogg area. "Ned's" job at the concentrator was to add forged steel grinding balls to the concentrator, which used these balls to grind every ton of ore. The balls were worn down from the grinding process and needed to be replaced. About a ton of these balls were fed into the concentrator over a period of forty-three hours. He retired in 1960 after working thirty years for the mining company. *(Courtesy Pierina L. Miller)*

Martorano Mine. Mike Martorano (left) and older brother, Sal Martorano (right), sit outside their family mine in Boncarbo, Colorado (about fifteen miles west of Trinidad), c. 1950s. Their aunt, Rose (center), visiting from Texas, wears a pair of Mike's overalls. The boys' father, Bernardo, from Bisaquino, Palermo, purchased a hundred and sixty acres when he married Giuseppa Mazzarise (from Alia, Palermo), in 1908 in the coal-mining town of Sopris. In 1929, when Sal was nine, Bernardo discovered a vein of coal on the land, and he mined the coal with the help of his three sons. Fifteen years later, on June 14, 1943, loose rocks fell and killed him, and Sal and Mike had to dig him out. Bernardo's sons continued working the mine; they closed the old entrance and opened a new one on another side of the hill. They provided coal for many businesses in Trinidad, including the Trinidad power plant, which provided the electricity for the city, the surrounding little coal camps, and suburbs. The Trinidad Power Company secured deferments for the Martorano brothers during World War II since they preferred the more efficient and hotter burning coal their mine provided as compared to other coal in the area. *(Courtesy the Salvatore Martorano family)*

Above the Mine. Guido Bugni (right) works as an ironworker (called ropeman) alongside electrician Bill Brunell as they lower a cage into the Modoc Mine in Butte, Montana, c. 1950. Born in Dewey, Idaho, Guido Bugni left the family dairy ranch in Elk Park when he was sixteen years old and moved to his sister Mary Ghiringhelli's home in Meaderville (the Italian section of Butte). There he worked for the Hansen Meat Packing Company. After he married at age twenty-one, he began working underground for the Anaconda Copper Company. The air was unsafe and the work was dangerous. So when Guido got a chance to work on the rope gang, he accepted, learning on the job how to keep the cages in good working order. Not long after his job switch, Guido's brother Fred died with three other men in a mine accident. Although Guido was on twenty-four-hour call, and during one year, the only day off he had was his birthday, he enjoyed the challenge of the rope gang and stayed with the company for forty years. (*Courtesy Virginia M. Bugni*)

Italian Hospital and Dispensary. Located at 169 W. Houston St., New York City, the *Istituto Italiano di Beneficenza* purchased a third house in 1904, and, on the upper floor, in March 1905, they opened an Italian hospital with forty beds. During its first year of operation, the facility administered outpatient *(ambulatorio)* treatment for approximately four-teen thousand people. The *istituto* also provided a dormitory and dining area for newly arrived immi-grants needing assistance. (*From* Gli Italiani negli Stati Uniti d'America, *1906*)

Ethnic Business. Salvatore Amato, a goat shepherd in Termini Imerese, Palermo, left Italy in 1897 to earn money in America. He spent a year in Montreal, Quebec, and returned home. In 1898, Salvatore left again, this time with his fourteen-year-old son, Calogero, and settled in Portland, Oregon. For the next seven years, he owned a grocery on the west side of the city at the foot of the Steel Bridge, which was built in 1888. During this time, he sent for three other children: Frank, Rosaria, and Joe. Fearful of the voyage, his wife Maria would not come. His daughter Josephine decided to remain with her mother who longed for her family. Salvatore sold the store and returned to Sicily in 1906; he died there in 1920. His children remained in Portland. In this photo, Salvatore is on the far right, standing next to his brother Michele. His sons, Frank and Calogero, are at the left. Notice the cans of tomatoes and olive oil lining the shelves. They also sold cheeses, pasta, candy, and household items, such as brooms. Their customers were people from the neighborhood and friends and relatives who knew them, especially *paesani* from southwest and southeast Portland. (*Courtesy Diane [Amato] Partain*)

Physician to Immigrants. Umberto Buffo, a native of Pratiglione, Torino, and graduate of Turin Medical School, was a pioneer physician who came to Krebs, Indian Territory, to begin practicing medicine around 1904. His patients were mostly Italian miners who worked in the area. This photo shows him examining a patient in his sanitarium, which served as an early-day hospital and rest home in McAlester, Oklahoma. Records show that he had three nurses, a cook, and two roomers living in this building. In 1908, he married Theresa Silotto. He enjoyed his work in Oklahoma, but when he became ill in 1910, he wanted to go back to Italy for treatment. He and his wife only got as far as New York City, where he died. She brought his body back to McAlester for burial. He was thirty-one years old. *(Courtesy Jane Tua Smith and Judy Tua Brown)*

Immigrant Employers—Immigrant Workers. Alpi and Company, owned by Angelo and Pietro Alpi, manufactured artificial flowers in their factory at 69 Houston Street, New York City. They employed over two hundred workers, mostly Italian immigrant women who chose to work with other women in locations near their homes. These employment choices conformed to Italian traditions, which relegated primary care of the home and family to women. Since most newcomers to the workforce found jobs through friends or family members, certain departments in certain industries reflected this concentration. It was an unusual parent who declared, "My daughters are not going to work in a factory." In 1922, Nicola Gerardi took his daughters to an employment agency in lower Manhattan to obtain a non-factory job. The young women tearfully left school to help support the family. They joined the typing pool at the American Addressograph and Telephone Company. *(From Gli Italiani negli Stati Uniti d'America, 1906)*

Bringing the News. The Italian press served the community in many ways. This picture was taken in front of *Il Progresso's* headquarters in New York City during a campaign the paper launched to raise money and clothes for the victims of the Messina, Sicily, earthquake of December 1908. Carlo Bassotti, an emigrant from Tuscany, founded the paper in 1880. It became a daily and reached a circulation of 125,000. In 1927, Generoso Pope, the owner of the world's largest building-construction-materials company, purchased the paper and fostered support for Tammany Hall candidates and for the Fascist regime of Benito Mussolini. By the outbreak of World War II, he was a vigorous supporter of the American war effort. (*From* Gli Italiani negli Stati Uniti d'America, *1906*)

Grass Roots Self-reliance. Almost exclusively Italian, gardeners joined together in 1916 to establish the Walla Walla Gardeners Association. They felt exploited by the two to three commission houses in Walla Walla, Washington, whom they believed favored some growers over others. The WWGA gave immigrant shareholders fairer access to the produce market, better distribution choices, and control over association policies. This new competition made it difficult for the older commission houses to practice favoritism. In addition, the WWGA operated a cooperative store that sold Italian products to the members on credit, to be paid from the member's portion of the sale of crops in the spring. (*Courtesy Walla Walla Gardeners Association, Inc.*)

Burial Services. Undertaker Tommaso Scarpaci established this combination real estate office and undertaker's business at 186 E. Twenty-first Street, Brooklyn, New York, around 1910. In the early part of the century, undertakers only embalmed the body and wakes were held in the home of the deceased. Italians followed their traditions of burial rituals, combining folk customs and Catholic practices. One grandson of emigrants from an Albanian settlement in southern Italy remembers the wailing chorus of women mourners that seemed primordial. *(Courtesy Anthony Scarpaci)*

Multiple Services. Domenico Pelaia settled in Wilmington, Delaware, in 1910. First, he opened a barbershop on West Front Street, and after his marriage in 1915, he opened a grocery store on West Second Street and served as *banchiere Italiano* (Italian banker) to expedite money exchange and money forwarding for fellow Italian immigrants. By 1924, Domenico was also a notary public, an agent for the American Express Company, and a representative for the Italian liner *Rex*. *(Courtesy Estate of Joseph A. Pelaia)*

Transplanting Skills. Here Angelo Brocato, Sr., and his sons, Angelo Brocato, Jr., Joe Brocato, and Roy Brocato, stand in their gelato and pastry emporium, c. 1920s. Born in Cefalu, Palermo, and apprenticed at age twelve to master gelato makers in the city of Palermo, he spent summers making *granite* (ices) and gelato and winters making cannoli, assorted biscotti, *frutta marzipane, torrone,* and many other confections. In 1905, he traveled with his four-year-old son, James, and his pregnant wife, Elizabeth, to New Orleans, Louisiana, and opened his first shop on Ursuline Street. Three months after the birth of a daughter, Giovannina (Mennie), Elizabeth became ill and died of yellow fever. In 1907, Angelo married Michelina Brocato (same last name but no relation). She worked in the shop with Angelo, making biscotti, cannoli, and running the store. Angelo's sister took care of Elizabeth's children and the five children born to Michelina and Angelo. Churning the ice cream by hand, Angelo produced flavors new to New Orleans, such as *torroncino,* a vanilla-based gelato with cinnamon and ground almonds. His lemon ice (*granita al limone*) was a favorite of his Italian-immigrant customers. James opened his own shop on Ursuline Street, moving later to McShane Place, where he remained active until his death in 1981. Angelo's other children and grandchildren continue the business today. *(Courtesy Angelo Brocato Ice Cream & Confectionary, Inc.)*

Ethnic Entertainment. Eduardo Migliaccio, known to audiences as Farfariello (translated as little butterfly, but also suggesting a rogue) was a famous Italian comedian from Salerno. Eduardo created character roles that portrayed the immigrant experience in cabaret performances in New York City, and he toured East Coast cities and from Chicago to California. He brought out the humor and pathos of the just-arrived immigrant, the laborer describing the "jobba," and the Italian woman, dressed in regional costume, describing life without her husband, a sojourner in America. He created these character sketches *(macchietta),* writing both the lyrics and monologues for all his skits and often the music as well. His use of the evolving Italian, English, American slang and dialect that flavored immigrant communication reflected the lives of his audience. *(Courtesy Eduardo Migliaccio Papers, Immigration History Research Center, University of Minnesota)*

Ethnic Accommodations, c. 1920s. Italian cross-country runners visit Dave Gentilini's stone hotel in Knobview (Rosati), Missouri. On the side of the convertible cover are the letters "LA to NY" (Los Angeles to New York, which refers to the cross-country foot race). Dave (far right) came from Stango, Bologna, to Mississippi before arriving in Knobview in 1912. An Italian constructed the stone building, and the Gentilini family lived in an old house behind the stone house. Dave's wife, Mary, cooked for the guests, who included wealthy people, such as the owners of Garavelli Restaurant in St. Louis and John Ravarino and Joseph Freschi, owners of R and F Pasta Company. By 1934, the building was being used as a convent for the Sisters of St. Joseph who taught in the local school. When the convent closed in 1937, a series of families lived in the building. Recently some of Dave's grandchildren purchased the building. *(Courtesy Steve Zulpo)*

Basic Ingredients. Giorgio Cataudella, from Modica, Ragusa, and two of his workers stand alongside his Harlem Macaroni Company truck, c. 1934. Giorgio's son, Stephen, is at the wheel. The truck transported wholesale bulk macaroni to stores in New York City. One of Giorgio's two retail stores is in the background with displays of pasta hanging in the windows. Giorgio used the first two floors and basement of this East Harlem tenement house, at 239 East 108th Street, for his factory and retail store. His extended family lived in two combined five-room railroad flats, housing his family of nine children and his eldest daughter's family, including five children—a total of seventeen. A second retail store was located on Second Avenue between 108th and 109th Streets. Ready-made products enabled many working immigrant families to eat traditional foods. *(Courtesy Grace Giorgina Marchese)*

Marketing Ethnicity. The radio station WDEL in Wilmington, Delaware, aired an Italian program in the late 1930s. The journalist Alfredo Tribuani, father of the fighter, Al Tribuani, 1940 winner of the New York Golden Gloves Tournament and the Diamond Belt, in the welterweight division, is at the microphone (Luigi Casapulla, founder of Casapulla's Sub Shop, is seated at the extreme left). This radio program was broadcast from the Sons of Columbus Hall at 1715 West Fourth Street. Programs in the Italian language enabled sponsors to promote their products to the widespread immigrant population. *(Courtesy Bonita Bandiera Episcopo)*

Holiday Fare. Frank Lucibello and the employees in his New Haven, Connecticut, bakery, c. 1930s, proudly display the array of Easter pastries they prepared. Frank came to New York in 1920 from Amalfi, Salerno. After trying various types of jobs, he found employment at an Italian bakery and decided to make that his trade. For nine years, he worked at several bakeries to perfect his skill, supplementing hands-on experience with research into the chemical properties of the ingredients. In 1929, Frank's cousin, Carolina Lucibello Amendola, encouraged him to rent a vacant store on Chapel Street in New Haven's Wooster Square. She lent him a modest sum and apprenticed her nine-year-old son, Joseph, to work with Frank. In 1931, Carolina's daughter, Theresa, was the first salesgirl, replacing Frank's wife, Filomena, who was pregnant with their second child. Frank continued to hire young people, such as eleven-year-old Sal Petonito and ten-year-old Frankie Faggio, whom he trained to become baker's assistants and then bakers. His young female employees were trained in customer relations, packaging techniques, and cash transactions. Filomena made lunch every day for the staff. *(Courtesy Norma L. Barbieri)*

Fellowship and Relaxation. After an eight-hour shift in the mine, a cold beer shared with friends at the Calusa Bar on Main Street in the Meaderville section of Butte, Montana, seemed the perfect way to end the day. Situated across from the Leonard Mine No. 1, where one thousand men, mostly Italians, worked three shifts, the Calusa served as a type of club for the men. Pictured in front of the bar right to left are unknown, Charlie Case, Barney Ciavori, Fred Stevens, Bill Bilto, Hal (salesman), Jack Harkins, Homer Haggins, Dan Hillen, Adolph Ossello, John Contralto, Bill Osborne, and Louis Bruna. Behind Bruna is Cye Oliver, and tending bar are the owner, Bronco Pete Troglia (right), and Frank Lavore. *(Courtesy World Museum of Mining)*

Internal Migration. Nancy Bowers (née Nunziata Pisani) stands in front of the store she opened with her husband, Felice D'Elia, in 1982 in Clearwater, Florida. In 1971, the couple, both from Contursi Terme, Salerno, opened a deli store in Patchogue, Long Island, with Felice's brother and brother-in-law. Nancy worked there from its beginning, using the skills she learned on her family's farm in Italy to make mozzarella, dry sausage, and salami. When Felice and Nancy decided to settle in Florida in 1981, they sold their interest in the three stores they cofounded in Patchogue. Their first store in Clearwater, Florida, pictured here, was at the Clearwater Mall on US 19, and later they opened a second store in a small strip mall in Clearwater near Largo. While they were still setting up shelves and refrigerator cases, they hung a sign announcing the opening of their pork store business and included their number. To their surprise, they were bombarded with calls from Italian Americans who "couldn't wait" for the store to open. This internal migration of many Americans settling in Sunbelt states, to work as well as retire, has created pockets of ethnicity and generated the formation and proliferation of Italian-American organizations and businesses offering Italian products. Nancy and her family also have introduced authentic Italian products, which she learned to make from her mother, Emilia, to a larger non-Italian clientele. *(Courtesy Nunziata Pisani)*

Economic Evolution. This artistic rendition of Roma Bank's newest headquarters, which opened in 2005 in Robbinsville, New Jersey, represents the journey from an Italian-supported building and loan institution to a full-service bank. A group of Italians, who wanted to promote lessons of savings throughout the immigrant community, started the Roma Building and Loan Association in 1920. They appointed committees from south Trenton, New Jersey, comprised of emigrants from the area of Venice and South and Central Italy; Chambersburg, emigrants from South and Central Italy; and north Trenton, emigrants from Sicily and southern Italy, to reach out into the Italian community including the lodges. They printed the association's constitution in English and Italian and placed advertisements in Italian newspapers. The board of directors reviewed and approved loan applications, mostly for home ownership, to those community members whose character and steady work record served as collateral. Over time, the bank has broadened its depositor base with nine branches serving a cross-section of Mercer County, and it employs people of many ethnic backgrounds. *(Courtesy Roma Bank)*

Serving the Pueblo, Colorado, Community. Considered one of the best Italian markets in Colorado, the Gagliano family store, in business since 1923, was started by Joe and Carmela Gagliano. They both came to America from Lucca Sicula, Agrigento, around 1910. Unable to find work in Sicily, Joe came to work in the steel mill, becoming employed by Colorado Fuel & Iron. In 1921, they purchased a dairy cow and began selling milk door-to-door. Eventually, because of the large Italian community in the area, they began to sell other items, such as vegetables, olive oils, and pasta, and they also made sweet Italian sausage. In July 1955, Joe's brother, Vincenzo Gagliano, came to Pueblo with his fifteen-year-old son, Anthony. Anthony Gagliano went to junior high and night school while he worked at the grocery store and other jobs. He traveled back to Italy, in 1963, where he met and married his wife, Josephine Gagliano. They settled back in Pueblo, and he worked as a shipping clerk for the Dana Corporation, a maker of auto parts. Josephine worked at the family store for the first fourteen years, and then she got a job at King Soopers, a supermarket. The couple continued to help their cousins during the holidays and weekends. Finally, in 1997, they assumed management of the business and changed the focus from grocery items to prepared Italian foods and homemade bakery items. Their two children helped on their off days. For the last seven years, their daughter Bonnie Gagliano has worked at the store full-time. Here Anthony and Josephine pose by the counter next to a 1930s picture of the store. The Gaglianos make their own sausage, biscotti, and other Italian delicacies. (*Courtesy* The Pueblo Chieftain, *photographed by John Jaques*)

www.italianheritagetours.com. Besides companies doing genealogy research, assisting Italian Americans to buy property, or applying for Italian citizenship, some entrepreneurs have targeted a market niche in reuniting Italian Americans with their relatives in Italy. Remo Faietta specializes in locating living relatives anywhere in Italy. A native of Pianella, Abruzzo, Remo sets up a booth at Italian festivals in Ohio and surrounding states to show potential travelers how he can help them find relatives in their ancestral villages. Most of his customers come from Ohio and Pennsylvania. Remo's tours usually combine "the best of Italy" (e.g. Florence and Rome) and a hometown visit. This 2002 picture shows Robert Bernardi of Dayton, Ohio, embracing his cousin in the town of Roccabernarda, Crotone, for the first time. On a higher level, this reconnection between descendents of immigrants and their Italian families provides economic opportunities for regional tourism and trade to replace the loss of remittances as the immigrant generation matures. (*Courtesy The Italian Heritage Tours*)

Memorializing the Departed. Italian stone carvers applied the skills they acquired in Italy to carving and ornamenting headstones. These memorials could be quite elaborate, according to the taste and financial means available to the family of the deceased. The Donatelli Brothers Marble and Granite Works in Pittsburgh, Pennsylvania, c. 1930, employed immigrants who had worked as quarrymen and stonecutters in Italy. Their business sign, "Successors to F. C. Brandt," suggests that the brothers purchased the firm. This transition also illustrates ethnic succession, with newly arrived immigrant groups "replacing" earlier occupants of businesses and neighborhoods in America's cities. *(Courtesy Italian American Collection, Senator John Heinz History Center of Western Pennsylvania; courtesy Nicholas Ciotola)*

International Clientele. Born in Arona, Novara, Pietro Di Silvestri carried his family skills as hoteliers and restaurant owners to many countries. In London, he owned a hotel and restaurant, and in 1901, he opened the Constantinople Restaurant at the Buffalo Pan-American Exhibition. After the exhibition closed, he established a beer cellar at 137 Bleecker Street in New York City, and in 1904, he traveled to the World's Fair in St. Louis to establish The Moulin Rouge Grande Restaurant. Returning to New York City, he opened the Sempione Restaurant at 114 West Twenty-sixth Street. In his leisure time, he participated in New York City's Italian Marksmen Club. *(From* Gli Italiani negli Stati Uniti d'America, *1906)*

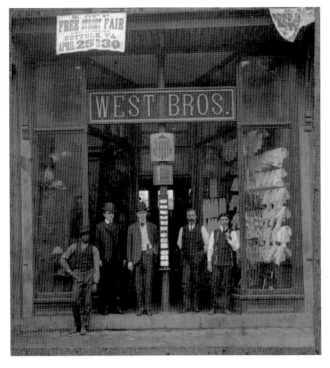

Tailor-made. Giovanni and Nicolantonio Gentile, brothers from Bomba, Chieti, arrived at Ellis Island in December 1893. Trained in Italy as tailors, they worked in New York City for a short time. Giovanni made several trips to and from Italy, and in 1900, returned there to marry Pulcheria Di Santo from Ponte San Antonio, Chieti, a short distance from Bomba. Together they returned to the United States and eventually settled in Suffolk, Virginia, where Pulcheria's brother, Nicola Di Santo, lived. Here Giovanni and his cousin, Nicola, also a tailor, pose with their employers. Pictured left to right are unknown; Joshua West, Jr.; Joshua West, Sr.; Nicola Gentile; and Giovanni Alessandro Gentile. There were several other Italian families in this community in addition to Pulcheria's brother, Nicola. Later in life, he dropped the "Di" from his last name, and his tailor business card read, "Santo." Suffolk was the home of Planters Peanut Company, founded in 1908 by Italian American Amadeo Obici. *(Courtesy the descendants of Pulcheria and Alessandro Gentile)*

Leisure-time Fare. Paul Rodin (nicknamed "Frenchy"), his wife, Edwina, and their seven-year-old grandson, Albert, staff their waffle stand on the Santa Monica pier, in California, c. 1924. Paul had started out in life as Ignazio Rodda in Roppolo, Torino, but he changed his name sometime before 1896. Paul also served as the business agent for a French company that manufactured waffle makers (note the sign at the back of the stand). They rode the Pacific Electric streetcar to Santa Monica from Venice, where they had built a six-unit court in 1923. In the warm California sunshine, the waffle stand operated year-round. *(Courtesy Peter Rodda)*

Decorative Arts. Olinto Scorci, born in Ancona, immigrated to the United States with his wife, Marietta, and their infant son, Gene, in 1904-05 and settled in Canastota, New York. Olinto brought his craft and trade as a cabinet-maker with him from Italy. He worked for local furniture companies until his early death from cancer. In 1924, Olinto sent his wife and two of his sons, Jesse and Leo, back to Italy for one year because Marietta was homesick. Jesse and Leo attended school while they were living in Ancona for the year. Olinto was instrumental in sponsoring other people from Ancona to settle in Canastota. *(Courtesy Jack Sorci)*

Embellishing Buildings. Secondo Freilino emigrated from Asti with his friend Giovanni "Frenchie" Perone in 1906. Once settled in Leechburg, Pennnsylvania, where many of the Italian immigrants came from the region of Piemonte, Secondo sent for his brothers Giuseppe and Luigi. This c. 1915 photo shows the beginnings of the Freilino Construction business. Joe Freilino is on the far left; Secondo is on the far right. To the immediate left of Secondo is Giovanni "Frenchie" Perone. Secondo's company built highways, a water treatment plant, homes, and business buildings, such as auto repair shops. His grand-daughter recalls, "He was always building something on the property [a huge old Victorian that Secondo bought in 1942]. After dividing up and adding on to the big house . . . Secondo lived downstairs, my family lived upstairs, my Uncle Ortanzo's family to the right side of the house, and my Aunt Clementina's to the left . . . all accessible by me, of course, without even having to go outside! Next door, he built two duplexes, where my Uncle Earl's family lived . . . Cousins, aunts, uncles, we were like one family. When Secondo got too old to build, he went back to making vases and benches, I still have some, and when he was too old for that, he made small mosaics." *(Courtesy Karen Freilino)*

Airplane Designer. Born in Sciacca, Agrigento, Giuseppe Bellanca studied at the *Istituto Tecnico* and the *Politecnico* in Milan, Italy, where he began experimenting in aircraft design, building his first plane in 1909. Arriving in the United States in 1911, Giuseppe first taught himself to fly, and then he taught flying from 1912 to 1916 at the Bellanca Flying School, which he founded in Mineola, New York. In this photo, Giuseppe (left) stands by his 1919 Model Ce 55-hp biplane (note the name Bellanca on the tail), with aviator Clarence Chamberlain, an ex-army air service instructor and mechanic, who purchased the first, and only, production Ce for thirty-five hundred dollars in May 1920. Using funding from millionaire Charles Levine, Giuseppe purchased and modified a WB-2 aircraft, named *Columbia,* that established an endurance record of fifty-one hours and thirty minutes in March 1927. Although Charles Lindbergh wanted to fly *Columbia,* a WB-2 aircraft, nonstop to Paris, Bellanca could not release his plane nor build another in time. Two weeks after Lindbergh's historic flight, Chamberlain flew *Columbia* from Roosevelt Field, Long Island, to Eisleben, Germany (just short of Berlin), a distance of 3,905 miles, 301 miles farther than Lindbergh's flight. The plane could have continued to Moscow but had to land for bad weather. Giuseppe made the cover of *Time* magazine's July 4, 1927, issue. In 1931, a Bellanca-designed plane, *Miss Veedol,* made the first nonstop flight across the Pacific from Tokyo to Wenatchee, Washington, completing the forty-five hundred-mile trip in forty-one hours. Bellanca's designs set records for safety, endurance, altitude, and speed. He is honored in the National Aviation Hall of Fame. *(Courtesy Francis A. Ianni)*

Paris Shoe Store. Pompilio Matteucci emigrated from Lammari, Lucca, to join his two brothers, Alessandro and Amadeo, in Albuquerque, New Mexico. Trained as a cobbler, he opened a small shoe repair shop, and, when it prospered, he named it The Paris. About 1915, Pompilio decided to expand the business to include retail shoe sales, and he located his retail store next to his repair shop. This c. 1923 photo shows Pompilio (center) standing next to his son Pete (center, leaning on the counter), who had worked at the store since his teenage years. By 1925, Pompilio had opened a second Paris Shoe Store, and, by 1930, he had added a third store, which Pete managed upon his father's retirement. By the 1960s, three generations of Mateuccis had participated in the family business, operating one of the largest retail shoe-store chains in the southwestern United States. *(Collection # 2002-020, Windows on a Community: The Italians of Albuquerque, Center for Southwest Research, University Libraries, University of New Mexico; courtesy Robert Matteucci, Sr.)*

Fish Market, Wilmington, Delaware, mid-1920s. Rocco Crisconi (right), who came from Olevano, Salerno, c. 1904, opened this fish market, c. 1920, at 225 King Street. This area hosted the farmers' market every Wednesday and Saturday, providing space for farmers to sell their meats and produce from their trucks. In 1926, not long after this photograph was taken, Rocco died when a car hit the passenger side of his company truck at five in the morning. He left his wife, Jane Viscount Crisconi, and six children. The oldest child, Madeline Lucia Crisconi, had to leave school to take care of the house and the younger children while Jane worked in the fish store from 1926 to 1932. When Jane's sons, Rocco and Tony, turned fourteen, they both helped in the fish store. Due to the Depression, Jane had to close the store. Between 1933 and 1934, she married Nicholas Mercante, who had three children of his own and worked at Youngco Leather Company's morocco leather shop on Monroe Street in Wilmington. Four years later, she opened a sub shop, and the family lived in the rooms behind the business. By then Jane's oldest sons were working for Del Campo Bakery, which made the rolls for the subs. Ultimately, five of the couple's combined children would work for Youngco. *(Courtesy Carmela Jane Marsilii Ianni)*

A Wider Market. The partners and employees of the U.S. Macaroni Manufacturing Company in Spokane, Washington, pose for this 1930 photo. *Left to right:* Fileno DeFelice, Carmen Julian, Joe DeFelice, John Amicarella, Vincent DeFelice, Bill DiLuzio, Tom DiLuzio, Sam Giampietri, Ted Verna is in the truck. Vincent and Tom are holding a pole displaying fresh pasta. Established in 1916, the company marketed pasta products under such generic labels as Taystee, Italian Chef, and Bette Baker. Partners Verna, Giampietri, DiLuzio, Amicarella, and DeFelice had all emigrated from Abruzzo. The DeFelice family, from Fara San Martino, Chieti, assumed full control of the company from 1945 until they sold it in 1989. *(Courtesy the family of Vinciguerro DeFelice)*

Selling and Repairing Cars, Trucks, and Farm Equipment, Trinidad, Colorado. Barney Iuppa (left) proudly stands in his garage, c. 1930s. His parents came from Geraci, Palermo, and farmed in Trinidad. Starting as a salesman for Essex and Terraplane Cars (possibly part of Hudson), Barney aspired to develop his own business. From this garage on Linden Avenue, he sold Diamond T trucks. Later he obtained a franchise from Allis Chalmers Farm Equipment and moved to larger quarters. During World War II, Barney employed his brother-in-law Fred Sola. And in 1946, Barney's brother Jim, a returning soldier, joined the company. By the mid-1950s, the Iuppas moved to a larger building in town. Currently, the business, still partly owned by the family, continues on Commercial Street. *(Courtesy the Sola and Iuppa family)*

Fisherman's Wharf, San Francisco, California, 1935. Italian immigrant fishermen from Italy's coastal villages continued their occupations in New England, California, Texas, and Louisiana. Early on, fishermen adapted the Mediterranean sailboat felucca to America. By the 1930s, most second-generation fishermen in California were using a gasoline-powered boat called the Monterey Clipper; pictured here are *La Famiglia Piazza* and *V. Primo.* The gasoline engine offered the crew options to fish more days, a wider range, and provided power to haul in nets and lines. In the background, Alioto's Fish House illustrates how the fishing industry provided Italian entrepreneurs with opportunities for related businesses. Mike Geraldi, who had been a fish peddler at the wharf since age ten, opened Fishermen's Grotto No. 9 in 1936. Immigrants, such as Salvatore Tarantino, were among the first major fish brokers at Fisherman's Wharf. Salvatore and his brother, Pietro, specialized in buying and selling sardines, anchovies, and herring. Accurrio La Rocca started the A. La Rocca and Sons Fish Company in 1902. His business became one of the major distributors of Dungeness crab at Fisherman's Wharf. Antonio Sabella opened the A. Sabella Fish Market in 1920. Vincenzo Rafella and his brother, Stefano, ran the Rafello Fish Market stall during the 1920s. *(Courtesy San Francisco History Center, San Francisco Public Library, AAB-8582)*

Soft Drink Enterprise. Denver-born Joe F. Iacino (left), owner of the Rocky Mountain Beverage Company, and Robert Haubert (right), deliver beverages to Harry Weinstock's (center right) Lincoln liquor store in Denver's Five Points neighborhood, c. 1935. Joe's father came from Grimaldi, Cosenza, and his mother was born in Missouri to Italian-immigrant parents. While in school, Joe worked at his father's Diamond A Market and also helped out an uncle who owned a soft drink business in Pueblo, Colorado. In 1933, he founded the Rocky Mountain Beverage Company in Denver, Colorado. Initially, the company had six workers and a small warehouse at Sixteenth and Market, selling only beer wholesale until Joe branched out into bottling and distributing soft drinks to corner grocery stores and supermarkets in the Denver metropolitan and northern Colorado areas until 1987. In 1977, Joe, an accomplished promoter of his products, partnered with the Denver Broncos football team to promote the team as the Orange Crush. As the Denver Broncos celebrated its first wildly successful season in 1977, Orange Crush fever dominated the city. People painted their houses and trucks orange; women dyed their hair orange; and many purchased Orange Crush hats, belt buckles, pencils, lamps and soda-pop cans. Even Governor Richard Lamm drank the soft drink in his office while proclaiming October 30, 1977, Orange Crush Day in Colorado. *(Courtesy Colorado Historical Society, CIPA Collection, image # PCCLI1431V2, and Joe and Frances Iacino, all rights reserved)*

Designing Woman. Frances Adams (née Francesca Adamo), a hat designer from Palermo, Sicily, advertises a fashion coup as a hat maker to Eleanor Roosevelt. She had studied singing with Enrico Caruso's coach but decided to give up a career in opera. "Money, money was the reason. Oh, I sang with [Giovanni] Martinelli and many others. They told me my voice was wonderful and that my future held bright things. But designing millinery fascinated me too, and besides, there was more money in millinery," Frances once explained. She became the exclusive hat maker for Caruso's wife; Lily Pons; Rosa Ponselle; Mdm. Gatti-Casazza, wife of the director of the Metropolitan Opera; and Mrs. Giovanni Martinelli. Frances' husband, Giovanni Flandina, whom she met while working for exclusive millinery companies, also came from Palermo. The 1910 census shows many members of Giovanni's (John) family employed in the fashion industry. One of his sisters, Renata Flandina, sang opera during the 1920s and 1930s until she married. By 1940, Frances and John were running their own business together at 711 Fifth Avenue, New York City. John did some of the finer handwork and Frances designed the hats. *(Courtesy Luisa Granitto)*

A Solid Foundation. Nick Innocenzi stands next to his Innocenzi and Sons' company car and fleet of trucks, c. 1942, in Hamilton Township, New Jersey. Nick emigrated from Monteleone di Spoleto, Perugia, to Trenton, New Jersey, c. 1900, to look for work in the pottery, wire rope, or rubber industries in that city. There he married Theresa Gatti, and they had nine children, eight boys and one girl. Although Nick had no trade and little education, he wanted to be his own boss. First, he opened a saloon, but once his oldest sons became teenagers, he employed his sons, and together they excavated cellars for new homes in Trenton. Over time, some *paesani* builders began urging Nick to manufacture cement blocks for their building contracts. By 1920, with the help of his six working-age sons (twelve to twenty) and some Italian-immigrant employees, he expanded his business to include selling building materials and moved outside the city to a 4.5-acre property. On the property, he built a new home, a plant for manufacturing blocks, a warehouse, sheds, and hoppers for sand and gravel. The bulk of their customers were Italian bricklayers, plasterers, tile setters, and concrete finishers. Eventually his sons filled the jobs of office worker, driver, warehouse keeper, and manual laborer. With the exception of World War II, when two sons were drafted, all eight sons continued in business together. *(Courtesy Richard J. Innocenzi)*

Creating a Culinary Empire, c. 1948. Mrs. Frances L. Roth and Harry Herman discuss a menu with Joe Amendola at the New Haven Restaurant Institute, which later became the Culinary Institute of America (CIA). Established in 1946 as a vocational training school for World War II veterans, the original institute offered a sixteen-week program featuring instruction in popular menus of the day. Instructor Joe Amendola, born in New Haven, Connecticut, to parents from Amalfi, Salerno, was a skilled pastry chef with a background in retail baking. He also spent time cooking for the military brass at the London Hotel during the war and then the hotel Plaza Athena in Paris after VE (Victory in Europe Day.) Attracting a student body from across the country, the institute changed its name in 1951, offering a two-year educational program and continuing education courses for industry professionals. By 1969, the CIA, seeking a larger site to accommodate over one thousand students, purchased a former Jesuit seminary in Hyde Park, New York, in 1970, and opened its new school in 1972. Beginning as baking instructor, Joe filled a variety of positions at CIA for over fifty years: dean of students, director of development, and acting president. His presence remains in the library and restaurant named for him at the CIA. Culinary schools in San Paolo, Brazil; Orlando, Florida; and Campbell, California, have also named libraries in his honor. He serves as senior vice president and principal of Fessel International, a consulting company for the restaurant industry and food service companies. *(Courtesy Joe Amendola)*

Textile Industry, June 1941. Many Italian-immigrant women and their daughters worked in textile mills in northeast communities such as Lawrence and Lowell, Massachusetts; Paterson, New Jersey; and Pawtucket, Rhode Island. The Meadox Weaving Company located part of its operations in the old Post Silk Mill Building at 60 West Prospect Street in Waldwick, New Jersey. Seated in the photograph, Andreana Totta, from Nola, Napoli, worked in different silk mills in the Waldwick/Paterson area throughout her career. During World War II, Meadox produced fabric for parachutes and soldiers' uniforms, and Andreana did piecework garment production, including making Eisenhower uniform jackets. *(Courtesy Andrea Mistretta Quaranta)*

Electrical Contractors. In 1902, when he was twelve years old, Giuseppe (Joe) Picatti's mining-engineer father, Gabriel, was killed by a team of horses in the coal mining town of Roslyn, Washington. After the accident, he quit school and went to work to support his mother and two younger brothers. By 1910, he had become a power company representative in Hanford/White Bluffs. He furthered his education by taking a course in electric instruments and meters from Fort Wayne Correspondence School. During World War I, he worked at the Bremerton Shipyards as an electrician, later returning to the power company. In 1928, he and his brother, George, started the Picatti Brothers Electrical Company in Yakima, Washington, selling, renting, and servicing the equipment supporting the area's agricultural industry. Their children and grandchildren still run the business, which also provides air conditioning and consulting engineering services. *(Courtesy Picatti Bros.)*

An American Idol. Jim Delligatti's first job at Isaly's, a combination dairy products store and restaurant in the East Liberty section of Pittsburgh, Pennsylvania, provided him with a basic knowledge of the food industry. After serving in World War II, Jim and his wife decided to move to California, where he worked as a manager of a drive-in restaurant in Newport Beach. When the first McDonald's drive-in restaurant opened in San Bernardino, Jim was inspired to follow suit in Pittsburgh. In 1953, Jim joined with a partner, John Sweeney, to set up a combination drive-in, sit-in restaurant, which did very well. Jim reconnected with a McDonald's restaurateur at a restaurant show in Chicago and promptly sold his business to franchise the first McDonald's in Pennsylvania. Other franchises followed. Within a few years, this grandson of immigrants from Calabria and Naples had developed a bigger hamburger sandwich, and, on April 22, 1967, the first Big Mac sandwich debuted at his Uniontown franchise. In 1968, Ray Kroc, the company's founder and president, promoted the Big Mac nationwide, eventually becoming the most recognized sandwich in the world. Jim's sons and two grandsons each operate McDonald's franchises. *(Courtesy Michael J. Delligatti)*

Construction Industry. Workers finish cement on the fourteenth floor of the Harbour Castle Hotel in downtown Toronto, Ontario, 1974. Many Italian-immigrant workers found employment in the construction industry and a large number of immigrants established their own companies. Today TRIDEL, founded by Jack Del Zotto, and FRAM Building Group, founded by John Giannone, are only two examples of Italian/Canadian-owned companies that develop and construct major building sites in the Toronto area and elsewhere in Canada and the United States. *(© Vincenzo Pietropaolo)*

From Hobby to Enterprise. Frank Isernio displays his family-recipe sausage at his company's plant in the Georgetown area of Seattle, Washington, 1989. Interestingly, the plant is only about a mile from Boeing Field where Frank's paternal grandparents, from Caserta, Napoli, operated a 124-acre truck farm until the 1950s when the landowner sold the property to Boeing. Growing up in an Italian family, Frank especially enjoyed the sausage his mother, Angie, made from a recipe she brought with her from San Marco, Foggia. Angie's sausage is also the "secret" ingredient in her ravioli. In the late 1970s, Frank decided to follow in his mother's footsteps and used his kitchen table to make the sausage for himself and friends. One day, in 1980, his friend, Flora Masio, who sold homemade ravioli with her husband from their basement, suggested that Frank should sell the sausage and invited him to share the space in their basement shop. Later Frank started selling to restaurants, and he quit his job at the Coca Cola Company to work nights at the shipyard to free up his days. By 1982, Frank had started selling retail, servicing the accounts, with driver-salesmen taking orders the previous day and delivering the sausage fresh, within hours of production. By 1985, Frank had moved out of the basement and into the plant occupied by Isernio Sausage Company. *(Courtesy Frank Isernio)*

Building for the Future. Architect Vincent S. Riggi and his son, Vincent J. Riggi II, stand next to the County of Lackawanna Transit System Bus Terminal facility, which they designed and built on N. South Road in Scranton, Pennsylvania, which was completed in 2007. Father and son continue the legacy of first-generation Vincent J. Riggi, from San Cataldo, Caltanissetta, who founded the company. *(Courtesy Vincent S. Riggi)*

Bringing Art into America's Homes. *Figurinai,* itinerant figurine makers from Barga, Lucca, produced and peddled plaster statuettes of famous people to customers in many countries. The craft of using plaster of Paris developed between the sixteenth and seventeeth centuries in the valley around Barga. By the eighteenth century, apprentices had traveled with their artisan teachers to Paris and London. Because the figurine makers carried their own tools and plaster molds, they could produce the statuettes on the spot and did not have to carry them from one locale to another. After an apprenticeship, the young men usually set out on their own, seeking new markets. Some of them crossed the Atlantic and journeyed to cities and towns in America, where they produced and sold statuettes of George Washington, Abraham Lincoln, William Shakespeare, and other well-known personalities. They brought art to the average home. Other craft and place connections were more practical. So many emigrants from Pinzolo, Trento, followed the scissor and knife grinder trade in America that a monument was erected in Pinzolo in 1969 to honor this tradition. *(Author's collection)*

Sousa of the South. For thirty-one years (1889-1920), Philip Memoli added luster to the musical world of Birmingham, Alabama. A gifted cornetist, Memoli studied music at the Royal Conservatory in Naples and composed such music as "Hero Hobson's March," which celebrated Alabama-born Richmond Hobson, an assistant naval constructor during the Spanish-American War. When he conducted the march on June 14, 1898, it was received with critical acclaim. Local critics also considered the mass he composed a "masterpiece." In 1899, in appreciation for his musical activities in band, orchestra, and teaching, the city of Birmingham gave Memoli a silver mounted gold cornet. In this c. 1918 photo of the band, Memoli, with glasses and a mustache, holding a trumpet, stands behind the drum. The inclusion of the Bricklayers, Masons and Plasterers' International Union No. 1 banner, featuring tools of the trade, suggests that the occasion might have been a picnic or a Labor Day celebration. In 1920, Memoli moved to Los Angeles where he taught music. *(Courtesy Birmingham Public Library, Department of Archives and Manuscripts; catalog # 829.3.2.84)*

ABBATICCHIO, PITTSBURG

Leading the Way, 1910. The first Italian American to play in Major League Baseball, Ed "Batty" Abbaticchio was born to Italian-immigrant parents in Latrobe, Pennsylvania. In addition to providing a leisure pastime, baseball also provided an avenue of upward mobility for Italian Americans hoping to avoid working in the mills and mines. In a career lasting from 1897 to 1910, Ed played professional baseball for teams in Philadelphia, Boston, and Pittsburgh. He stole more than twenty bases three times and more than thirty bases twice during his career. In 1910, he returned to Latrobe and ran a hotel, purchased from his father, until his retirement in 1932. "Batty" was also a good football player. In fact, in 1895, he played for the Latrobe volunteer firemen football team, the first professional team in the United States. He quite possibly was the first man of Italian descent to become a professional football player. *(Courtesy Nicolas Ciotola Collection)*

Architectural Sculptor. Angelo Bartolomeo Zari completes his model of the State Capitol building in Harrisburg, Pennsylvania, in 1906. Arnold Brunner designed the Italian Renaissance-style building. Born in 1873 in Pisa, Zari graduated from its university in 1894 and left for America in 1895. He excelled in creating architectural models and produced them for several structures, including the Lincoln Memorial, the National Gallery of Art in Washington, D.C., the New York Public Library, approaches to the Holland Tunnel, Temple Emanu-El, and the Graybar building in New York City. In 1927, the Italian Chamber of Commerce of New York City awarded him the *Gran Premio e Medaglia D'Oro* for his contribution to the arts in his adopted country. *(Courtesy Giovanna Zari Scano)*

The Second Room of Antique Sculpture, Caproni Galleries, Boston

Public Art. Pietro Paolo Caproni was born in Barga, Lucca, and left Italy for Boston, Massachusetts, in the late 1870s. Caproni excelled in the art of creating quality reproductions, traveling through Europe to make molds directly from masterpieces in museums such as the Louvre, the National Museum in Athens, the Vatican, the Uffizi Gallery, and the British Museum. In 1900, Pietro and his brother Emilio built the Caproni Gallery at 1920 Washington Street in Boston. The gallery had illustrated catalogs of over twenty-five hundred casts, including the full-size *Winged Victory of Samothrace* and the head of Michelangelo's *David,* and supplied art schools, such as the Pennsylvania Academy of Fine Arts; major universities, such as Yale, Princeton, and Harvard; and museums, such as the Portland (Oregon) Art Museum, with quality reproductions. The brothers assisted in the final productions of some of America's best-known civic sculptures. Cyrus Edward Dallin's statues *Appeal to the Great Spirit* and *Paul Revere* were modeled in Caproni studios. Daniel Chester French, Loredo Taft, and Leonard Craske worked with Pietro and Emilio to model original plasters before their major pieces went to a bronze foundry. *(Courtesy Roger M. Griffin)*

Serenading America. After gaining a following in Europe, Count Guido Deiro left Salto Canavese, Torino, where his family, ennobled in the late 1500s, raised dairy cattle, grew wine grapes, tended fruit orchards, and operated general stores in which they sold their produce. Guido traveled to America at the request of Ronco Vercelli, the accordion manufacturer, to demonstrate his *sistema fisarmonica* (piano accordion) at the Alaskan-Yukon-Pacific Exposition held in Seattle in 1909. When one of Vercelli's accordions needed repair, Guido contacted Guerrini Company in San Francisco, California. Owners Pasquale Petromilli, Antonio Petromilli, Finan Piatanese, and Colombo Piatanesi made "chromatic" or "semitone" (button) accordions. In 1910, Guido played a concert in the street in front of the Guerrini factory and was immediately booked in vaudeville, earning six hundred dollars a week. When the 1915 Panama Pacific Exposition opened simultaneously in San Diego, San Francisco, and Seattle, Guido used a Guerrini accordion to participate in a musical competition before a crowd of eight thousand people at the San Diego site where he won first prize. Guido played popular hits of the day, light classical and operatic fare, and his own original compositions. Guido's composition *Kismet* became the theme song of a successful Broadway musical (1911) and later was featured in two Hollywood movies. Guido was one of the first piano accordionists to be recorded and to play on the radio and in sound motion pictures. *(Courtesy Count Guido Roberto Deiro)*

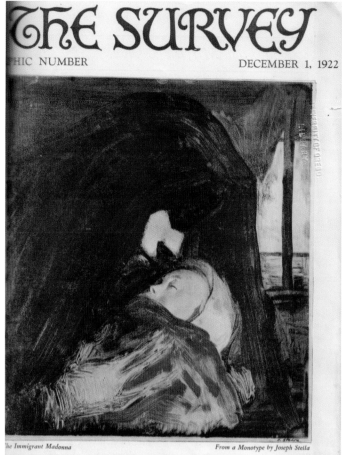

The Immigrant Madonna. Joseph Stella's first published drawing, depicting immigrants at Ellis Island, appeared in the December 1905 issue of *The Outlook* magazine. Stella left Muro Lucano, Potenza, at nineteen, in 1896 to join his brother, Dr. A. Stella, a respected physician in New York City's Italian colony. He studied medicine for two years but gave it up to attend the New York School of Design. Sent to West Virginia in 1907 by *Survey* magazine to record the aftermath of the Monongah mine disaster, he gained acclaim for his expressive drawings. Of the 381 dead, who could be identified, 171 were Italian immigrants. Stella's drawings of immigrants and industrial workers and his paintings of American scenes and religious subjects were admired by art critics and by fellow immigrants. He exhibited at the famous Armory Show of 1913. This reproduction of a monotype drawn on Ellis Island appeared as the front cover of *Survey*'s December 1922 issue. The nurturing Madonna portrayed the universality of family sentiment. *(Author's collection)*

Monumental America. Born in Siena, sculptor Giuseppe Moretti studied in Florence and Carrara. Coming to the United States in 1888, he was commissioned to produce the interior marble friezes and statuaries for William K. Vanderbilt, Sr.'s new home in Newport, Rhode Island. Not only was the marble imported from Italy for this project, but also most of the artisans and workers. During his prolific career, he produced fifteen World War I memorials, nineteen monuments, six church sculptures, twenty-four memorial portrait tablets or busts, fourteen cemetery memorials, and other pieces. Moretti stands next to his forty-three-foot-tall Italian marble and bronze monument, completed in 1927, commemorating the Civil War Battle of Nashville. He wrote, "I love this monument more than any other work that I have done . . . the youth standing quietly in the clouds of tumult holds, calms, and unites the struggling forces with something of the strength and vision of the Angel of Peace who inspires him." In 1974, a tornado destroyed the obelisk and angel. In 1999, Moretti's bronze sculpture of the youth and horses was mounted on a new base, with a new obelisk and angel carved in granite, and relocated to a new park in Nashville. *(Courtesy Birmingham Public Library, Department of Archives and Manuscripts; catalog # 617.1.36)*

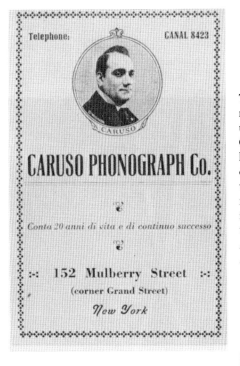

The Great Caruso. Famed tenor Enrico Caruso lent his name to this New York City phonograph company. The company was established in 1905, only two years after Caruso's triumphant debut performance as the Duke of Mantua in *Rigoletto* at the Metropolitan Opera. One of the first singers to use the phonograph, Caruso's voice could be heard in modest homes of Italian immigrants and refined salons of music lovers across the globe. He recorded songs in his native Neapolitan dialect, and patriotic songs, such as "Over There," for the war effort. His recordings have been reissued in new formats and remain popular. His 1907 recording of "Vesti La Giubba," from *I Pagliacci* (first recorded with piano accompaniment in Milan and re-recorded in 1904 for Victor USA, with full orchestral backing), became the first record to sell over a million copies. In 1987, the National Academy of Recording Arts and Sciences recognized Caruso with a posthumous Grammy Lifetime Achievement Award. (*From* Columbus Revista *magazine*)

Beautifying the Home. Maria Dellama Albertini and her daughter, Emma Elisa, left Val Di Ledro, Trento (then a part of Austria), c. 1899, and established an embroidery/fine-sewing business in New York City's Italian East Harlem. Maria supervised Emma Elisa and other Italian-immigrant women who embroidered linens and made clothing and pictures in needlepoint for hanging like the one shown here. Italian women sewed their own linens or purchased them as part of their wedding trousseau. Contemporary Italians still purchase finely embroidered linens for this purpose. In 1913, Maria hired and brought over Vladimiro Lutterotti, an artist from Riva del Garda, Trento, to create designs for her factory. The terrain in this hanging resembles the mountainous Dolomites near Riva del Garda. Maria later returned to Italy, leaving the business to Emma Elisa and her new husband Vladimiro. When Vladimiro died in the flu epidemic of 1919, his wife continued the business, which ended with her death in 1936. (*Courtesy Dr. Emelise Aleandri; photographed by Tom Arkin*)

Setting the Standard. Hank Luisetti stands in Stanford University's Maples Pavilion next to the bronze statue of himself, sculpted by one of his teammates, Phil Zonne, in 1988, to immortalize Hank's outstanding contributions to the game of college basketball. The son of Italian immigrants, Angelo Enrico Luisetti was born in San Francisco, California. His father, Stefano, had arrived shortly after the 1906 earthquake and worked clearing the rubble. Hank developed his one-handed shot on San Francisco's playgrounds. He explained, "Shooting two-handed, I just couldn't reach the basket. I'd get the ball, take a dribble or two, and jump and shoot on the way up." Hank led San Francisco's Galileo High School to city championships in 1933 and 1934, winning a scholarship to Stanford. In January 1938, using his one-handed running shot, he scored fifty points, becoming the first collegiate player to do so in one game. His innovative shooting and dribbling revolutionized the game. He was a three-time All-American and recognized as Player of the Year twice. His total of 1,596 points in four years was a national record. During World War II, he joined the navy where he contracted spinal meningitis. After recovering, he coached briefly and went on to succeed in the travel business. In 1950, the Associated Press named Hank the second-best player in the first half of the twentieth century. He was named to the Basketball Hall of Fame in 1959. *(Courtesy Chuck Painter/Stanford News Service)*

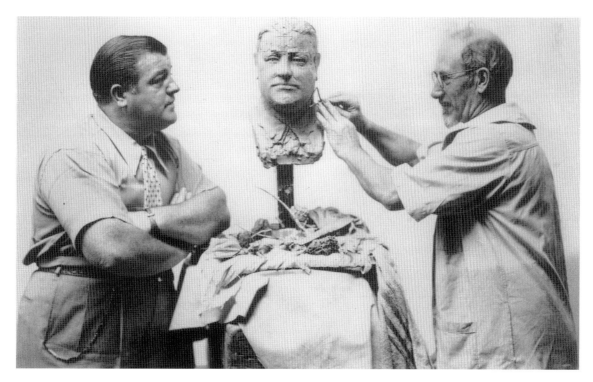

Two Guys From Paterson. Paterson-based Italian-born sculptor Gaetano Federici works on a bust of Lou Costello in 1942. Born Louis Francis Cristillo in Paterson, New Jersey, to an Italian father and a mother of French and Irish descent, Lou excelled in basketball and boxed under the name Lou King. After a brief stint in Hollywood as a laborer and stunt man in studio films, he landed a job in St. Joseph, Missouri, as a Dutch-accented comic at a local burlesque theater. He eventually changed his name to Costello and moved to New York to continue working in vaudeville theater and burlesque. While in vaudeville during the 1930s, Costello met Bud Abbott, a talented straight man. They formally teamed up in 1936 and signed with Universal Studios in 1940, playing supporting roles in *One Night in the Tropics,* their first film. In the film, they steal the show with an abridged version of their classic routine "Who's on First?" This routine, in which Bud confuses Lou by naming members of an imaginary baseball team, became their signature piece and earned them a tribute from the Baseball Hall of Fame. The duo started their own radio program and, in 1952, debuted their television sitcom *The Abbott and Costello Show.* Jerry Seinfeld admitted that this show, with its major emphasis on funny situations rather than life lessons, inspired his classic sitcom *Seinfeld. (Courtesy Patricia Federici-Fiorina)*

Artistic Enhancement. Remo Petrini, a blacksmith from Nocera, Umbria, arrived in Dunmore, Pennsylvania, in 1903. He opened his first shop on 512 Ripple Street; he then built a shop behind his home on 921 Prospect Street, where he made beautiful wrought iron railings. Starting in the 1920s, he worked year-round to construct a display for a crèche in his home and added to it yearly. He rigged up a jigsaw from an old sewing machine and used it to make wooden models of buildings in Scranton, Pennsylvania, e.g. Sacred Heart Catholic Church. He used gold leaf for some façades. He used motors from other appliances to provide running water for a waterfall and fountains in his display, and he even converted a discarded sink into a pond with live fish. He used living greenery, such as moss, in the display, and enclosed his work of art and love with his own miniature wrought iron railings and scrollwork. Each year the display filled the family living room, and people would come from miles around to see it. Although none of his children became blacksmiths, some did express their love for design as upholsterers. *(Courtesy Felix DiRienzo)*

A Family of Players. The Yankee Clipper, Joe DiMaggio, is cheered by the fans at Yankee Stadium on a day commemorating him in October 1949. Joe's parents came from Sicily and settled in San Francisco, California, where his father fished. Joe's older brother, Vince, was the first in the family to play professional baseball. A member of the San Francisco Seals, Vince pleaded with Seals' manager Ike Caveney to let Joe try out, and Joe ended up taking Vince's position. Vince "moved up" to play with National League teams, including the Boston Bees, Cincinnati Reds, Pittsburgh Pirates, Philadelphia Phillies, and New York Giants. Dom, the youngest of the brothers, played for the Boston Red Sox from 1940 to 1953, and Joe played for the Yankees from 1936 to 1951. Another San Franciscan, Frank Crossetti also started with the Seals and then played shortstop with Babe Ruth and Lou Gehrig. Frank and fellow Yankee teammate Tony Lazzeri were a dynamic double-play combination. DiMaggio's younger teammate Philip "Scooter" Rizzuto got his nickname for his speed moving from shortstop to second base. After leaving baseball in 1956, he broadcast the New York Yankees games and was known for his spontaneous saying, "holy cow," to describe an exciting play. *(Courtesy Italian Tribune)*

Golf Pro. Ken Venturi gained national prominence in 1956 when, as an amateur, he finished second in that year's Masters Golf Tournament. Born in San Francisco, California, where his father was a golf pro at a driving range, Ken turned pro at the end of 1956 and played in PGA Tours during the late 1950s and early 1960s. Ken again came close to winning the Masters in 1958 and 1960, but he lost both times to Arnold Palmer. A back injury in 1962 severely affected his game. Refusing to give up, Ken competed in the 1964 U.S. Open at the Congressional Country Club during scorching heat that undermined Arnold Palmer and other stars. Nearly collapsing during the record thirty-six-hole final, he struggled on and won, a feat that earned him *Sports Illustrated* magazine's Sportsman of the Year award. Immigrants like Ron Caperna (born Romeo) from Veroli, Frosinone, also aspired to the trappings of the American leisure class by working as a golf caddy and ultimately becoming a golf professional in California and then in Astoria and Medford, Oregon. *(Courtesy* Italian Tribune*)*

Close up of the Assumption of Mary
Saint Anne of Woonsocket, R.I. USA
Mary's chapel - East transept
Fresco done sometimes between 1940-48

Studio Boccini Nincheri 2007

Michelangelo of North America. Born in Prato and trained in Florence, Guido Nincheri moved to Montreal, Quebec, in 1914, where he began work as a theater set and interior designer. After 1920, Nincheri received commissions to decorate dozens of church interiors, in Canada and in the United States, with frescos and stained-glass windows. During the 1940s, the parish of St. Anne in Woonsocket, Rhode Island, hired him to cover the church's interior walls with religious images. Learning that the walls had never been given their final coat of plaster, Nincheri decided to adorn the ceilings and walls using the fresco technique made famous by Michelangelo and Rafael. He worked for eight years to record the history of the Old and New Testaments as well as the Apocalypse onto twenty thousand square feet of fresco surface. For the six hundred characters he painted in specific scenes, Nincheri selected parishioners as models. Here we see his rendition of the Assumption of the Virgin Mother. He used this fresco as a model for a stained-glass window he completed at Corpus Christi Church in Toronto, Ontario. Although the diocese closed St. Anne in 2000, the building has been reopened as an arts and cultural center. *(Courtesy R. Boccini Nincheri, Boccini Nincheri Studio)*

Dedicated to Music. Born in New Orleans, Louisiana, to parents from Palermo and Bisacquino, Palermo, Marguerite Piazza left for New York at age eighteen and, to critical acclaim, became a star at the New York City Center Opera Company. She gained television fame singing in Sid Caesar and Imogene Coca's *Show of Shows,* which aired from 1950 to 1954. She made her Metropolitan Opera debut in 1951, becoming the first singer to achieve television fame before joining the Met. After marriage and six children, she diverted her career to supper-club appearances to allow for more time with her family (who enjoyed her spaghetti sauce). After surviving skin cancer, she served as national crusade chairman for the American Cancer Society. She serves as permanent vice president and board member of the Memphis Symphony. She published an autobiography, written jointly with her daughter Marguerite Bonnett, titled *Pagliacci Has Nothing On Me! (Courtesy Marguerite Piazza)*

Solo and Ensemble Guitarist. John "Bucky" Pizzarelli was born in Paterson, New Jersey, to American-born parents of Italian ancestry (the Abruzzo and Naples areas). He learned to play the guitar from his uncles Bobby and Peter Domenick. His career began in 1943 with the Vaughn Monroe Orchestra, and he has played White House concerts with Benny Goodman, with whom he toured and recorded, Frank Sinatra, and Claude "Fiddler" Williams. He played in the Doc Severinsen Band on NBC's *The Tonight Show.* Bucky has appeared at Carnegie Hall and jazz festivals around the world and performed with the Boston Pops. He taught guitar at William Paterson University from 1971 to 1988. In New York, he worked mainly as a freelance musician in the studios, appearing on many recordings as part of the rhythm section; he was in high demand to provide propulsion and background for other musicians. Starting in the 1970s, he made his own recordings some of which were historic guitar compositions from the 1930s. More recently, he has recorded with his son John, a guitar player. Another son, Martin, often performs on double bass with John's jazz trio. *(Courtesy Bucky Pizzarelli)*

Star Crossed. Comedian Jimmy Durante compares vocal chords with singer Mario Lanza. Born in New York City's Little Italy to parents from Salerno, Jimmy was a classically trained piano player. As a young man, he formed a five-piece jazz band, and in the late 1920s, he created a nightclub act with Eddie Jackson and Lou Clayton. The team capitalized on improvisational clowning, physical humor, and self-parody, with much of it directed at Jimmy's large nose, which gave him the title *Schnozzola.* Jimmy's ability to distort and fracture polysyllabic words and use malapropisms in his distinct New York accent became his trademark. He wrote dozens of songs, including "Inka Dinka Doo," "Umbriago," and "Start Off Each Day With a Song." Jimmy also appeared in musicals, films, and his own television show, winning the Emmy award for best comedian in 1952. Singer Mario Lanza was born Alfredo Arnold Cocozza in Philadelphia, Pennsylvania, to an Italian-American disabled veteran and a seamstress. In 1942, Serge Koussevitzky auditioned Mario and helped him get a scholarship to the New England Conservatory of Music. During World War II, he was assigned to special services and sang on the radio for American troops. After the war, he starred in the MGM musicals *The Student Prince, The Great Caruso,* and *The Toast of New Orleans.* He died at age thirty-eight. (*Courtesy* Italian Tribune)

Racing Colors. Throughout the world Mario Gabrielle Andretti's name is synonymous with auto racing. Mario grew up in Montona, near Trieste, during World War II, in a region troubled by warring factions of Yugoslav nationalists and communists. Moving to Lucca, Mario helped support the family by parking cars, while his father Louis worked in a toy factory. Although his father forbade him to drive because he thought Mario too reckless with cars, Mario began driving competitively. In 1955, the Andretti family left Italy and settled in Nazareth, Pennsylvania, where Mario competed in stock car races and later began racing Offy (Offenhauser) midget racers. In 1965, he began his first full campaign in the United States Automobile Club circuit, was awarded Rookie of the Year, and finished third in the Indianapolis 500 race. Mario also won the USAC championship in 1969, 1984, and 1987, and he ranks second all-time in Indianapolis car victories. His sons, Michael and Jeffrey, are also racecar drivers, following in their father's footsteps. (*Courtesy* Italian Tribune)

Musical Bridges. Gia and Louis Prima perform with Sam Butera and The Witnesses in Las Vegas, Nevada, in 1967. Louis' career reflected his ability to bridge music of one era with another, starting with his seven-piece New Orleans-style jazz band in the 1920s. He successively led a swing combo in the 1930s, a big band in the 1940s, a Las Vegas lounge act in the '50s, and a pop-rock go-go band in the '60s. Louis grew up in New Orleans, Louisiana. His mother, Angelina Caravella, emigrated from Ustica, Palermo, and his father, Anthony, from Palermo. His performance style reflected his Italian heritage, and he wrote songs depicting immigrant culture, such as "Angelina," "Bacciagaloop-Makes Love on the Stoop," and "Felicia No Capicia." He wrote or cowrote many other pieces, including "Sing, Sing, Sing," which is considered by National Public Radio as one of the three hundred most important American musical works of the twentieth century. His easy ethnicity made room for other Italian-American singers to connect publicly with their roots. (*Courtesy Prima Music, L.L.C.*)

Top Defensive End. Named top defensive end of the National Football League's first fifty years, Gino John Marchetti ranks as one of the premier players in professional history. As a member of the Baltimore Colts, he played in eleven Pro Bowls, missing one due to an injury, and was named All-Pro seven times, every year from 1957 to 1962 and again in1964. He was elected to the Pro Football Hall of Fame in 1969 and named to its 1960-1984 All-Star Team. He was born in West Virginia and raised in Antioch, California, where his father was a tavern owner. When Gino was fourteen years old, his family had to move to a detention camp, because his noncitizen immigrant father was one of ten thousand Italian enemy aliens required to vacate the West Coast military zone. Gino retired in the mid-1960s, and he spent time tending his successful restaurant business. (*Courtesy* Italian Tribune)

"The Brockton Blockbuster." Rocky Marciano was born Rocco Francis Marchegiano in Brockton, Massachusetts, to shoe factory worker, Pierino, from Chieti, and his wife, Pasqualena Picciuto. At sixteen, he quit school to work at odd jobs. Drafted into the United States Army in 1943, he served abroad. Later, when he was stationed at Fort Lewis, Washington, he began boxing as an escape from routine GI duties. Turning pro in 1947, his first sixteen bouts ended in knockouts, with nine in the first round. Ready to challenge for the heavyweight crown, he stopped legendary ex-champion Joe Louis in eight rounds. Rocky defended his title six times, scoring five knockouts and earning a fifteen-round decision over former champion Ezzard Charles. In April 1956, Rocky retired as the nation's only undefeated heavyweight champion. He won all forty-nine of his pro fights, including forty-three by knockout. This scene from the *Art of Boxing* shows Steve Acunto to Rocky's left. Rocky hosted a weekly boxing show on television in 1966. The story of professional boxing has included many Italian Americans, with some achieving outstanding careers. (*Courtesy* Italian Tribune)

Symbols of Romance, Tradition, and Love. The careers of Dean Martin, born Dino Paul Crocetti in Steubenville, Ohio, Judy Garland, and Frank Sinatra include recording albums and performances on television and in films. Both men were sons of Italian immigrants. Sinatra symbolizes for many Italian Americans the success story with flair—from Hoboken to Hollywood. Music critic John Rockwell considered Sinatra "by any reasonable criterion [to be] the greatest singer in the history of American music." Dean Martin's warm, romantic "Everybody Loves Somebody"-style endeared him to an audience that bridged generations. His recording of "That's Amore" remains one of America's favorite tunes. Perry Como, born Pierino Ronald Como, in Canonsburg, Pennsylvania, to immigrant parents, left his barbershop at twenty-one to join Freddy Carlone's band. Perry had 148 Top-40 hits during his career. His "unaffected and pleasantly wholesome manner" made him a perfect host for his weekly variety show from 1955 to 1963. (*Courtesy* Italian Tribune)

The Star-Spangled Girl. Connie Stevens entertains troops during one of Bob Hope's USO tours in Vietnam. Concetta Anna Ingolia was born in Brooklyn to an Italian-American father and Native-American mother, both jazz musicians. She performed with vocal groups and made teen movies until she was cast in 1959 as Cricket Blake in the television detective series *Hawaiian Eye.* In the 1970s, she reestablished herself as a singer, starting with commercials before moving up as a headliner in Las Vegas. She won a Theatre World Award for her 1967 performance in the Broadway show *The Star-Spangled Girl.* She and Connie Francis, another Italian-American *Concetta* from Brooklyn, are often mistaken for each other. Both singers topped the pop charts in the 1950s and '60s. In the 1990s, Stevens launched a new career promoting skin care and make-up products, and she has been financially successful in developing a beauty products line. She has received Humanitarian of the Year awards from the Sons of Italy in America and the National Italian American Foundation. *(Courtesy Lena Abatangelo)*

The Pride of Pizzoferrato. Bruno Sammartino flexes his muscles for family and friends gathered at a surprise party for his seventieth birthday at his Pittsburgh, Pennsylvania, home in 2006. Bruno started wrestling in 1959 and won his first world championship in 1963, defeating "Nature Boy" Buddy Rogers in just forty-eight seconds. He held the World Wide Wrestling Federation title twice, keeping it first for a span of nearly eight years—the longest in wrestling history. He kept the second title for three years. He holds the record for 211 appearances at Madison Square Garden, selling out the venue 187 times. His dynamic style in the ring, including power moves and showmanship, plus his good will endeared him to countless fans, especially on the East Coast. Bruno grew up in Pizzoferrato, Chieti, during World War II. He was nine when the German SS moved into his village, forcing the townspeople, whom they believed were partisan sympathizers, to leave. Most families fled to Valle Rocca, including Bruno's mother, Emilia, and her three children, where they hid for fourteen months before returning to their devastated village. Bruno's father, Alfonso, had immigrated to Pittsburgh to find work in the steel mills when Bruno was three. Bruno almost died on that mountain from rheumatic fever, and in 1948, he was unable to pass the physical required for an entry visa to the United States. His family had to wait another two years before they could leave. In December 2000, a statue was dedicated in his honor in his hometown. *(Courtesy Bruno Sammartino)*

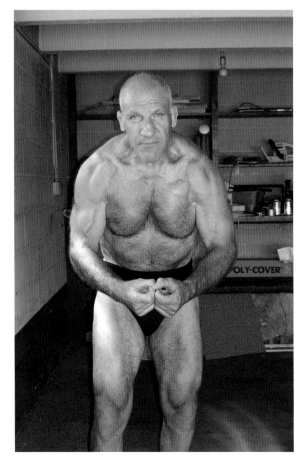

Hockey Star. Phil Esposito grew up in Sault Ste. Marie, Ontario, where he and his younger brother, Tony, who later became an accomplished goalie, learned the game of hockey together. Phil broke into major hockey with the Chicago Blackhawks from 1963 until 1967 when he was traded to the Boston Bruins. In 1969, he became the first National Hockey League player to score over one hundred points in a season, a feat he accomplished six times in his career. Phil set a new record when he scored seventy-six goals in the 1970-71 season—a record not broken until Wayne Gretzky scored ninety-two goals in the 1981-82 season. As the leading individual scorer—with seven goals and six assists—for Team Canada against the Soviet Union's ice hockey team in the 1972 Summit Series, Phil, with his teammate brother, exalted in Canada's victory. Playing for the New York Rangers during the 1976 season, he set a then league record of 152 points. Elected into the Hockey Hall of Fame in 1981, Phil served as the general manager for the New York Rangers from 1986 to 1989, and in the early 1990s, he was the first general manager for the Tampa Bay Lightning. Phil's hometown named a park in his honor featuring an outdoor skating rink mainly for hockey practices and pick-up games. (*Courtesy* Italian Tribune)

Dance in America. Italian-American Edward Villella, from Bayside, New York, entered the School of American Ballet at the age of ten. He also excelled in sports, and while at the New York Maritime Academy, he played baseball and became a Golden Gloves boxing champion. At age nineteen, he returned to the School of American Ballet and two years later joined the New York City Ballet under George Balanchine. In one year, he became a soloist, and in 1960, he was promoted to principal dancer. Balanchine created many roles for Edward, but he is probably best known for his rendition of the 1960 revival of Balanchine's 1929 ballet *The Prodigal Son.* His autobiography, *Prodigal Son: Dancing for Balanchine in a World of Pain and Magic,* was published in 1992. Edward was the first American dancer to perform with the Royal Danish Ballet and is the only American ever to be asked to dance an encore at the Bolshoi Theater. He founded the Miami City Ballet in 1986. Awarded the National Medal of Arts in 1997, Edward also received the National Society of Arts and Letters Award for Lifetime Achievement Gold Medal, making him only the fourth dancer thus honored. (*Courtesy* Italian Tribune)

Composer and Director. Growing up in a musical family—each of Agostino and Maria Zasa Coppola's seven sons had to learn an instrument—Anton Coppola and his brother Carmine Coppola became professional musicians. (Carmine and his children Francis Ford Coppola and Talia Shire won Oscars for the film *The Godfather*.) As a director, Anton has displayed versatility, ranging from Broadway musicals to grand opera. He directed the Broadway musicals *Silk Stockings* and *The Boy Friend* and conducted the world premieres of the operas *Lizzie Borden, Deseret,* and *Of Mice and Men* and important revivals of the operas *Zaza, Mireille,* and *Falstaff.* After serving four years as an army band-master during World War II, he moved on to conduct at Radio City Music Hall. For fifteen years, he was the director of both the symphony and opera departments at the Manhattan School of Music. Having composed a symphony, a violin concerto, and numerous film scores, Anton claims his opera *Sacco and Vanzetti,* which ran at Opera Tampa in 2001 and 2007, as his "major professional achievement." Critics have described this opera as "compelling . . . in a highly accessible musical style, with lyrical and attractive arias and ensembles," and they predict that *Sacco and Vanzetti* could become the "operatic sleeper" of this era and experience "a greater shelf life than other works launched with much greater fanfare." *(Courtesy Anton Coppola)*

Documenting Immigrant Lives. Photographer Vincenzo Pietropaolo, whose family emigrated from Maierato, Vibo Valentia, to Canada in 1959, focuses on the lives of working class people. This 1983 photo shows Angelo Garro (holding a pole, second from the right), an Italian wrought-iron artist, and Italian-Canadian municipal employees installing the bower that he created for St. James Park in Toronto, Ontario. The photograph captures the hard work and determination of the men installing a work of art in the harsh winter environment. It also expresses the wish to embellish their man-made world with an aesthetic appreciation. Pietropaolo has included this image in a new book, *Not Paved With Gold: Italian-Canadian Immigrants in the 1970s.* The experience of his construction-worker father struggling to support the family during their first lean years in Toronto influenced his art. He explained that at home "the notion of work was very important. . . . Work was fundamental, and photographing the Italian workers became inevitable for me. [When] they would ask me why I wanted to take their picture, I would say it was like a monument on paper, and I would tell them of my intentions to do a book on the Italian immigrants. . . . One person said to me 'Immigration has not been easy, make sure you tell the truth.' I thought . . . What is the truth? How can you convey that in photography? . . . Photography is such an international language, after all, [and] I think that those experiences, crossing barriers, are the essence of the photographic experience for me." *(©Vincenzo Pietropaolo)*

Painter Laureate of Baltimore's Little Italy. Tony DeSales grew up on the streets of Baltimore, Maryland. His father Gaetano Salvatore De-Sales, the son of emigrants from Palermo, worked at the shipyard by the inner harbor painting the inside of cargo ships. His mother Genevieve Dolores Sokolowski, daughter of Polish emigrants from Warsaw, suffered from mental illness during a pregnancy when Tony was three. At age eight, he worked in Impallaria's Italian Bakery and served mass at St. Leo Catholic Church. For thirty-five years, this self-taught artist sketched the restaurants, Catholic Church, and ordinary houses of his neighborhood. Usually working on the corner of Fawn and High Streets, he became a Baltimore institution, engaging tourists and local people in lively conversation. Using ordinary paper, colored pencils, a Bic® ballpoint pen, simple paints, and crayons, Tony conveyed a native son's personal view of Baltimore in his drawings. This drawing features Baltimore's Star-Spangled Banner Flag House in which Mary Pickergill sewed the flag used at Fort McHenry during the War of 1812. Francis Scott Key celebrated that flag in America's national anthem. By 1905, this historic building housed Dr. Giampiero's Dispensario Medico Chirurgico. Velleggia's restaurant at the left, started in 1937 by immigrant Enrico Velleggia, continues into its second generation. *(Courtesy Rita DeSales French; © Genevefa Press 2003)*

Franco's Italian Army. Franco Harris was the third of nine children born to an African-American serviceman, Cad Harris, and his Italian-immigrant war bride, Gina Parenti Harris. Although he grew up in a predominately African-American neighborhood and considered himself black, his mother brought the Italian language, food, culture, and family values into the home. In the summer of his sophomore year, he traveled to Italy to learn more about his Italian heritage. Named high school All-American in football in the city of Mt. Holly, New Jersey, he accepted a full scholarship to play at Penn State University. In 1972, he was drafted by the Pittsburgh Steelers as a first-round pick, and the rookie player thrilled fans when he rushed for over one hundred yards in six consecutive games. During this streak, Italian Americans in East Liberty (a traditional Italian section of Pittsburgh) "appropriated" Franco's Italian heritage as a way to express their Italian ethnic pride. Tony Stagno, the son of immigrants and owner of an East Liberty bakery, and some second-generation Italian Americans talked to Franco about creating a fan club in his honor. Franco accepted the proposal as a tribute to his accomplishments and perhaps because of the link to his Italian heritage. "Franco's Italian Army" debuted on November 12, 1972, at a game with the Kansas City Chiefs. Gaining ten thousand-plus yards rushing during his career, Franco is arguably one of the greatest players in the history of professional football. *(Courtesy Historical Society of Western Pennsylvania, Senator John Heinz History Center)*

A View from the Bridge. Tony LoBianco plays Eddie Carbone, the lead role in Arthur Miller's play *A View from the Bridge.* A *New York Times* reviewer praised Tony's mastery of the role, and he received an Outer Critics Circle Award and a Tony nomination for his starring role in this 1983 revival of the play. A former Golden Gloves boxer, his New York-native-born-and-bred tough guy attitude serves him well, playing streetwise Italians in a variety of blue-collar roles, initially on stage and then on film and television. He has portrayed both sides of the law—the determined, streetwise cop and the corrupt politico and syndicate boss. His 1984 performance as Fiorello H. La Guardia in the one-man show *Hizzoner!* (written by Paul Shyre) was described by the *New York Times* as "never dull, emphasizes the comic, the energetic and the ebullient; his La Guardia is a folksy, populist crusader." When the show was adapted for public television, Tony received an Emmy award for his performance. Tony was appointed as a national spokesman for the Order Sons of Italy in America to raise awareness about negative stereotyping in the film industry. (*Courtesy* Italian Tribune)

Ben Gazzara as Yogi Berra. Born Biagio Anthony Gazzara to Sicilian immigrants living in New York City's Lower East Side, Ben and Yogi's lives seemed parallel. Ben decided to pursue an acting career at age twelve when he performed in a play at the Boys' Club. He attributed that success to saving him from a life of crime during his teenage years. He received a scholarship, enabling him to attend Erwin Piscator's Dramatic Workshop at the New School for Social Research. Ben was a success in the Actor's Studio production of *End as a Man* (1953) and had starring roles in the original 1955 Broadway productions of Tennessee Williams' *Cat on a Hot Tin Roof* and Michael V. Gazzo's *A Hatful of Rain,* for which he received his first Tony nomination. Peter Bogdanovich, who would later direct him in several movies, said, "I've never seen a more exciting stage actor." The *Cape Cod Times* review of the 2005 road show *Nobody Don't Like Yogi* praised "the understated dignity" that Ben Gazarra brought to his portrayal of Yogi:

> When Yogi leaves the clubhouse for the field to give his speech, his words reverberate with authenticity. A backdrop of Yankee Stadium and its famed façade further enhances the setting. But it's Gazzara and the understated dignity that he brings to Yogi Berra that make it work. "Baseball has given me more memories that I can remember," says Yogi. And Gazzara's memorable performance will only add to the lovable legacy ("Gazzara in a poignant 'Yogi,'" March, 11, 2005).

Son of brick-maker, Peter, and shoe-factory worker Pauline (Longsoni) Berra, of Italian heritage, Lawrence Peter "Yogi" Berra left school at age fourteen, worked in a coal yard, drove a soft-drink truck, and toiled as a tack-puller in the shoe factory in St. Louis, Missouri's "Hill" section. At seventeen, he tried out for the St. Louis Cardinals, but the New York Yankees signed him. In 1951, 1954, and 1955, Berra was named the American League's most valuable player. In *Nobody Don't Like Yogi,* playwright Tom Lysaght captured Yogi's example of "the importance of pride in integrity, trusting convictions, and believing in oneself. It's a reminder that a man's humanity and his ability for empathy are the true marks of leadership." (*Courtesy* Italian Tribune)

Lessons for Life. Actors Joe Mantegna and Pierrino Mascarino talk earnestly with each other in a scene from the film *Uncle Nino* (2003). Uncle Nino (Pierrino) comes to America from Italy for the first time to visit his nephew, Robert Micelli (Joe), who is in the rat race of a demanding job and the father of a disconnected family. Nino becomes the lifeline that reminds them of the importance of savoring the simple pleasures that bring joy and fulfillment. There was a hometown connection between several of the production's cast members. Both Joe and the screenwriter-director Bob Shallcross grew up in Chicago, Illinois, suburbs, and Pierrino was born in Illinois. Pierrino's father, an Italian teacher, taught Joe's brother, Ron, in high school. Joe's daughter, Gina, auditioned and got the role of "Gina," Robert's daughter in the film. Joe's career has included stage, film, and television. He received a Tony award for his portrayal of Richard Roma in David Mamet's play *Glengarry Glen Ross*. *(Courtesy Uncle Nino Productions, LLC)*

CHAPTER 5

ITALIANS AND THE LAND

While a majority of the Italians who came to America in the nineteenth and early twentieth centuries emigrated from rural areas, only a small portion showed up in the census as agriculturalists. Many of them sought readily, available work in industrial settings in order to save money and return to Italy. Others lacked the capital necessary to purchase land and market crops. Regardless of these and other barriers, Italians did make their mark on the land, mostly as truck farmers with specialty crops, such as broccoli, peppers, and strawberries, and as grape, sugar cane, peach, and cotton growers.

Yet, regardless of how Italians earned their primary source of income, they continued to connect with American soil. In backyards, vacant lots of cities, suburbs, and remote areas, Italians tilled gardens to feed their families, to sell produce to neighbors, and as a secondary source of income. During World War II, the government urged Americans to grow more of the food they consumed so that farmers could provide enough for the armed forces; however, most Italians did not need encouragement. Vincenzo Blundi from Spezzano Albanese, Cosenza, continued to tend his vegetable garden in South Philadelphia while his wife and her aunt cooked, canned, and dried the vegetables. In addition, Vincenzo also grew the flowers he donated to Saint Rita Catholic Church, an Italian national parish.

My grandfather, Nicola Gerardi, "expropriated" undeveloped land adjacent to his home in Bensonhurst, New York, to increase his garden. Although he had left his father's farm in Calatafimi, Trapani, he recaptured the essence of that life each summer Sunday as he sat with his family at the picnic table in his backyard shaded by his peach tree. He would end his meal by pulling a peach off the tree, peeling it, cutting it into slices, and putting them in a glass of his homemade red wine. He had achieved the best of all possible worlds.

The connection between railroad construction and Italian agriculturalists in America has various implications. Section crews building and maintaining railroads in Wisconsin, Idaho, Iowa, and New York took advantage of opportunities to buy land for farms. Often the men continued to work in nearby lumber mills or in distant mines and railroad sites to supplement income while their wives and families cultivated the land. Women in Italy had maintained the land while their husbands, brothers, and sons worked abroad. In 1914, David Ranieri and his brothers, Theodore and John, applied for 160 acres each of land to homestead in Fergus County, Montana. In order to claim the land, the families built homes, barns, and fences. The husbands continued to work at the smelter, which was forty-five miles away. On their days off, they would ride the train for fifty cents to the town of Square Butte, then walk the twelve miles to their farms near Round Butte. Large families with ten to fourteen children provided ready labor for the fields. As one immigrant in Canastota said, "The more children you have, the more acres you can cultivate." These strategies adapted well to the work cycle in America.

Some immigrants learned about agricultural opportunities when they worked harvesting crops. In Independence, Louisiana, Italian immigrants traveled from New Orleans to harvest strawberries each year. Many of these seasonal workers invested in unimproved land, which they developed into productive farms.

Northern Italian farmers used partnerships to establish themselves on the land. A group might sell shares in the agricultural enterprise or two or three partners would jointly own and work the land. This system was common on the West Coast, in the San Francisco Bay Area, in Sacramento, and in the Portland and Seattle/Tacoma areas.

Italian truck farmers settled near cities such as Seattle, Denver, Houston, New Haven, and along transportation lines connecting them to markets for their goods. In 1905, Eliot Lord commented, "There is not a single one of the cities of this country yet reached by the Italians, where there is available market land near by, that is not now receiving vegetables and fruits as the produce of Italian labor."

California's climate and availability of land enabled a number of immigrants to develop agricultural corporations. Two D'Arrigo brothers, Stefano and Andrea (Andrew), born in the province of Messina, moved to San Jose, California, in 1925. Using seed sent by their father from Italy, they developed the broccoli market by advertising their "Andy Boy" brand. The western tomato industry began with Camillo Pregno, who, in 1900, taught Merced farmers how to grow tomato vines on stakes, as was the custom in Italy. He and other Italians became tomato purée packers, their product being in demand for pasta sauces.

Italian agricultural entrepreneurship often created a base for wholesale and retail trade. Immigrant peddlers and storekeepers purchased produce from their farmer *paesani*. In some areas these merchants had themselves started out as agricultural workers. In addition, Italians who sold fruit and produce on the streets of Chicago, Philadelphia, Portland, Cleveland, and elsewhere became marketing agents as they introduced native-born Americans to "new" items, such as Italian beans, artichokes, asparagus, zucchini, broccoli, and peppers, grown by their countrymen. In most cities across America, Italians distributed produce to the general population from their market stalls, grocery/produce stores, or peddlers' carts and trucks. In many cases, the produce they sold was grown by Italian-immigrant farmers and purchased from Italian wholesalers. Moreover, by making a variety of fresh produce more easily available to urban populations, Italian agricultural enterprise transformed the eating habits of the native population.

Wholesalers became intermediaries between the grower and the consumer. The Phillips (Filippi) produce company in Erie, Pennsylvania; Salvatore Di Giorgio in Baltimore; and Rinella Produce and Pioneer Fruit Distributors in Portland, Oregon, facilitated the distribution of produce throughout the country.

In Baltimore, Boston, Seattle, Tampa, and countless other places, produce markets still reflect a heavy concentration of Italian enterprises. In today's markets, Italian greens—arugula and radicchio—create the "designer" salads served by leading chefs. Customers regard garlic not only as a flavor enhancer, but also as a "health food" supplement. Healthy-heart menus incorporate the traditional Italian peasant diet of vegetables and pasta, dishes favored by the general public.

ON THE LAND

Migrant Workers. Italians were also migrant workers who left the city during the summer to harvest crops in the rural areas of New York, New England, New Jersey, Delaware, and Louisiana. Ann Parion, thirteen, and Andenito Carro, fourteen, pick berries at Newton's Farm in Cannon, Delaware, around 1910. They traveled from Philadelphia each summer with their mothers to live and work in the fields. In Italy, women carried baskets of fruit or wheat and jars of water on their heads. (Boxes of berries ranged in weight from twenty-five to sixty pounds.) *(Courtesy Library of Congress, Prints and Photographs Division; reproduction # LC-USZ62-19563)*

Italian *Barrelle* in Portland, Oregon, c. 1900. The man in front of the *barrelle* (a platform with handles on the front and back), second from left, is Lorenzo Lavagetto from Vignole/Seravalle Scrivia, Alessandria. Lorenzo traveled to San Francisco and then by stagecoach to Portland, where he grew row crops for city residents. Many Italian farmers found an agricultural niche in Portland's open areas. The location of this picture might be in the Reed College area near Steele Avenue. Notice the turnips, beets, and lettuce stacked on the *barrella*. Two men would use the handles to move vegetables for sorting or for display. *(Courtesy Stephen Montecucco and the Montecucco family)*

They Knew What They Wanted. Sidney Howard's play *They Knew What They Wanted,* about Italians in the Napa Valley, later made by Frank Loesser into the musical *The Most Happy Fella,* appears re-created by the Gromo family in Healdsburg, California, one county (Sonoma) west of Napa Valley. Ernesto Gromo, from Sestri Levante, Liguria; his wife, Maria Picetti Gromo, from Varese Ligure, La Spezia; and children Michael, John, and Frank, born in Varese Ligure, arrived together in 1905. Here they stand in 1907 in their orchard posing behind a gallon wine bottle with a glass on top. Maria's enterprise paved the way for the family's success. She worked picking tomatoes and gradually used family earnings to purchase parcels of land within the city, including three acres of grapes, a grocery store with apartments above, and homes with good-size lots for all three boys. *(Courtesy JoAnne Gromo Perkins)*

From Dairy to Dairy. Rosina Dalpaz Piazzola stands near her children while her husband, Angelo, is in the back standing next to a horse on their dairy ranch in Sheepsgulch, Montana, 1913. Both of their families had dairy farms in Piazzola, Trento. Angelo came over first, c. 1900; Rosina, accompanied by her seventeen-year-old brother, arrived in 1904 to marry Angelo. They had seven children. Angelo homesteaded and retailed milk house-to-house for residents (many of whom were Irish Americans) along his ten-mile route to Walkerville. He sent for his brothers, Celeste and Max, to come from Italy to help with the Walkerville route. The Piazzolas' Sheepsgulch Mountain Dairy had about five hired hands—mostly Italian—and owned about two hundred head of dairy cows. About 1929, Angelo left to join the Christian Scientists, but by then the children were already working on the farm. After Angelo died in 1931, Rosina married a ranch hand, Andrew Varischetti. Andrew had emigrated from the area of Sondrio in 1917 and began working at the Piazzola dairy in 1921. He modernized the farm with machinery, and eventually they sold off the dairy cows and raised beef cattle. Today Angelo and Rosina's grandson runs the ranch. *(Courtesy Mary Carol Orizotti)*

Fresh Produce. Giuseppe Desimone arranged his produce artistically to attract customers to buy the vegetables he grew. Leaving Passo DiMirabella, Avellino, in 1888, he spent a few years in New York, then went west to Seattle where an uncle lived. He found work among the Italian-immigrant truck farmers who had settled primarily south of the city in the Rainier and Duwamish Valleys. Many referred to the Rainier Valley as "Garlic Gulch." Here the agricultural skills of the immigrants applied to the rich soil reaped quality produce as illustrated in this image. Giuseppe rented land to farm until he was able to purchase his own. Assunta, his wife, worked at his side. Giuseppe's grandson speculates that the signage on the truck in this image was devised as a marketing device. Note the final "e" is left off Desimone, perhaps as an attempt to Anglicize it, and the business name—Desimon Bros. & Co.—implies that Giuseppe was in partnership with his brothers, which was not the case. He first sold his produce at Westlake Market and moved to Pike Place Market in 1922. In the 1930s, he acquired shares in Pike Place Market and ultimately became director/owner. *(Courtesy Richard Desimone, Jr.)*

An Italian Farm Town, c. 1917. Originally from Recoaro Terme, Vicenza, Louis Zulpo left Sunnyside Plantation in Mississippi where he worked with other immigrants as a sharecropper. Disillusioned by the conditions of work and the unhealthy living conditions, Zulpo helped establish Knobview, Missouri, as a mostly Italian farm community. From first settlement in 1898, immigrant families grew berries and vegetables on land they purchased from the St. Louis and San Francisco (Frisco) Railroad. They planted grapes and fruit trees and raised cows, pigs, and chickens. Several families made cheese to sell. Louis' married Maria Vitali Zulpo, who came from Bologna in 1903, in January 1905. By 1908, the town contained two stores, a saloon, canning plant, post office, school, depot, and a church. *Left to right:* Maria (Vitali) Zulpo; Louis; Pietro; Virginia; Louis, Jr. (boy in front); Taresa (Frizzo) Zulpo; Josephine; Domenico; Caterina Zulpo. In 1934, Knobview residents petitioned the post office to rename their community Rosati, Missouri, after Bishop Joseph Rosati, the first bishop of St. Louis and the first bishop west of the Mississippi. The Zulpo family still farms the land and proudly displays their Century Farm certificate 1901-2003 in their home. *(Courtesy Steve Zulpo)*

A Different Crop. In the early 1880s, some Italian railroad workers, mostly from Poggioreale, Corleone, and Salapurta, Sicily, accepted the Houston and Texas Central Railroad's offer to sharecrop with the option to buy land. Subject to flooding, this river bottomland, located about eighty miles from Houston, was cheap. Local American or Bohemian (Czech) and German farmers judged this soil too heavy for cotton. However, by cultivating their crops with the help of their entire family, the immigrants kept production costs down, and their intensive labor produced yields per acre that exceeded those of their neighbors. By 1909, nearly fifty of the 350 families owned their farm. Some Italians eventually increased their holdings to over three thousand acres on which they raised cotton. This 1920s photo shows (left to right) an Italian worker, name unknown; Luke Patranella; girl unknown; Bonnie Patranella; Ed Sanders; John Patranella; and Francesco Paulo Patranella picking cotton on the Patranella farm on Old Reliance Road in northeast Bryan, Texas. The Patranella family emigrated from Corleone. *(Courtesy Marilyn Grizzaffi Halleran)*

Sustenance from the Land, 1928. Giuseppe Gambero cuts clover to feed the milk cow while his three-year-old nephew, Carlo Latuda, watches. Arriving from Buscate, Milano, c. 1913, Giuseppe worked in the mines near Du Quoin, Illinois, but he soon decided to leave that work and return to growing food. Giuseppe bought the ten-acre farm in 1914 near Christopher, Illinois, just before World War I. He built a house and then sent for his wife, Luigina, and two children. He raised corn, grapes, cows, and pigs; made sausage; and sold produce in Christopher (about twenty miles north of Herrin). Each summer Luigina's sister Rosa Scampini Latuda traveled with her children from Trinidad, Colorado, to visit. *(Courtesy Charles D. Latuda)*

Italian Styles, American Settings. Filippo Cusimano emigrated in the 1880s from Piana degli Albanesi, Palermo, where his family raised goats and farmed. He joined his brother, who worked as a coal miner near Trinidad, Colorado. Filippo also worked in the mine but quit after he witnessed a cave-in. He then worked as a dishwasher and for the railroad. He married Brigidia Maria Perri, whose brothers farmed and delivered the vegetables they raised in Trinidad. When Brigidia died in the flu epidemic of 1918, she left Filippo with three small children to raise. He wrote to his sister (a nun) in Italy to help find him a wife. In 1920, she chose Giusippina DeGregorio (whose sister was also a nun in the same convent) in Piana degli Albanesi. Filippo left the children with friends and went to Italy. When the couple returned to Trinidad in 1921, they started a goat dairy farm on land they rented from the coal company (it was too expensive to purchase). At one point, they owned one thousand goats they milked twice a day. They sold the ricotta and other kinds of cheeses they made to customers who came out to the dairy. They also sold cheese locally and to buyers in California and New York. Later on, they purchased cows and horses. Filippo believed he had achieved a better life than he would have had in Italy. This 1930 photo shows (left to right) Mary, Filippo, and Giuseppina Cusimano (others unknown). *(Courtesy Loretta Cusimano Martin)*

Still Farming in Hammonton, New Jersey. Tony Rizzotte (far right) and his Glossy Fruit Farm employees painstakingly lay sweet potatoes in a hotbed. Laid by hand, the potatoes were warmed from underneath by water heated by burning wood in metal barrels or by an electric current. This method accelerated their growth, creating new seedlings that were planted and that produced the next year's sweet potato crop. Italians, mainly from Gesso (Catania), Palermo, and Casalvelino, near Naples, arrived in this southern New Jersey community, not far from Vineland, to work as seasonal harvesters, in the 1870s. Some stayed to buy cheap land, which they cleared of pine growth. Others purchased land from the native farmers. By 1907, farms in Hammonton were averaging twenty acres. Berries, mostly strawberries and raspberries, predominated, but sweet potatoes and white potatoes were also grown. In 2002, the Rizzotte family celebrated 115 years of farm operation. (The Hammonton Gazette, *courtesy Evelyn Penza*)

Home on the Range. *From left:* Jelindo Tiberti, Rocco Sola, and Fred Sola brand a calf at Boldini and Sola's farm in the early 1930s. Rocco and his cousin, Andrea Boldini, from Savaiore, Lombardia, purchased two hundred acres to start a dairy farm in 1923 on land south of Trinidad, Colorado. A sheepherder in Italy, Rocco came to the United States in 1901, at age twenty-one, and found work in the mines in Starkville, Morely, Hastings, and Wooten, Colorado. He married Margaret Pantoni in 1908. Margaret was born in Starkville to parents also from Savaiore. In 1923, when the mines offered work only one to two days a week, Rocco and Andrea decided to change occupations. The family, including two sons and one daughter, worked the farm and sold milk to the mining camps, one delivery a day. On Saturdays, they made butter and used the leftover milk to make Toma cheese, which was aged for six months. At the time of Rocco's death in 1943, the family was raising beef cattle on three hundred acres. In 2006, they were still running cattle on their land. *(Courtesy the Sola and Iuppa family)*

Celebrating a Good Crop, c. 1940s. Concetto Stagnitti, American-born son-in-law of Santo Farfaglia, gives the victory sign for a good crop of seed onions. Born in Castiglione, Catania, Santo decided to emigrate after his vineyards were destroyed by eruptions of Mount Etna. About 1913, he brought his family from Sicily, and they settled in Stamford, Connecticut, where he worked as a laborer. When they heard tales of "getting rich" by raising onions in Canastota, New York, they decided to relocate. First, the Farfaglias sharecropped on the Klock Farm, living in one of the houses Mr. Klock provided for his immigrant workers. The entire family cleared the undeveloped land by hand and with one horse. They worked for Klock until they could buy their own land and become onion farmers. (In 1905, Michael Patterelli became the first Italian sharecropper to buy his own land.) Instead of following the traditional pattern of living in the town of Canastota and going out to the farms each morning and returning in the evening as they had done in Sicily, the Farfaglia family built a house "on the muck," where they lived during the summer to cultivate and harvest their crops. *(Courtesy Lynne Stagnitti Ahnert)*

Ties to the Soil. Louis Sonazzaro left Cossombrato, Asti, with his family in 1895 at age four. His father Raimano found work shoeing oxen in North Haven, Connecticut's brickyards, and by 1900, he had purchased, for $1,700.00, the already established thirty-acre Cedar Crest Farm on Elm Street in the town center. Louis worked as a sign painter until 1928 when he took ownership of Cedar Farm upon his father's death. Both men sold their produce at the farmers' market in New Haven. Here Louis displays his pepper crop, c. 1940. The land yielded Indian artifacts as well as produce. Louis' niece Laura Castiglione remembers him bringing some of his finds to her school in North Branford. He donated his collection to the North Haven Historical Society. Louis stopped farming around 1960 and sold his land. He kept a house and two acres. On this land, he planted vegetables, which he sold at a stand in front of his house until his death at age ninety-three. Although his son Raymond showed little love for full-fledged farming, he continues, at age eighty-four, to tend his own garden and looks forward to planting tomatoes each year. *(Courtesy Laura Castiglione Sabatino)*

Continuing a Tradition in Pueblo, Colorado. The hog on the table has had its jugular severed, and its blood is being drained. Ralph Williams is at right, a distant cousin of the Williams family who lived across the road from the Granato farm on Highway 50 East. John Panepinto, the grandson of farmers Biaggio and Vincenza Troppea Granato, from Spezzano della Grande, Cosenza, took a series of photographs to document the pig slaughter ritual with the Brownie camera he received for his sixteenth birthday in 1956. He remembers feeding this hog often with leftovers and grain. John's eight-year-old cousin Billy Williams looks on. Beyond him is six-year-old cousin Larry Sanfillipo. Italian farm families across America slaughtered a pig each year to make salami, *capocollo* (commonly spelled *capocolla* in the U.S.), soppressata, prosciutto, and sausage. *(Courtesy John Panepinto)*

Farm Family Traditions. In June 1956, Louis Calcagno succeeded in sponsoring his youngest brother, John, and his family, including his wife, Julia, and three children, Betty, Dino, and Joe, to immigrate to Portland, Oregon. *Back row, left to right:* Mary and Louis Calcagno; Julia and John Calcagno; Bernie Calcagno, the son of Mary and Louis Calcagno. *Front row, left to right:* Dino and Joe Calcagno, the sons of Julia and John Calcagno. Louis' uncle Jimmy had sponsored him in 1923 to leave Varazze, Liguria, and come to Portland. In Portland, he entered into a farming partnership in 1925, but he had to relocate his farm a number of times: in 1942 when the government purchased the land for military housing and again in 1956 to make way for the Portland International Airport. His family had just moved their farm to Sixty-eighth and NE Columbia Boulevard when John arrived. John, who was a mason in Italy, worked on his brother's farm for a while and eventually went to work for Jim Parks' Cement Company until he started his own business, Calcagno Cement, in the 1960s. The Calcagno family still farms at Sixty-eighth and NE Columbia. *(Courtesy the Rossi family)*

Work as Play, Canastota, New York, c. 1950. Taking a work break, members of the Concetto Stagnitti family peek through the pyramid of ten bushels of onions, which they just completed stacking in order to dry. Pictured (left to right) are Amalia (Mary) Stagnitti and her children, Joseph, Lynne, and Judith. The Canastota School System determined its spring break based on the onion-planting season, which would vary. Many of the children walked to school while some were fortunate enough to ride the "early" school bus. *(Courtesy Lynne Stagnitti Ahnert)*

Continuing a Tradition—The Dirty End. *Left to right:* Ruth Williams, Amelia (Allay) Kastelic, Florence Panepinto. The women are cleaning the pig's large intestine, which Ruth "did not care to do." This was a dirty job because the colon was still filled with digested food. However, Amelia and Florence Panepinto, Ruth's grandmother and neighbor, respectively, insisted she participate in the task of rinsing the tubing multiple times until clean. They would use this to make a special sausage, which they called Super Six. All the meat cut from the bones would be ground up and made into sausage. The sausage was either hung to dry or placed in five-gallon pottery crocks and covered with liquid lard that congealed as a preservative. With either method, the sausage had to be stored in a cool basement. *(Courtesy John Panepinto)*

Starting Early, Parkrose, Oregon, 1964. Joe Rossi, age one, "helps" his neighbors Arturo Garbarino and his son-in-law, Allen Sisson, thin carrots on the Garbarino-Sisson family farm. Arturo and Allen farmed next door to the Rossi-Giusto Farm in Parkrose (now part of Portland, Oregon). The barn and land in the background center are owned by Joe's father, Aldo Rossi. Besides being neighbors, Allen's wife was Joe's *comare* (godmother), one of the highest honors Italians bestow on relatives and friends. A *comare* and her family share a special relationship with her godchild. Although the Garbarino-Sisson barn on the right has been replaced by Garden Crest Apartments, Rossi Farms, managed by Joe and his father, continued to operate as one of the few remaining Italian-owned-and-operated enterprises in the Portland area until 2007. *(Courtesy the Rossi family)*

Southern California Greetings, 2004. Fourth-generation agriculturalists Steve, Scott, and Brian Emanuelli juggle lemons on the land their father, Donald, purchased. The farm produces citrus and dates and is located in Imperial Valley, California. Currently Steve (left), the eldest, is the only son to work the farm. In earlier days, the boys' great-grandfather Giuliano Emanuelli would send crates of citrus fruit to his relatives in Belluno Veronese, Verona, at Christmastime because they didn't have much fruit in the winter there. *(Courtesy Sharon K. Emanuelli; photographer Joy Cramer)*

Family Occupation. Ben Cavalli, Jr. sells his crop of Walla Walla Sweet Onions in 2004. Italian gardeners in this community developed the unique onion that matures early in the season. Francesco, Ben's grandfather, arrived in Walla Walla, Washington, from Valstagna, Vicenza, in 1913, and Ben's father, Benevento, arrived in 1920 to reunite with his family on their farm. Ben, Jr. worked at Sears and Teague Motor Company before taking over the family farm shortly after the death of his father in 1977. Francesco, a charter member, received tag number seventy-five, which his grandson now uses. Ben grows onions and spinach, and eighty percent of his onions are distributed by the Walla Walla Gardeners Association. He and his wife, Roberta, sell the rest locally, and, through their Cavalli Onions Acres Web site, Roberta also ships about five hundred boxes of onions each year. Not only does he take pride in the crops he produces, but he also makes salami and sausage according to traditional recipes with his Italian-American friends. *(Courtesy Peter Rodda)*

Country Living. Stonemason Pasquale "Pete" Petosa traveled from Vinchiaturo, Campobosso, to Chicago, Illinois, in 1880. In Chicago, he met Maria, who was from the same village; they married in 1882 and had thirteen children. In 1900, stonemason/architect Mike Jacobs (Jacobucci) recruited Pete to work at the stone quarry he leased in Columbus, Montana. Pete's family farmed on the Kovanda ranch while he worked in the quarry. Later they bought a small farm of their own on the lower Stillwater River and used the saleable farm produce, especially eggs, to supplement their income in order to support the family. Here, c. 1915, the Petosa family, with friends and neighbors, enjoys one of Maria Petosa's (at left) traditional outdoor spaghetti meals on the farm. When the quarry closed, c. 1920, the Petosas moved into Columbus where Pete and sons Henry and Chris established a monument business. *(Courtesy Sharon Meredith)*

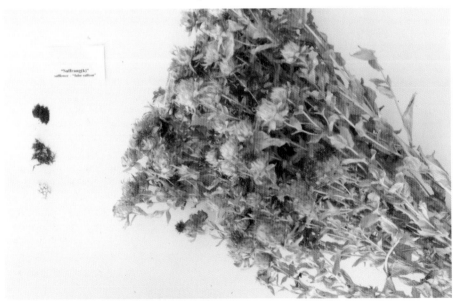

Saffrang = Saffron. Emigrants from Italy near Milano who settled in Walla Walla, Washington, raised safflower plants to produce a substitute for saffron. In Lonate Pozzolo, Varese, as well as in Walla Walla, the immigrants ground dried safflower petals into powder to season risotto dishes. Most used the dialect word "saffrang" although others called it "saffrank." According to Giuseppe Locati's granddaughter, Marilyn Locati McCann, "There is no equivalent English word, because outside of the Italian community here, no one else grows it for this purpose, nor calls it by anything else. But it was grown in Lonate Pozzolo by our families for use as false saffron." *(Courtesy Marilyn McCann; photo by Peter Rodda)*

Animal Husbandry. When Tony Bernardo, the son of a *contadino,* came to the United States from Aiello Calabro, Cosenza, in 1913, he found work at the Kennecott Copper Company mine in Bingham Canyon, Utah. Yet he continued his connection with the land by raising goats. This c. 1925 photograph shows Tony tending goats in Butterfield Canyon, located close to Magna, Utah, where he worked at Kennecott's smelter. Tony, who never learned to read or write, partnered with Louis Nicoletti to raise goats and make cheese. Louis later became famous for his goat cheese, which he sold across the United States. Tony spent his days off and some evenings working at the ranch. By 1928, he was working as a car repair helper on the railroad. In 1937, the family moved to Sandy where Tony had a few goats and continued to make cheese. *(Courtesy Rose Marie Sicoli-Ostler)*

Going to the Source. Although immigrants couldn't raise pigs inside American cities, they could buy whole slaughtered pigs from nearby farmers. Each year Nazzareno Parigi from Quarata, a *frazione* (hamlet) of Arezzo, traveled from his home in Monessen, Pennsylvania, to visit a local farm, owned by an Italian immigrant, in Star Junction. He chose a piglet from a newly born litter and paid the farmer to feed the animal according to his instructions. (Each family had their own preferences.) Here we see Nazzareno and family coming to "visit" their pig. Once the farmer slaughtered the pig, the family carted it back to Monessen where they spent three nights processing the meat in their cold basement. Many immigrants continued the tradition of butchering one or two pigs each year in the wintertime and, using traditional methods, made *capocollo,* headcheese, sausage, roasts, and prosciutto. *(Courtesy Cassandra Vivian)*

Owning Land. Concetta Annaloro Tamburo and her grandson, Frank DiGregorio, stand on the family's three-acre farm in Des Moines, Iowa, c. 1939, while her husband, Pietro, works with a horse and plow in the background. Pietro Tamburo left San Basile, Cosenza, in 1889 to follow a Protestant missionary to America. Although he spoke seven languages and was quite well versed in the Bible, he worked as a day laborer, a coal miner (with other Italian immigrants), and a construction worker. Pietro met Concetta in Des Moines. She was born in Roccapalumba, Palermo. They were married in 1901 by a justice of the peace. They raised nine children. In 1925, after waiting nearly forty years, Pietro, age sixty-one, and Concetta, age forty-one, purchased a farm at 204 Kirkwood Avenue, on the city's outskirts. Pietro did most of the planting and harvesting and made wine from the grapes they grew. He built a *forno* (an oven for making bread) in the barn. Concetta sold the vegetables they raised in the downtown market. At the end of the day, unsold produce might be traded for other items, given to neighbors, or shared with neighbors who were invited to their house on Sunday after church for a big meal. However modest, home and land ownership brought status in Italy as well as in America. *(Courtesy Vickie Tamburo Sengbusch)*

Second Income. Frank and Amelia Orsi harvest vegetables on their land located in Dishman, Washington, in Spokane Valley on Argonne Road in 1931, as their friend, Leda Commellini, watches. They grew beans, potatoes, tomatoes, peppers, corn, pickling cucumbers, zucchini, garlic, and many herbs to supplement the income Frank earned firing bricks for the Washington Brick and Lime Company. Customers, many of them Italians, came to the stand (visible behind Frank) to buy fresh produce. Frank and Amelia came from sharecropper families in Ponte Buggianese, Pistoia. Frank immigrated to Spokane in 1913 and sent for Amelia, his childhood sweetheart. They married in Spokane in 1920. *(Courtesy Lee B. Busch, née Orsi)*

Open Land. Some New York City dwellers jumped at the opportunity to farm on undeveloped city land in the late 1940s and early 1950s. Essentially these families were squatters (no permits were required) who planted crops, sunk wells for watering the plants with buckets they hand carried, and built shacks to store their gardening tools. In some ways, these small plots, located a subway ride away from their homes, replicated the land patterns of southern Italy. In Italy, families would walk or ride a cart out to their parcels of land and spend the day harvesting crops and enjoying a hearty meal. Here Joseph (Giuseppe) Gerardi, whose family had farmed in Calatafimi, Trapani, plays with his children on the two-acre plot they cultivated in Canarsie (south Brooklyn, New York). The family built an outside dining room by using old telephone poles, and they also built a *forno* on the side of a hill. They would set up wire snares by the fences to catch rabbits. Italian immigrants in the Bronx used the area of Hunt's Point for their "summer gardens." *(Courtesy Frank Gerardi)*

Homemade Wine. Joseph Catanzaro (center) and his son-in-law, Charles Mancuso (right), relax after grape picking in North Boston, New York, 1955. Joseph came to Buffalo, New York, from Castelamare del Golfo, Trapani, about 1913. He operated a fish store in Buffalo and took advantage of the farm his daughter, Grace, and her husband, Ernest Jablonski, owned, twenty-two miles south of the city. Joseph and his wife, Maria, visited occasionally and delighted in harvesting grapes and foraging for *cardoon* (wild artichoke plant stalks, sometimes referred to as burdock) to take back home. Joseph would supplement the concord grapes he harvested with grapes he purchased to make wine, using an old grape press he stored in the basement of his Buffalo home. *(Courtesy Nina G. Jablonski)*

Gardening in a Mining Town. Mary D'Andrea Truant carries strawberries from her garden in the bowl on her head in Kellogg, Idaho, in 1957. Her parents, Carlo and Lucia Tonti D'Andrea, came from Forli del Sannio, Isernia, to Harrison, Idaho, in 1901, and lived with Lucia's parents. Dominic and Josephine Tonti had arrived in 1894 and settled on a plot of land he won in a government lottery of Indian lands, close to Anderson Lake near Harrison. The families grew vegetables and fruits for their own consumption. Carlo worked in the Harrison sawmill until his death in 1916 in a mill accident. In 1925, Mary married Natale (Ned) Truant from San Martino al Tagliamento, Pordenone, and moved to Kellogg, where Ned found work at the Bunker Hill Concentrator. On their 50-by-200-foot city lot, Mary and Ned continued to grow vegetables for their family. Ned brought soil from outside the city for his garden, and he used compost and manure from farms in the area to fertilize the plants they grew. *(Courtesy Pierina L. Miller)*

Urban Gardens. An Italian-Canadian family sorts the tomatoes they harvested from their backyard garden in Toronto, Ontario, c. 1958. After World War II, thousands of Italians immigrated to Canada to fill jobs on railroads, in factories, and in construction. Many of these newcomers came from rural areas in southern Italy where they sharecropped. In urban Canada, they exalted in growing vegetables for the table, even on the small plots of land behind their homes. This combination of owning a home with a garden represented an important achievement for these new Canadians. *(Courtesy The Multicultural History Society of Ontario)*

Bred in the Bones. In 1920, when Carmelo Facciponti arrived in New York City at the age of sixteen from Castrofilippo, Agrigento, he left behind his farming life. Living in Manhattan with his brother, he worked making cigars in order to repay his brother for his passage and to save money. By 1922, Carmelo had married Palma Alaimo and started a grocery business in South Brooklyn, a predominately Italian neighborhood. Yearning to reconnect with his agrarian past, Carmelo purchased a four-acre farm in Lindenhurst, Long Island, in the early 1950s. His grandson, Carl, remembers Carmelo spending weekends during the summer living in the small house he and his son built on the farm and doing what he really loved to do—grow vegetables. Carmelo grew plum tomatoes, and Palma would cook down the tomatoes for sauce and make a paste *(conserva)* by cutting the tomatoes in half, salting them down, and drying them in the sun on a big porcelain tray. They raised so much produce that they gave most of it away or sold it in their store. In this c. 1963 photo, Carmelo beams with pride on his bountiful crop of zucchini. After they closed their grocery in Brooklyn in 1972, the family remained in the city but spent their summers on the farm. *(Courtesy Carmelo [Carl] J. D'Orazio)*

A Family Heritage. Philip Cosentino chips branches while pruning his fruit orchard in San Jose, California. In 1946, his parents Dominic and Isabelle Cosentino, from Termini Imerese, Palermo, moved their family from Youngstown, Ohio, to a ten-acre farm in San Jose where they grew apricots and other fruit for local canneries. As a teenager, Phil and his three brothers helped cultivate, harvest, and cut fruit. Phil participated in the 4-H club in high school. Later the family moved into selling produce at Cosentino's Vegetable Haven and then expanded into a full supermarket. Phil continued to care for the orchard, bringing most of his harvest to sell in the produce section he managed at the family's market. In 1992, the state appropriated 8.1 acres by eminent domain to construct Highway 85, leaving Phil with 1.9 acres. In retirement, nevertheless, Phil still cares for this small remaining bit of his family land and sells his fruit at the J&P stand in front of his house. His crop includes twenty-five varieties of peaches, five kinds of grapes, and three kinds of prunes. Some of these items, e.g., nectarines with white skins, are no longer grown commercially. He enjoys talking about orchard cultivation to groups such as the Greenbelt Alliance and to school groups who request tours. *(Courtesy Philip Cosentino)*

Dairy Farming to Ice Cream. Salvatore Reina sits on a stallion while Castenzio Ferlita stands holding the white horse hitched to a wagon, on their dairy farm in Tampa, Florida, c. 1894. They arrived in 1886 from Sicily, and in less than ten years, they built this successful business. Later, using their dairy products, they established the Cosmopolitan Ice Company and the Tropical Ice Cream Company. *(Courtesy Special Collections, University of South Florida Tampa Library, Anthony Pizzo Collection)*

Market Niche. Alessandro Alfano (foreground in suit) stands in front of his place of business in New York City's lower Manhattan, circa 1902. He left Marano Principato, Cosenza, at age seventeen, in 1893, and settled in East Harlem. In the late 1890s, he met Rosa Ottato, the daughter of Italian immigrants who owned a produce wholesale business. They bought celery from immigrant Italian farmers in upstate New York that they sold as "King of Hearts" brand to groceries in Manhattan. After his marriage to Rosa in 1900, Alessandro expanded the business. His fellow produce dealers nicknamed him, "The Celery King." During the first three decades of the twentieth century, the family earned approximately forty thousand dollars a year. This enabled them to purchase a sixty-acre farm in Saratoga Springs, New York; a house in Brooklyn; and beach property in Rockaway Beach, Queens. After Rosa's death in the early 1930s and with the onset of the Great Depression, the business suffered dramatically. Alessandro managed to hold on to the property, but family members had to find other jobs. Alessandro ended up working in the shipyards in the late 1930s. *(Courtesy Cynthia Savaglio)*

Fruit Magnate. Giuseppe (Joseph) Di Giorgio left Cefalu, Palermo, at age fourteen, for New York City. His experience working in his father's lemon groves and at a local packer's cooperative enabled him to find work with a fruit jobber (wholesaler). In the 1890s, he became a middleman by establishing a fruit importing company in Baltimore, Maryland. With a loan from a Baltimore bank, he began to import oranges and other fruit. This picture of the first Di Giorgio Fruit Company truck was taken in 1904. Eventually he held a controlling interest in the Baltimore, New York, and Pittsburgh fruit exchanges and purchased the Earl Fruit Company, a well-established California shipper. Joseph became a grower in 1918 when he acquired land in Florida for citrus, thus extending his control to the source. A year later, he bought 5,845 acres of land north of Arvin in California's southern San Joaquin Valley. By 1929, the company had the largest fruit-packing plant in the nation. By the end of World War II, Di Giorgio Fruit occupied thirty-three square miles in the San Joaquin Valley and was the largest grape, plum, and pear grower in the world. It was also the second largest producer of wine in the United States. Moreover, the company held about fourteen square miles of land in Florida and was the largest producer of citrus in that state. Joseph's nephew, Robert Di Giorgio, became president of the company in 1964. He expanded into processing, distributing, and marketing foods and sold most of the land. *(Courtesy The Maryland Historical Society, Baltimore, Maryland)*

Civic Pride. The Gardeners and Ranchers Association of Portland, Oregon, exhibit their crops on the float they designed for one of Portland's Rose Parade Festivals in the 1920s. In 1906, one hundred Italian gardeners sold shares at fifty dollars each in order to build a covered market facility to sell their produce. Many shareholders, most of whom originated from the northern provinces of Italy, purchased multiple shares. Those with the most shares got the best-placed stalls in the building. Although all shareholders were Italian, any farmer could rent a stall. They would drive their wagons into the building at Union (now Martin Luther King Blvd.) and Main Streets and sell the produce from the wagons. The market was open all year. The gardeners sold any produce left at the end of the day to private homes, saloons, boarding houses, and small businesses along their way. The association paid dividends to the shareholders even through the Depression years. As the number of gardeners declined, the association rented space in their buildings, or sold them outright and used the money to purchase other buildings, which still provide income for shareholders. *(Courtesy Oregon Historical Society; Image # 59694)*

Grape and Wine Production. While the names of Robert Mondavi, Joseph Gallo, Samuele Sebastiani, and Louis Martini are familiar to wine lovers around the world, Italian grape growers and wine makers established businesses wherever grapes would grow. Here the Cardetti family and friends process concord grapes from their Knobview (Rosati), Missouri, vineyards. *Top row, left to right:* Angelo Tessaro, Richard J. Cardetti, Pete Deluca, Richard Cardetti. *Front row:* Joseph Cardetti, Martina Piazza, Anna Deluca, Lena Donati Marchi, Rose Deluca. Their wine label reads, "Rosati Natural Concord Wine, manufactured and bottled by R.M. Cardetti and Sons." The winery, producing wines from "the finest Ozark vineyards" operated from 1933, the end of Prohibition, until 1942, when Richard Cardetti had to close down operations due to a lack of sugar and labor in wartime. The Welch Grape Juice Company purchased the winery building and bought grapes from local growers to make jam and jelly for the armed forces. Besides selling their grapes to Welch's, many growers with land along Route 66 also had their own roadside stands. Today some still sell grapes along I-44. *(Courtesy Steve Zulpo)*

Land Baron. Originally recruited as field hands to pick strawberries in Tangipahoa Parish, Louisiana, Italian immigrants gradually bought farms of their own and were instrumental in revitalizing the state's strawberry industry. From the 1920s until 1931, Louisiana was the leading strawberry state in the nation. Joe DeMarco, pictured here, established a cooperative association for strawberry farmers and served as their broker, sending berries via the Illinois Central Railroad to markets in Chicago and elsewhere. Born in Villafrati, Palermo, he arrived in Louisiana at age twenty in 1905. He worked as a laborer in a sawmill in Des Allemands, near Raceland in southeastern Louisiana, and then as a strawberry picker in Tangipahoa Parish. Over time, he acquired land to raise strawberries and dairy cattle and left an estate of over one thousand acres. Successful immigrant strawberry association leaders and brokers invested thousands of dollars in banks, loan associations, ice-manufacturing companies, canneries, and box and veneer factories, and in March 1924, the Independence Bank was established with a majority of Italian depositors and bank officers. *(Courtesy Southeastern Louisiana University, Center for Southeast Louisiana Studies)*

Indoor Markets. *Left to right:* Jess Mazzeo, Anthony (Bevi) Bevilacqua, Albert Phillips, Marion Phillips, Al Mazzeo, Louise DiFonzo, Julia Bevilacqua. They are working at B & M (Bevilacqua and Mazzeo) fruit and produce stand in Erie, Pennsylvania's Central Market. Erie's most important commercial food source from about 1900 to World War II, Central Market was located on State Street, between Sixteenth Street close to Union Station on Fourteenth Street and adjacent to "Little Italy," which stretched west for several blocks and south to Nineteenth Street. Some of the other Italian families with market stalls were Ange, Grande, Yapello, Sansone, Comi, Sunseri, Arnone, and Pistori. Other ethnic groups such as Germans, Poles, and Eastern Europeans also operated stalls at the market. Farm communities like Hammonton and nearby Vineland, New Jersey, supplied Italian wholesalers and retailers from Philadelphia to New York City with the produce they sold to the public, thus creating an "ethnic chain" of commerce. *(Courtesy Dora E. Mazzeo)*

Cannery Technology. The Gennaro Filice and Joseph Perrelli families had been sharecroppers in Cosenza, Calabria. They settled in Gilroy, California, in 1908, where the men worked at the Bisceglia Brothers Cannery and on the railroad. When the plant burned down in 1913, the Bisceglias moved operations to San Jose. The Filices and the Perrellis decided to buy the Gilroy plant and rebuild it on a corner of the sixty acres Gennaro leased in order to plant their first crop of tomatoes. Joseph supervised construction of the new F & P plant. With very little machinery, the families worked mostly by hand. By 1920, the company was producing 350,000 cases of canned fruit and tomatoes. In 1929, F & P transferred their operations to a plant they built on South Tenth Street on the Richmond, California, waterfront. They relocated seventy-five of their former employees and hired over six hundred more workers, mostly women, many Italian, from the Richmond area. As one of the largest independent canners in California, F & P remained a major employer in Richmond until 1958. Joe Perrelli designed a cling peach pitter that revolutionized the industry. Gennaro and Joseph created a new company, the Filper Corporation to produce and distribute the pitter worldwide. *(Courtesy The Richmond Museum of History Collection)*

Wine Marketing. Anthony Chauppette stands to the far right in this c. 1930s photo at his New Orleans Wine & Liquor Cellar located at Claiborne Avenue near Broad Street, in New Orleans, Louisiana. Tony's father, Gaetano (Chiapetta), came to Plaquemine Parish from Salaparuta, Trapani, where he and his brothers operated truck farms. Tony decided that farm work was not his thing, so, during Prohibition, he partnered with Louis Jeanfreau to smuggle alcohol from Cuba into Louisiana. The men produced whiskey and other liquors, which they served at their "three bar" speakeasy in New Orleans. They avoided arrest by paying the authorities to look the other way. After Prohibition, Tony bought barrels of bulk wine (mostly made from negro rubio grapes) from Italian grape growers in San Joaquin Valley, California; he blended the wine, bottled it, and supplied liquor stores and bars, which were open on a 24/7 basis in New Orleans. He employed cousins and friends to make deliveries. Unfortunately, his bookkeeper, a childhood friend, embezzled from the company, and Tony had to declare bankruptcy in 1939. Left with eight thousand dollars, he purchased Nola Bottling Company and produced a variety of soft-drink flavors, including a flavor he developed named Doctor Nut; the label pictured a squirrel with an acorn. Somehow, a major beverage company acquired the formula, modified it, and produced the now famous Dr. Pepper. Later the Gulf Bottling Company merged with Nola to produce and distribute soft drinks including Pepsi Cola. *(Courtesy Ron Cannatella, Greg Chauppette, and Frances Nudo and family)*

Northwest Pioneers. Employees of the Pioneer Fruit Distributors pose for a group picture, c. 1933, in front of the company's building at S.E. Tenth Avenue and Belmont Street in Portland, Oregon. Salvatore Dindia and his son, A.J. "Gus" Dindia, started the company as Dindia and Son in 1920. Their first building was directly west of the Gardeners and Ranchers Association on First Avenue where they had easy access to purchase produce. Most of the early customers were peddlers who sold produce to households along their routes. Salvatore had had his own route that covered Southwest Morrison and Burnside Streets and First and Third Avenues. He came to Portland from Termini Imerese, Palermo, in 1900. Dindia and Son also distributed produce to grocery stores and other markets in the city. The company was one the first family-owned produce houses in Portland. The family changed the company name to Pioneer Fruit in 1931. They supplied hospitals, restaurants, and other institutions. Besides buying produce from local farmers, Pioneer bought partial carloads of produce that brokers had shipped by rail. As local agriculture declined, more products came from elsewhere. The green-and-white Pioneer Fruit trucks covered a radius of thirty miles, going into Washington as far as Longview. Don Dindia, Salvatore's grandson, sold the business to Rinella Produce in 1985. *(Courtesy Donald Dindia and Steve Dindia)*

Building on Tradition. Gary Figgins (center) works with his uncles, William Leonetti (front) and George Leonetti (rear), planting the first Cabernet Sauvignon vines in the Walla Walla Valley in spring 1974. Gary's maternal grandparents, Frank and Rose Leonetti, came from Serra Pedace, Cosenza, to Walla Walla, Washington, in 1906, where they operated a twenty-acre farm. Frank grew black prince grapes for his annual winemaking, which Rusty Figgins, Gary's formally vintner-trained younger brother, later identified as black malvoise or cinsault. Frank and his sons, George and Bill, made five barrels. Annually, as a young boy, Gary observed this family ritual. Gary and wife Nancy established Leonetti Cellar Winery in 1977, and his first vintage of Cabernet Sauvignon, released in 1978, earned an award from *Wine & Spirits* magazine as the Best Cabernet in the nation. One day Bill Leonetti received a phone call from Ernest Gallo who wanted to purchase a bottle of the 1978 cabernet. Bill replied, "Whatsa' matter, you don't have enough wine you have to have mine too?" Then switching into Italian, Bill continued the conversation. Several days later, a Gallo representative arrived at the winery and picked up a bottle, which the Gallo winery proceeded to analyze. Although the 1978 vineyard no longer exists, Leonetti Cellar, produces about 6000 cases each year divided among Cabernet Sauvignon, Merlot, Sangiovese, and a Reserve Cabernet. *(Courtesy Gary Figgins)*

Unto the Fourth Generation. Anthony DiMeo III (left) and his grandfather, Anthony DiMeo, Sr., stand in a field of blueberries at their farm in Hammonton, New Jersey. On their thirty-five-acre farm, established in the early 1900s by Michael DiMeo, who emigrated from Sulmona, L'Aquila, the family raised sweet potatoes, raspberries, and black diamonds (a form of blackberry). His son, Anthony, Sr., purchased more land during the 1930s, '40s, and '50s and added apples, peaches, tomatoes, butternut squash, and also pumpkins and gourds for Halloween. Today the family operates one of the largest blueberry farms in the world, spanning well over six hundred acres. DiMeo Farms, LLC is managed by fourth-generation grandchildren (including Anthony III) who will continue the family-farming legacy. *(Courtesy Anthony DiMeo III)*

King of Onions. As a young man, Joseph Graziano of Portland, Oregon, often helped his family hand-chop lettuce, cut carrot sticks, and peel potatoes in his father's kitchen and basement at Thirty-fifth and Franklin. Joseph's grandfather, Agostino Graziano, from Termini Imerese, Palermo, peddled produce through Portland Heights and downtown Portland. His son A.J. expanded the business into Graziano Produce, specializing in supplying restaurants, including the Hilton Hotel, with precut produce. Agostino's grandson Joe expanded the business to become the largest northwest supplier of cut produce, with customers such as Taco Bell and Pizza Hut. By 1998, Joe decided to sell Graziano Produce to Del Monte and Company and created a new business, Rivergate Farms. He purchased land in the Columbia Basin to grow high-quality onions, which could be cut and packaged for distribution. This vertical business (from field to final product) has grown into a national company, one of the largest onion stripping/peeling operations in the United States. Joe plans to develop a line of peeled onions to sell in supermarkets. *(Courtesy Joseph Graziano)*

CHAPTER 6

RELIGION AND THE
RITES OF PASSAGE

For Italians, the Roman Catholic Church and their public devotion to God and the saints were almost inseparable from everyday life. Roman Catholicism was the established faith of the Italian nation, supported by the state, and most adhered to its teachings.

The history of Italy is rich in the variety of cultures and the beliefs that have influenced its people. The coming of Catholicism (Christianity) provided another way to worship and understand the supernatural. Many forms of worship combined characteristics of the Near Eastern religions with the new faith. The use of oil, the ceremony of baptism, and the belief in the transformation of bread and wine into the body and blood of Christ had parallels in other religions known to the Italians (Romans). Many people accepted their faith without knowledge of theological explanations. The mysteries and drama of Christianity offered a way to express their concerns and questions about life.

For many Italian Catholics, worship meant the personal bond between the individual and his or her patron saint. Vows or promises were sealed with gifts of money, food, or activities such as fasting or other physical sacrifice. Celebrations of saints' days filled the calendar and each town and region had its own favorite devotions. Special societies were formed to aid in the annual celebration, which took on a festive atmosphere. The church was decorated with flowers, with statues adorned in rich clothing and candles ablaze. A procession was formed to carry the saint's image through the streets. Bands joined the procession, and the young men of the town carried the statue. Many devout worshipers walked barefoot as a penance or for a special vow.

Many of these traditions remained part of the Italian-American experience. Yet it was difficult for the newcomers to continue this form of worship, since the Irish-American hierarchy in the American Catholic Church disapproved of many of the religious traditions of the Catholics from southern and eastern Europe. They viewed their different styles of worship as pagan and attempted to transform the newcomers into "American" Catholics.

The Americanization policy of the church hierarchy appeared discriminatory to the immigrants. Polish Catholics, as well as Italian Catholics who wished to worship in their native language, were assigned space in church basements. Most bishops fought requests to establish separate parishes or to assign immigrant priests to conational congregations. Continued ethnic advocacy helped bring about a compromise to create national parishes. These parishes did not have geographic (neighborhood) boundaries. Any person of that nationality could join the congregation. Italian immigrants joined in initiating ethnic parishes. They collected funds, donated their labor, and built churches across America. By the end of World War I, there were between five and six hundred Italian parishes in operation, some of which included schools.

Italian bishops feared the loss of religiosity of immigrants settled in a predominately Protestant country. They encouraged the founding of special religious orders, like the Salesians, the Scalabrinians, and the Congregation of the Missionary Sisters of the Sacred Heart (founded by Mother Frances Cabrini), to offer solace and support to Italian immigrants who settled throughout the world. Bishops in Italy and America realized that Protestant missionaries interpreted the lack of Catholic services tailored for Italian immigrants as an opportunity for proselytization. In fact, the first and second Italian churches in Trenton, New Jersey, and in Ensley, Alabama, were not Catholic but Presbyterian and Baptist. Church hierarchy took action to ward off missionary incursions.

Born in Sant'Angelo Lodigiano Lodi, Mother Frances Cabrini, the first American saint, established hospitals, orphanages, and schools in many communities, including New Orleans, Chicago, and New York. Right Reverend Monsignor John Zarrilli, born in Calitri, Cosenza, came to Minnesota in 1905 at the behest of Bishop James McGoldrick of Duluth, Minnesota to organize a parish and build a church for the large number of Italian Catholics on the iron range in Hibbing, Minnesota. In 1906, he officiated at Saint Peter Catholic Church, located in Duluth's Little Italy. In 1912, Zarrilli became dean of all the Italians of the diocese. He organized the parishes of Good Shepherd in West Duluth, Immaculate Conception in Eveleth, and Sacred Heart in Virginia, and he recruited Italian priests for those churches.

Not all Italians belonged to the Catholic Church or practiced Catholicism. For some, it was a matter of belief. The Waldenses of northern Italy had embraced Protestantism during the Reformation. A group of Waldenses founded Valdese, North Carolina, in 1893. During the nineteenth century, Protestant groups established missions in Italy. Some of their converts became ministers and were assigned to immigrant missions in American cities. Protestant missions in North American cities catered to the needs, physical and spiritual, of the immigrants. Methodist, Presbyterian, and Episcopal groups opened soup kitchens and dispensed clothing, food, and money to needy families. Their centers offered recreational and educational services for the community. Day schools, vacation schools, citizenship classes, and health-science classes attracted local residents. Most Italians who attended appreciated the kindness of the organizers but saw no need to convert. The few who did (approximately twenty-one thousand) participated fully in church activities, helping to construct buildings and attempting to convert their neighbors.

Proselytizing efforts reaped minimal results in America because Protestants misinterpreted Italian religious behavior. They assumed that the absence of men from church meant repudiation of the faith, but many Italians separated their religious devotion from church membership. They accepted their faith but saw little need to attend mass or visit church. Their faith was a personal commitment expressed in devotions, such as shrines at home, participation in saints' feasts, or special activities (for example, not eating wheat products on the feast day of Santa Lucia—December 13—or making trips to religious shrines).

In America, as in Italy, lay people formed organizations for providing mutual benefits and celebrating the feasts of patron saints. Societies, such as the *Società Italiana di Mutuo Beneficenza Maria Immacolata Concezione* (established in 1904 in White Castle, Louisiana), provided sick and death benefits for its members before the days of unemployment insurance and health-care programs, and the organization coordinated the annual feast dedicated to the members' patron saint (the Blessed Mother). Special devotion to individual saints took on a new meaning in America. Residents of Baltimore, Maryland's Little Italy believed that Saint Anthony of Padua had protected their homes from the disastrous fire of 1904. To commemorate this miracle, they formed a society to celebrate Saint Anthony's feast day on June 13. The feast lasted over a week and bands would travel from Philadelphia to play during the celebration. Not all groups incorporated both mutual aid and religious functions.

Some immigrants held strong opposition to the established church. In Italy, the landowning church often exploited the *contadini*. Some local priests gave little of their time to the needs of the poorer congregants and viewed the priesthood as a means to gain social acceptance among the landowning classes. This "liaison" between the clergy and the landowners created resentment.

Also among the immigrants were individuals who did not accept church theology at all. These ranged from skeptics to anarchists. Their numbers were small, but in America, they expressed themselves openly in the radical press and in organizations. These groups sometimes directly challenged the clergy and attempted to convince conationals that the church worked with the agents of exploitation, or at least represented obsolete, unscientific views.

The immigrant community gradually adopted many American religious practices. Men, especially the second generation, attended mass and joined Holy Name societies. Clergy encouraged the establishment of activities and organizations to parallel those of the native Protestant society. Scout troops, church basketball teams, and mothers' clubs were established for parishioners.

Although the second and third generations formalized their participation in American church activities, they retained some of the traditional forms of devotion. The traditional Christmas Eve fish dinner and special foods designed for holiday celebration still grace family tables. In New Orleans, the annual St. Joseph's Day parade (March 19) continues a devotion established by the immigrants. Each year in September, the Feast of San Gennaro held in New York City and Los Angeles attracts tourists who enjoy the food and festive atmosphere that accompany the religious celebration. Many immigrants and their children have maintained a connection with their *paese* parish by sending money to restore and enhance aging buildings and supporting local devotions to particular saints.

Naming Their Church. At first the Sicilian immigrants in Bryan, Texas, attended Saint Joseph Catholic Church along with German, Czech, and Polish settlers, but they soon wanted their own church. When a parish was established for them in 1896, the immigrants could not agree on a name. Those from Poggioreale, Trapani, wanted Saint Anthony, and those from Corleone, Palermo, wanted Saint Leo Luca. They drew straws and Saint Anthony "won." Although immigrants from each Sicilian town settled in different sections of Bryan, they came together to worship in their church and maintained the customs associated with Saint Joseph's and Saint Lucy's feast days. *(Courtesy Marilyn Grizzaffi Halleran)*

Neighborhood Shrine, Portland, Oregon. The Amato family decorated a shrine to commemorate a religious feast in Portland, Oregon, in 1910. *Starting at the top left and working downward in a half circle ending top right:* Rosaria (Sarah) Catanese (Natala's daughter), Joe Amato (Natala's son), August and Pete Catanese (Rosaria's sons), Charles and August Cacicia (Natala's grandsons), Philip and Jim Amato (Natala's sons), Natala Amato (Rosaria's mother). Young Charles had crippled feet, and the family prayed for a miracle to enable him to walk normally. He eventually did. This extended family continued their fervent devotion lighting candles regularly at the shrines they created inside their homes and backyards. *(Courtesy Diane [Amato] Partain)*

Chiesa Italiana di Santa Maria del Carmelo

UTICA, N. Y.

STATI UNITI d'AMERICA

Fede Di Battesimo

Il Sottoscritto *dichiara che Mariantonia Maggio nata il 15 Maggio 1900*

da Donato Maggio - Gaetana Pepe

fu battezzata dal Rev. A. Caselli il 8 Luglio 1900

Padrino Felice Sabato   Madrina Gaetana Sangregorio

Utica, li 5 Maggio 1916   Per Il Parroco

Libro   Pag   Rev. F. Valitutti

Language and Style of Worship. Italian national parishes in America enabled Donato Maggio and Gaetana Pepe (Petrone) Maggio, parents of Maria Antonia Maggio, to maintain the familiar traditions and language of the faith they learned growing up in Pignola, Potenza. Rev. A. Caselli of Santa Maria di Carmelo Church in Utica, New York, baptized Maria on June 8, 1900. Maria's godparents not only participated in this religious ceremony, but also became part of the family with a special connection and responsibility to their godchild. *(Courtesy the Maggio family)*

A Royal Funeral. Joseph Tachi's funeral in 1912 at Saint Patrick Catholic Church in Walla Walla, Washington, showcased his prominence in the community. Although the Italian community considered him a "millionaire," his property was worth closer to $300,000. Originally from Lonate Pozzolo, Varese, he started out modestly, buying garden land in choice areas and renting acreage to incoming immigrant gardeners, many from the same area of Italy; he invested his money in more land and business property in town. By 1909, Tachi owned some 110 acres of fine garden land west of Fort Walla Walla, some forty acres in east Walla Walla, the major portions of two business blocks, and other interests, including two homes located on East Isaacs that he owned jointly with his nephew, Tony Locati. Tachi died in a runaway-horse accident, leaving his wife, Antonia, and no children. *(Courtesy the Saturno family photo collection)*

Extended Family Baptism, Portland, Oregon. The extended Amato family gathers in the backyard of Joseph and Mary Amato Cacicia's family home at SE Nineteenth and Tibbetts on June 3, 1917. Three children born to three Amato sisters were baptized that day at the predominantly Italian Saint Philip Neri Catholic Church at SE Eighteenth and Division. The children being baptized are (first row, seated at right) Marina, who is held by her mother Mary Cacicia (Marina's father Joe Cacicia stands in the second full row of men, second from right, holding her sister, Sarah); (second row, second from right) Rose (Rosina), who is held by her mother Marina Amato (Rose's father Joe Amato—yes, same last name—stands in the second full row of men, far right, holding her brother, Sam Amato); and (third row, fourth from left) Pete, who is held by his mother Rose Gatto (Pete's father Joe Gatto, with cap, stands at the left in the first full row of men). The fourth Amato sister, Sarah Amato Catanese (first row, first on left), was married to Joe Catanese, holding railing on left. All four sisters were born in Termini Imerese, Palermo. The remaining people are brothers, sisters, aunts, uncles, cousins, in-laws, and friends. *(Courtesy Jane Antrosio Mace)*

Protestant Outreach Activities among Italian Immigrants. In 1892, the Presbyterians established a mission on Larimer Avenue in Pittsburgh, Pennsylvania, to offer spiritual guidance to Italian immigrants living in that neighborhood. By 1903, the mission had evolved into the First Italian Presbyterian Church of Pittsburgh, later called Trinity Presbyterian. Here Rev. Anthony DiStasi, the longstanding minister of the church, stands at the pulpit. Trinity provided a place for religious rites of passage, sponsored religious and secular events, and activities for its members. In some urban areas across America denominations such as the Christian Scientists stocked religious tracts in Italian as well as secular Italian newspapers in their reading rooms. Italian immigrants enjoyed reading their native language and keeping abreast with news from home. This type of social support sometimes resulted in conversion. *(Courtesy Italian American Collection, Senator John Heinz History Center of Western Pennsylvania, and Laurette Bradnick)*

Marriage Patterns. Many Italian immigrants and their children continued the pattern of marrying people whose families originated from the same or nearby towns in Italy. Calogera "Callia" Chippo, born in Sacramento, California, to parents from Piana degli Albanesi, Palermo, married Tommaso Mezzanares, who was born in Piana degli Albanesi on June 22, 1919. In fact, the entire wedding party was related to either the bride or the groom. Callia's niece, Josephine Catania, is the flower girl at left; Tommaso's niece, Maria Filpi, is the flower girl at right. Callia's cousin, Annie Riolo, is the maid of honor. Tommaso's brother-in-law, Giorgio, is the best man. Father D. Taverna officiated at Saint Mary Cathedral in Sacramento. The couple was engaged for a year before they married. Tommaso soon opened a shoe repair shop on K Street, just blocks from the state capitol building. *(Courtesy Jo Saunders)*

Crowds in the Streets. Founded in 1900 in New Haven, Connecticut, by emigrants from Amalfi, Salerno, Saint Andrew's Society celebrated its twenty-third anniversary on Wooster Street on June 27, 1923. Each year the society commemorated his death on November 30 with a solemn mass. Emigrants from Amalfi credited Saint Andrew with the miracle that saved their lives and homes from a sea invasion led by the pirate Barbarossa in 1554. While the invaders prepared to land ashore, an old man was seen walking along the embankment whittling a stick. As the shavings hit the sea, a storm came up and all the ships were lost. During the festival in Amalfi, Saint Andrew's statue is carried to the sea. In New Haven, they carry his statue around the square and into Saint Michael Catholic Church. *(Courtesy Theresa Argento)*

Protecting the Faithful in Alabama. In the early 1900s, Birmingham, Alabama's bishop asked the Pope to send an Italian priest to serve the immigrant population he hoped to protect from Protestant missionaries in the area. The Presbyterians had already opened a church with an Italian minister in Ensley. Father John B. Canepa, originally from Genoa, arrived in 1904 to establish a church. While Republic Steel, a major employer, donated the land, Italian families raised money to build Saint Mark Catholic Church, completed in 1905. Canepa (standing on the porch in this picture) celebrated the first mass on March 19. In 1913, he established a second Italian Catholic Church, Saint Joseph, for the Italian settlement in nearby Ensley, and in 1923, he built Saint John Catholic Church in East Lake. In order to bridge generational acculturation, Father Canepa would ask altar boys serving mass to read important letters from the bishop, written in English, to the congregation to motivate the immigrants to learn English. *(Courtesy Birmingham Public Library, Department of Archives and Manuscripts; catalog number 829.3.2.75)*

A Strong Foundation. As early as 1891, Italian priests invited by Bishop O'Hara of Scranton, Pennsylvania, to administer the spiritual needs of the Italian community, recorded the baptisms and marriages at which they officiated as "Pastor of the Italian colony of Scranton." Established in 1901, the Saint Lucy Italian National Parish Church and school occupied an old public school building purchased by Bishop Hoban on Scranton's west side. The Missionary Sisters of the Sacred Heart conducted classes. In 1913, Father Gurisatti built the foundation for a new church, and for a decade, both church services and school classes were held in this foundation. Finally, in 1924, Louis Caputo's construction company began building the upper church, which was completed in 1928. *(Courtesy Historic Saint Lucy's Catholic Church, Scranton, Pennsylvania)*

Boarding House Romance. Adolfo Visintainer, born in Cles, Trento, married Carolina Imana in Chicago, Illinois, on July 18, 1925. Carolina, born in Rock Springs, Wyoming, in 1904, returned to Banco (north side of Lake Giustina) with her parents at age one. In 1922, Carolina's aunt in Chicago loaned her money to return to the United States. To repay that loan Carolina worked in her aunt's boarding house, located on the near northwest side, settled with Italians from the regions of Tuscany, Piedmont, Veneto, and Sicily. Adolfo, one of the boarders, observed that Carolina's workload was closer to exploitation, and he became her advocate and then fiancé. They married at Saint Maria Addolorata Catholic Church, which was established as an Italian parish in 1903 soon after the Scalabrini Fathers, an Italian order of clergy, assumed jurisdiction. The Scalabrini extended the church's role in the community, supporting parish societies and neighborhood feasts and providing a kindergarten, a day nursery, and catechism classes staffed by the Italian Missionary Sisters of the Sacred Heart. (*Courtesy Leonard J. Visintainer*)

The *Festa dei Ceri* in Italy and Pennsylvania. Three *ceri* (candlelike structures) holding statues of Saints Ubaldo, George, and Anthony Abbot are carried through the streets for the Feast of Saint Ubaldo. Emigrants from Gubbio, Perugia, settled the area of Jessup, Pennsylvania, where they continued the tradition each year in May. The Race of the Saints challenged the *ceraioli*, a group of ten, to keep their platform steady and upright so that the *cero* did not fall thereby humiliating the team. The *ceri* travel in single file through the streets. Saint Ubaldo, Saint George, and Saint Anthony Abbot are considered respectively protectors of stonemasons, tradesmen and merchants, and laborers and peasants. For the immigrants, work was their life and the source of substance for their families. (*Courtesy Museo Regionale dell'Emigrazione "Pietro Conti," Gualdo Tadino, Italy*)

A House of Worship. Newly dedicated Saint Ann Catholic Church, Ossining, New York, celebrates its first communion and confirmation in 1929 with pastor Rev. John Eula and assistant pastor Rev. Louis Masciola. Italian immigrants led by Mr. Giulio Tuono sent a petition to Cardinal Hayes for a new church. In February 1927, Tuono rented a vacant store in the old Olive Opera House at Central and Barandreth Streets and equipped it with seats and a temporary altar for the first mass held on December 16, 1927. From there, the church moved to an abandoned theater, the Parthenon, on lower Main Street. Finally, on October 14, 1928, the cornerstone was laid for Saint Ann Catholic Church. *(Courtesy St. Ann's Church, Ossining, New York)*

Teaching Religion. A First Communion class poses with their pastor at Saint Anthony Catholic Church on Clinton Avenue in Hamilton, Ontario. For most immigrant and second-generation children, religious education was taught after regular school hours. Parochial schools charged a nominal tuition, and many working-class parents decided to take advantage of the free public-school system. *(Courtesy The Multicultural History Society of Ontario)*

Holy Trinity Italian Evangelical Lutheran Church, Erie, Pennsylvania. Founding pastor Rev. Fortunato Scarpitti (on left in suit) poses with Daily Vacation Bible School attendees in 1942. Fortunato left Italy at fourteen for Butler, Pennsylvania. He converted and helped Presbyterian missionaries work among the Italians in Pittsburgh. When the Presbyterians decided to end their proselytizing efforts, the Lutherans offered their support. As a Lutheran minister, Scarpitti moved to Erie in 1921 to start a mission. First, he preached on the corners of Sixteenth and Seventeenth Streets, and with the support of the Lutheran church and some Italians in the neighborhood, he purchased a wood frame house on West Seventeenth Street in 1922, which he converted into a chapel. His free Bible school offered movies, singing, embroidery, woodworking, and Bible lessons to all who attended. Even some nonconverted Italians enjoyed this summer option. During the Great Depression, Scarpitti raised money to help all the people in the neighborhood regardless of their affiliation. His church was among the first congregations to build a gymnasium and to become racially integrated. *(Courtesy Holy Trinity Lutheran Church, Erie, Pennsylvania)*

Community Prayer During World War II. Italians from southern New Jersey and Philadelphia gathered in Hammonton, New Jersey, to express their devotion to the Lady of Mount Carmel and to pray for the safe return of their sons fighting in the military. This annual celebration dates from the founding of the Our Lady of Mount Carmel Society in 1875. Although the practice of carrying statues of saints through the streets during religious festivals was common in Italy, in America, most non-Italians, especially the Irish, and some northern Italian priests did not approve of the practice. During the 1920s, an Irish priest in New Castle, Delaware, permitted only banners with images of the saints. Eventually the parishioners' persistence won the day and statues rejoined the outdoor parade. (The Hammonton Gazette, *courtesy Our Lady of Mount Carmel Society)*

Lifetime Devotion. Vito and Rosa Machi, from Sant'Elia, Palermo, pose in front of their elaborate Saint Joseph table in their Mason Street flat in San Francisco, California, in 1940. They arrived in San Francisco before 1906, and Vito continued a livelihood of fishing, which he had practiced in Sicily. While living in Sant'Elia, Rosa had prayed to Saint Joseph to help them overcome their poverty, and she transferred her annual devotional observance to America. She provided an elaborate table, made large quantities of food, and invited all the parishioners of Saints Peter and Paul Catholic Church, an Italian national parish in North Beach, to her home during the period from March 19 until Easter. She continued this tradition until her death in 1978. *(Courtesy Charles Farruggia)*

Personal Devotion, late 1940s, early 1950s. Antonio Tropea created this Nativity scene that filled the entire back wall of his grocery store in Monongah, West Virginia. He came to America from Gioiosa Jonica, Reggio Calabria, in 1898 at age twenty, and he practiced his trades of shoemaking and barbering in town. He met Rosa Loss from the Tyrol (located in southern Austria), and they married in 1906. In 1919, Antonio learned that the Catholic Church building was going to be sold, and he immediately contacted the bishop of the diocese and purchased the property. The family converted the main section of the church into a grocery store and transformed the priest's residence into their home. People admired Antonio's sincere faith, and each Christmas season, they came from miles away to share his joy in celebrating this special occasion. *(Courtesy Christine Tropea Jacobin)*

Religious Pilgrimage. Antonietta Greco (on third step at the right) departs from Boston in 1950 with Franciscan priests from Pittsburgh, Pennsylvania, as part of a Holy Year Pilgrimage to Rome. The group first traveled to France to visit the shrine at Lourdes and then continued onward to Rome and Assisi. Antonietta Greco had married and left Italy in 1927. This was her first visit to her family in Tricarico, Matera. On this trip, she decided to adopt her nephew, Michael Greco (her husband's brother's son), a war orphan. *(Courtesy Michael Greco, Bronx, New York)*

Family Blessings, 1954. Newly ordained Rev. Leo Spizzirri bestows his first blessings as a priest upon his parents, Susan (Pellicore) and Marion Spizzirri, while his younger brother William holds the prayer book. William followed his brother's path to Saint Mary of the Lake Seminary in Mundelein, Illinois, joining the priesthood in 1967. One of the young men's uncles, Henry Pellicore, had become a priest in 1937. *(Courtesy Jeffrey Caracci)*

Innkeeper at the Vatican. In 1982, Sister Prisca Dardano began her assignment as directress of Saint Francis Convent Pensione—a lodge that houses priests, nuns, and their families during visits to Rome and the Vatican. During her forty plus years in Rome, she obtained Papal Blessings for family members' nuptials. Here Pope John Paul II greets Sister Prisca. Born in 1930 in Utica, New York, to parents from Siracusa, Sicily, she entered the Sisters of Saint Francis and professed her final vows in August of 1952. For many years, she taught and served as principal for schools in Syracuse, her home parish of Utica (Saint Anthony of Padua School), and Albany, New York, and in Camden, Hoboken, and Riverside, New Jersey. *(Courtesy the Maggio family)*

Women's Tribute. In about 1935, Sicilian immigrant women and their daughters in Monterey, California, transferred out into the streets their in-house rosary group devotion to Saint Rosalia, the patron saint of Palermo, Sicily. Most of these emigrants came from the fishing villages of San Vito da Capo, Palermo, and Isola delle Femmine, Palermo. The women created a living rosary to march behind the statue. After World War II, this annual event evolved into more of a political and cultural event as the men participated in organizing the feast, expressing Italian pride, and including all Catholic groups, such as the Knights of Columbus. This photo shows the 1986 Saint Rosalia feast as the parade moved along Fishermen's Wharf. *(Author's collection)*

Giglio Tradition. The parade of the *Giglio* (lily), dedicated to St. Paolino (c. 400 A.D.), in the Williamsburg section of Brooklyn, New York, features a large structure, weighing about four tons and standing sixty-five-feet high, that is carried through the streets by 112 trained *paranze* (lifters). The parade, which takes place in July, was started by emigrants from Nola, Napoli, in 1903 to honor their patron saint. A band and singer stand on the platform base of the tower to provide music for the dance of the *Giglio.* The *capo* (leader) choreographs the beginning steps of the dance to songs, such as "O' Giglio è Paradiso" (written by Pasquale Ferrara and trumpeter Phil Caccavale in the late 1950s). This picture shows a children's *Giglio,* which will be lifted by youngsters, wearing caps, kerchiefs, and special T-shirts. Their participation provides training for the future; for at age sixteen, they can become adult lifters. The official band for the *Giglio* Feast is the Vecchiano Festival Band led by Danny Vecchiano. His great-grandparents came from Palma, east of Nola, near Naples, and he is the third generation to be actively involved in the festival. In 1999, descendants from the Williamsburg, East Harlem, and Astoria *Giglio,* who had moved to various towns across Long Island, formed the Long Island Giglio Association. They celebrate a five-day-long *Festa del Giglio* at the Sunrise Mall in Massapequa, New York. *(Courtesy Jerry Krase)*

Together for Eternity. In 1899, the Italian Mutual Benevolent Society (founded in 1858) purchased about thirty-five acres on F Street in Colma, California, to create the Italian Cemetery. The society proceeded to transfer the remains of its members from the City Cemetery in San Francisco. After 1901, San Francisco banned new burials within its limits. This 1948 view illustrates the peaceful setting as well as the extensive and varied monument styles. Gravesites of prominent immigrants still impress the visitor. For example, the forty-five-foot tall ornate chapel of John Fugazi, travel agent and founder of Fugazi Bank, features a carved life-sized bust atop the doorway arch. The chapel of G. B. Levaggi, the Olive Oil King of California, displays a beautiful and sad weeping angel. Although the monuments reflect a predominant Italian presence, one can find other traditional Catholic ethnicities, such as Hispanic, French, Portuguese, and Filipino, represented. *(Courtesy Italian Cemetery, Colma, California)*

Odyssey of San Gennaro. The Feast of San Gennaro, traditionally associated in the United States with New York City's Little Italy, has become part of the landscape in Peoria, Arizona; Las Vegas, Nevada; and Los Angeles, California. This photo shows Gregg Cannizzaro, Mike Marino, and members of the San Gennaro Foundation carrying the saint's statue past the corner of Hollywood and Vine, in Los Angeles on September 20, 2003. This annual event began in 2002 when a group of Italian Americans decided to combine the legacy of Saint Gennaro, the patron saint of Naples, Italy, who helped people in need, with an effort to promote and preserve cultural identity and solidarity within the Italian-American community. Each year, the San Gennaro Foundation donates funds to help resource-challenged children through various programs, such as mentoring, scholarships, and educational workshops, and the foundation also subsidizes Feast4All, a feeding program for the homeless. *(© 2008 Kayte Deioma)*

Civil Ceremony in San Francisco, California, March 29, 2003. Giuseppe DeMaio, born in Sarno, Campania, and Ursula Eva Glandon (of Alsatian and Bohemian descent) met in Paris in April 2002 when she was an American college student. Giuseppe, as did two of his brothers, left Sarno, where there was little work, and moved to France. Giuseppe had attended a cooking school in Florence and was working as chef at Caruso's Restaurant near the Place des Vosges in the Marais district when Ursula and her mother dined there one evening. He came to their table and asked them how they were enjoying their meal, and the rest is history. The couple chose to marry in the restored rotunda of San Francisco's City Hall. Although a Roman Catholic, Giuseppe does not attend church often. However, at the time of the wedding, his mother, Maria, made it clear that their first child would be baptized in Sarno's church. Giuseppe is chef at Brunello Ristorante in Menlo Park. *(Courtesy the DeMaio family)*

CHAPTER 7

BECOMING AMERICAN

The majority of immigrants who made America their home worked hard at becoming a part of their adopted country. They participated in the major activities of American society and incorporated its values. Although they remained aware of the events taking place and of the conditions back in the land of their birth, they were concerned about their immediate world. They expressed the transition from immigrant to ethnic in a variety of ways: participating in patriotic celebrations, becoming involved in the political system, facing the joys and sorrows of everyday life, and learning to live together with their non-Italian neighbors and coworkers, as American society responded to national and international issues.

Italian immigrants and their children proudly joined their neighbors in celebrating civic events. In 1936, for the parade held in Madison, Wisconsin, during the State's Centennial Celebration, the Italian-American community constructed floats depicting their heritage and featuring local occupations such as railroad workers. In 1948, the Italian societies of Monessen, Pennsylvania, built a float to celebrate the fiftieth anniversary of the City of Monessen.

Italian Americans often combined their identity with Columbus when they participated in other patriotic events. For example, in 1876, the Italians of Philadelphia, Pennsylvania, celebrated the centennial of the Declaration of Independence by erecting a statue to Columbus in West Fairmount Park as part of this national exposition. The 1876 Columbus statue was the first funded entirely by public subscription.

While immigrants' lives reflected the customs and traditions they learned in Italy, they, and especially their children, learned the traditions of American society. Both parents and children dealt with cultural contrasts as native-born educators, social workers, labor leaders, and politicians encouraged the newcomers to adopt "American" lifestyles.

The settlement house movement hoped to mitigate the substandard lives of many working-class immigrants by teaching them the tools to navigate in America. They offered civics and English classes, provided recreational and vocational opportunities for children, and offered space to hold meetings to discuss community issues, such as inadequate housing conditions and government services. For example, after World War I, the staff of Haarlem House in New York City, organized 1,250 families into the Harlem Tenants League, which forced landlords to moderate rent increases and make the needed repairs and improvements to their properties. Settlement house workers also recognized the importance of honoring folk customs and traditions as a way to reassure immigrants with familiar icons.

Immigrants also formed organizations to meet the new conditions of their lives. Italians who attempted to participate in politics discovered that older immigrant groups, particularly the Irish, had gained power in Democratic Party urban-ward politics, and some were reluctant to share their control. Local Republican parties often welcomed Italians to compete against other immigrant voting blocs. Ward-level politics could "influence" votes, but on the other hand, local party leaders dispensed aid and comfort to residents in need, helped them get jobs, gave out turkeys at holiday time, and supported reforms for worker safety and the elimination of child labor.

Political clubs affiliated with one of the major

parties promoted the official nominees and encouraged immigrants to become citizens. At first, political associations supported the party candidate, who was usually a non-Italian. In most areas, Italians did not have a sufficient number of registered voters to determine elections, but by the early twentieth century, both parties were appealing to the Italian-American voter, either by appointing a conational to a status position in the party or in government, or by endorsing a conational for elected office. By the 1930s, Italian-American votes could influence the outcome of elections in some cities. Finally, Italian-American political organizations promoted candidates from their own community. Angelo Rossi of San Francisco, Fiorello La Guardia of New York, and Robert Maestri of New Orleans became mayors; Thomas D'Alessandro of Baltimore and Vito Marcantonio of New York became United States Congressmen.

During the Depression, many Italians who benefited from the pro-labor and social welfare programs of President Franklin D. Roosevelt switched to the Democrat Party. Since then, Italian-American elected officials in both major parties have filled offices from city council member to governor, senator, and congressperson, and their political achievement has increased exponentially. In 1984, Geraldine Ferraro, the first Italian American and the first woman nominated for vice president by a major party, started her congressional career in a New York City district with a core of Italian voters. More recently, Arizona governor Anne Napolitano and Vermont senator Patrick Leahy succeeded in areas having a more diverse electorate. Many presidents have selected Italian Americans to serve in their cabinet as agency directors and as judicial appointees.

By the mid-1980s, Italian Canadians' representation in Ottawa—five percent of the House of Commons—was on par with their approximately four percent of the entire Canadian population. Italian Canadians have served as cabinet members and have been selected as senators.

Immigrants also shared the impact of events outside of their control, such as depressions, wars, foreign trade, epidemics, Prohibition, and domestic policies. They fought with others for social justice. While these issues affected everyone, in some instances, ethnic groups responded differently.

Most Italians, and many Germans and Irish, disapproved of Prohibition because drinking was part of their social culture. Some immigrants violated the law by manufacturing or selling alcohol, and they rallied to support Alfred Smith in the 1928 presidential election because he pledged to repeal Prohibition.

Italians joined with coworkers from other immigrant and ethnic groups to organize and strike to protest inadequate working conditions in many industries. Major strikes of the first half of the twentieth century illustrate the ability of workers from different nationalities to overcome linguistic and cultural differences to take action. The movie *Matewan* documents a coalition of Italian, African-American, and native-born Appalachian miners unified in their grievances against the mining company.

In everyday life, Italian immigrants interacted with the larger society. My grandmother, Vincenza Gerardi, shopped in the Jewish-owned stores and push-cart stands in Brooklyn's Brownsville section. She would use the little English she knew to purchase food items. When she wanted a breast of lamb or veal, she would ask for "tit," which the butcher understood. Neighbors and coworkers socialized, exchanging food specialties, recipes, nature's bounty, chatting over the fence, and sweeping the sidewalk.

The trial, appeal, and execution of the anarchists Nicola Sacco and Bartolomeo Vanzetti and the rise of Benito Mussolini, while central to Italian-immigrant concerns, resonated across ethnic lines. Workers and others throughout the world committed to social justice rallied to the cause of the two men convicted of a payroll robbery and murder in 1920. Many felt that the Massachusetts judge and jury allowed their dislike of Italian immigrants and radical ideology to prejudice the judicial process. In America, a cross section of writers, Boston "blue blood" socialites, artists, socialists, syndicalists, communists, and trade unionists joined with Italian immigrants to protest the conviction.

Reaction to the rise of Fascism in Italy varied in tone and content in America. Initially many non-Italians admired the swift action taken by Mussolini to modernize Italy's infrastructure, eradicate malarial infested swamps, and stabilize the economy. Some immigrants read glowing accounts of *Il Duce* written during the 1920s by American journalists, philosophers, and politicians. By the early 1930s, the New Deal program of Franklin D. Roosevelt echoed some of the programs introduced by Mussolini, and many Americans believed that the United States would benefit from strong leadership—fascist style. Things changed when, in 1935-1936, Italy invaded Ethiopia and added it to their colonies of Eritrea and Italian Somaliland. The United States and Canada supported the League of Nations' weak economic sanctions against Italy.

Italians across North America broke ranks according to political ideology, religious allegiance, and pride in a refurbished *la patria*. Pro-fascist and antifascist immigrant groups fought each other in the press, in public debates, and, at times, in the streets. Leaders, such as Fiorello La Guardia and Luigi Antonini, opposed Mussolini's regime. Other groups and individuals cheered Mussolini's success. Immigrants sent gold rings and jewelry to support the goals of *la patria*. In 1935, at a ceremony in San Jose, California, Guido Deiro gave the gold medals he had received in recognition as a renowned accordionist to the Italian American Legion (a pro-fascist organization). Many immigrant children attended *dopo scuola* (after school) classes, which used Italian-language materials filled with pro-Mussolini propaganda.

But for most, their pride in a powerful Italy was more a reaffirmation of their ethnic identity and the need for respect and recognition in America rather than an endorsement of the actual form of government and tactics of Mussolini. They were happy to see the emergence of Italy as a world power, but their loyalty to America was stronger. The same men and women who sent their gold rings to *Il Duce* in 1935 proudly sent off their sons to the armed forces of Canada and the United States in 1940 and 1941. The immigrants had chosen.

World War II served as a watershed for Italians in America. First, noncitizens became enemy aliens. The issue of war-time restrictions and internment of Italian Americans and Italian Canadians, once *la storia segreta,* (the secret story), has been researched and portrayed in several documentaries, such as *Prisoners Among Us* and *Il Duce canadese, le Mussolini canadien.* Italian was the language of the enemy and many organizations changed their names and dropped the use of Italian at their meetings. Parents also stopped speaking Italian at home.

Second, large numbers of immigrant children served in the armed forces. Some estimate that Italians were the largest single ethnic group in the U.S. armed forces. They fought on all fronts and distinguished themselves in battle. They participated in the invasion of Italy, where many still had relatives. Their parents cheered as they helped to defeat the Italian army in 1943. (Ken Burns' PBS series *The War,* about World War II, includes examples of these aspects.) Italian-American soldiers also played an important role in restoring self-government, the free flow of resources, and rebuilding the judicial system in Italy.

America's non-Italian soldiers stationed in Italy "discovered" its rich heritage as they visited that nation's historic sites and savored the variety of cuisine. Many met and married Italians whom they brought back to America. Some of this new awareness is reflected in the movies *The Secret of Santa Vittoria,* based on a novel by Robert Crichton, and *A Bell for Adano,* based on a novel by John Hersey.

The immigrant's need to join with others of common background or interest fostered the formation of associations for Italian Americans. Most groups limited membership to men. *Paese* or regional origins served as a basis for establishing many groups. The Calascibetta Society of Baltimore admitted men who were born in that central Sicilian town. In San Francisco, the *Lucchesi del Mondo* followed similar criteria. All these groups sponsored formal and informal social activities, ranging from annual dinners or picnics to card playing at club headquarters. Most offered mutual-benefit services. Members paid dues that gave them illness and death insurance. A sick member could go to a doctor retained by the association. He was entitled to a sum of money to help his family when he could not work. Upon his death, his widow received a sum from the association. Social obligations accompanied the benefits. A delegation visited the sick, and the entire association attended the funeral of any member. Such organizations existed in Italy, but they had greater significance in America, where the immigrant was distant from the extended family networks that offered social and economic aid in times of emergency.

The Order Sons of Italy in America (OSIA), established in 1905, represented another type of response to the New World. This organization promoted a love of the motherland and loyalty toward the adopted countries of North America. The order attempted to dispel the anti-Italian prejudice that associated immigrants and their descendants with the crime and vice that plagued American cities. Lodges formed across North America, supporting worthy causes in Italy, such as the Italian War Relief of 1918, and in America, such as orphanages. Pride in the Italian heritage grew in proportion to the anti-immigrant policies of the 1920s and 1930s, and OSIA considered itself the major guardian of immigrant self-respect.

Becoming American came at a personal cost. For some, the price was too high, and they returned to Italy in defeat and bitterness. Others endured their sorrow and suffering in a world of strangers as penance for leaving their familial world. These life-altering losses produced permanent scars that passed down to descendants. (Susan Caperna Lloyd's film *Lost Baggage* provides a vivid example of ambiguous loss.) While every family experienced these reverses, few "remember" them during holiday gatherings or when interviewed by a family historian or a researcher. The "shame" of illegitimacy, mental illness, domestic abuse, and other "unpleasant" events are filtered out. Instead, grandchildren learn about battles won and problems resolved. These empty spaces in Italian heritage distort the picture and deprive posterity of a full understanding of the experience.

By stressing conformity to the English language, American society deprived immigrants of their native tongues, an essential part of their identity. Most of the languages were regional and provincial dialects, not the language of Dante or Manzoni. My parents and their siblings spoke Sicilian until they started school. They did not teach us children "Italian" because they remembered being ridiculed by their fellow schoolmates. Many second-generation children remember their embarrassment and shame when they sat in Italian classes taught by teachers who laughed at their pronunciation or use of dialect terms—or worse—when they said *baccauso* (the Anglicized version for backhouse) for *gabinetto* (toilet). Their Italy was not the world of Henry Adams or Margaret Fuller, but the reality of workers focused on life from moment to moment.

The loss of place became a double-edged sword for immigrants who lost their *paese* and then, as urban dwellers in postwar America, lost their ethnic enclaves, mostly through urban renewal and the postwar housing policies, which promoted suburban expansion. Anthony Riccio's book *The Italian American Experience in New Haven: Images and Oral Histories* provides graphic detail of how deeply Italians of New Haven felt about the loss of their homes. The sad irony of their uprooting is that some of the land they vacated for the bulldozer remains undeveloped wilderness.

The immigrants' appreciation of simple pleasures enjoyed with family and friends heightened their ability to live in the moment. Tasting newly made wine, relishing a feast of *pasta fagioli* (*fazool*), polenta with cheese, risotto with wild mushrooms, or spaghetti with anchovies, and tending their gardens were celebrations of life. Grandchildren remember grandparents who introduced them to the smells of fresh basil, mint, and pungent garlic as they sautéed in olive oil.

The 1920s and '30s were years of transition. Children (the second generation) of immigrants began to participate more fully in the social and economic life of America. Their achievement was recognized in the formation of professional organizations, such as the Italian American Graduate Club of New Orleans, which admitted persons who acquired a bachelor's degree, and the Justinian Society of Chicago for Italian American lawyers. These two organizations, which celebrated ethnic achivments, became a source of pride for the Italian-American community.

In other areas of their American experience, immigrants and their children adopted and adapted to the mores and attitudes of the native-born population. Italian Canadians recognized how modern lifestyles had altered the traditional attitudes toward elder care. The concept of multigenerational households changed as elderly immigrants preferred independent living without the responsibility of caring for grandchildren full-time. In 1976, a group of Ontario businessmen came up with the idea of a home for the aged. They spearheaded a campaign to establish the Villa Colombo to provide culturally sensitive care.

Traditional concepts of gender roles also evolved as Italian-American women combined careers with motherhood. Founded in 1980, the National Organization of Italian American Women developed a network to promote the educational and professional aspirations of its members while honoring the role of women as keepers of culture. Women also gained leadership positions in organizations traditionally dominated by men. Joanne L. Strollo was the first and only woman to serve as national president of the Order Sons of Italy in America (1993-1995). Although the national chapter has had no woman president since Ms. Strollo, in the twenty-first century, most state lodges have had women presidents.

The National Italian American Foundation (NIAF) was founded in 1975 to promote the best of Italian-American culture and heritage through a wide range of programs. NIAF provides information and educational materials on Italian-American history and culture and highlights the contributions of Italian Americans to the United States.

The experience of Italians in America results from the interaction of two cultures. Not only were immigrants exposed to new and different lifestyles and values, but they also introduced new ways to the host society. Sometimes the two fused into a new combination. For example, in 1971, the Italian Canadian Benevolent Corporation, founded in Toronto, built a multipurpose complex with senior citizens' housing and a community center offering recreational, cultural, and social services. Similar projects followed in Italian communities across Canada.

In the process of becoming American, the descendants of Italian immigrants did not lose the strength of intergenerational influence. The imprint of family businesses, professions, and community involvement continued to shape the individual. The threads connect the past with the present. Older generations handed down their traditions, modified by time and adaptability, to their grandchildren as a legacy to treasure.

American Citizenship. This impressive 1885 certificate printed in red and blue with a gold seal grants citizenship to Gaetano Castellano. He arrived from the area of Salerno about 1860. By 1875, he had returned to Italy for his wife, Rose Caserta, and daughter Maria, and they settled on Fourth Avenue and Carroll Street, in one of the earliest Italian neighborhoods in Brooklyn, New York, close to Our Lady of Peace Italian National Parish Church. Gaetano prospered, running a grocery store, selling steamship tickets, and lending money to his Italian *paesani*. However, he gambled most of his money away. Maria married Vincent Libretti, another successful merchant, who owned a bar and had a concession to salvage items from the dump in Brooklyn. *(Courtesy Dr. Luciano J. Iorizzo)*

Honoring Canada. Michele Rigali from Barga, Lucca, arrived in New York just before the Civil War; he married Mary Ann Putnam and enlisted in the U.S. army. In 1865, he relocated his family to Canada and eventually settled in Quebec. Between 1891 and 1910, Michele maintained a sculptor's studio and workshop at 134-132 Rue Saint-Jean. In this photo, the façade shows bunting honoring the Dominion of Canada and Italy. Claiming to offer the "finest and most complete assortment of religious statues in the dominion," Michele made plaster models for interiors and cement ones for exteriors that were less expensive than figures carved in wood. His work enhanced many churches and public buildings in southern and eastern Quebec. His cement statues (recently restored) set in the façade of Saint Jean-Baptiste Church in Quebec represent one of his major artistic accomplishments. *(Courtesy Pauline Rigali Kuehnel)*

Teaching American Values. Little Italy Neighborhood House, a social settlement, at Ninety-eight Sackett Street in Brooklyn, New York, offered woodworking, sewing, sports, and violin lessons for immigrant children. The staff believed that through the process of learning these skills the children would absorb the "American spirit of cooperation and self-government." While the staff respected the children's Italian heritage, they hoped to provide a bridge toward assimilation. (*From* Gli Italiani Negli Stati Uniti d'America, *1906*)

American-Indian Territory. Italians, working in coal mines in the southeast section of Indian Territory, incorporated into the state of Oklahoma in 1907, created opportunities for immigrant-owned commercial development. Italians established businesses and cultural activities in McAlester and nearby Krebs, Oklahoma. Joe and John Fassino, from Canischio, Torino, opened a wagon and carriage factory and repair shop, which can be seen in this photo behind the float they constructed for a Fourth of July parade, c. 1904. The brothers also owned the McAlester Macaroni Factory, which distributed Eagle Macaroni in Kansas, Texas, Missouri, and Arkansas. Joe Fassino served as consular agent for Italy until 1910. (*Courtesy Jane Tua Smith and Judy Tua Brown*)

A Royal Welcome. The duke of Connaught, the governor general of Canada, and a cousin of King George V visited Vancouver, British Columbia, in 1912, to dedicate a bridge named in the duke's honor. Citizens turned out to greet the duke as his entourage traveled on Hastings Street. Many of the city's ethnic groups joined in building commemorative arches along the route. Italian Canadians dedicated their archway at Homer and Hastings Streets to the governor as a symbol of their loyalty to the Crown. Designed by a local Italian sculptor, the sixty-four-foot-high arch replicated the Arch of Constantine in Rome. The solid wood structure had Corinthian columns of plaster to imitate marble. Above the arch was inscribed, "Italian Colony, In Honour of His Royal Highness." When the new bridge was officially opened to traffic, Alberto Principe, a Sons of Italy Society member, became the first person to cross the Connaught Bridge in a horse-driven wagon. *(Courtesy Vancouver Public Library, Special Collections, VPL4192)*

Claiming America. Italian gardener families gather together in Walla Walla, Washington, to mark the Fourth of July. Concetta Morrone and Maria Pizano left Pedace, Cosenza, in February 1915, to meet the men they had agreed to marry in Walla Walla, Domenick Loiacono and Vincenzo Ciarlo. *Standing, left to right:* Frank Venneri, Vincenzo Ciarlo, Domenick Loiacono, Baptista Barca, Julia Arcuri (Maiuri). *Middle row:* Pete Venneri, Josephina Venneri, Raffelina Venneri (baby), Maria Pizano Ciarlo, Concetta Morrone Loiacono, Vincenza Barca, Marietta Barca (little girl). *Front row:* Louis Venneri, Frank Barca, Joe Barca. The three women sitting at the right, including the new brides Maria and Concetta, are pregnant. Julia is Josephina's niece, and Vincenza and Josephina are Vincenzo Ciarlo's sisters. *(Courtesy David A. Ferraro and Domenick and Concetta Morrone Loiacono)*

Making Citizens. Vito Volino, born to parents from Albania Di Lucania, Potenza, attends a Citizen's Military Training Camp at Camp Custer, Michigan, c. 1922-1923. President Warren Harding declared that the CMTC would establish a voluntary military training for at least 100,000 men each year for peacetime preparedness. Candidates read that this training was designed "to bring together young men of all types, both native and foreign born; to develop closer national and social unity; to teach the privileges, duties, and responsibilities of American citizenship; to show the public . . . that camp instruction . . . would develop them physically, mentally, and morally; and will teach Americanism in its true sense." At camp, the United States military tattoo played each night; it was derived from the British "First Post." The tattoo originated from an old Neapolitan Cavalry call, "Il Silenzio," written by Rosso-Brezza. *(Courtesy Raffaella Ventura Volino and the Higgins family)*

Pride in Citizenship. Members of the Regina Elena Society of St. Michael Catholic Church in New Haven, Connecticut, wear crowns similar to the Statue of Liberty to celebrate their path towards citizenship, c. 1923. When James Cardinal Gibbons approved the formation of national parishes, which allowed immigrant groups to worship in their own language, he believed that the second and third generations would make the transition to "American" styles of worship and use of the English language. *(Courtesy Theresa Argento)*

Bringing America into the Home. Older women in Italian-American enclaves had limited opportunities to learn English or the traditions of their new country. They usually stayed at home to care for their families, and when they did venture outside, they shopped in stores owned by *paesani* or worked nearby with other Italian women. Guided by the adage "Never too old to learn," Jennie Weaver, director of the Italian Neighborhood House in Wilmington, Delaware, sent instructors into the homes of older women immigrants. Here grandmothers, ages 63, 65, 73 and 83 years, have their first English lesson, May 1925. After World War I, Pierre S. du Pont, one of the major employers in Delaware, promoted the Service Citizens of Delaware to implement the Americanization of Delaware's immigrants through such agencies as the Italian Neighborhood House. *(Courtesy Louise Ciconte Giliberto)*

Citizenship Classes. The Department of Labor training service supported English and civics classes for immigrants at the YMCA in Newark, New Jersey. This class met in the 1920s. Many agencies of all levels of government and nonprofit organizations like the Y, religious groups, and public-school boards promoted these efforts. Since many immigrants worked ten- to twelve-hour days at hard physical labor, they did not have enough energy to sit through a class that required their full, undivided attention. For those who succeeded in becoming citizens, the reward reflected their personal determination. (*Courtesy* Italian Tribune)

Color-filled Celebrations. Vitale Fireworks Manufacturing Company, in New Castle, Pennsylvania, supplied the pyrotechnics essential to celebrate festive events. Italian immigrants in western Pennsylvania organized annual feasts, resembling village fairs, to honor their patron saints. An elaborate firework display ended the *festa*. Constantino Vitale, originally from Naples, arrived in New Castle in 1922, bringing with him the tradition of fireworks design and manufacturing. By 1926, his company was one of the largest producers of fireworks in the area. However, it was Antonio Zambelli, who owned a rival company in New Castle, who ultimately became one of America's preeminent fireworks maestros. He extended his patron base by providing fireworks displays at bank openings, baseball games, and Fourth of July celebrations. George Zambelli, Antonio's son, developed the art into entertainment spectaculars, providing special performances for presidential inaugurations and the annual opening of the Kentucky Derby. Throughout the United States, Italian-owned companies continue to dominate the field. *(Courtesy Italian American Collection, Senator John Heinz Pittsburgh Regional History Center of Western Pennsylvania)*

Pledge of Allegiance. Children at the Beulah Brinton Center in the Bay View section of Milwaukee, Wisconsin, salute the flag in 1932. The center, at Potter and St. Clair Streets, served a neighborhood of mostly *Piemontesi, Marchegiani,* and *Toscani* residents. The building had been an old firehouse before the Beulah Brinton Center began operations in 1922. Named for the philanthropic wife of the steel-rolling mill owner, the center offered a variety of classes, sports, and entertainment in which entire families participated. Children found playmates and enjoyed activities that caught their interest. Many children remember that they took their first showers at the center. As one such beneficiary remarked, "No more wash tubs in the kitchen on Saturday night!" Italian-American associations also encouraged the second generation to "become Americans." For example, the Italian Center in Stamford, Connecticut, sponsored Boy Scout Troops 18 and 20 and also initiated a swimming team. *(Courtesy Italian Community Center of Milwaukee, Wisconsin)*

Patriotic Symbols. Laden with the fruits of harvest, this float acknowledges the 125th anniversary of the Liberty Bell in 1931. The Rizzotte Brothers of Hammonton, New Jersey, combined Italian-American traditional celebratory food—the roast pigs seen on the back of the float—with a replication of the bell at the top of the float. The tentlike sign over the top of the bell reads, "LIBERTY BELL'S FIRST COUSIN 125 YRS. OLD ain't cracked yet." (The Hammonton Gazette, *courtesy Evelyn Penza*)

Teaching Acceptable Social Behavior. Throughout America, school systems focused on the goal of enabling immigrants and their children to adapt standard middle-class culture and values. Similar lessons were part of the regular home-economics classes taught to all working-class children. However, the combination of class and culture created a special challenge for educators. Here, Clarence Fulmer directs a class of first- and second-generation Italian immigrants in the "proper" way to set a table in 1940. Fulmer later became principal of Wilmington (Delaware) High School. *(Courtesy Louise Ciconte Giliberto)*

Becoming American 183

American Themes. Butte, Montana's mostly Italian section of Meaderville established a volunteer fire department in 1910. Many of the volunteers worked in the mines, yet they spent part of their leisure time planning and constructing decorative civic displays. In 1945, the men produced their first annual Christmas display. The hoist at the Leonard Mine can be seen a block north of the piece. Each year, until the 1960s, they featured a new theme with elaborate designs. They also decorated a float for Butte's July 4 parade. Their 1949 prize-winning float on the theme of Playtime Unlimited measured fifty-two feet in length and featured a locomotive with operating wheels and a turntable inside the cab displaying Schmoos, cartoon figures from the "Li'l Abner" comic strip, which were the rage at that time. The volunteers won first prize for their floats almost every year. *(Courtesy World Museum of Mining, 96258 and Smithers Studio)*

State Seal of Oklahoma. Architect-sculptor Angelo Zari points to a detail in the Oklahoma state seal he designed and cast in 1951. Zari produced seals of the United States and possessions (forty-eight states and four territories: Alaska, Hawaii, the Virgin Islands, and Puerto Rico) to border the ceiling in the House of Representatives in Washington, D.C. In 1993, Zari's daughter, Giovanna Zari Scanno, presented plaster casts of these seals to the College of Staten Island at Willowbrook, New York. The first president of the college, Edmond Volpe, accepted the gift and had the seals mounted in the atria of the North and South Administration buildings. *(Courtesy the Giovanna Zari Scano family)*

A Special Birthday. Born Anna Izzo on May 22, 1921, in the small Italian village of Torchiati, Avellino, Anna Izzo Russo became a naturalized American citizen on her thirty-fifth birthday, May 22, 1956. Her mother, Raffaela, died when she was sixteen, leaving her to keep house for her father and brothers. At nineteen, Anna attended the *Academia Italiana di Taglio* in Naples, where she learned the skills of fabric cutting and pattern making. In Torchiati, she taught the young girls how to design and sew clothing. During World War II, Anna survived the German occupation and the Allied bombing of her town. In 1948, she met William Russo, the son of Antonio and Emilia Russo, who traveled with his mother to vacation in Italy. Emilia and Raffaela had been childhood friends. Anna's brother, Espedito, a Franciscan Capuchin, married the couple on February 20, 1949. When Anna arrived in America, she moved into the Russo family home in the Coney Island section of Brooklyn, New York. Knowing little English, Anna found work in a local doll factory where she painted eyes. Soon she got a job in a nearby dress factory and earned a reputation as an exceptional seamstress. After the death of Antonio, they moved to a new home. William died shortly after, in February 1962, leaving Anna again responsible for the entire family. *(Courtesy William Russo)*

Paths of Glory. Frances A. Ianni stands next to his father, Francesco Ianni, during a Memorial Day parade in Newark, Delaware, 1985. Francesco came to Philadelphia in 1913 from Tortoreto Alto, Teramo. He moved to Baltimore and worked on the docks unloading banana boats. When World War I began, he joined the army and fought in France where he was awarded a Silver Star. After the war, he worked in the steel mills in New Castle. His son, Francis, graduated from West Point in 1954, and as a lieutenant colonel and battalion commander of the First Calvary Division, he received a Silver Star during his second tour of duty in Vietnam. Francis retired in 1981 as a major general. *(Courtesy Francis A. Ianni)*

The Greatest Gift. By the 1930s, Giuseppe (Joe) Desimone had acquired more than three hundred acres of farmland in the Seattle, Washington, area. Starting with ten acres, he sold the produce on the road and later sold at a stall at Seattle's Pike Place Market. By the 1930s, Joe had acquired much more land and was director of the Pike Place Market. Known for his "peasant" belief that a farmer's highest achievement was land ownership, he would not sell his holdings. Yet, in 1936, when the Boeing Aircraft Company, a major area employer, needed land for expansion but couldn't find suitable sites for sale, and was reportedly considering an offer to move to Southern California, Giuseppe saved the day. He sold land to Boeing along the waterfront for one dollar. This picture shows Boeing President Claire L. Egtvedt presenting Giuseppe with a plaque in appreciation for his "Civic Consciousness, his Unselfishness and his Patriotism." After diverting the Duwamish River and filling in the old channel, Boeing started construction of Plant II, which began operation just before World War II, providing the space needed to build the famous B-17 bombers. *(Courtesy the Boeing Company)*

Honoring Veterans of Foreign Wars, 2004. During the annual Feast of San Gennaro in Federal Hill, Providence, Rhode Island, parade organizers pay tribute to Veterans of Foreign Wars. Ciro Giorgio, dressed as Pulcinella from the traditional *Commedia dell'Arte,* leads the column of marchers. Born in Naples, Ciro aquired many skills—actor, singer, magician, comedian, piano and keyboard player, street performer, director, and writer. Portraying Pulcinella has become one of his signature roles, which he has performed at Italian festivals in scores of American cities. *(Courtesy Ciro Giorgio; photographer Gianna)*

Concerns for Earthquake Victims, 1909. Chicago, Illinois, judge Bernardo Barasa supervises counting the receipts from a fundraiser, which was held to assist the victims of the December 1908 Messina, Sicily, earthquake. Italian immigrants living in the crowded tenements of New York's Lower East Side participated in a community-wide fundraising effort by tossing their contributions of money and clothing from their windows to collectors standing with horses and carriages on the street below. Later, many of the survivors sought refuge through emigration. Bernardo Barasa was the Republican candidate for the circuit court in the June 6, 1921, election. Although he was defeated soundly in a later primary bid for mayor of Chicago, Barasa came closer than any other Italian American to becoming mayor. *(Courtesy Italian American Collection, IAC 110.19; Special Collections Department, University Library, University of Illinois at Chicago)*

Supporting Italian Refugees, c. 1915. Caterina Venneri d'Ambrosio Curcio collects money to help Italian refugees during World War I. Italy entered the war against Austria and fought their enemy in the territory of the Southern Tyrol, which later became part of Italy. Caterina's first husband, Francesco d'Ambrosio, had emigrated from Pedace, Cosenza, to New York for work. Physically devastated by pneumonia, he returned home to die. Left with two children, Caterina decided to join her brother, Frank Venneri, in Walla Walla, Washington, where she could work on his farm. She arrived in 1904 with her son Tony. There she met and married Joe Curcio, a widower with two children, c. 1905. Caterina worked on her husband's farm and raised the combined family until she died at the age of ninety. *(Courtesy the Pasquale Criscola family)*

Worldwide Flu Epidemic, 1918. The toll of the "Spanish Flu" touched the lives of thousands of families. When Ernesto and Rose Manetti's infant child died of influenza in White Castle, Delaware, the community shared their grief. Young girls, including Mary Marcozzi (Ianni), at the front to the right of the casket, served as pallbearers. Mary's father, Carlo Marcozzi, wearing a black hat stands near his daughter. Ernesto and Rose are in the center of the picture, behind the girls carrying flowers. Ernesto stands to the left of the downspout, and Rose, in the black hat with the veil, stands to the right of it. Ernesto emigrated from Teramo, Abruzzo. Rose came from a town nearby. Carlo also came from Teramo, and his wife, Maria, from Giulianova, Teramo. The procession moved solemnly through the streets to the church. *(Courtesy Francis A. Ianni)*

Prohibition Network, c. 1920. Joe and Mary Riggio (on left) go courting in Jansen, Colorado, on the hay wagon of their neighbor Sam Cimino (wearing fur coat). The Cimino family raised hay and made whiskey. Joe dispersed the hay-covered barrels of whiskey to his customers at the Jansen saloon, which he owned with his father and operated with his brother-in-law. The Riggios came from Palazzo Adriano, Palermo. Prohibition began in 1916 in Colorado, and Joe, who was convicted of a liquor law violation in June 1918, served eight months at the Colorado State Penitentiary. Across the country in the Bushwick section of Brooklyn, New York, John's bar closed down in 1919 at the start of national Prohibition. The partner-owners John Scoca and Vito Galgano from Calitri, Avellino, manufactured liquor in the apartments above and the basement below the closed facility. They purchased raw alcohol, which was delivered, usually late in the evening, in a hearse. They boiled water and alcohol in huge metal pots and poured the liquid into stills with booze-flavored additives. They stored the pint bottles in walls and closets. As needed, they would bring bottles down via a trap door under a bed that led to a secret stairway. *(Courtesy Pauline Riggio Bonfadini)*

A Universal Cause, 1927. Well-known poet Edna St. Vincent Millay pickets in Boston, Massachusetts, for the cause of Italian anarchists Nicola Sacco and Bartolomeo Vanzetti. Her sign reads, "Free Them and Save Massachusetts! American Honor Dies With Sacco and Vanzetti!" It was not just Italian immigrants who believed the two men had not received a fair trial and were unjustly executed, but also many members of the working class and their supporters in the United States and across the world (Australia, Argentina, France, and Italy). The men were executed after seven years of failed appeals for the murder of a guard and paymaster of a Massachusetts factory during a robbery. Many felt that the two men suffered injustice because they were Italian immigrants and anarchists. Many American writers and artists, including Ben Shahn, John Dos Passos, Katherine Ann Porter, and Upton Sinclair, "found their voice" during the intensive efforts to support the protest. *(Courtesy Boston Public Library, Rare Books Department; courtesy of the Trustees; Ms. 2030.10 N9)*

Supervising the Project. Immigrating to Portland, Oregon, in 1913, Pietro Granata applied his skills as a stonemason, which he learned in Celico, Cosenza. His on-the-job experience helped him to secure a position as supervisor on a Works Progress Administration flood control project in 1936 or 1937. He installed riprap and other structures along Johnson Creek in Portland. Pietro's mostly Italian-American stonemason crew added a distinct European style to their work. *(Courtesy Oregon Historical Society; COP # 02931)*

Supporting the Government. The Fedeli's Blue Eagle Fruit Market in Trenton, New Jersey, proudly adopted the symbol of President Roosevelt's National Recovery Administration as the name of their business. They offered a place to buy cheap fruit and vegetables during the Depression. *(Courtesy Center for Migration Studies, Robert Immordino Collection)*

Mussolini in Church. In 1930, the archbishop of Montreal, Quebec, commissioned fresco painter Guido Nincheri to produce a design for the Madonna della Difesa Catholic Church (Italian emigrants from the area of Campobasso and Molise built the church in 1919). The fresco would celebrate the Lateran Treaty of 1929 by which Benito Mussolini, prime minister of Italy, permitted the Pope to rule Vatican City as a separate and sovereign state. The treaty also authorized Roman Catholicism as Italy's only recognized religion. In return, the Papacy accepted the seizure by Italy of the Papal States in 1860 and of Rome ten years later. Devout Catholics applauded Mussolini's policy. Nincheri's contract specifically requested a triumphant Mussolini on a horse, and while he was reluctant to paint the dictator, he fulfilled his commission. Years later at the outbreak of World War II, the Royal Canadian Mounted Police arrested Guido as a fascist sympathizer and imprisoned him for three months at Petawawa, a prisoner-of-war camp outside of Pembroke, Ontario. *(Courtesy R. Boccini Nincheri, Boccini Nincheri Studio)*

Protesting Mussolini's Involvement in the Spanish Civil War. The Italian Anti-Fascist Committee in New York City sponsored a protest demonstration in the 1930s, during the Spanish Civil War. Immigrants, such as writer Domenico Saudino, who came to the United States from Drusacco, Torino, in 1912, and in 1924 joined the National Council of the Italian Socialist Federation in America, helped to organize and publicize the protest. As a longtime contributor to *La Parola del Popolo* (Chicago, Illinois) and *Il Corriere del Popolo* (San Francisco, California), Saudino became an outspoken critic of Fascism. American worker organizations joined the protest in support of the Spanish workers' Republican government. During the Spanish Civil War, the Roman Catholic clergy of North America praised Mussolini's support for Francisco Franco, who led the Nationalist forces against the leftist Republican government. Italy sent eighty thousand men and supplied several thousand guns, tanks, and planes. *(Courtesy Domenico Saudino Collection, IM000640, Immigration History Research Center, University of Minnesota)*

GI Bill. Benedetto Domenico Luigi Alfano Savaglio was born in Saratoga Springs, New York, in 1926, to parents from Marano Principato, Cosenza. He went through basic training late in World War II—in 1944, while the Battle of the Bulge raged. As the war in Europe ended, he was assigned to the Pacific to be part of the planned first wave to invade Japan. When the Japanese surrendered after the horrific bombings of Hiroshima and Nagasaki, the army transferred him to a postwar mission in the Philippines. Like thousands of other GIs, Ben Savaglio (standing in front of the board addressing the class) used his GI benefits to further his education. He attended Brooklyn's Polytechnic Institute, graduating in 1950 with a degree in engineering. Ben was the first in the Savaglio family to attend college. *(Courtesy Cynthia Savaglio)*

Cold War Concerns. At the beginning of the Cold War, Leonard H. Pasqualicchio, a lobbyist in Washington, D.C., for OSIA (Order Sons of Italy in America) commented that although "the Communist party in Italy was larger than it should be, God-fearing and freedom-loving people, the Italians will never submit to Communism." At the end of 1947, OSIA's Supreme Venerable Spatuzza instructed Pasqualicchio to argue "the Marshall Plan will effectively combat the spread of Communism" in order to pressure Congress into passing it and including Italy among its beneficiaries. Pasqualicchio also helped craft the Refugee Relief Act of 1953, which President Eisenhower signs in this photo. This legislation provided forty-five thousand visas to refugees of Italian ethnic origin residing in Italy or in the free territory of Trieste and fifteen thousand visas to persons of Italian ethnic origin in Italy or the free territory of Trieste who qualified under any of the preferences in the 1952 Immigration and Nationality Act (McCarran-Walters). United States labor unions with large Italian-American memberships supported efforts to stifle Communism in Italian trade unions and also sponsored direct aid through programs such as "adopt a child." *(Courtesy Robert P. Pasqualicchio, col. USAF, ret.)*

Worldwide Celebration. Over 500,000 people—among them many Italians—take to the streets in Toronto, Canada. This was the scene on Toronto's St. Clair Avenue West after Italy won soccer's World Cup in July of 1982. The win has historically been seen as a coming-out party; one writer called it "an epiphanic moment" for the Italian-Canadian community in Toronto. In honor of this victory, Toronto Italians referred to St. Clair Avenue as *Corso Italia,* and it replaced College Street as the center of the community. Similar scenes occurred in other countries with large Italian populations, e.g., Australia and Argentina. *(Courtesy Roberto Portolese)*

War as Adventure. Grant Caproni was born in Chicago, Illinois, December 1880. His father, Antonio, from Barga, Lucca, ran a saloon and imported olive oil and wines. Grant's native-born American mother died three weeks after his birth, and Antonio died when he was eight years old. For a while, he lived with his mother's relatives in Sandwich, Illinois. By the time he turned thirteen, Grant had stowed away on a ship in New Orleans, eventually landing in Abyssinia, where he joined the Italian army. "In the excitement of the Abyssinian campaign," he explained, "everyone thought I was an officer's son and let it go at that." He fought in the battle of Aduwa (or Adowa), March 1, 1896, with thirteen thousand Italian soldiers and was one of the four hundred who returned. Once the officers realized he was not part of their entourage, they "fired" him on the spot. Grant returned to the United States and, in 1897, he "procured . . . [his] guardian's consent to join the army, necessary because [he] was not of age." Grant stated, "I was so excited and overjoyed when the paper came in that mail that I actually shook. I went to Chicago to see if [I] would be accepted. I was worried because I looked so much younger than I really was." He fought in the Philippines during the Spanish-American War and in the rebellion (called the Insurrection) that followed. By 1902, Grant had returned to Illinois, where he studied to become an engineer, graduated, and moved west; during World War I, he served as a cavalry officer, training troops at the Presidio in San Francisco, California, but he was discharged because of physical disability before he could join the war in France. *(Courtesy Ken Caproni, Tucson, Arizona, and Corinne Godfrey, Salt Lake City, Utah)*

Registering for Service. Giacomo Sartorio, from Cadrezzate, Varese, registers for Canadian national service in June 1918. He and his brother, Pio, worked in the coal-mining area of Crowsnest Pass, Alberta, one of the major transportation passes across the Canadian Rockies between Alberta and British Columbia. Coal helped to fuel the ships and industrial steam engines for the war effort. Giacomo's wife, Brigida, whom he married in 1901, remained in Cadrezzate, as did Pio's wife Chiarina, whom he married in 1907. Giacomo and Pio eventually returned to Italy. *(Courtesy Ernesto Milani collection)*

Italian Day in Birmingham, Alabama, 1918. Italian Americans sponsored this float in celebration of May 24, 1918, which marked the third anniversary of Italy's declaration of war against Austria-Hungary in 1915. The banner urges spectators to support the Liberty Loan—buy Liberty Bonds to support America's war effort. Childe Hassam's famous painting *Italian Day 1918* illustrates this celebration on the Fifth Avenue parade route in New York. *(Courtesy Birmingham Public Library, Department of Archives and Manuscripts, catalog # 829.3.3.27)*

Military Bands. In 1918, Dr. Amos DuBell, a physician from Mount Airy and Germantown, Pennsylvania, formed the 103rd regiment of the Pennsylvania National Guard. He asked Luigi Giorno, a musician from Luzzi, Cosenza, to recruit musicians and conduct a military band to support the regiment. The players, mostly Italian emigrants from Calabria, Abruzzo, Sicily, and Salerno, played music to raise morale during and after World War I. In 1923, the band became La Banda Giorno and played in processions during religious feasts and gave a concert on the ending night. Luigi chose marches and symphonic music that reflected the Italian origin of the feast sponsors. He often played compositions by other Italian immigrants, such as composers Domenico Villoni, who emigrated from Salerno to Cleveland, Ohio, and Jack (Concetto) Lentini, who migrated from Lentini, Siracusa, to New Britain, Connecticut. *(Courtesy Norman Giorno-Calapristi)*

Serving America, 1918. Mike Cancassi, from Sciara, Palermo, served as a bugler with the Twenty-first Infantry in Alsace. When he enlisted in New York City in 1917, at age eighteen, Mike worked as a laundryman. His discharge papers, issued in June 1919, noted Mike's excellent character. This commendation enabled Mike to obtain a peddler's license, which granted those who honorably served their country the privilege to hawk, peddle, or vend merchandise in New York State. *(Courtesy Mari Grace Montemuro/Schede)*

Going off to War, Butte, Montana, May 29, 1918. These men, the Meaderville Contingent, stand on a flat bed with a large cannon decorated with bunting as they prepare to go off to war. Mostly Italian immigrant mineworkers and their children lived in the Meaderville section of Butte. Written on the cannon in chalk is the phrase *"Il Piave non si passa"* ("the foreigner will not pass over the Piave"), which refers to a river in northern Italy that flows from the Alps into the Adriatic Sea north of Venice. Here the Italian army prepared to push across into territory occupied by the Austro-Hungarian army. In June, the Italian army, aided by Allied forces, pushed the enemy across the Piave and held firm. The Austrians lost thousands of soldiers and were unable to recoup from this defeat turning the tide of war in favor of Italy. Giovanni Gaeta, a well-known Neapolitan musician wrote the famous song "La Leggenda Del Piave" (The Legend of the Piave) to commemorate this event. The Austrian armies capitulated at the battle of Vittorio Veneto in October 1918. *(Courtesy World Museum of Mining)*

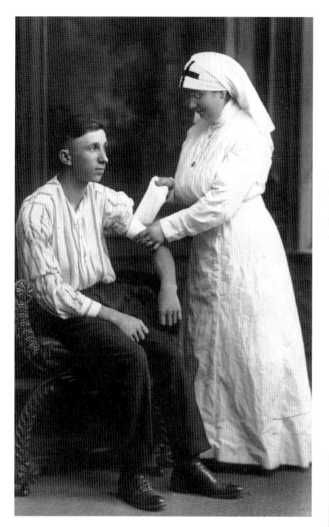

Doing Her Part. Claurinda Giannantonia Iannidinardo from Ripalimosani, Campobasso, volunteered for the Red Cross in Rochester, New York, during World War I. Here she practices bandaging on her son, Tony. During World War II, she knitted items for American soldiers. *(Courtesy the Iannidinardo family)*

Interned during World War II. Because he was a member of Circolo Giulio Giordani, an organization under suspicion by the Canadian government, Santo Pasqualini, born in Turida, Friuli-Venezia Giulia, was arrested at his home within a few hours of Italy's declaration of war against Great Britain and France, June 10, 1940. Most of the people arrested in the area of Vancouver, British Columbia, were members of this organization. He had joined the Circolo only to acknowledge the group's patronage of his bakery and in hopes of benefiting from the discount fares to Italy they offered to take his wife and children to visit their families during the Holy Year of 1940. The police roused him from bed, where he had been sleeping after returning home from his night-shift work at his Paris Bakery. The next day Santo's wife, Alice, and their two children Lina, six, and Lino, three, went to the immigration facility in a futile attempt to see Santo. Instead, Alice received this formal message from her husband two days later. Alice's inability to communicate adequately in English and her inexperience in running the family business resulted in the bankruptcy of the Paris Bakery, which was the sole source of the family income. During Santo's internment of twenty-five months, Alice became sick and was hospitalized. Friends cared for her children until Alice's health started to improve after Santo's release from the Kananakis, Alberta, internment camp in July 1942. *(Courtesy Ray Culos)*

PRISONER OF WAR MAIL   FREE

(THIS SIDE FOR ADDRESS ONLY)

8 PM
1940
B.C.

Mrs. Alice Pasqualini

834 East Geogia Street

Vancouver

British Columbia

FOR DELIVERY IN CANADA ONLY

FORM I.O: 13

I have been interned under the Defence of Canada Regulations. I will write you more details soon.

Address my letters:

c/o INTERNMENT OPERATIONS,

Department of the Secretary of State,

OTTAWA, Ontario.

Date........12th June 1940

Signature

(Nothing except signature and date are to be written on this side.)

Imprisoned at Ellis Island. In early 1942, Italian residents on the East Coast, including the famous Italian basso of the Metropolitan Opera, Ezio Pinza, joined the Italian nationals held as enemy aliens at Ellis Island. His granddaughter recalled, "In March of 1942, two strange men . . . came right in the house and proceeded up the stairs and . . . asked him, 'Are you Ezio Pinza?' He admitted he was. They pulled out their FBI badges. One of them said, 'In the name of the president of the United States, we place you under arrest.'" He was not told the charges against him nor was he allowed a lawyer during his hearings. Many believed that people who disliked him had alleged fascist sympathies. The *Washington News* headline read "FBI's Been Watching Him: Pinza, Met's Basso, Jailed as Duce's Pal." Fortunately, well-known friends, such as author Thomas Mann and antifascist leader Carlo Tresca, wrote letters to the federal authorities, and they helped gain his release by late spring 1942. "Paroled" after only eleven weeks, on condition that he report weekly to "a reliable United States citizen," he returned home to his family and resumed his career. Of the roughly two thousand Italians living in the United States who were detained for questioning after Pearl Harbor, only three hundred were deemed sufficient security risks to warrant confinement in Fort Missoula, Montana. *(Courtesy Alfredo Cipolato)*

Sincere Pledge of Loyalty. Anticipating the entry of Italy into the European war, Angelo Branca gathered a group of Italian Canadians in Vancouver, British Columbia, in June 1940 to declare their allegiance to the Commonwealth. Born in Vancouver to parents from Turbigo, Milano, Angelo, an attorney, had helped many Italian Canadians with legal problems over the years. At the meeting, he advised the more than three hundred Italian-Canadian attendees to form the Canadian-Italian War Vigilance Association of Vancouver. This new association endorsed the cause and donated cash to support Canada's war effort (at this point fighting Nazi Germany). The group placed this advertisement in the *News Herald* shortly after Italy's declaration of war in June 1940. *(Courtesy Ray Culos)*

Bella Vista—Fort Missoula, c. 1942. In the spring of 1941, fifteen hundred seamen were taken from twenty-eight Italian ships seized in United States waters and interned at Ellis Island to prevent sabotage. After a brief stay at Ellis Island, the Italian seamen were sent to Missoula, Montana, during the summer of 1941. By December, the authorities began sending some men back to Italy. However, after the declaration of war, following the December 7 attack, all the detainees' radios and cameras were confiscated. Impressed with the setting of the fort, the Italians called the area Bella Vista. About one hundred internees were entertainers—largely musicians, singers, dancers, and choreographers from the luxury cruise ship that was caught in the Panama Canal. One detainee, Alfredo Cipolato recalled, "We had a regular theater—a comedy one week, an opera the next." Alfredo met his future wife Ann D'Orazi while singing in the choir at Saint Frances Xavier Catholic Church in Missoula. Some of the men worked as orderlies in the hospital. Others picked sugar beets or worked on the railroad. In this photo, Alfredo stands behind the accordionist while his buddies laugh at the lyrics. *(Courtesy Alfredo Cipolato)*

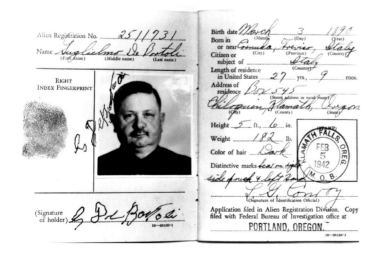

Enemy Aliens. In 1940, the United States required all noncitizens to register, and once registered, they were issued cards. Then in February 1942, all aliens of "enemy nationality" were required to obtain a passport type of identification issued by the FBI. At that time, there were some 600,000 Italian resident aliens, the largest immigrant group in the United States. This image shows Guglielmo DeBortoli's document. Born in Cornuda, Treviso, Guglielmo had settled in Chiloquin, Oregon. Enemy aliens had to obey regulations and instructions printed on the back page of this document governing "travel, change of residence, occupation, possession of various articles like cameras, radios, firearms, ammunition, explosives, signal devices and similar articles." If found, these articles were confiscated. They could not reside near "certain areas of military character" and could not go to other areas "without permission from an authorized government officer." Those violating the restrictions could be interned for the duration of the war. *(Courtesy Tina M. DeBortoli-Frostad)*

Question of Loyalty. Because some enemy aliens lived in designated military areas, such as the western military district in California, they were required to move (sometimes only across the street) from their homes in 1942. As a result, ten thousand people had evacuated their homes and another fifty thousand lived under curfew. Some of them suffered economic deprivation if they had had jobs that required them to be away from home between 8:00 P.M. and 6:00 A.M. Members of the Buccellato and Cardinalli families from Pittsburg, California, are pictured in front of the housing they found at substandard migrant worker bungalows in Oakley, California. About two thousand Italians were forced to move from Pittsburg. The Buccellato family had moved from Detroit, Michigan, with their seven boys and three girls, to California in 1930. Mr. Buccellato passed away in 1941, and when the war broke out his sons Rocco and Nick joined the navy. While they were both on battleships—USS *South Dakota* and USS *Idaho*—fighting in the Pacific, Mrs. Buccellato, a noncitizen, had to move from Pittsburg, bringing her American service flag with two stars. No one was spared.

Sash Donated By Bob Strano

Pictured are various styles of badges used by the Society throughout the years. In earlier years the writing was in Italian. One of the most significant changes in style occurred during World War II when, out of loyalty to their country, the membership decided to replace the original Italian colors, green, white and red, with the more patriotic American colors, red, white and blue.

Demonstrating Loyalty. During World War II, Our Lady of Mount Carmel Society in Hammonton, New Jersey, redesigned their official badges. Previously the organization's name was in Italian, with ribbons in the colors of the Italian flag, green, white, and red. In 1942, the membership decided to change their badges to show the "more patriotic American colors" of red, white, and blue. Across America, most Italian-language radio shows ceased to broadcast, and many immigrants and their children felt it best not to "speak the language of the enemy." *(Courtesy Our Lady of Mount Carmel Society)*

End of World War II. To celebrate the end of World War II, this banner, displaying one star for each of the eighty-five residents of Baltimore, Maryland's Little Italy who left for war in 1942, was hung across Eastern Avenue to welcome the returning veterans. In 1942, the banner had been blessed at Saint Leo Catholic Church, an Italian national parish. During the war, many families in Little Italy worked in defense industries or provided laundry services and meals for men who worked in the nearby shipyards. *(Courtesy The Maryland Historical Society, Baltimore, Maryland)*

Returnee Becomes Goodwill Ambassador, c. 1931. At age fourteen, Bernardino Maffucci left Calitri, Avellino, for Dunmore, Pennsylvania, where he pulled coal carts for fifty cents a day. "Barney" fled that life for New York City, and he worked in different saloons and tended bar by the age of seventeen. He tried a number of businesses—a shoe repair shop, a saloon, the concrete business, and fruit vending—until he finally achieved financial success with a taxi company and real estate company in Lynnbrook, New York. He was about forty-two when he sold his Long Island business in 1928. He decided to settle in a villa he purchased in Marzano Di Nola, Avellino, his wife's hometown, where he applied his American sense of practical innovation. Marzano had no running water, so he drilled an artesian well to obtain water for his olive-oil mill process. He also sold water and delivered it to other landowners through a system of pipes he constructed. The grateful townspeople elected him mayor. Barney had learned German dealing with the predominately German immigrant population in the Bushwick section of Brooklyn, and during World War II, this helped him communicate with the Germans. Later his command of English worked well with the Allied forces. He also brought his eighteen-year-old American-born son, Barney, Jr., to the United States army headquarters to register for the draft. Barney, Jr. spoke no English, and the army found it difficult to give him a steady assignment. So he stayed around headquarters and went home each night on his motorbike, often bringing other GIs with him. *(Courtesy Gerard Maffucci)*

Collecting Scrap Metal. Wilmington, Delaware-born William J. Marsilii, Sr. opened Bear Safety Service in 1940 at 1900 Lincoln Street. Due to wartime restraints on new cars, William focused on keeping his customers' cars in good condition by providing wheel alignment, brake adjustments, and replacing and straightening out body frames bent in accidents. In 1942, "Bill" parked an old car in front of his station with the slogans "Dump Metal Inside" and "Let's Go USA Keep 'Em Flying," and he invited people to put their scrap metal, aluminum cans, and chewing gum wrappers in the car. He painted the names of friends and relatives in the service on the car. "Mando," his cousin, the first name on the car, flew B-17s, was shot down over Germany, spent a year as a prisoner, and suffered greatly when forced to march in the winter away from the advancing Russians. *Left to right:* Joseph Renzetti (William's brother-in-law), Joseph Kemp, unknown. All three worked with William who took the photo. Nardy Spitelli, William's cousin, crouches in front. *(Courtesy Carmela Jane Marsilii Ianni)*

Serving Her Country. Emily Salerno poses with her brothers, Tony and Frank, in 1943, before leaving to serve in the Women's Auxiliary Army Corps. Before the war, Emily taught grades fourth through sixth in Tercio, Colorado. Three of ten children in the Salerno family, whose parents came from San Fili, Cosenza, went into the service during World War II. Emily made quartermaster (T-5) and served in New Guinea and the Philippines. She received the Good Conduct Medal, two Victory Medals, the American Theater Medal, and the Asiatic/Pacific Medal. *(Courtesy the Salerno family by Teresa Compton)*

Reporting the War. During the war, Girolamo Valenti, editor of *La Parola,* his progressive, anti-fascist weekly, continued to publish with the support of the American government. Here he corrects proofs in February 1943. The few Italian-language papers still operating during the war provided news for immigrants anxious to read about the impact of the fighting in Europe, especially Italy. Later that summer, the Allies invaded Sicily and began the campaign to liberate Italy. Italians in America worried about their families in Italy and their sons fighting to defeat fascism. *(Courtesy Library of Congress, LC-USW3-017539-D; photo Marjory Collins)*

Welcoming Victory, 1943. Louise Scarpelli of Portland, Oregon, shows her pleasure at the Allied victory in Italy as she draws muscatel from a wine barrel to share with her friends in celebration. Her husband, Giovanni, and his two brothers Salvatore and Antonio owned the Porter-Scarpelli Macaroni Company at 3510 NE Broadway. Louise and Giovanni lived at Twenty-eighth and Division. Overnight, Italy, freed from the yoke of fascism, joined the Allies. Still, most of the peninsula remained under German occupation and had to be taken agonizingly in some of the bloodiest battles of the war. *(Courtesy Oregon Historical Society, image # 015815)*

Return of a Native, Spring 1944. Sergeant Matteo Fioretti enjoys this scene of his grandmother Fiorinta behind the steering wheel and his mother Stella as assistant in the U.S. army jeep he drove to his hometown of Carbonara, Bari. In 1933, at age thirteen, Matteo had left Italy with his father, Luigi, to live in Lester, Washington. Once he arrived in Italy in October 1943, he longed to see his family and "borrowed" an army jeep to do so. Called to report to his Naples-based executive officer, he encountered an intelligence officer from G2 holding his personnel file; the questioning began, "Sergeant, we know your family is in Bari." Matteo anticipated being "court-martialed and shot." Then the G2 officer gave Matteo a book in Italian and told him to translate. Matteo immediately displayed his language facility, and the officer interrupted to say, "Sergeant, you are going to be a translator," and assigned "Matt" to the 2675th Regiment, Company E of the Allied Military Government. He would spend the rest of his military duty translating for the military court, which was established during the period of martial law. He assisted in cases ranging from espionage to bootlegging. *(Courtesy Matt and Antonetta Fioretti)*

Italian POWs in the United States. Eustacchio Antonio Guardiani and his wife, Cesidia (Cecilia), from Tocca Casauria, Chieti, traveled from their home on Staten Island, with their daughter Mary, to visit an Italian POW, Antonio, held at Camp Kilmer, New Jersey. *Left to right:* Cecilia, Antonio, Mary, Eustacchio. A coworker at Wallerstein Company, which made malt for beer and bosco, read a list of Italian POWs printed in an Italian newspaper and noticed that Antonio also came from Tocca Casauria. After Antonio returned to Italy, they corresponded briefly, but they did not stay in touch. Wherever the estimated 51,156 Italian POWs stayed in America, Italian Americans in nearby communities connected with people from the same areas of Italy, often bringing the POWs home for dinner. After Italy had surrendered, this practice became commonplace. In Seattle, Washington, POW Mike Prontera (from Lecce) met his wife, Mary Vacca, when she came to dances held near his barracks at East Marginal Way. In 1944, the United States army offered the POWs the option of signing up to form Italian Service Units. Close to thirty-four thousand enlisted men and officers chose to join these units. They wore American army uniforms with a green armband with "Italy" in white letters. They provided much needed support in ordnance, transportation, and quartermaster functions. *(Courtesy the Guardiani and Sticca families)*

Flying to Japan. Joseph Anthony Barecca, from St. Louis, Missouri, worked as a radar technician on this B-29, called *The Lucky Lady,* during World War II. Stationed in India, Joe flew over the Himalayas to bomb Japan. Before the war, he worked on airplanes at Curtis Wright, which later became McDonald Aircraft in St. Louis. He did not become a pilot because he was colorblind. His parents, Anthony Joseph and Rosa Venterella Barecca, had immigrated to St. Louis from Castelbuono, Palermo. Joseph, the oldest of seven children, used his GI benefits to obtain a law degree from the University of Washington. *(Courtesy Joseph A. Barreca, Jr. and family)*

Four Stars of Courage. Joseph Pellicore from Rende, Cosenza, poses with his grandsons Leo and Billy Spizzirri in front of the home they shared at 2059 North Kilpatrick Avenue in Chicago, Illinois, during World War II. The Armed Service Flag framed in the window behind them has four stars, one for each of Joseph's sons in the military: William (army), Philip (army air corps), Albert (navy Seabees), and Raymond (navy). Two of Joseph's other sons George and Henry also served stateside in the army during the war. Edward, the only son not in the military, was a Roman Catholic priest. *(Courtesy Jeffrey Caracci)*

Family Reunion. Felix DiRienzo, from Scranton, Pennsylvania, takes a picture of his grandfather, Felice (standing front, second from left in dark work clothes) in Villamaina, Avellino, during World War II. The two had never met. When Signal Corpsman Felix ("Phil") met his grandfather, he was surprised to hear him speak some English. Phil learned that his grandfather had traveled to the United States three times in the early part of the twentieth century to work on railroads. He also recruited people for the American rail companies. When he returned to Italy, Felice and his family cultivated olive groves and vineyards. Stationed at the palace in Caserta near Naples, Phil often invited his buddies—Italian-American James Fitch from Binghamton, New York (standing in front of the door frame), and Anglo-American Russell Rhodes (standing in the doorway), who was Phil's mechanic in the motor pool—to accompany him to Villamaina. The GIs arrived with gifts of candy, Spam™, biscuits, and canned chicken. Years later, Felice proudly wore the belt buckle his grandson gave him at their first meeting. (*Courtesy Felix DiRienzo*)

"Rosalie the Welder." From 1943 to 1945 Rosalie Taggi left her North Beach, San Francisco, California, home at 5:30 in the morning and walked to the Ferry Building where she caught a boat heading to the Kaiser Shipyards across the bay in Richmond, California. Rosalie received numerous certificates for outstanding work. She had qualified to do flat, vertical, and overhead welding, and, because of her small size, she could also work in difficult-to-reach places. In 2005, Rosalie donated her welding leathers and helmet to the Richmond Museum. The actual poster image of Rosie the Riveter was named after Rose Bonavita, who was called to duty at the former General Motors Eastern Aircraft Division in North Tarrytown, New York. Bonavita and her factory partner, fellow Italian-American Jennie Florio, drilled a record nine hundred holes and placed 3,300 rivets in an airplane tail within six hours. FDR sent them a letter of praise. (*Courtesy The Richmond Museum of History Collection*)

Italian-American Soldiers Restore Stability to Liberated Italy. Pictured are members of AMGOT (Allied Military Government for Occupied Territory), also known as the Allied Commission. *Left to right:* Fred Pierce, Phil Mallozzi, Charles (Chuck) Inga, Al Cardello, Ed Barsetti, Bill Lanni, Tony Romano (center), Al Guarnieri, Pat Marano (crouching), Al Popolizio, a British soldier. The men pose as their buddy Nicholas Granitto, from Brooklyn, New York, snaps the picture in Pesaro, Italy, October 1944. AMGOT units were attached to the standard divisions (e.g., infantry, quartermaster, tank corps, etc.) and were dispatched shortly after the Germans were routed, town by town, to provide the expertise and supplies needed to reestablish civilian life. Working through the rubble, the soldiers helped to restore roads, provide transportation, oversee the administration of public health, and restore industrial and agricultural operations. They conducted judicial proceedings and helped to reinstate municipal governments. Approximately ninety percent of the 270 soldiers in AMGOT were Americans of Italian-born parents or grandparents. Many of the officers, such as Pennsylvania Supreme Court Judge Michael Musmanno and New York Lieutenant Governor Charles Poletti, plus several specialists, such as medical doctor Joseph Ruisi of Rhode Island, also participated. While the soldiers were often selected at random from a cross-section of military units because of their Italian names, many of them were not fluent in the standard Italian language. However, their cultural/ethnic backgrounds equipped them with some empathy for the everyday lifestyles of the Italian population. *(Courtesy Nicholas Granitto)*

Helping to Win the War. Born in Lehigh, Oklahoma, where her father worked in the coal mines, Gene (Jenny) Bonino's family moved back to Balangero, Torino, when she was five. She married Domenico Airaudi in 1920, and soon after, they came to the U.S., and Domenico found work in the copper mines in Butte, Montana. Eventually they moved to Redwood City, California. In 1942, when one of her sons, Claudio, was in the marines, she started to work at the S & W Cannery in Redwood City to supplement Domenico's income as a city gardener. She first worked on the canning line to ensure that the cans of carrot juice would not jam and cause the work to come to a halt. Carrot juice was provided for United States pilots because it was believed the juice would improve night vision. By 1943, Gene was promoted to supervisor. Some of the workers, who had been employed longer at S & W resented her promotion and complained that her broken English was a problem. The administration supported their choice and Gene continued as supervisor until she left the company in 1959 when she returned to Balangero after Domenico was killed in a car accident. *(Courtesy Denise Calvetti Michaels, granddaughter of Jenny Bonino Airaudi)*

Invading His Ancestral Homeland. Fighting with Princess Patricia's Canadian Light Infantry, Elmo Trasolini stands by the tail of a German plane in Oderburg, Germany, c. 1945. Born in Vancouver, British Columbia, in 1922, to Luigi Trasolini (from Torrice, Frosinone) and Raffaella Raino, Elmo wanted to follow his three older siblings into the service. Elmo participated in Operation Husky (invasion of Sicily), landing in Italy in the summer of 1943. He fought in battles along the Hitler Line, west of Monte Cassino, in late May 1944, during the Allied advance northward to Rome. Toward the end of August, the regiment moved back to the Adriatic and took part in the assaults on the Gothic Line from Ancona to Rimini. Following the liberation of Torrice and Frosinone, southeast of Rome, Raffaella wrote, asking Elmo to visit his relatives in his father's hometown of Torrice. "I obtained permission from my commander to go back and attempt to find my relatives," he said. When his family saw him still in full battle dress, they brought him to their home and "invited [him] to sit at the head of the table." Elmo remembers, "I couldn't speak Italian, which I really regretted. But I was treated as a god, the centerpiece. And everybody just stood there smiling, talking and looking at me . . . I only had meager rations . . . cigarettes and chocolates. I gave them all I had." *(Courtesy Ray Culos)*

Above and Beyond the Call of Duty. Immediately after his junior year at Blakely High School, in Peckville, Pennsylvania, Gino Merli tried to enlist. He was turned down, given a 4F for medical reasons, and told to go home. He appealed, demanded to retake the physical, and passed a day or so after July 4, 1943. On September 4, 1944, Gino was the last man standing as his gunner position was overrun outside Sars-la-Bruyère, Belgium. Twice Gino took bayonet thrusts to his back as the German troops probed for life. Twice he was up and firing after being taken for dead. At daybreak the next day, a squad of United States infantrymen found Gino, exhausted and half frozen, and fifty-two dead enemy bodies. Instead of resting, Gino went into a chapel and prayed for the dead, including the soldiers he had killed. His wife Mary recalled, "Just like my Gino to do that. Those German soldiers were like him, only nineteen or twenty years old with girlfriends and families—that's war, you know." In this photo, President Truman stands on the portico of the White House, June 15, 1945, with four war heroes to whom he awarded the Congressional Medal of Honor. *From left:* Maj. Everett P. Pope, Wollason, Massachusetts; Pfc. Gino J. Merli, Peckville, Pennsylvania; Pfc. Luther Skaggs, Henderson, Kentucky; Lt. Carlton R. Rouh, Lindenwold, New Jersey. Gino was in the army, and the other men were marines. Rouh's niece, Floretta Graham, is in the center of the photograph, and on Truman's right is General George Marshall; on his left is James Forrestal, secretary of the navy. *(Courtesy AP Images)*

Brothers in Arms, June 1953. Army Private First Class Domenic Codella, Jr. (sitting) and his twin brother, Marine Private First Class Anthony, meet in Korea. Anthony, assigned to the First Marine Division, received permission from his commanding officer to make a fifty-mile trip from his sector of the battlefield to the front in Kumwha Valley (east-central part of Korea) to spend three days with his brother. The twenty-one-year-old soldiers sent this picture back to their widowed father, who had emigrated from Calitri, Avellino, to Newark, New Jersey, in 1920. *(Courtesy Mario Toglia)*

Love with the Proper Stranger. Lucia Galizia at age seventeen, chaperoned by her mother Ann, dates a sailor at the NATO military club in Naples. The American sailor was a customer at her parents' coffee/wine bar in Naples where she worked. Although Lucia did not marry this sailor, she accepted the proposal of another sailor and, like many of her contemporaries, left for the United States as a serviceman's bride. *(Courtesy Lucia Galizia)*

Return to the Front. Frank Abatangelo, a navy veteran of World War II, worked as a civilian contractor for a company that did utility installation for the military in Vietnam, 1969-1970. Before and after Vietnam, Frank maintained electrical equipment for State Farm Insurance Company. Born in Brooklyn, New York, to Italian-immigrant parents from Monreale, Palermo, and Calabria, Frank had fought in the Pacific theater during World War II and then escorted German and Italian prisoners-of-war back to Europe. While stationed in Naples, he cooked for the officers billeted in Il Duce's palace. Italian civilians assisted him just as Vietnamese civilians had assisted him in 1969. *(Courtesy Lena Abatangelo)*

Army Family. Retired Army Major General Francis A. Ianni, whose father was from Tortoreto Alto, Teramo, and had settled in New Castle, Delaware, poses with his daughter, Lieutenant Colonel Marisa Tanner, after attending the burial of an army friend at Arlington National Cemetery in 2001. A West Point graduate (1954), Francis served two tours in Vietnam. In 2001, Marisa worked at the Pentagon. She served in Iraq in the initial invasion in March 2002. Promoted to colonel, she is on her second tour in Iraq, stationed in Baghdad as director of operations for intelligence for IFOR (International Force), the top headquarters in Iraq, commanded by General David Petraeus. *(Courtesy Francis A. Ianni)*

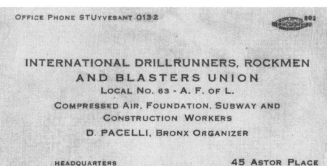

Organizing for Justice. Dominick (Dionisio) Pacelli emigrated with his family from San Sebastiano al Vesuvio, Napoli, to New York City in 1899. New York City was building its subways and tunnels, and the workers who blasted through rock faced constant danger. In the Bronx, Dominick helped organize the Rockmen, Drill Runners, Tunnel, Subway, Compressed Air, and Construction Workers Union. Originally affiliated with the American Federation of Labor, they moved into the Congress of Industrial Organizations in the 1930s. He treated union members with sympathy when they couldn't work or had difficulty paying their dues. In 1937, he formed the D. Pacelli Association, which sponsored annual dances in the Bronx to provide social events for working-class families. The fifty-cent subscription helped to pay for the two bands and the facility. *(Courtesy Sharon Pacelli Haddox)*

Job Discrimination. At the McCloud River Lumber Company in McCloud, California, Italians comprised approximately two-thirds of the labor force, working in the planning mill, the box factory, and in the woods cutting and hauling timber. Most workers were single men who worked seasonally from April to the first snows in December. They lived in tent cabins with few facilities and paid a dollar a day for room and board out of a total wage ranging from $1.75 to $2.00 per day. Protesting their poor working conditions and the failure of management to implement a twenty-cent-per-day raise, more than a thousand immigrants went on strike in 1909. They believed that the company discriminated against them because they were Italian. After Salvatore Rocca, Italian consul in San Francisco, arrived to investigate, he filed a complaint with the governor of California, protesting management's assumption that "Italians belonged ethnographically to a darker-colored race." This characterization of Italians, especially those from southern Italy, was common during the period of mass migration. He also wrote to the commissioner general of emigration in Italy that Italian lumbermen in McCloud were "subjected to systematic insults and to demeaning appellations." *(Courtesy Sacramento Archives and Museum Collection Center, 1983/71/1923, Hazel Pendleton Collection)*

Freedom of Assembly. During the 1913 strike in the silk mills of Paterson, New Jersey, mill owners pressured city officials to deny the strikers permits to assemble for meetings within the city limits. William Brueckman, the German socialist mayor of neighboring Haledon, invited the strikers to assemble in his jurisdiction. Haledon residents and silk workers Pietro and Maria Botto invited strike leaders, mostly members of the Industrial Workers of the World, to use their home as headquarters. Each Sunday, speakers, such as writer Upton Sinclair and Industrial Workers of the World leaders Elizabeth Gurley Flynn, "Big Bill" Haywood, and Carlo Tresca, addressed more than twenty thousand workers from the balcony of the Botto home. The strikers, mostly Italian immigrants, filled the open fields around the house. The *New York Times* printed advance notice of these meetings. *(Courtesy American Labor Museum/Botto House National Landmark)*

Protesting Injustice. After the Ludlow Massacre in Trinidad, Colorado, in 1913, which resulted in the deaths of thirteen women and children, striking miners in Louisville, Colorado, members of the United Mine Workers of America, became more militant. The 2,700 men had been on strike since 1910. In 1913, the state militia, led by General Chase, was called in to restore order. The troops favored the mine owners and also employed some of the mine guards. On Monday, April 27, a week after the Ludlow Massacre, riots started. If anyone was seen on the street after dark, the militia would shoot at them from a high tower near the Hecla Mine, equipped with a spotlight and machine gun. During a union meeting, the miners heard gunfire and rushed to their homes for weapons to attack the mine. Machine-gun bullets sprayed homes and buildings in Louisville. Families evacuated if they could or retreated to basements for protection. In 1914, President Wilson sent in army troops to establish an impartial control and peace, which prevailed until the strike was settled in early 1915. The settlement provided a wage increase but did not recognize the UMWA as a bargaining agent. *(Courtesy Louisville Historical Museum)*

Supporting Fellow Strikers. Demonstrators in New York City protest the arrest of Italian anarchist Carlo Tresca during the iron ore miners' strike in Hibbing, Minnesota, in 1916. Support for common causes crossed international borders. During the 1912 strike in Lawrence, Massachusetts, when Industrial Workers of the World organizers Joseph Ettor and Arthur Giovannitti were jailed, Italians in Vancouver, British Columbia, collected and sent fifty dollars to the IWW defense committee to support "fellow countrymen . . . who have been falsely imprisoned." *(Courtesy Library of Congress, Bain Collection, LC-DIG-ggbain-23310)*

Police Violence. Jerry Carabetta (Corbetta), a veteran of World War I and a member of a prominent family in Denver, Colorado's Italian community, was shot in the back by a Denver detective during a bootleg raid on a soft drink parlor (Corbetta Bros. and Guida) in north Denver in June 1919. The entire community was outraged. The next day, members of the Italian American Protective Association assembled more than four thousand Italians who marched to City Hall where they demanded that the officer be punished for the shooting. On June 13, 1919, a jury exonerated the officer responsible for the death of Carabetta. This photo shows the funeral cortège. *(Courtesy Colorado Historical Society, image # PCLLI1475)*

United in Common Cause. The United Mine Workers of America local in Avella, Pennsylvania, stopped work for a day, c. 1925, in support of a ten-county strike in West Virginia as a show of union strength. One of western Pennsylvania's largest labor unions in the first half of the twentieth century, UMWA and its members reflected the different ethnic backgrounds of the miners organized to improve worker safety, reduce hours, and increase wages. Note that one of the signs says, in Italian, "We will never tolerate reduction of wages. We are ready for any sacrifice, but we will not accept any reductions." *(Courtesy Italian American Collection, Senator John Heinz Pittsburgh History Center of Western Pennsylvania)*

Support for the Cause. Anarchists Nicola Sacco and Bartolomeo Vanzetti are escorted onto a trolley in Boston, Massachusetts, c. 1927, during one of their appeals for a new trial. With their appeals denied, the men awaited execution for the 1920 murder of two men in a payroll robbery. On August 5, 1927, fifteen thousand cigar makers in Ybor City, Tampa, Florida, staged a two-hour general strike when the lector in the Perfecto-Garcia factory read the news that Governor Alvan T. Fuller of Massachusetts refused to grant the men executive clemency. The workers spread the word to other factories and held a mass meeting in protest. They planned to strike again on the day scheduled for the electrocution. In November, the Industrial Workers of the World (IWW) evoked the martyrdom of Sacco and Vanzetti to protest the use of strikebreakers at the Columbine Mine in Serene, Colorado. *(Courtesy Boston Public Library/Rare Books Department: courtesy of the Trustees, MS. 2030.10N.61)*

Supporting their Talisman. Frank Forges and his anti-fascist friends tossed these leaflets about art and freedom from the top balcony of Carnegie Hall during a concert conducted by Arturo Toscanini. They applauded the conductor's public anti-fascist sentiments and actions. When police rushed in and tried to arrest the activists, Toscanini came to their aid, asking the police to free them, which they did. Toscanini had left Italy for New York City because of his opposition to Mussolini's government. In 1931, he had been attacked by fascist thugs in Italy for refusing to play the party's official anthem at the start of the concert. He became conductor of the New York Philharmonic in 1928. As a guest conductor in Europe, he refused to perform in Germany or Italy in protest against Nazism and Italian Fascism. He traveled to Palestine at his own expense in 1936 to conduct a new orchestra in Tel Aviv whose members were largely Jewish refugees from Central Europe. *(Courtesy Sylvia Forges Ryan)*

Mussolini and his black shirts do not represent the spirit of Italy.
Viva ARTURO TOSCANINI!

Down with Fascisti, the Savages of Modern Age!
Long Live ARTURO TOSCANINI!

Liberty Is Essential to Art!
Down with Fascism!
Viva Arturo Toscanini!

Women United. Emma Adami and Rose Lancilotti picket in front of the Woolworth five-and-dime store at 1343 Stockton Street in San Francisco, California, in August 1937. Some 450 other striking employees of Retail Department Store Employees Union, Local No. 1100, many of them Italian- and Chinese-American women, employees of Woolworth and Newberry stores, also participated throughout the city. The women carry signs in Italian and Chinese to inform the people of this North Beach/Chinatown neighborhood that twelve to sixteen dollars a week is not a living wage. Most customers chose not to cross the picket line. The persistence of the union members paid off with a settlement reducing weekly work hours to 44 and a weekly pay increase to twenty dollars. *(Courtesy San Francisco History Center, San Francisco Public Library, AAD-5376)*

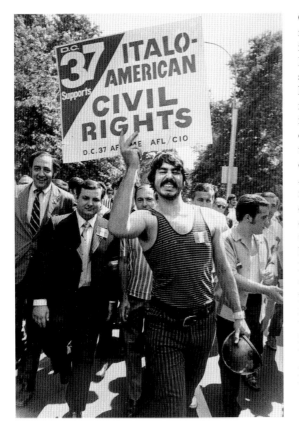

Campaigning for Civil Rights, 1972. During the late 1960s and early '70s, many ethnic groups found inspiration from African Americans who gained civil rights as a result of mass demonstrations. The Italian-American Civil Rights League was formed to combat pejorative stereotypes about Italian Americans, specifically their association with the Mafia. The league's founder, Joseph Colombo, had complained of unfair harassment by various federal law-enforcement authorities who alleged that he was the boss of one of New York City's five Mafia families. Colombo gathered thirty demonstrators to picket the offices of the Federal Bureau of Investigation in April 1970. Within a few days, five thousand demonstrators were participating. In June 1970, the league attracted a crowd of fifty thousand, a cross section of New York-metropolitan-area Italian Americans, to a rally in Columbus Circle. African Americans, including Godfrey Cambridge and Adam Clayton Powell; Puerto Ricans; and Jewish Americans also participated. Many Italian-owned businesses closed that day, and dockworkers joined the rally to protest the government's and the media's broad use of the term Mafia and other negative stereotypes. This picture shows members of District Council 37 of the American Federation of State, County, and Municipal Employees, AFL-CIO, New York's largest public employees union, demonstrating for the cause. Some held signs reading, "Does your name make you a criminal?" At this time, thirty thousand, or one-third, of District Council 37's membership, was Italian American, many of them in blue-collar positions. United States attorney general John Mitchell and New York governor Nelson Rockefeller responded with a declaration that the term "Mafia" would no longer be used within their jurisdictions. The league also threatened to boycott companies that produced objectionable television commercials, and they got Macy's to stop selling a board game called The Godfather Game. *(Courtesy Catherine Ursillo,* Italian American Demonstration, Central Park, 1972, *Museum of the City of New York, gift of the photographer, 03.104.2)*

Labor Strife. Italian-immigrant workers walk the picket line during a strike at the Artistic Woodwork Factory, a manufacturer of fancy picture frames, in North York, Ontario, then a suburb of Toronto, 1973. Mostly emigrants from Italy, Greece, the West Indies, Portugal, and Latin America, 120 out of 150 workers experienced their first strike for the right to form a union. Company owners had emigrated from Estonia in the 1950s and transferred their anti-communist, anti-union, and conservative politics into the work place. It was a long and bitter strike, which was marked by violence on the picket line when the company hired scabs to cross the picket line and keep the factory running. As a result, it galvanized the attention of the city and the Industrial Workers of the World, whose organizers suffered a number of arrests. Police abuse of the strikers prompted the Ontario Federation of Labour to join the picket lines. The immigrant workers learned about labor relations first hand. *(© Vincenzo Pietropaolo)*

Tragic Loss

Falling Short of His Dream. Emilio Donati left Fiumalbo, Modena, in 1900 to work in the coal mines near Higbee, Missouri. He returned to Italy and married Francesca Amedei, and they arrived in Higbee in September 1906. This picture of the couple and their first two children, Louis and Anita, c. 1911, was taken after they moved to nearby Bevier, another mining town. Six years later, some of the immigrant coal miners, who wished to leave this dangerous occupation, went to the Italian consulate in St. Louis. They learned about the Italian agricultural community at Knobview and were encouraged to meet the Castelli family for a tour of available farms. Emilio purchased a farm and returned to his job in Bevier, and over the next two years, he managed to build a house and purchase farm equipment. He moved his growing family there in 1919. Two years later, he went back to Bevier to earn money to tide the family over, but within a few months of reaching that goal he died in a mining accident. Francesca was left to raise eight young children on her own. Her sons helped her by caring for the apple trees and raising dairy cows. Eventually, one of her sons, Michael, took full control of the operation. *(Courtesy Steve Zulpo)*

A Life of Sorrow. Francesca Cirillo sits on a rocking chair in an alley near her Bridgeport, Connecticut, home. She died from tubercular meningitis on Christmas Eve 1917. The following year her brother Michael and another sister died in the flu epidemic and their bodies were buried in a mass grave. This left their mother, Cesaria, from Melito di Napoli, with one surviving child, Angelina. Cesaria had lost her mother at an early age and was raised by an aunt before going into a convent for four years. She married Antonio Cirillo, from Succivo, Caserta, an experienced chef who had studied in the Middle East. They settled in Bridgeport, where he established the successful restaurant Vittoria. Although his wife and daughter lived above the restaurant, Antonio did not allow Cesaria to help him or to attend the parties he catered. His addiction to gambling, drinking, and womanizing depleted his income, and sometimes his family did not have enough to eat. Cesaria made artificial flowers at home to ease the strain. Her religious devotion provided some comfort, and she became a member of the Third Order of the Franciscans (lay people devoted to following the rule of St. Francis). When Antonio died at age fifty, he left his wife with nothing. Cesaria chose to live alone and supported herself by making flowers, rather than intrude upon her daughter and son-in-law. *(Courtesy Cecilia Ferrara)*

Abandoned and Defenseless. Maria Maggio and Artillio Rossi married in 1919, at St. Anthony di Padua in Utica, New York. The couple lived with Maria's parents. Soon after their second child, Catherine (Gaetana), was born in 1921, Artillio abandoned his family. The police caught him in February 1922, fined him one thousand dollars, and gave him a choice between jail time and resuming full responsibility for his family. Although Artillio seemed contrite to the judge, he soon abandoned his family for good. Maria and her two children, Philip Anthony and Catherine, remained with her parents, Donato and Gaetana Petrone Maggio. These traumatic events eroded Maria's health, and she died in 1926 at age twenty-three. Gaetana and Donato adopted their grandchildren who assumed their grandparents' surname. Donato, who had emigrated from Pignola, Potenza, worked on the railroad and had to stretch his wages to support his own seven children as well as his two grandchildren. *(Courtesy the Maggio family)*

The *American* Illness. A healthy, alert Maria Robotti arrived in New York City from Fubine, Alessandria, in 1909. Maria married Luigi Ravizza from Zanco di Villadeati, Alessandria, in April 1912. They had four children, with one dying in infancy. In 1922, Luigi was diagnosed as schizophrenic and sent to Central Islip Hospital on Long Island. Maria was similarly diagnosed and sent there in December 1923. She gave birth to a fifth child a few months later. This picture of Maria, copied from her hospital record, shows a woman ravaged by the fear, confusion, and disillusion she experienced attempting to adjust to a new environment. In Mario Puzo's novel *The Fortunate Pilgrim,* the mother, Lucia Santa, commits her husband to an institution because she fears his unpredictable behavior. In Puzo's own childhood, his father, Antonio, a railroad trackman, married late, became increasingly erratic, and was finally diagnosed as schizophrenic and institutionalized. For those immigrants who were also illiterate as well as non-English speaking, life in an institution was like being in isolation. Staff did not relate to the cultural or linguistic backgrounds of their Italian patients. Most families could not tolerate the pain, indignity, and disruption they suffered when a member became mentally ill, and many chose to hide the loss and never told their children. Maria's eight-and-a-half-year-old daughter Rosa was placed in the Cabrini orphanage in West Park/Esopus, New York, and remained there until 1931 when Luigi's brother, Quinto, sent for her to join his family in Greenwich Village. *(Courtesy the Tanzilo/Faiola family)*

Severing the Community. The North End of Boston, Massachusetts, played an important part in the American Revolution. By the late nineteenth century, however, this area was the Little Italy of Boston, and Faneuil Hall was an important market site. But after World War II, Boston decided that it needed an arterial highway. Planners routed it through the North End severing Faneuil Hall (foreground of picture) from the neighborhood. It also obliterated the 1907 Hanover Street Station of the Post Office. After 1911, immigrants had access to the U.S. Postal Savings system, which was similar to the one they knew in Italy. Some of the postal clerks spoke Italian and others learned enough to assist the patrons, typically immigrant women, accompanied by their babies, who made deposits or had interest added to their accounts. The new highway opened to traffic in 1959. The city's planning board labeled the area along Poplar, Chambers, Everett, Lowell, Blossom, and adjacent streets in the North End as an "obsolete neighborhood." Buildings would be demolished in this densely populated part of Boston to make room for multistory-elevator apartment buildings and open areas. While city officials considered the area blighted, the inhabitants who had migrated from urban villages in Italy to re-create a close-knit largely Italian community within Boston did not agree. *(Courtesy Boston Public Library, Print Department, 02146; Leslie Jones)*

Urban Renewal Condemns a Treasured Past. In the early 1960s, hundreds of people who lived in an eighty-three acre section of southwest Portland, Oregon, were displaced from their homes and businesses. This area, roughly four blocks wide and fourteen blocks long, had served as a predominately Jewish and Italian neighborhood nestled near the Civic Auditorium. Italian families living close-by often hosted dinners for visiting Italian opera singers who performed in the auditorium. As the city was formulating the Portland Development Commission in 1959, property values in the area began to fall. Residents protested Portland Urban Renewal's staffs' description of the area as "blighted and economically isolated" and claimed that these very pronouncements precipitated the neighborhood's decline. This photo records the demolition of a four-story apartment house at SW Third and Montgomery, c. 1964. The renewal project, designed by Skidmore, Owings & Merrill, was hailed as a breakthrough in urban design that complemented the natural landscape. Saint Michael the Archangel Church, built by the Italians in 1901 at SW Mill and Fourth Avenue to replace a chapel they had been using since 1894, remains the sole witness to a once vibrant ethnic past. *(Courtesy Oregon Historical Society, image # CN007085)*

Somber Despair. One thousand workers, mostly Italian immigrants, attend the founding meeting of the Union of Injured Workers (UIW), May 19, 1974, at Bloor Collegiate Institute, Toronto, Ontario. On this Sunday, entire families came as witness to the reality that *"L'America non è oro; è lavoro. E il santodollaro non è altro che dolore"* (America is not gold; it is work. And the sacred dollar is nothing but pain). They sought changes in the labor standards enforced by the Workers' Compensation Board (WCB). Italian workers, the predominant immigrant group in heavy construction, despaired that, when injured on the job, they received insufficient compensation and lower than adequate disability assessments and had limited recourse for appeal. There were many reports of unfair actions against workers. For example, Saverio Vardaro, injured when the roof collapsed at the construction site where he worked, charged that the WCB doctors used drugs like LSD and truth serum to prove that his injuries were largely psychosomatic and that he should return to work. After eight years, Saverio, with the help of the UIW, won his case and was declared fully disabled, which qualified him for monthly insurance payments. However, no one could compensate for the loss of dignity and physical impairment these workers suffered. (© *Vincenzo Pietropaolo*)

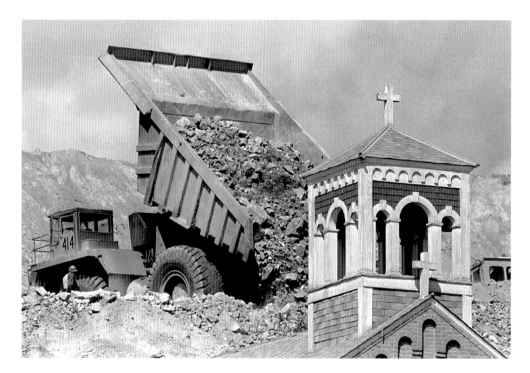

Requiem for a Community. About 1960, the Anaconda Company decided to expand its operations in Butte, Montana, with open-pit mining. The company's decision doomed the predominately Italian Meaderville neighborhood. Family-owned homes sat on company land, and Anaconda started buying up all the buildings in 1963. Digging the pit continued day and night, creating dirt and noise. People had to move to new undeveloped areas and assume the burden of installing water and sewer lines. The community sent protests to elected officials, but the company diverted their "inspection tour" of the devastation by inviting them to a popular café. The final mass was said at St. Helena Catholic Church in 1964 before the building was moved to another location, where it is part of the World Museum of Mining. In this photograph, Holy Savior Church, along with its school and nun's residence, is being buried intact by rock excavated from the pit in August 1979. Holy Savior had served residents of Meaderville and the predominately Croatian McQueen neighborhood in Butte. During the 1960s, Italian national parish churches in Milwaukee, Wisconsin, and St. Paul, Minnesota, were demolished to make way for highway construction. *(Courtesy Walter Hinick)*

Engulfing the Land. The Genzale family had been farming twenty acres of land in the Sunnyside neigborhood of Burien, Washington, since the 1930s. Frank Genzale's grandparents, Francesco and Angelina, and his father, Tony, had emigrated from Calore, Avellino in the 1920s. His mother, Antoinette Camerota, emigrated from Atena Lucana, Salerno. Besides farming, the Genzales sold their produce at Pike Place Market. In the 1970s, the Port of Seattle bought fifteen acres of the land as part of Sea-Tac (Seattle/Tacoma) Airport's noise mitigation program. In this 1999 photo, Frank Genzale works on the remaining five acres of his family farm, which is about to be incorporated into a third runway for the airport. Frank reasoned with the authorities: "Look, we don't really want the money, what we want is a [replacement] farm." Unfortunately, there was no available farmland with such favorable growing conditions within easy commute to the market. Finally accepting the inevitable, Frank sought a financial compensation that would equal the development value of the land. *(Courtesy* The Highline Times, *Robinson Newspapers)*

Relaxing with *Paesani*, c. 1914. Neighbors in Priest River, Idaho's "Italian Settlement" sample homemade beer at Charlie Naccarato's house. Frank Rizzo has his hand on the bucket, Angelo Naccarato is seated on the other side. *Second row, left to right:* Joe Naccarato, George Naccarato, Tony Albi, Henry Falsetto (holding the cane). *Back row, left to right:* Brothers Marion and Delio (last name unknown), Charlie Naccarato, Tony Naccarato, Tony Lorenzo. Sport relaxes in front of the barrel. *(Courtesy Priest River, Idaho, Museum)*

Remembering the Departed. The Ventura/Cairo family visits the grave of Roberto Ventura at Mount Carmel Cemetery, Chicago, Illinois, on Memorial/ Decoration Day, 1914. Born in Chicago to Maria (Cairo) and Frank Ventura, from Gesuiti, Cosenza, Roberto died of pneumonia a few weeks after his second birthday. In Italy, November 1 is All Saints Day, the traditional time to visit gravesites. But the Ventura family embraced the tradition of their new country and decorated the grave with American flags in a tribute to their American-born son Roberto. *Left to right:* Frank Cairo, Raffella Ventura (seven), Maria Cairo Ventura, Joe Ventura (five), Frank Ventura. *(Courtesy Jeffrey Caracci)*

Youthful Exuberance. Vickie Toffoli, left, kicks up her heels with fellow office workers at the California Wine Association (CWA) at Point Molate in Richmond, California, 1918. The Winehaven facility was the home of the CWA, then the largest winery in California. Marc Fontana served as its president. Vickie left Venice with her mother and three siblings in 1911 to join her father who had been working with other Italians at the winery for several years. Vickie worked as a stenographer in the office and is pictured here with Vera Glasby, Carrie Bariros, Violet Holt, and Sheila Murphey. Vickie's mastery of English and clerical skills, as well as her exuberant spirit, contributed to her selection later that year as "Queen of Richmond." *(Courtesy The Richmond Museum of History Collection)*

Urban Adventure. Eight-year-old Rita Blundi enjoys a pony ride in front of her parents' home on Ellsworth Street in south Philadelphia, Pennsylvania, 1923. Rita's parents had to pay not only for the cost of the ride, but also for the picture. Most peasant families considered such activities frivolous, but as wage earners, parents could choose to indulge in such treats. This photo might have been sent to relatives back in Italy to document a new life of prosperity. Rita's father, Angelo, decided to ignore the traditional naming sequence followed by most Italian families. Since Angelo's mother was named, Letizia, the first-born daughter should have been baptized with that name. Instead, Angelo named his daughter Rita because of his great devotion to St. Rita. The nearby parish church, built in 1915, was also dedicated to St. Rita and is now a national shrine in south Philadelphia. *(Courtesy Vincent F. Blundi)*

Thanksgiving. Immigrant families adopted and adapted American customs. Here the Candeloras of New Haven, Connecticut, celebrate Thanksgiving in 1938. Salvatore Candelora (face partially visible on left) was found on the steps of a church in Atrani, Salerno, by Sister Maria Bernese. He was named Salvatore Canneloro and raised in an orphanage until adopted by the Esposito family who brought him to the United States, c. 1897. Salvatore married Carmelina Amarone (from the area of Atrani), and they had fourteen children but only ten survived. (Each child's birth certificate has a different variation of the Candelora/Canneloro surname). Salvatore worked as a locksmith for the Sargent Company in New Haven. Carmelina presents the turkey, the centerpiece of the meal. The Thanksgiving dinner also included pasta, an essential ingredient for any celebration. *(Courtesy Laura Castiglione Sabatino)*

Casual Pastime. Italian Americans relax together on Decatur Street, near the levee along the Mississippi River, in New Orleans, Louisiana, c. 1938. The men in the center appear to be playing the traditional game of *morra*. In this ancient game, dating back to the early Greeks, the player shouts out his guess of the total number of fingers extended by himself and his opponent at the same time. The numbers range from zero to ten, with zero symbolized by a closed fist. The competitive aspects of the game can escalate into confrontations, but usually the loser treats the winner to a glass of wine. Some areas of Italian settlement, like Hazelton, Pennsylvania, sponsored *morra* tournaments as do Italian towns, like Barga, Lucca. *(Courtesy The Historic New Orleans Collection, accession # 1979.212.32)*

Mayor Robert Maestri at Home. Robert Maestri, New Orleans' first Italian-American mayor, watches his mother, Angele Maestri, cook in her kitchen at 2602 Esplanade Street, 1938. The mayor and wife Hilda Bertoniere, who had been his secretary for thirteen years, lived with Angele. Francis and Angele Maestri emigrated from Italy in the 1880s. In 1896, Francis and his two brothers opened the Maestri Furniture Company at Rampart Street on the corner of Iberville Street. Robert inherited his father's business. He also invested in real estate and acquired substantial property in the city. In 1926, Governor Huey Long appointed him head of Louisiana's Conservation Commission, which controlled production quotas in Louisiana's oil industry. He served until 1936 when Mayor T. Semmes Walmsley of New Orleans suddenly resigned. Robert ran for mayor without opposition and served until 1946. He traveled around the city seeking out problems and welcomed both complaints and suggestions at open-door sessions in his office. His personal governing style, delivered in his colorful New Orleans accent, and folksy manner of expression gained him a loyal following. *(Courtesy Collection of The Louisiana State Museum, Gift of Ms. Roberta Maestri, 1986.103.2.101)*

Specialty Trade. Alfred Grasseschi, born in Santa Maria Del Giudice, Lucca, works with his twenty-five-year-old son Maurice in his shoe repair and boot shop in Hayward, California, c. 1946 (note the NRA sign in the background). Alfred had worked as a shoe- and boot-maker in Italy. First working in the brickyards in Niles, California, he sought better paying work at the Anaconda copper mines in Montana. He moved his family to Hayward in 1931 and opened his shop. The family baked bread on the wood-heated brick oven Alfred constructed in their backyard. All of his children, Maurice, Romeo, Al, and Rudy, worked in the shop after school as soon as they were able. The business, called The Cobblers, is operated by Rudy, age seventy-two, and his sons Dino and Rodney and Dino's two sons, Dominic, twenty-two, and Kenneth, nineteen. Such generational continuity of skills often crossed the ocean with the immigrants. Giovanni Mastracchio, who came to New York City from Sassinoro, Benevento, in 1921, represented the fifth generation of his family as shoemaker. In 1960, Giovanni invited his nephew, Antonio, to join him. Currently Antonio has a shoe repair shop in Ossining, New York. *(Courtesy Rudy Grasseschi)*

Urban Games. Joe Granitto, age thirteen, plays stickball on West Eleventh Street near Avenue T in the Bensonhurst neighborhood of Brooklyn, New York, 1946. Before World War II, popular New York street games were punch ball, box ball, ringalevio, roller skate hockey, touch football, and johnny on the pony. More organized sports were boxing (every night during the 1936-1937 summer), gymnastics, and swimming at Coney Island. Stickball became popular in the 1940s. *(Courtesy Nicholas Granitto)*

Singing Italian Songs. Tenor Umberto Rovere, accompanied by his friend Guido Deiro (the accordionist), sings in his popular night club the Paris Inn, 1947. Located on North Broadway (in the Italian quarter) in Los Angeles, California, the club featured singing waiters. The waiters sang operatic chorus songs like the "Libiamo" (Let Us Drink) from *La Traviata,* and the "Toreador Song" from *Carmen.* But they also sang popular tunes of the World War II era. A weekly radio program was broadcast from the premises. During World War II, Bert and Guido entertained Italian POWs, who also enjoyed Italian dishes prepared by immigrant women. *(Courtesy Count Guido Roberto Deiro)*

Sunday Memories, Waldwick, New Jersey. Members of the Totta family enjoy a daylong repast in their Waldwick, New Jersey, backyard in 1949. Luigi Totta emigrated from San Giovanni Rotondo, Foggia, and his wife, Andreana Ragosta, from Nola, Campania. Eating outside did not signal a light meal. Andreana, who worked in the silk mills, prepared different types of sauces to complement the rigatoni, ziti, and cavatelli she served with the Pecorino Romano cheese she hand-grated each week. Her granddaughter, Andrea Mistretta Quaranta recalls Andreana (aka 'Ndrianella)"making meat-based sauces with tomatoes from their own garden. . . . She could pick weeds and make a gourmet *minestra* soup. . . . Sometimes she would throw flavorful wild wood mushrooms into *coniglio cacciatore* [made with rabbits caught eating the greens in Luigi's huge garden.]" Inspired by these splendid meals, Andreana's daughter, Rose, wrote this winning motto for the Buitoni Macaroni Company's contest, c. 1960: "FROM ANTIPASTO TO SPUMONI—IT'S NOT A MEAL WITHOUT MACARONI." *(Courtesy Andrea Mistretta Quaranta)*

Family Pugilists. Carmine Basilio, 1955 Welterweight Champion, tosses onions with his prizefighter nephew Billy Backus during the 1964 Onion Olympics festival in Canastota, New York. Billy began boxing in the early 1960s, and in 1970, he became the Welterweight Champion of the World when he defeated the then champion Jose Napoles by a technical knockout, surprising and delighting many of his fans who never thought he would win. His uncle Carmine, watching from ringside, exclaimed, "Billy winning the world title is the best thing ever to happen in my life, even better than me winning the world title." *(Courtesy Rocchina Vecchio Russitano, American Italian Heritage Association)*

Outdoor Recreation. Since the 1950s, there have been tournaments at the bocce ball courts at East Portal Park in east Sacramento, California. This picture was taken between 1955 and 1960. While some thought this traditional Italian game might disappear with the deaths of second-generation Italian Americans, its popularity has continued to attract both Italian and non-Italian players. A recent documentary, *Watch the Pallino,* tells the story of how the tradition of bocce was introduced to the small mining town of Toluca, Illinois, and evolved into one of the largest tournaments in the country. *(Courtesy Sacramento Archive and Museum Collection Center, 1983/146/slide #29 Italians, Sacramento Ethnic Survey Collection)*

Nature's Beauty. Claurinda Giannantonia Iannidinardo tends lilies, her favorite flower, at her home in Rochester, New York, c. 1950. She loved to grow flowers and vegetables. In 1902, she left Ripalimosani, Campobasso, with her two young children to join her husband, Angelo, who worked as a tailor for Hart, Schaffner, and Marx in Rochester. Author Jerre Mangione described the desire of immigrants in Rochester to own "a home with a 'yarda' in which to grow vegetables and flowers. . . . [They] moved into the neighborhoods where real estate values had begun plummeting as soon as the first Jewish, Italian, and Polish immigrant families moved in. One neighborhood, formerly known as 'Little Dublin' . . . [became known as] 'Mount Allegro.'" This area served as the setting for Mangione's semi-autobiographical novel by the same name. *(Courtesy the Iannidinardo family)*

New Discoveries, April 1954. Giuseppina, age fourteen Salvatore, twelve, and Prisco Vacca, eighteen, from Calore, Avellino, sample their first ice cream soda (chocolate) upon their arrival in Seattle, Washington. Antonio D'Ambrosio, a cousin who escorted them from Italy, stands behind. The children's aunt and uncle, Madeline and Giuseppe Vacca, adopted them in 1949. However, they waited five years (because of quota restrictions) before they could welcome them to Seattle. The teenagers decided they preferred Seattle bakery bread to the heavier bread made from the wheat raised on their family farm in Italy. Prisco went to work while Giuseppina and Salvatore attended school. After school, Salvatore helped his cousin Pre, owner of Pre's Garden Patch. In the summer months, after the store closed, he would help park cars for baseball games at Sick's Stadium. By age fifteen, Salvatore had saved $250 and won a $100 U.S. Savings Bond as Junior Dealer of the Month, delivering the morning *Seattle Post-Intelligencer.* The children's father, Vincenzo, emigrated to Seattle in 1963 to work with his brother, Giuseppe, in construction. In 1966, the children's mother, Amalia; brother, Antonio; and two sisters, Sofia and Elisabetta, completed the unification of the family. *(Courtesy* Seattle Post-Intelligencer, *Stuart Hertz, photographer)*

A Rising Star. Vincent J. Riggi and his son, Vincent S. Riggi, mark the beginning of the younger Vincent's freshman year at the University of Pennsylvania. Born in San Cataldo, Caltanissetta, Vincent J. Riggi arrived in Pennsylvania in 1902, at age fourteen, with his mother to join his brother and father. His sisters would come later. He had studied barbering in Italy, and he opened his own shop next to the family house in Throop, Pennsylvania. When the family moved to Dunmore, Pennsylvania, he opened a new barber shop and dreamed of becoming an architect. At age twenty-four, Vincent went back to school; he obtained his high-school diploma two years later and entered the University of Pennsylvania. He studied architecture for five years, supporting himself with work as a barber. He graduated in 1929, and by 1933, he had established his own architectural firm, best known for designs of churches, rectories, convents, and schools. Vincent J. Riggi married Irene Napolitano and they raised two sons, Dr. Stephen J. Riggi, a research scientist who became president of a national pharmaceutical company, and Vincent S. Riggi, who graduated from the University of Pennsylvania School of Architecture in 1958 and assumed management of his father's firm in 1961. Currently he runs the business with his son, Vincent, who serves as director of operations. The firm has received numerous national and local awards for its innovative designs. *(Courtesy Vincent S. Riggi)*

Access to Leadership. Mike Prelee interviews Eleanor Roosevelt for WERE in Cleveland, Ohio, 1960, where she received an award for her work on the Universal Declaration of Human Rights. That same year Mike interviewed John Kennedy during the Minnesota primary. Mike was born in Sharon, Pennsylvania, to Joe (Prili) (from Paliano, Frosinone) and Mary Rose Prelee (from Baia e Latina, Caserta). During the Korean War, he worked for Armed Forces Radio. After being discharged, Mike returned to Sharon and then went to Akron, Ohio, to apply for a job as a street reporter at the radio station WCUE. His father, a steel worker, gave him advice and support: "Here's twenty dollars for the bus, go get the job. When I came to this country, I couldn't speak the English language and you, my son, are going to make your living from it." Joe tuned in for years to listen to his son report from Akron and Cleveland. Mike's parents were especially proud when he interviewed Eleanor Roosevelt. Although Mike's "Italian look" often seemed a handicap for media positions in the '50s and '60s, the owner of the radio station in Cleveland, Jim Story, who happened to be blind, told Mike that if he increased the WJW news program ratings in Cleveland, he'd send him to New York. Fifteen years after Joe's twenty-dollar send-off, Mike became a news director in New York City at WHN and later for NBC and WNEW. *(Courtesy the Prelee (Prili) of Sharon, Pennsylvania)*

Traditional Foods. The Sciorra family (standing, left to right): Joseph, Nicholas, John, Anna, and (sitting) Enrico Sciorra savor the array of Anna's Christmas cookies in their Brooklyn, New York, home, 1981. Both Anna and Enrico were born in the United States, and, as children, they returned with their families to Italy. As adults in the 1950s, Anna left Formia, Latina, and Enrico left Carunchio, Chieti, to settle in New York City. The confections pictured here reflect continuity, ethnic interaction, and acculturation. *Back row, left to right:* bows (fried serrated dough in shape of bows that Anna learned to make in Italy), Tre colori (baked layered cookies from a recipe Anna clipped from a magazine). *Front row, left to right:* zeppoli (fried dough, served with powdered sugar or honey, learned in Italy), struffoli (fried dough, served with honey, Anna adopted from an Italian friend in New York), snowballs (baked dough with powdered sugar that Anna also got from a magazine). The variety of traditional holiday sweets differed from region to region and sometimes from town to town in Italy. *(© Martha Cooper)*

Country Style. The youth group of the Pisticci Club enjoys an American-style Corn Roast and Barn Dance in Woodbridge, Ontario, in 1978. Woodbridge is now part of Vaughn, a suburb of Toronto, and this barn is now part of a shopping plaza. Woodbridge is a predominately Italian-Canadian neighborhood, with the majority of its homes built by Canadian Italian-owned construction companies. The Pisticci Club of Canada was organized in 1960 by post World War II immigrants—brick masons, laborers, steelworkers, hairdressers, shoemakers, tailors, railroad workers, miners, and factory workers. In 1972, they established the Pisticci Youth Club of Canada to attract the younger generation who had different interests and expectations. *(Courtesy Pisticci Club & Pisticci Youth Club of Canada)*

Culinary Ties. Three-and-a-half-year-old Christine Bennett makes cappelletti at her great aunt Lena Vellani DeNucci's home in Columbus, Ohio, 1981. In 1915, the Vellani family, from Canolo di Correggio and Bibbiano (both in Reggio-Emilia), transplanted this traditional regional dish to their new home. These "little hats," modeled after the tri-corner hats of Napoleon's army, are most often made and eaten at Christmas, Easter, and other important occasions. The pasta generally is stuffed with meat (beef, pork, or veal), Parmigiano-Reggiano, grated breadcrumbs, and salt and cooked in chicken broth. Each cook has his or her own personal variation. Lena's recipe also includes grated mortadella, egg, and a little nutmeg. Christine's mother, Amy, treasures her memories of making cappelletti. "Of course everyone wanted to eat them, but not everyone wanted to make them. So my mother [Helen Vellani Sabino] would tease that you got to eat as many as you made. I remember my mother entering cappelletti in a Pillsbury cooking contest. She didn't win, and thought it was because no one took the time to make cappelletti to test the recipe. [Years later when] I picked up my youngest daughter Jenny from preschool the day before Thanksgiving, the teacher asked me what we were going to eat on Thanksgiving . . . Jenny, of course, [had] said, cappelletti. The teacher couldn't understand . . . Jenny was confused because she thought everyone ate cappelletti before the turkey on Thanksgiving." *(Barbara DiNucci Hendrickson, for the Vellani and DiNucci families)*

Adapting Tradition. Dominick Russitano holds a box of grapes while his brother, Tony (second from left), his nephews, Tony (far left) and Alfred (second from right), and son, Anthony (far right), look eager to begin wine making, 1983. Dominick began making wine under his father's supervision in 1953. He remembered how the "old Italians made their own wine and kept it in jugs in the ditches between the muckland fields" so they could drink during breaks as they cultivated the onion fields in Canastota, New York. Dominick explains, "The men would go fishing on Chittenango Creek and toss a rope across the water so they could pass the jug of wine back and forth between the banks of the creek. Then, as now, they would compete for recipes and critique each other's wine and cry over the bad barrel that was poured out of the glass." Their sons participated in this ritual. Dominick has modified his father's recipe, and for one barrel of wine he uses, "fourteen boxes of Muscat grapes, six boxes of alicanti, and a lot of tender, loving care." Domenick's wine won fifth place at a state fair wine competition in 2005. He waits until San Martino Day (November 11) to tap his wine, following his Uncle Lawrence's advice: "If you tap your wine on that day, the barrel will never go dry." *(Courtesy Rocchina Russitano)*

Dancing the Tarantella. Each year people from the village of Civita di Boiano, Campobasso, celebrate the Feast of the Madonna della Libera at the end of August. Here, in 1998, an elderly couple dances the tarantella in the field of Mary Lake Monastery, in King City, Ontario, just north of Toronto. The setting is perfect for such celebrations—partially a working farm, with a large modern church, a hilltop wooden chapel, and open fields. During the summer, different *paesani* groups organize their individual town's feast day to venerate their town's saint at the monastery. The feasts begin with a mass followed by a procession from the church, which dominates the landscape like a cathedral in the wilderness, to the hilltop chapel, and back. Next, they have a picnic, replete with regional specialties, followed by bocce, song, and dance. Sometimes the group invites a professional choir who dress in traditional costumes and sing traditional songs from all over Italy. *(© Vincenzo Pietropaolo)*

Honoring Ancestors. Marilee and Luciano Iorizzo and family celebrate their fiftieth wedding anniversary in 2002 in Alexandria Bay, Thousand Islands, New York. By adding photos of (left to right) Luciano's grandfather, Luciano, his great-grandfather, Giovanni, and his father, John, the group spans six generations. Marilee and Luciano's five children and ten grandchildren complete the genealogical line. Giovanni, a businessman, came from Ariano Villanuova, Benevento, to New York City in the 1870s. His son, Luciano, a stonemason, arrived later and worked on the Croton Dam. His grandson, John, was a factory worker and jazz musician. Marilee, of Native-American, English, and German heritage, added ethnic diversity to the family. Their children chose spouses of Irish, Polish, Czech, French-Canadian, and British descent. Although the fifth- and sixth-generation family members achieved high levels of education, none of the boys of the first, second, or third generation went beyond high school. Surprisingly second- and third-generation daughters aimed high—one second-generation daughter received a Ph.D. in educational administration and two others taught history and English respectively. One third-generation daughter became a physician and another became a pharmacist, an exception to the generalization that females were taught only domestic skills in preparation for marriage and a life as a homemaker. *(Courtesy Dr. Luciano J. Iorizzo)*

Pasta Dynasty. Governor John Hoeven of North Dakota (right) thanks Luke Marano, Jr. (left) and his father Luke Marano, Sr. for expanding their wheat milling operations, which brought jobs and income to his state, 2003. Plans for their Philadelphia Macaroni Company's second plant (completed in 2004) are displayed on the easel. Luke, Sr.'s grandfather, C. Antonio Marano, came from Montella, Avellino, to Philadelphia, Pennsylvania, before 1900. He operated a variety of businesses but specialized in food, including wholesale and retail imported macaroni. Antonio established the Philadelphia Macaroni Company (PMC) and immediately solicited business from the Campbell Soup Company located across the river in Camden, New Jersey. Campbell continues to purchase products from the company. Other companies that patronize PMC are Betty Crocker, Lipton, Ragu, Annie's, and Marie Callender's. The company also introduced the ramen noodle to the United States. PMC's headquarters remain in Philadelphia although the company has macaroni plants in Spokane, Washington, and Grand Forks, North Dakota. Presently, Luke's son, Luke, Jr., and his grandson, Luke J. Urban (representing the fifth generation), work together to guide their company in the twenty-first century. *(Courtesy Luke Marano, Sr.)*

Cross-Cultural Christening. Nicole Carrington is held by her godfather and uncle, Joseph Gerardi, after her christening in March 2005, at All Saints Episcopal Church in Baldwin, New York. Nicole's parents, Mike Carrington (who took the photo) and Nancy Gerardi Carrington (middle row, third from left), whose four grandparents came from Sicily, met while attending the New York Institute of Technology on Long Island. Nancy's sister-in-law, Tammy Gerardi, Tammy, stands in the middle row left; Nancy's father, Rosario (Sardi), is in the middle rear, with one hand on his daughter, Jane Gerardi (Nicole's godmother), and the other on his wife Josephine's shoulder. Mike's mother, Christine, and his sister, Lisa Bundy, complete the row. Mike grew up in Columbia, Maryland. Nancy recalled that at her wedding her father "gave a pretty funny toast; in one part he said that he had Mike investigated before the wedding and, of course, the place went nervously silent. . . . Then he finished with saying he found out that Mike wasn't Italian! Well the place just roared with laughter." Nancy makes traditional Italian cookies during the holidays. When they spend Thanksgiving with their relatives in Maryland, they enjoy a traditional Southern meal. *(Courtesy Michael S. and Nancy Gerardi Carrington)*

Common Origins. Members of the *Lega Abruzzesi* Lodge, a mutual benefit society, gather in front of the mine company store at Dawson, New Mexico, c. 1910. The founding members came from the Abruzzo region of Italy and used their common heritage to forge a safety net of financial assistance in times of personal crisis, e.g., mine accidents, sickness, and family deaths. Eventually the lodge opened membership to all Italian immigrants. Lodge member Francesco Latuda (far right at top, full view in a dark suit), from Magnago, Milano, ran the company store and saloon. He dealt fairly with the mine families who appreciated his empathy for their well-being. Miners faced dangers every day so the establishment of a common fund to help in time of need was essential. *(Courtesy Charles D. Latuda)*

Worker's Association. The Scavenger's Protection Association members accompany the body of a member in a funeral procession on Columbus Avenue in San Francisco, California, c. 1910. Emigrants from the region of Liguria, who owned shares in the Scavenger Company and worked as refuge collectors in that city, formed the mutual benefit association. *(Courtesy Alessandro Baccari Historical Photographic Collection)*

National Affiliation. Vincenzo Sellaro, M.D., and five other Italian immigrants, founded *L'Ordine Figli d'Italia,* the Order Sons of Italy in America, in New York City's Little Italy, June 22, 1905. Other groups of immigrants formed local lodges of OSIA across America. OSIA provided services for its members, ranging from health and death benefits to assistance with becoming American citizens. Many lodges established schools to teach English and to offer citizenship preparation classes. This photo shows a meeting of the Giuseppe Garibaldi Lodge #211 in Brooklyn, New York, in 1913. OSIA promoted pride and respect for Italian heritage along with a commitment to assimilate. Today the organization continues to promote OSIA's original objectives, monitors and protests the defamation of Italian Americans, publicizes the achievements of Italian Americans, and contributes to a variety of humanitarian, educational, and cultural programs. *(Courtesy Dona DeSanctis for the OSIA)*

Photograph was donated by new on-line member John Scafordi who is joining the new Manhattan Lodge. His grandfather was a member of the Giuseppe Garibaldi Lodge #211 formed in 1913 in Brooklyn.

Family Haven. Immigrants from about ten towns in the region of Friuli established the Venetian Club in Laverock, Pennsylvania, c. 1924. Most of the members lived in Chestnut Hill and worked as tile layers, stonemasons, and in construction. *La Barracca* (the shed), at Cheltenham Avenue and Waverly Road, was constructed on the site of an old stone quarry. This social club encouraged sports, such as tennis and bocce, and sponsored banquets. Club membership was never exclusively *friulano;* Irish, German, and emigrants from other parts of Italy were welcome. The club events were especially popular during the days of Pennsylvania's blue laws, which prohibited the sale of alcohol after midnight and on Sundays. In 1930, the club moved to a brick building on Germantown Avenue in Chestnut Hill. Today, bowling, pool, shuffleboard, card playing, and other events, such as dinner dances and marching in Philadelphia's Mummers Parade, rather than the bocce shown in this 1920s photo, engage the membership. An annual polenta dinner continues the *friulano* tradition. *(Courtesy The Venetian Social Club)*

The Dante Club. The Dante Club celebrates the grand opening of its renovated building at 1511 P Street, in Sacramento, California, 1926. The group started meeting in 1923 at St. Mary's Italian Parish Church with the purpose of encouraging music, drama, art, literature, athletics, and social activities among the immigrant population and to ease their entry into American society. A woman's auxiliary was initiated in 1926 to "encourage . . . Americanization and good citizenship; to engage in religious, charitable, social, and educational activities; to encourage music, drama, art and literature." The auxiliary supported the opera and raised money for hospital equipment. As one of the dominant clubs in Sacramento, the Dante Club sponsored a variety of events such as dinners, fencing tournaments, pool and card games, bocce, and soccer and baseball teams. Members remembered that bets on the bocce games ranged from three hundred to one thousand dollars during the 1920s and '30s. The members built new quarters in 1960, and today the club operates as rental property open to anyone wishing to hold a dinner, dance, or wedding reception. *(Courtesy Sacramento Archives and Museum Collection Center, 1983/146/Slide#23 Italians, Sacramento Ethnic Survey Collection)*

Provincial Ties. Emigrants from the province of Siracusa, and especially the town of Ferla, formed the Siracusa Lodge, c. 1920, in Wilmington, Delaware. The first meetings were held in private homes. Later the lodge purchased a lot and built this structure on East Fourth Street to accommodate a membership of approximately two hundred. This all-male mutual-benefit society did not have any religious affiliation. The lodge sponsored social events to include women and children. Families used the building for wedding receptions and special family gatherings to play cards and socialize. *(Courtesy Estate of Elva del Grosso Lentini)*

Combining Business with Pleasure. The Cristoforo Colombo Club of Herrin, Illinois, was started before 1906 and lasted until 1974. Most of the two hundred members were Italian miners, carpenters, bricklayers, and small-business owners. Each member purchased shares in the club's co-op—a tavern and restaurant with a dance hall above that featured big bands. Called the CC Club, it was a popular spot in Herrin and members earned quarterly dividends. Newcomers might join only if a member died or sold his share. Another organization, the *Lombardia* Society of Herrin, owned a grocery co-op and peddled produce throughout the town. *(Courtesy Bob Carnaghi, www.cuggionesi.com, bob_carnaghi@cuggionesi.com)*

Bridging Generations. In the 1930s, the Sons of Italy Lodge in Framingham, Massachusetts, established the Maria Montessori Junior Lodge for teenage women. Four cousins in the Cella family are in this 1937 photo of the precision drill team: Ermina Cella (front row, first on left), Bob Agostini (the group's trainer, far right), Verna Sartori (second row, third from the right), and Alice Ghilani (the group's captain, first row center). The team competed against other teams in the region and won the trophy displayed here. *(Courtesy Irma Crocetti Carter)*

Reformation. The Italian Sons and Daughters of America enjoy their bowling league banquet and dance in Pittsburgh, Pennsylvania, 1941. In 1928, six Sons of Italy lodges in Pittsburgh decided to merge and hold meetings in English. The Grand Lodge of the State of Pennsylvania rejected this action and expelled the dissident members. By 1930, those western Pennsylvanian Italians who had left the Sons of Italy had established a new mutual aid society—the Italian Sons and Daughters of America (ISDA). John S. Aldisert, Pennsylvania State president, who was among the expelled dissenters, sits to the immediate left of the floral piece on the head table. After World War II, Aldisert became national president of the ISDA when new lodges were created in Cleveland and West Virginia. The ensuing legal and polemic struggle caused a nationwide division of the order that was not healed until 1943. ISDA still functions as a separate national organization of some two hundred local lodges, mainly in seven Midwestern states. An effort in 1990 to reconcile the separation was unsuccessful. *(Courtesy Italian American Collection, Senator John Heinz History Center of Western Pennsylvania)*

Cultural Connections. *Calcio Squadra del Club Italico* (*Italico* Club's soccer team) of Trail, British Columbia, pose for this group picture in 1960. They played in soccer tournaments that included Nelson, Grand Forks, and Cranbrook, British Columbia, and Spokane, Washington. The club was organized in 1959 by newly arrived immigrants to Canada to promote Italian culture, arts, and athletics. Besides soccer, the club presented dramas, Italian films, and invited local artists to perform. *(Courtesy Carlo Piccolo)*

Service Above Self. Dr. Antony P. Vastola, M.D., an emigrant from San Valentino Torio, Salerno, gathered fifteen men at his home at 103 North Main Street, Waterbury, Connecticut, in October 1922, and founded UNICO (Italian for unique), a civic organization of Italian Americans. Dr. Vastola believed that Italians in America needed an opportunity to counteract the negative stereotypes following WWI and the Sacco-Vanzetti trial, which questioned the immigrants' loyalty to their adopted country. The existing service organizations, such as the Elks, did not, as a rule, welcome Italians as members. The purpose of UNICO was to unite Italian-American professionals and businessmen and motivate them to become more civic-minded, placing service before self in promoting charitable, patriotic, and educational programs. In the ensuing years, the meaning of UNICO became an acronym that stood for Unity, Neighborliness, Integrity, Charity, and Opportunity. In this photo commemorating the groups' fiftieth anniversary (1972), UNICO National president Dr. John X. Basile stands second from left and founder Dr. Anthony P. Vastola stands at the far left. In recent years, UNICO has broadened its focus from charitable and scholarship support to endowing chairs of Italian and Italian studies at a number of universities. *(Reprinted with permission of UNICO National, Inc.)*

Working Fellowship. The Columbia Association of New York City's fire department marches in the 2006 Columbus Day parade. In 1934, Fire Commissioner John McElligott and Deputy Fire Commissioner Francis X. Giaccono approved a request from Italian-American firefighters for a program to instruct Italian immigrants, especially those in tenement buildings, what to do in case of fire. Fire Captain John Capillo of Engine 28 helped draft a simple set of rules to distribute. They then recruited other firefighters of Italian descent to implement the program. Ultimately the association expanded "to promote and provide opportunities for the social and fraternal betterment" of its members. In 2007, the Columbia Association had three thousand members, nearly one-quarter of the entire fire department. *(Courtesy Vincent A. Tummino, ambassador, International Columbia Association)*

Immigrant Politicians. Vincent Palmisano, an emigrant from Termini Imerese, Palermo, ran for city council in Baltimore, Maryland, in 1915. Italian Americans in the third-ward Democratic club formed a power base for his career. He was elected to the U.S. House of Representatives in 1926. Ethnic loyalty in addition to personal interaction with political leaders created a voting bloc that continued to elect Baltimore's Italian-American candidates to city and national offices. *(Courtesy The Maryland Historical Society, Baltimore, Maryland)*

Visiting Congressman. Fiorello Henry La Guardia of New York meets with Sam Raine, Sr. (left) and John Antonio (right) in Bessemer, Alabama, 1931. Both men, of Sicilian heritage, had distinguished themselves as resourceful community leaders. Raine amassed a fortune in real estate dealings and "retired" at age thirty-six. Antonio became Bessemer City Alderman in 1937 and was involved in establishing the TVA (Tennessee Valley Authority). La Guardia's reputation as an independent-minded politician preceded him. Born in New York City to an Italian father and a Jewish mother from Trieste, he felt comfortable in the city's multiethnic environment. He joined the Republican Party to challenge the Irish-controlled Democratic machine and served in Congress from 1916 to 1932 when he was defeated in the Democratic groundswell that put Franklin D. Roosevelt into the White House. La Guardia, however, became New York's first Italian-American mayor in 1933 and served until 1946. *(Courtesy Birmingham Public Library, Department of Archives and Manuscripts, Catalog # 829.3.2.76)*

United for Workers' Rights. Mayor Thomas D'Alessandro, Jr. of Baltimore, Maryland, stands shoulder to shoulder with Angela Bambace of the International Ladies Garment Workers' Union (ILGWU) at a strategy planning session in 1948. Charles Kreindler, ILGWU vice president, stands at the left. D'Alessandro, the son of emigrants from Abruzzo, supported the effective employer/employee negotiating procedures that the ILGWU advocated. Born to Italian parents in Santos, Brazil, Angela founded the first women's local in Baltimore in 1936. In 1956, she became the first and only Italian woman to become a vice president of the ILGWU. Her union supported D'Alessandro as a congressman (1938-1946) and later as mayor of Baltimore (1947-1959). The first Italian American to hold this office, D'Alessandro enjoyed wide support across the city. His son, Thomas D'Alessandro, III, served as mayor from 1967 to 1971. *(Courtesy Bambace Collection, Box 1 Folder 2, IM000644, Immigration History Research Center, University of Minnesota)*

First Italian-American Senator. John Orlando Pastore was born in the Italian neighborhood of Federal Hill in Providence, Rhode Island. His parents came from Potenza. In 1916, when his father died, John, who was nine, started working after school to support his family. Struggling to get ahead, he took night courses to complete his law degree. He was elected to Rhode Island's Assembly in 1934 and served as the state's assistant attorney general from 1937 to 1938 and from 1940 to 1944. Elected as lieutenant governor in 1944, John became governor in 1945 when Governor James Howard McGrath resigned to become U.S. solicitor general. He ran and won on his own in 1946 and was re-elected in 1948. Elected to the U.S. Senate with a landslide victory in 1950, he became the first Italian American to serve in that body. He combined political expertise and pride in his Italian-American heritage as a founder of the National Italian American Foundation. (*Courtesy* Italian Tribune)

Philadelphia's Mayor. Frank Rizzo gazes out from this mural at Eighth and Montrose Streets in South Philadelphia, Pennsylvania. Diane Keller created the mural in 1995. Born Francis Lazzaro Rizzo to Italian parents, Frank joined the police force in 1943, patrolled city streets, and distinguished himself as an energetic leader of vice squads. He became a pivotal figure during the grass roots activism of the 1960s by his confrontational stance toward groups such as the Black Panthers. His reputation for preventing disruption and rioting earned him the votes needed to become mayor in 1971. As the first Italian-American mayor of Philadelphia, he drew strong support from his South Philadelphia base. His administration took a conservative approach to social and economic issues. Although he was a Democrat, his support of Richard Nixon's re-election in 1972 brought federal contracts to the city. His supporters became known as Rizzocrats because they placed loyalty to leader above loyalty to party. The mural illustrates Rizzo's Italian ties and his roots in *bella vista* (Philadephia's name for Little Italy). This spot remains a popular backdrop for public appearances by political candidates. *(Courtesy Jerry Krase)*

Ethnic, Working-Class Advocate. Father Geno Baroni, Housing and Urban Development Assistant Secretary for Neighborhood Development, Consumer Affairs and Regulatory Functions, stands next to President Jimmy Carter on Air Force One during a trip to Kansas City, Missouri, in October 1979. Baroni was born in Acosta, Pennsylvania, to Italian immigrant parents. As a priest and social activist, he became active in community affairs and organized credit unions for the needy in Johnstown and Altoona, Pennsylvania. He was assigned to Washington, D.C., in 1960 to integrate the black and white (respectively) parishes of Saints Augustine and Paul. His emphasis on Catholic social doctrine, and his dedication to civil rights, impressed Attorney General Robert Kennedy, who recommended Baroni to become treasurer of the first Head Start Program in D.C. He became executive director of the Office of Urban Affairs of the Washington Archdiocese and then director of the Urban Task Force of the U.S. Catholic Conference. With the backing of the Ford Foundation, he established the National Center for Urban Ethnic Affairs in 1972. Its purpose was to rebuild traditional neighborhood institutions through community organization. In 1975, Baroni was instrumental in establishing the National Italian American Foundation in Washington, D.C., to work for Italian-American interests, and he served as its first president. In 1977, President Carter appointed him to work with inner-city groups. *(Courtesy Jimmy Carter Library)*

Star of Watergate. Congressman Peter Wallace Rodino and Essex County Clerk Nick Caputo campaign with 1972 Democratic Party nominee George McGovern. Born in Newark, New Jersey, Peter studied law, served in World War II, and ran for Congress in 1948, with strong support from the Italian-American voters in his district. He worked on voting rights, immigration legislation, and crime prevention. However, he is best known as chairman of the House Judiciary Committee during the impeachment hearings of President Nixon. Judge John Joseph Sirica, born in Westbury, Connecticut, to an emigrant father from a small village near Naples, obtained his law degree from Georgetown University and then worked for a law firm in Washington, D.C. In 1957, President Dwight Eisenhower appointed him to the federal bench. In his book *To Set the Record Straight,* Judge Sirica detailed his role on the Federal District Court in D.C., adjudicating the Watergate break-in, cover-up, indictments, guilty pleas, battle over the tapes, and the jailing of the men associated with these illegal activities. The careers of these two men refuted Nixon's notorious allegation (recorded on the White House tapes) that "you can't find one [Italian American] that's honest." (*Courtesy* Italian Tribune)

Endorsing Candidates. Fabio Schettini, a union organizer for the International Ladies Garment Workers' Union, makes a speech for New York City's mayoral candidate John Lindsay in 1966. Lindsay won support from his own Republican Party as well as the Liberal Party (successor to the Labor Party) in New York City. Born in Brooklyn, Schettini grew up in Trebezzano, Salerno. In 1969, Democrat Mario Procaccino (born in Bisaccia, Avellino) ran against Lindsay (supported by the Liberal Party) and Republican John J. Marchi (born in Staten Island) in a three-way race for mayor. While Procaccino led Lindsay in the early polls, his badly managed campaign contributed to his defeat. As a result of this close election, New York City revised its election law to require a runoff election if no candidate carries at least forty percent of the vote. (*Courtesy Antoinette P. Schettini*)

National Limelight. New York City Mayor Rudolph Giuliani waves to the Columbus Day crowd on Fifth Avenue by Rockefeller Center, October 8, 2001. (Michael Bloomberg, then mayoral candidate, is at right.) Born in Brooklyn, New York, to Italian-American parents, Giuliani attended New York University Law School and became a U.S. attorney in New York's Southern District. In 1981, he was named associate attorney general by President Ronald Reagan. Two years later, he was appointed head U.S. attorney of New York's Southern District. His prosecutions of white-collar criminals, organized crime, and corrupt politicians earned him national recognition. Elected mayor in 1993, he was overwhelmingly re-elected in 1997. In the aftermath of the September 11, 2001, terrorist attack on the World Trade Center, his decisive actions and statements impressed the entire country. Term limits prevented him from running for a third term, and in 2002, prostate cancer caused him to drop out of the race for the U.S. Senate. In 2007, Giuliani entered the Republican Party's presidential primaries, the first Italian-American to seek the highest office. *(Mayor Rudolph W. Giuliani, Columbus Day Parade, 10/20/2001, Courtesy of the NYC Municipal Archives)*

ACCENT*i*

The Canadian Magazine with an Italian Accent

January – March 2004, Vol. 2.1

Paving the Way for an
Italian Canadian
Prime Minister?

Also in this issue

Mediterranean Shadows on Corydon Avenue

Interview with Steve Galluccio

Word on the Street Makes an Italian Connection

Publication Mail No.: 40731052
ISSN 1705-4125

$6.99

Italian-Canadian Aspirations. A 2004 cover of *Accenti: The Canadian Magazine with an Italian Accent* posits the question of when will be an Italian-Canadian prime minister. Canada's parliamentary system selects the head of government from the majority party, usually its leader, in the House of Commons. Often this person has served in the prime minister's cabinet. *Accenti* noted that no major party has featured "a candidate whose background was other than English or French Canadian." However, as Canada's demographic changes reflect the increase of Southern Europeans, South Asians, East Asians, Middle Easterners, and South Americans, the political establishment will have to solicit their support; Nick Discepola, member of Parliament for Vaudreuil-Soulanges, stated, "It will be a matter of political expediency. People vote for leaders who are a reflection of them. As the ethnic face of Canada changes, the political apparatus . . . must make room for prime ministerial candidates who are of neither English nor French descent." Italian politicians are quick to note that Canada's multiethnic population would not accept a prime minister who favored one ethnic group over another. When Paul Martin selected six Italian Canadians for his cabinet in 2004, the potential pool of prime minister candidates increased. (*Courtesy* Accenti Magazine)

Canadian Senate. Canadian prime minister Stephen Harper plays bocce at Villa Columbo in Toronto, Ontario, May 2005. Ralph Grittani, chairman of Villa Columbo, stands to his left, and Senator Consiglio DiNino to his right. Members of Canada's Senate are selected, not elected. (The Senate consists of 105 members appointed by the governor general on the advice of the prime minister. Seats are assigned on a regional basis, with each region receiving twenty-four seats.) DiNino was a successful banker and community leader. He was the third Italian Canadian appointed to the Senate. The DiNino family's transition from agricultural workers in Pratola Peligna, L'Aqulia, in 1951, to construction and factory workers in urban Canada exemplifies immigrants' belief in the promise of America. *(Courtesy Villa Charities, Toronto, Canada)*

Salute From the Top. President George W. Bush welcomes members of the American Society of the Italian Legions of Merit in the Oval Office, June 2, 2006. *Left to right:* Dr. Aileen Sirey of Chappaqua, New York; Stephen Acunto of Mt. Vernon, New York; Rosemarie Gallina-Santangelo of Rye, New York; Dr. Lucio Caputo of New York City; Justice Dominic Massaro of Pelham Manor, New York; Larry Auriana of Greenwich, Connecticut; and Dominic Frinzi of Milwaukee, Wisconsin. (Robert A. Messa, Sons of Italy Foundation president, was present but not pictured). Italian Independence Day, June 2, celebrates the establishment by referendum of the Italian Republic in 1946. The group presented the president with a medal commemorating the fortieth anniversary of the national society. The Italian government awards the *Cavaliere della Repubblica* to individuals who have gained personal achievement or have rendered a special service to Italy. Approximately seven hundred Americans to date have received this honor. In 2007, the society awarded its medal to Arizona's governor Janet Napolitano. *(White House photograph by Kimberlee Hewitt)*

Sunbelt Ethnicity. Mayor Pam Iorio of Tampa, Florida, congratulates Jeral McCants, the first homebuyer of InTown Homes on March 17, 2006. This project offered a mortgage initiative for first-time homebuyers with household incomes at or below the median income level. Mayor Iorio's father, John, traveled, at age two, with his parents from Casandrino, Napoli, to Trenton, New Jersey. At ages eleven and seventeen, Pam Iorio spent two semesters in Florence, Italy, where her father taught at the University of South Florida's Florence campus. The family made an unannounced visit to Casandrino and experienced spontaneous hospitality with a seven-course meal. Iorio began her political career in Florida in 1985 at age twenty-six when she became the youngest person ever elected to the Hillsborough County Commission. Elected three times to the office of Supervisor of Elections for Hillsborough County (1993-2003), Iorio was elected mayor in 2003 and re-elected in 2007. She is the first female Italian-American mayor of Tampa. She combined her Italian heritage with her love of cooking by giving a cooking class, with her father, on the "Mayor's Hour," a monthly show appearing on Tampa's local government access channel. *(Courtesy City of Tampa)*

Highest Court. Supreme Court Justice Samuel Alito, Jr. speaks to students in Professor Carlo Cirillo's Latin Club at Columbia Middle School in Berkeley Heights, New Jersey, January 2007. Alito's father immigrated to the United States, settled in Trenton, New Jersey, and eventually found employment with the State Office of Legislative Services. Alito, Jr. served in different positions in the Department of Justice until he was named U.S. attorney for the District of New Jersey during Ronald Reagan's presidency. In 1990, President George H.W. Bush appointed him to the Federal Appeals Court. Supported by leading Italian-American organizations for his nomination to the Supreme Court in 2006, he became the second Justice of Italian heritage joining Justice Antonin Scalia who was appointed to the Supreme Court in 1986. Like Alito, Scalia was also born to an Italian-immigrant father in Trenton. After graduating from Harvard Law School, Scalia taught at the University of Virginia, served various government legal agencies in Washington, D.C., and then returned to teaching at the University of Chicago Law School. President Ronald Reagan appointed him to the Federal Appeals Court in Washington, D.C., in 1982. *(Courtesy Mary Ann Re, New Jersey Italian and Italian American Heritage Commission)*

Pioneer Gardeners, Walla Walla, Washington. Hoy Tom hauls 4,370 pounds of onions from onion field to city in a "belly good truck," c. 1918. In the 1870s, the Chinese leased land and worked with partners to supply local homes and town markets with vegetables. Others worked for native-born farmers. Italian gardeners began to arrive in this rural community in the mid-1870s, and some settled in close proximity to the Chinese. A number of Italian-immigrant children worked for them, and their parents sometimes leased their land to the Chinese. Charles Paietta remembers working for a nearby Chinese farmer, Ching-shu, and his family. *(Courtesy Walla Walla Gardeners' Association, Inc.)*

Bilingual Attraction, c. 1910. Alessandro Matteucci's Champion Grocery and Meat Market, on the corner of Seventh Street and Tijeras Avenue, Albuquerque, New Mexico, used their delivery wagon to provide door-to-door service. He brought over his brother, Amedeo Matteucci, from Lammari, Lucca, to help operate the business. The brothers and their mostly Italian clerks, cashiers, butchers, and deliverymen employees reached out to attract the city's Hispanic community by stocking chili peppers in addition to fresh vegetables and featuring signs written in Spanish as well as English. This strategy proved successful, and the brothers soon moved out of the apartment they occupied over the store into a two-family home. *(Courtesy Nicholas P. Ciotola / University of New Mexico, Center for Southwest Research, Paul and Patti Marianetti)*

Ethnic Dynamics. Immigrants, beginning with the Irish, then eastern European Jews, and finally Italians, settled sequentially into the crowded, older housing in Boston's North End, where they established communities. On a Saturday morning in 1909, an Italian boy on Salem Street in Boston calls out, "Fire. Fire. I want to make the fire." Since observant Jews could not do any work on their Sabbath, non-Jewish children earned five cents for lighting a fire in the wood stove in Jewish homes. The lure of a nickel per home motivated neighborhood children in locales such as Brownsville, in Brooklyn, New York, and Baltimore, Maryland, to compete for this service. As adults, some of these *shabbos goys* remembered how their customers remained loyal to them when the "competition" tried to take their place by answering to the inquiry, "No thank you, the Gerardi kids help us each *shabbos*." *(Library of Congress, Prints and Photographs Division, LC-DIG-NCLC-03303, attributed to Lewis Hine)*

Crossing the Color Line, New Orleans, Louisiana, 1915. Vito Scorsone, a successful Italian-immigrant businessman, serves two black customers in his French Quarter barroom located at 2259 Dryades Street, at the corner of Philips Street. In the Jim Crow South, most native-born whites refused to serve African Americans. Italian immigrants, even those like Scorsone, who became an American citizen in 1904, tended to extend simple courtesies of fellowship to all their neighbors, sometimes risking condemnation by local society. In many other Southern communities in Louisiana and Alabama, Italian immigrants provided retail services for their African-American and immigrant neighbors. Italian immigrants also lived and worked with African Americans on Louisiana's sugar plantations. *(Courtesy Sydney J. Mazerat III)*

A Tribute of Respect. In Stamford, Connecticut, the immigrant population benefited from Dr. J. Nemoitin's medical care. As a member of the Jewish immigrant community, the doctor sympathized with the plight of those not able to afford fees for service. Not only did he allow patients extra time to pay their bills, he often would prepay for their prescriptions. In tribute, the Mutual Benefit Society, Provincia di Caserta, gave him a certificate of membership, dated October 18, 1914. Ironically, his fellow physicians in Stamford did not invite him to join their organizations because of his religious affiliation. Immigrant neighborhoods were not completely segregated; in New York and Baltimore, Italian immigrants and their Jewish neighbors found many commonalities. *(Courtesy Stamford Historical Society)*

Worker Solidarity. Italian, Cuban, and Spanish cigarmakers at Factory No. 1 of the Sanchez & Haya Company in Ybor City, Tampa, Florida, pause for a photograph, c. 1910. Italian workers learned Spanish to communicate with their Spanish-speaking coworkers. In a segregated society, the presence of some Cubans of African descent (visible in this photo) among the workforce reflected the bond of mutual support. During their leisure hours, cigar workers joined in lively domino games played at various ethnic clubs and sidewalk cafés. Frank Urso's book *A Stranger in the Barrio: Memoirs of a Tampa Sicilian* offers a personal view of the everyday life of these immigrants. *(Courtesy Gary Mormino)*

United in Struggle. Famous Industrial Workers of the World (IWW): union organizer Elizabeth Gurley Flynn (right) is next to Mary Gallo at Eva Botto's (standing) family grape arbor in Haledon, New Jersey, in spring 1913. Elizabeth Gurley Flynn, the daughter of Irish immigrants, helped to energize the silk workers on strike in Paterson, New Jersey. She had played a major role in the 1912 strike in Lawrence, Massachusetts, where she worked with Italian syndicalists and other members of the IWW. Some of the same leaders, e.g., Big Bill Haywood and Carlo Tesca, rallied to the cause of the Paterson workers. Elizabeth's autobiography, *Rebel Girl*, vividly describes her interaction with Italian-immigrant workers. *(Courtesy American Labor Museum / Botto House National Landmark)*

Celebrating the Harvest. Francesco Paolo Patranella and his good friend and employee Ed Sanders (right) wave towards the camera in triumph of completing the harvest in Bryan, Texas, c. 1920s. Francesco found Ed, his wife Minnie, and five children starving and without a place to live. He offered Ed a three-room house and wages if he and his family would work for him. The Patranella and Sanders families became very close, eating almost all of their meals together, and their children always played together. Francesco's son, Sam, remembers that he would always "get into trouble" because he spent more time at Ed's house than his own. *(Courtesy Marilyn Grizzaffi Halleran)*

Living on a Reservation, Chiloquin, Oregon. Alfeo Minato's third-grade classmates in 1932 included members of the Klamath Indian Tribes in central Oregon. Alfeo and his brothers made friends with some of the Native Americans. They remembered these boys as being very intelligent, talented, and good friends. Because a lumber company leased land on the reservation, Native-American families received payments from the timber sales. During the Great Depression, the non-native children of immigrants often benefited from the treats their friends generously shared. *(Courtesy Alfeo E. Minato)*

Trading Recipes. Delfino Antrosio, from the Piemonte region of Italy, delivered produce daily to customers along his route in what was called German-Russian town, in the Northeast Fremont area of Portland, Oregon. In the 1920s, he retired his horse and bought a 1923 Model T Ford truck to make deliveries until he retired in the early 1950s. One of his customers was Elizabeth Beard, the mother of the famous chef James Beard. A November 18, 1990, *Oregonian* article describing the book *Epicurean Delight: The Life and Times of James Beard* noted that Delfinio Antrozzo—note the misspelling—had taught Elizabeth to make polenta. Elsewhere in America, Italian-immigrant peddlers would bring the produce they sold into other immigrant neighborhoods and also to the homes of native-born. *(Courtesy Jane Antrosio Mace)*

Enduring Friendship, c. 1947. Emily Gregori and Japanese-American Ima Kozen became best friends in their first-grade class in San Francisco, California, in the 1920s. Emily and her husband, Joseph, served as witnesses when Ima married George Kozen on April 5, 1942, just before they were sent to Tanforan Assembly Center in May. When Ima gave birth to a daughter, Lynne, while in the Topaz Relocation Camp in Arizona, Emily sent baby shower presents. Here Emily and Ima stand with their daughters in front of the Gregori home on Connecticut Street. Emily's in-laws, who rented an apartment to the Kozen family before and after the war, stand at the right. One of their neighbors circulated a petition questioning the Gregori's patriotism since their son, Joseph, was still serving in the Pacific theater. No one in this mainly Italian- and Greek-immigrant neighborhood would sign. *(Courtesy JoEllen Gregori Waldvogel)*

Second Generation Intermarriage, July 13, 1947. When Philomena "Mamie" Pullo married Anthony Mosellie at Our Lady of Mt. Carmel Church in Roseto, Pennsylvania, she told her father, Frank Pullo, that Anthony was Italian. Frank, from Roseto Val Fortore, Foggia, worked as a stonemason and farmer. When his wife, Marie Cacciarro Pullo, died in childbirth after having eight children, Frank raised the children alone. He grew all the food for his family, butchered pigs, smoked meats, and canned food. He was strict, gentle, self-taught, religious and traditional, and when he expected all of his children to marry Italians, seven did. Had he known that Anthony Mosellie was Syrian, although the name sounded Italian, he would not have given Mamie his blessings to marry. Mamie did confess a year after the marriage when she was pregnant with her first child, but by then, Frank looked forward to the birth of a grandchild and all was forgiven. *(Courtesy Mamie Pullo Mosellie and Weda M. Mosellie)*

Fairness in Business, 1950. After World War II, some native-born Americans, especially on the West Coast, refused to conduct business with Japanese immigrants or their American-born citizen children. In Portland, Oregon, Paul Montecucco disagreed with this sentiment, and when acquaintances questioned his decision to sell produce to Seimi (Sammy) Kuribayashi, he replied, "Well we both were on the losing side of the war." Here Seimi poses with the Montecucco family as he prepares to drive to Seattle with a full load of cabbage, plus boxes of parsnips bound for United States military in the Pacific. (*Courtesy Steve Montecucco and the Montecucco family*)

A Trophy Season. The mostly Italian-American members of Hammonton (New Jersey) All-Stars receive the winner's trophy in the Little League World Series in 1949. In 1947, the year Jackie Robinson broke baseball's "color line" barring African Americans from the major leagues, Otha Crowder (center) was one of the first African Americans to participate in a Little League World Series. When Albert Mulliner, founder of the Hammonton Little League, and his team managers, Robert Colucci and Barney Ricci, were told that Otha could not play in the 1947 Little League Series because he was black, they told the league that either Hammonton's entire team would play or they would not come at all. The league relented and Otha went to the 1947, '48, and '49 World Series. (The Hammonton Gazette, *courtesy William Ordille*)

Campaigning across Cultures. When Boston, Massachusetts, lawyer Edward W. Brooke campaigned for Massachusetts Secretary of State in 1960, he addressed this audience from the Watertown Italian American Social Club in fluent Italian. During World War II, he served with army intelligence, working with Italian partisans. Besides learning the language, he married an Italian woman, Remigia Ferrari-Scacco. In 1962, Brooke was elected Massachusetts attorney general, becoming the first African American in the United States to lead a state's legal affairs division. In 1966, Brooke became the first African American since Reconstruction elected to the U.S. Senate. His wife helped to rally Italian-American voters to support his candidacy. *(Courtesy Library of Congress, Prints and Photographs Division, LC-L9-60-8982-Q26, Doug Kirkland, photographer)*

Ethnic Combination, c. 1978. Contact between ethnic communities resulted in a combination of Italian and Portuguese baked goods in Toronto, Canada. The area, formerly Italian, now includes more recently arrived Portuguese. Businesses originally designed to serve the Italian ethnic community are expanding and attracting the newcomers. *(Courtesy The Multicultural History Society of Ontario)*

Seeking Justice. Nina Miglionico stands to the right of a group of Birmingham, Alabama, officials at the opening of Birmingham Fire Department Station Number One in 1971. Her parents came to Birmingham from a town near Naples. They ran a store selling sundries and served African Americans as well as other working-class customers. Nina worked in the store while she attended school. She went to the University of Alabama Law School, graduated in 1936, and is still practicing law at age ninety-five. A lifelong advocate of women's rights, she helped gain the right of women to serve on Alabama juries. In 1963, she ran for Birmingham city council at a time when the city's media image was "police dogs." Nina reached out to all segments of the community and was not afraid to speak out in black churches as well as at meetings with whites. Crosses were burned in her yard, and there were phone threats. A bomb was placed on her front porch, but her eighty-year-old father discovered the bomb when he stepped outside for the morning newspaper and noticed a green box. "I thought it was a gift," he said. But when he saw what was inside, he "took the clock out and threw it out of the yard." The box held thirty-eight sticks of dynamite. The police, alerted, rushed to the homes of the mayor and eight other council members. At Mayor Albert Boutwell's home, they found a powerful time bomb containing fifty sticks of dynamite, enough to level the house—more than was used in the bombing of the Sixteenth Street Baptist Church where four young girls were killed in 1963. Nina was the first woman to attain certain city and state positions. *(Courtesy Birmingham Public Library, Department of Archives and Manuscripts; catalog # 1556.38.29)*

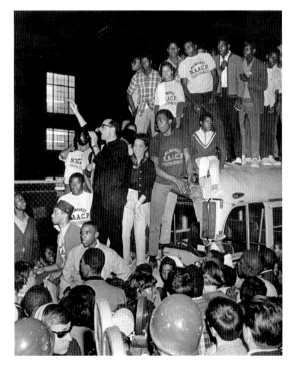

Civil Rights Activist. Using a portable loudspeaker, Father James Groppi speaks to a large group attending a National Association for the Advancement of Colored People (NAACP) Youth Council rally in the parking lot in the rear of Saint Boniface Catholic Church, Milwaukee, Wisconsin, September 1967. Groppi's immigrant parents had settled in Milwaukee's "Guinea Hill." Growing up, he resented the way Italians, including his parents, were treated, and he eschewed any form of ethnic humor. In 1965, he became the advisor to the Milwaukee chapter of the NAACP Youth Council and began protesting segregation in Milwaukee's public schools. He also mounted a lengthy, continuous demonstration against the city of Milwaukee on behalf of fair housing. He was arrested many times, including the time he led a march on August 31, 1967, even though Mayor Henry W. Maier had issued a proclamation banning demonstrations at night. (Urban rioting had occurred after the summer riots in Newark, New Jersey, and in other cities.) The group was challenging the ban and Groppi urged them to march to Maier's house on the Saturday following the march. The *Milwaukee Sentinel* editorial suggested that it was time for Archbishop William Cousins to take disciplinary action. However, Cousins supported Groppi's goals while rejecting his methods. Groppi also was an organizer of the "Welfare Mothers' March on Madison" (1969).Though he was denigrated and arrested on numerous occasions for standing firm in his beliefs, he was instrumental in dramatizing the segregated housing situation in Milwaukee. This led to enactment of an open-housing law in Milwaukee. Groppi also raised the consciousness of many to other inequities. *(Courtesy Milwaukee Journal Sentinel, 9/2/67, © 2005 Journal Sentinel Inc., reproduced with permission, NEG No. 671654, all rights reserved)*

Inclusive Celebrations. Ray Martire prepares to step out into the Saint Patrick's Day parade in Spokane, Washington. In 1988, Irish organizers opened up participation to guests, and the American Italian Club joined the march. Spokane does not hold a Columbus Day parade (they celebrate with a dinner), so this occasion provides an opportunity for Italians to gain recognition. In New Orleans, Italians and Irish Americans join forces for a combined Saint Patrick and Saint Joseph's Day celebration. *(Courtesy Ray Martire)*

Mexican Farm Labor. Before the end of World War II, Italian gardeners in Portland, Oregon, usually employed Italian immigrants to help cultivate and harvest the crops. By the 1970s, Mexican immigrant workers began to take over agricultural work from a mixture of native-born casual laborers and high-school kids. The same development occurred much earlier in a majority of Western states. Today's Italian-American agriculturalists, like Aldo Rossi, shown here supervising tomato transplanting, are usually second- to fourth-generation Americans who discover that their understanding of Italian helps them communicate with their Spanish-speaking workforce. After the passage of the Immigration Reform and Control Act of 1986, which granted amnesty to undocumented immigrants, second-generation Italian-American Paul Montecucco of Portland, Oregon, used the information he had learned in 1942, while helping his Italian immigrant father study for his citizenship exam, to coach his Mexican workers to succeed in their applications. *(Courtesy the Rossi family)*

Customer Focus. Trained as tailors in Austria, brothers Jacob and Morris Teitel left the tailoring shop where they worked on Essex Street in New York City to open a provisions store for Italians in the Belmont section of the Bronx in 1915. They lived where they worked, in an apartment over the store, and used the trial-and-error method to stock their store with the cheeses, cans of tomatoes, pasta sold by the bulk, and olive oil that appealed to their customers. Jacob would bang on the water pipe to summon his wife to come down to the store and help make change. Other Jewish-owned stores in the overwhelmingly Italian area sold groceries, clothing, and other items. Competition was healthy, focusing on price with no hostile overtones. Customers would bargain over a penny or half-cent difference. The brothers learned some Italian before they mastered English. Over time, with the help of the store clerks they hired from the neighborhood, they learned a bit of the different Italian dialects. During the '30s, Jacob had a Star of David set in tile in the entrance to the store as a gesture against Fascism. Although the area's population changed from Italian to Albanian/Yugoslavian and then Mexican, Puerto Rican, and Colombian, the Teitels' customer base is still mostly third-generation Italians. *(Courtesy Peter Rodda)*

CHAPTER 8

ITALIAN-AMERICAN ISSUES

The passage from immigrant to ethnic not only involves sensitivity to how your group is viewed by fellow Americans, but also how your group adjusts to change. In the twenty-first century, many Italian Americans work to erase negative attitudes toward Italians in America. Current issues, such as the celebration of Columbus Day and the popularization of the Italian crime figure in the media, are troubling to those who feel that these images damage the reputation of the entire group.

European Americans viewed Columbus as the "discoverer" of a "new" continent. Harvard historian Samuel Eliot Morison, writing in the 1940s, praised Columbus as a "master mariner" who opened America to European commerce and settlement. Leaders in the Italian-immigrant community felt that Columbus' legacy allowed them to claim "Mayflower" status as equals to the pilgrims who established permanent residence. The use of Columbus as a name for Italian clubs, and the proliferation of statues and plaques memorializing Columbus, illustrated the strong identification of the immigrant. As Italian immigrants became more influential in politics and business, native-born Americans eagerly participated in the annual Columbus celebration ceremony, usually a formal banquet and sometimes a parade. Soon, Columbus Day became a holiday in some states, later becoming a national holiday.

Since the quincentenary of Columbus' 1492 voyage, Native-American groups have targeted this event as the first assault upon the native peoples of the Western Hemisphere. These groups maintain that Columbus and his crew initiated a genocide and the subjugation that

followed. For Italian Americans this viewpoint has created a dilemma of faith.

Many Italian Americans regarded this assault on Columbus as a condemnation of a national symbol. Other Italians feel that the image of Columbus lies at the center of Italian-American identity and fear that an alteration of this association would erode national recognition of the Italian presence. Dismayed at the fervor of Native-American groups, and scholars who described Columbus as a destroyer of civilization, many Italian Americans rejected the new scholarship, and leading organizations produced treatises to modify the negative interpretation.

Others endeavored to acknowledge this reassessment. In 1992, Italian Americans for a Multicultural United States (IMUS) formed to assist the Italian-American community to recognize the benefits they enjoyed as Europeans in a society that has denied these benefits to its non-European population. They pointed out that Italy does not celebrate Columbus, nor does Canada. They also welcomed the new scholarship that added the role of sixteenth-century Spanish and Native Americans into post-1990 U.S. history textbooks. (Before this time, most history textbooks started with the founding of Jamestown in 1607.)

In Chicago, Italian-American groups forged a détente based on mutual respect and avoided open conflict. While some Native Americans continued to oppose any connection with the quincentenary, a majority of their leaders negotiated with the Joint Civic Committee of Italian Americans (JCCIA). The committee offered to drop the term "discovery" for the terms "landing" or "encounter." Native-American leaders voted unanimously to support an art contest celebrating the quincentenary and noted that it was the first time that whites had asked their permission on how to portray American Indians.

The Italian government travel office, and several Sicilian organizations, who felt a bond with the Native Americans because of their own history of being a "conquered nation" for three thousand years, invited Native Americans to Italy between April 6 and 15, 1991. The Pope, elected officials, and the public greeted the contingent of Native Americans enthusiastically. Pope John Paul II noted that the "evangelical zeal of the colonizers often failed to seek the links between native spiritualities and Christian tenets" and thus destroyed the indigenous culture and way of life.

Dominic Di Frisco, president of the JCCIA, called for "more cultural exchanges, always remembering that our two groups have both been victimized by ugly stereotyping." Fred Gardaphe, while a professor at Chicago's Columbia College (presently at Queens College—CUNY), felt that Italians placed too much emphasis on a parade and suggested that both groups needed "to get beyond the rhetoric and help each other. Our next step is to see what we can jointly do to educate the population."

During the annual parade in Chicago, in 1991 and 1992, a contingent of Native-American leaders marched in the parade. Some Native-American war veterans wore black armbands to mourn the destruction of the indigenous culture that followed European settlement. This direct interaction and cooperation has faded over the years.

In Denver, Colorado, a center of American Indian movement activity, angry dissent created an atmosphere so charged with tension that the parade committee decided to cancel the 1992 parade to avoid the possibility of physical violence. In 2000, Denver's Italians resumed their celebration to a chorus of protestors, some of whom attempted to block the parade route. Each year some demonstrators are arrested. In the 2004 Columbus Day parade, the float of the *Tirolesi-Trentini* of Colorado combined a depiction of their Italian homeland with the celebration of Columbus. Interestingly, Cristoforo Colombo, who sailed under the Spanish flag, is not a national hero in Italy. The Order Sons of Italy's Commission for Social Justice issued a pamphlet, "Columbus: Fact vs. Fiction," in 2005, to provide a broader historical context of Columbus' voyages. Dona DeSanctis, OSIA's deputy executive director, maintained that Columbus should be "judged by the standards and ethics of his own time."

Some Denver Italians want to end this discord, which they feel turns Italian pride into hero worship. They propose changing the emphasis from Columbus Day to Italian Heritage Day to honor all the Italians who played a role in the development of America, such as Philip Mazzei, William Paca, Charles Bonaparte, the Civil War generals Francis Spinola and Luigi Palma diCesnola, and countless others.

Many nations of the Western Hemisphere accept Columbus as part of their past. While the arrival of the Europeans to the Western Hemisphere decimated native peoples and their cultures, it also created a new population combining indigenous peoples with Europeans and Africans. Most countries in Latin America celebrate October 12 as *Día de la Raza* (Day of the Race). In Costa Rica, it is called *Día de las Culturas* (Day of the Cultures). This focus commemorates the intermingling of Africans and Europeans with Native-American peoples following Columbus' voyage as the beginning of a new *raza*. As Richard Rodriguez, whose ancestors came from Mexico, said on October 12, 1992, during a news commentator spot on PBS, "This is the birthday of my people." He expressed the hopes of many that October 12 would expand into a day to commemorate all the cultures now part of the Americas by celebrating the richness of the Americas, its foods, political forms, and its acceptance of the first European settlers and the Africans and Asians who followed. He hoped that Americans would bring understanding, reconciliation, and mutual commitment to develop a social ethic that respects and treasures all ethnic groups.

Historian Dominic Candeloro noted that Italian Americans can learn from this historical reassessment, stating "that developments often have unintended consequences, excesses of faith and power have ugly results for all, and that cultural isolation is impossible. . . . There are no easy answers. Debate will sharpen our analytical skills and sensitize us in dealing with the problems of the future in our diverse society . . . and despite his flawed record as an administrator, businessman, and diplomat, [we can join together in acknowledging] Columbus' achievements [in bringing] together two continents to create a new world—our world."

The other major issue for contemporary Italians is the stigma of crime and prejudice. Since the days of yellow journalism, the media has used highly charged issues to sell papers. While organized crime in America was not a product of Italian immigrants, the popular image, reinforced by successful films and books, perpetuates a harmful stereotype. Most Italian-American organizations have developed antidefamation units to indicate how this negative association damages the image of an entire group.

Sensational accounts of Italian misbehavior and wrongdoing have always helped to sell newspapers. This one-sided view of the immigrant fueled fears of the native-born. Mary Antin, in her 1914 book *They Who Knock at Our Gates: A Complete Gospel of Immigration,* said of this phenomenon, "Half a dozen Italians draw knives in a brawl on a given evening, and the morning newspapers are full of the story. On the same evening hundreds of Italians were studying civics in the night schools, inquiring for classics at the public library, rehearsing for a historical pageant at the settlement—and not a word about them in the newspapers."

In the twentieth century, as America's cities grew, crime increased, housing deteriorated, and the political process became more corrupt. Most Americans blamed these changes on the foreign element. The existence of crime among the immigrants, the negative image of the *padrone,* and the radical political beliefs of some newcomers contributed to the suspicions and prejudices held by many Americans. The American press wrote lurid accounts of Black Hand activities—kidnappings, extortions, thefts, and killings—usually restricted within the immigrant community, but whenever crime spilled over into the general population, the public overreacted.

During Prohibition, Italian-American criminals formed organizations with veteran criminals from other ethnic groups to operate regional and national bootlegging, gambling, and prostitution syndicates. Most scholarship documents the emergence of Italian-American crime as part of the assimilation of the children of immigrants to a nation that exalted ostentatious wealth and power. Mary Antin's defense still rings true in a nation in which, according to a study of the U.S. Justice Department, only 0.25 percent of all Italian Americans have criminal records, one of the lowest percentages of any ethnic group. While most ethnic groups—the Irish, Jews, Poles, Germans, Chinese, and Japanese—suffered from biased and discriminatory criticism, such generalized labeling has declined for most of them. Yet for Italians, the criminal label remains. One leading Italian-American scholar, Rudolph Vecoli, who visited a Southern state, was asked if he had Mafia connections. He retorted, "Do you belong to the Ku Klux Klan?" Alleged connections with criminal activity still limit opportunities for political candidates and restrict freedom of expression.

In 2002, the Columbus Citizens Foundation barred two Italian-American actors, Dominic Chianese and Lorraine Bracco, from marching in New York's Columbus Day Parade because they appeared on the HBO series *The Sopranos.* The presence of actors from a TV show about the Mob would be an insult to Italian Americans, claimed the foundation. Dona De Sanctis, deputy executive director of OSIA, writing in the February 2006 issue of *Fra Noi,* observed, "For more than seventy-five years—since the 1930 premiere of *Little Caesar*—Hollywood has persistently portrayed Italian Americans as crude and violent gangsters. Many Italian Americans have ignored such stereotyping, believing that no sensible person would

think they were really like those characters on television and in the movies. . . . [Yet] several years ago . . . a study by the Princeton-based Research Analysis Corporation found that three of four people in this country associate Italian Americans with crime."

Writer Lawrence DiStasi suggests, "*The Godfather* is about mobsters with Italian family life as background. . . . With *The Sopranos,* on the other hand, the main story is the Italian-American family, dysfunctional to be sure . . . That's why it's more devastating to Italian-American culture. It says, more strongly than ever, that this is a typical Italian family—that its violence, criminality, betrayal are typical of the Italian-American family. . . . Organized crime is one of the last areas in the depiction of Italian-American life—*at least in the media versions of it*—which has not yielded to Americanization." DiStasi concludes that for many Italian Americans, their most vivid sense of what it means to be Italian is the veneer of gangster culture that undermines true Italian culture.

However, the fact that the characters reflect their Italian-American ethnicity should not be surprising. If they were Jewish-American criminals, we probably would see them eating bagels with lox, putting money in Chanukah gift cards for their relatives, or watching their wives attend a Hadassah luncheon. In addition, historian Gary Mormino notes that the claim of the gangster epic replacing the American Western as a cultural icon reflects a fascination with the characters of Tony Soprano and Michael Corleone because "they can solve any problem with a simple command. . . . Tony is a fabulously successful businessman—with a dysfunctional family and friends, to be sure, but he has mastered the art of politics, compromise, and conflict resolution—American values." These images resonate with many viewers.

Some organizations criticize actors for accepting these roles. However, when many of the leading Italian-American actors and directors came of age, these were box-office opportunities. Remember when African Americans and Asian Americans were typically cast as maids or butlers? And realistically in today's profit-driven world, networks and movie companies market to the largest audience. One might argue that *Survivor,* the reality show, equally damages young audiences who tune in to watch people elbow and connive their way to a prize. America's entertainment media proliferates sensationalism and elevates power.

On February 8, 2005, representatives of more than twenty Italian-American groups stood on the steps of New York's City Hall to protest the negative stereotyping of Italian Americans in Steven Spielberg's animated children's movie *Shark Tale.* Jack Como, chairman of the Italian American Political Action Committee (I AM PAC), lobbied the city council for a resolution banning the showing of the movie and the related curriculum the film producers made available to public schools. These organizations formed the Coalition Against Racial, Religious, and Ethnic Stereotyping (CARRES), a multiethnic activist group. The Order Sons of Italy in America also directed their anger at actor Robert De Niro who, along with Martin Scorese, provided the "Italian-American" street gang accents for the "bad" sharks in the film. OSIA appealed to the Italian government to cancel its plans to grant De Niro honorary Italian citizenship, claiming that he had damaged the image of Italians and Italian Americans by portraying them in criminal roles. The ceremony was postponed, but the offer was not rescinded.

Although some Italians have been involved in criminal activity, there is no question that media images exaggerate this connection. Yet, more importantly, a significant number of Italian Americans have gained acclaim as agents of law enforcement. These upholders of the law include Louis Freeh, former director of the Federal Bureau of Investigation, and Rudolph Giuliani, who served as U.S. attorney for the Southern District of New York. Many, but not all, outstanding lawmen of Italian heritage earned distinction apprehending or prosecuting Italian-American criminals. OSIA's 2005 report "Italian American Crime Fighters: A Brief Survey" documents the presence and achievements of this group.

Stereotyped images of Italians included the street musicians, mainly organ grinders, who "disturbed" the quiet, residential tone of middle- and upper-class neighborhoods, and the *padrone* who supplied immigrant labor and sometimes votes. While the organ-grinder's appearance and music were unpleasant to some Americans, the *padrone* was seen as the symbol of foreign corruption brought to American shores. American workers were convinced that *padroni* imported men who would flood the labor pool and decrease wages. American authorities condemned the practices of unscrupulous bosses who exploited these immigrant workers by charging them a fee for obtaining a job (while also collecting payment from the employer), overcharging them for transportation to the job and for room and board on the job site, and exacting high interest rates for money loaned to them. Official accounts of such criminal practices made the word *"padrone"* synonymous with thief or felon. Yet, not all *padroni* exploited workers. Many served as employment agents, channeling job seekers to work opportunities. They profited as businessmen who provided services needed by the immigrant worker, and they were regarded as community leaders.

A rapidly changing society that was subject to unpredictable economic cycles and social maladjustments often found a release for its confusion and frustration in anti-immigrant sentiments. The Italians' outdoor recreation and their extroverted daily life, their eating habits—including foods strange to the American palate, such as garlic, spices, snails—and their public practice of Catholicism, replete with feasts and processions, separated them from a society that followed Anglo-Saxon-Protestant values. Efforts to restrict immigration, especially from southern and eastern Europe, grew in intensity as the number of newcomers increased and as Americans became convinced that foreigners threatened to undermine American democracy and Protestantism and cause economic chaos.

Native-born Americans applied derogatory names to immigrants, such as wop, guinea, and dago. These labels reflected an opinion that the newcomers, who labored in low paying jobs, crowded together in substandard housing, and were semiliterate, were in fact an inferior "race." The prevailing belief held by some government officials and social scientists in Italy, and in the United States, equated the low status of southern Italians with an inherent inability. Native-born white Americans have used similar beliefs to characterize African Americans, Native Americans, Chinese, and Mexicans, none of whom were considered to be equal to the dominant culture.

Discriminated against because of their ethnic identity, these targeted groups faced socioeconomic restrictions. Some Italians, especially those of the laborer and industrial workers class, were not perceived as a white or Caucasian population. Their legal, political, and cultural stance showed a kind of racial non-whiteness or in-betweenness, especially visible in the American South and New York's Harlem. They were paid less and given the jobs spurned by "white" workers. In a race-conscious society, they were treated as a separate group. They were not welcome in churches, social activities, or housing in middle-class neighborhoods. American cinema's portrayal of Italians as darker, more impulsive, and violent relegated them to a racial group considered threatening to the social and economic system. As a result, they were targeted, along with immigrants from southern and eastern Europe, by the restrictionist laws of the 1920s, which drastically reduced the number of Italians, Greeks, Bulgarians, etc., who could enter the United States.

Even in jest, the use of pejorative terms caused problems. Jerre Mangione recalls an incident told by shortstop Phil Rizzuto. At a crucial moment during a game, when a New York Yankee coach hollered, "Throw it to the dago, the dago," the catcher, not knowing which "dago" to throw it to—DiMaggio, Crosetti, or Lazzeri—froze. The runner scored.

Sociologists argue that the self-image of a group declines in proportion to the way it is perceived by the dominant culture. A combination of the *contadini* experience of low expectations and a lack of support from the American school system played an important role in impeding socioeconomic progress. Francesco Cordasco described how the *Casa Italiana* of Columbia University (Italian language studies center) replicated the seigniorial system of Renaissance Italy. Although the Italian-American community raised the money to construct the *Casa,* Cordasco bitterly remembered how its staff seemed unconcerned, and, in fact, were inhospitable toward the few Italian-American students who attended a school they perceived as "a WASP fortress of social class and privilege." Such feelings have contributed to insecurity and, at times, oversensitivity of Italian Americans toward their personal and group history. Some suggest that they seek approval from the larger society by parading their success stories as if that was the total value of their heritage.

However, this is not to say that Italian Americans should not single out those among them who achieve success. Role models are important for every group who aim for the stars. The banner year of 1941, when Fiorello La Guardia was mayor of New York; Angelo Rossi, mayor of San Francisco; and Joe DiMaggio, the most famous ball player in America, established a "new frontier" of achievement. Still today, each one of us experiences a sense of pride when we watch Oscar, Tony, and Emmy awards presented to Italian-American performers; note Italian names on the bestseller list; and read about Americans of Italian heritage pioneering in medical research.

Italian immigrants learned firsthand how inequality damaged America. They joined labor unions, protested poor working conditions, unfair rents, and formed political coalitions to combat these injustices. However, the fact that Italians originated in Europe ultimately distinguished them from non-European groups. As immigrants relinquished the behavior that displeased the majority culture, they gained entry into the mainstream although, at first, not into the executive suite. In the process of moving from inferior to acceptable, some Italians disengaged themselves from those still at the bottom of the socioeconomic ladder.

Not all Italians moved up and out; some of them remained in working-class neighborhoods. Many felt threatened by the post-1960 societal changes and protected their "turf" from outsiders. When Italians reacted violently, the media labeled them racist. Sociologist Jerry Krase reminds us that the technique of "Pitting people who should be working together, against each other is a long-standing American tradition. . . . [Blaming] Italian Americans for American racism is not unlike blaming Irish Americans for anti-Catholicism or Jews for anti-Semitism." Krase stresses the need to combat defamation "with accurate information" rather than denial, and he feels that "the reluctance of most Italian-American organizations and their leaders to honestly address the problem of racial and ethnic bias [by denying] the extent or degree of the problem or [making] defensive statements . . . [exacerbates the problem] . . . because it projects an appearance of lack of remorse or sympathy for victims of bias-related violence."

Unfortunately, some have forgotten or, more likely, never learned how their immigrant ancestors joined with other exploited groups to combat injustice, to embrace the principle that an injury to one is an injury to all. We need only to look to our past leaders, such as Geno Baroni, Vito Marcantonio, and Angela Bambace, to reconnect with the values our ancestors practiced. A coalition of groups working toward a more equitable society would extend this tradition. How will Italian Americans resolve the issue of societal inequality that assaults the dignity of all? The road ahead, as people like Candeloro, Vecoli, and Krase recommend, is a joint exploration of our heritage in order to understand our place in American society and to share this unique experience with our neighbors. Learning from the many dimensions of Italian-American reality will enable us to influence future generations.

Establishing a Presence, 1892. The Italian community of Scranton, Pennsylvania, celebrates the four hundredth anniversary of Columbus' landing in America as depicted in this float. After the parade, people gathered on North Washington Avenue to dedicate a statue of Columbus, created by the Italian sculptor Alberto Cottini. According to the *Scranton Times,* the police worried that "[t]he excited crowd might become unruly" and considered using fire hoses, but mounted police cut a path through the crowd to avoid injuries. The statue portrayed the explorer as the "Admiral of the Indies," holding a chart in one hand and pointing to the newly sighted land with the other. (*Courtesy Vincent S. Riggi*)

Claiming Columbus. Sixty-two members of the Albuquerque, New Mexico, Italian community formed the *Associazione Italiana di Mutua Protezione Cristoforo Colombo,* April 4, 1892. Founding members of this mutual benefit association promoted construction of Columbus Hall at 416 North Second Street. In this c. 1910 photograph, the imposing three-story building housed a bar, banquet room, dance floor, and a card room where members played *briscola, tresette,* and *scopa.* A bocce court was constructed outside the building. The all-male organization welcomed women to the dinners, dances, and theatrical performances they sponsored, and people rented the hall for wedding receptions and special events. (*Courtesy Nicholas P. Ciotola / University of New Mexico, Center for Southwest Research*)

Immigrant Initiative. Italian immigrants throughout America believed that celebrations of Columbus enhanced their image in their adopted country. The symbol of Columbus gave Italians a sense of ownership that paralleled the arrival of the Mayflower. In the Walla Walla, Washington, Italian community, major contributors toward construction of a statue to Columbus received these badges to wear at the October 1911 dedication ceremony. The names of all ninety-eight immigrant donors were engraved on the back of the pedestal. The statue, produced by the Roberts Monument Company of Walla Walla for one thousand dollars, stands in front of the county courthouse. (*Courtesy the Saturno family photo collection*)

Community-Wide Celebration. Each October Italian immigrants reminded Americans that it was the Italian explorer Christopher Columbus whose voyages initiated European settlement in the New World. During a period when immigration restrictionists believed that the peoples from southern and eastern Europe could not assimilate into American society, Italian immigrants reminded everyone that an Italian opened the golden door. Here in Tampa, Florida, around 1910, a group of Italian Americans dressed as sailors and Native Americans pose in front of a streetcar driven by Columbus. Ybor City's community of Cubans, Spaniards, and Italians all identified with this annual commemoration. (*Courtesy Special Collections, University of South Florida Tampa Library, Anthony Pizzo Collection*)

Dedicating a Statue. The Italian sculptor Carlo Brioschi created the Columbus statue, which is still covered in black cloth. It was erected in front of the Minnesota State Capitol in St. Paul in 1931. The Minnesota State Federation of Italian American Clubs commissioned the statue for this state with its predominately Scandinavian and German population. Most Italians worked for the railroad or as miners in the Iron Range, so their modest contributions made during the Depression years speaks for their zeal. Twenty-five thousand people attended the dedication. Representatives from the Italian areas of Buhl, Gilbert, Ely, Hibbing, Eveleth, St. Paul, and Minneapolis carried flags, each with their town name. In 1933, Brioschi designed another Columbus statue for Grant Park in Chicago, Illinois, as part of the Chicago Century of Progress Exposition, which celebrated the centennial anniversary of the incorporation of the city. (*Courtesy Fred A. Ossanna Papers, IM 000413, Immigration History Research Center, University of Minnesota*)

Canada's Preference. Italian Canadians in North Bay, Ontario, reminded their neighbors that the explorer John Cabot, who sailed to the area around Newfoundland in 1497, was born Giovanni Caboto. In the 1930s, this drama group performed a play illustrating Cabot's travels in order to raise money for a statue commemorating the Italian explorer. Italian Canadians do not rally to the symbol of Columbus who did not sail their northern waters. In fact, the second Monday in October is Canada's Thanksgiving Day. More often, Canadian politicians refer to John Cabot's voyage to Newfoundland and Nova Scotia. He reached land on June 24, 1497, and claimed it for King Henry of England. Some, including Italian-Canadian senator Peter Bosa, have proposed that day as a national holiday. However, June 24 would conflict with Quebec's provincial holiday celebrating St. John the Baptist. (*Courtesy The Multicultural History Society of Ontario*)

Adopting the Legacy. By June 1941, the organization founded as the Vittorio Emanuele Club in 1891, in Great Falls, Montana, had evolved into the Cristoforo Colombo Lodge No. 2. This group of first- and second-generation Italian Americans celebrated the club's fiftieth anniversary under threats of another war in Europe. President Roosevelt and Congress had already frozen Italian assets and impounded Italian civilian and military ships in U.S. waters. A focus on Columbus reinforced allegiance to America rather than a connection with the "homeland." (*Courtesy Larry Ranieri*)

Reconciling the Past. Samson Keahna, a member of the Chicago, Illinois, American Indian Center, marches in the Columbus Day parade, October 1991. Some American Indian Center members and war veterans marching in the parade wore black armbands signifying the destruction of the indigenous culture precipitated by Columbus' arrival in the Western Hemisphere. Other Chicago ethnic communities joined the Native Americans in the event. Earlier in 1991, Chicago-area Italian and Native Americans agreed to work together to develop a mutual understanding. The president of the Joint Civic Committee of Italian Americans, Dominic Di Frisco, expressed concern about the changing interpretation of Columbus, which depicts the explorer as starting the exploitation and violence against native peoples, thus undermining his stature as an ethnic hero. He also acknowledged the need to show compassion by lending "a hand to our Native-American brothers and sisters." James Yellowbank declared that the Native-American community recognize Italian Americans "as a minority community that has gone through many problems" and acknowledge that Italians "have deeply rooted religious connections similar to ours, and we don't want to take a similar pride from people." (*Courtesy* Fra Noi)

At Odds Over Columbus. The American Indian Movement, led by Russell Means, challenged the meaning of Columbus Day in 1991. That year Means and fifty supporters blocked Denver, Colorado's parade for forty-five minutes. After the 1991 parade, Russell Means stated, "We're going to put an end to this holiday. The holiday started in Colorado [1905]. We plan to make it stop in Colorado." On the day of the quincentennial celebration in 1992, threats of violence prompted the organizers to cancel the event. A reintroduction of a parade in 2004 brought more than three hundred protesters into the street. They linked arms and knelt in the parade's path, halting the event for more than an hour. Italian-American organizations demanded ordinances making it unlawful for any person to "significantly obstruct or interfere" with any "lawful meeting, procession, parade, or gathering" by "physical action, verbal utterance, or any other means." Enacted by the Denver City Council in 2005, the ordinances did not stop protests but did reduce disorderliness. Native Americans have been lobbying the Colorado legislature to change Columbus Day to All Nations Day. This 2004 photo shows members of New Generations Lodge of the Sons of Italy riding motorcycles in the parade to prevent protesters from breaking into the parade route. This display contrasted with traditional floats, such as the *Tirolesi-Trentini* of Colorado, which featured a tribute to their Italian homeland. Some protesters hold posters entitled "STOP THE CELEBRATION," with an image of Columbus covered by the word "savage" and a slogan reading "Stop genocide, racism, and imperialism." *(Courtesy Colorado Historical Society, CIAPA collection, CPC0020.16, Michael "Spydr" Wren, photographer)*

CRIME AND DISCRIMINATION

Immigrants as Terrorists. In 1890, dozens of Sicilian immigrants were rounded up as suspects in the assassination of New Orleans' police chief Dave Hennessey. Twelve men were tried, most were acquitted, and the others freed by mistrial. On March 14, 1891, some of the city's leading citizens incited an outraged crowd to demand vengeance. They headed to the jailhouse, dragged out the men, and lynched them. The Italian government protested, demanded reparations, and broke off diplomatic relations with the United States. Newspapers across America declared that the victims were Mafia members and deserved their fate. This Thomas Nast cartoon, "The Lesson of New Orleans," which appeared in *New York World,* captures the hostility towards Italy and the character of its emigrants. A sinister figure writes on the side of a mausoleum near Jackson Square, "The American Must Go." A *carabiniere*-type figure empties the boot of Italy filled with small figures to which Nast replies, "Americans! Prohibit the dumping of criminals at your hearth." Another image shows the Italian boot crushing the scales of justice. Although Italian officials attempted to identify the leaders of the lynch mob, the State of Louisiana would not cooperate, reinforcing the cartoon's words, "When Justice becomes a farce, the People will act Tragedy." Eventually the U.S. government paid indemnities to the families of the immigrant victims. But the memory of this episode fueled the popular taunt hurled at Italians thereafter, "Who killa da chief." *(Courtesy The Historic New Orleans Collection, accession number 1974.25.25.225)*

Crime-fighter. Law enforcement often looked the other way when crimes of extortion and kidnapping attributed to the Black Hand or Mafia occurred within immigrant communities. Many Americans suspected all Sicilians, Calabrians, and Neapolitans of belonging to or shielding the criminals and doing little to help immigrants eliminate crime from their own communities. Italian-American detective Charles Carola receives a gold badge from city officials in appreciation of his success in breaking up an Italian gang in Cleveland, Ohio, 1915. Even in New York City, Giuseppe (Joe) Petrosino's success in apprehending criminals did not counterbalance the negative image. Petrosino came from Padula, Salerno, in 1874. In 1883, he joined the New York City Police Department, and in 1895, became detective sergeant of the Homicide Division, the first Italian American to hold this position. In 1908, he was promoted to lieutenant and placed in charge of an elite corps of Italian-American detectives (The Italian Squad) specifically assembled to deal with the criminal activities of the Black Hand and other illegal organizations. On March 12, 1909, Petrosino was gunned down in Piazza Marina in Palermo, Sicily, while on a secret mission to combat the Mafia. Yellow journalism sold newspapers and even petty crime dominated the headlines—many crimes were attributed to The Black Hand or Mafia. The Order Sons of Italy in America's 2005 report "Italian American Crime Fighters: A Brief Survey" reflects the contradictions of Italians in crime, since many outstanding lawmen of Italian heritage earned distinction apprehending or prosecuting Italian-American criminals. *(Courtesy Charles Ferroni)*

Condescending Attitudes. "I Break-a da Stones." This sheet music represents an aspect of American humor that capitalized on the image of the ill-educated immigrant worker whose lack of English and industrial/technical skills forced him to take low paying jobs. Americans considered the men in these low-paying, backbreaking jobs uneducated and inferior. A popular parody of Italian railroad-track workers ran, "Where do yu work'a John? 'I work on the Lackawann.' What do you do'a there? 'I pusha, pusha, push.'" Others added the refrain, "What do yu do'a Marie? 'I maka spaghetti.' How do you do'a that? 'I pusha, pusha, push.'" Ironically this lampooning song was written by Italian-American songwriter Harry Warren, née Salvatore Anthony Guaragna. *(Courtesy The Historical Society of Pennsylvania, Balch Institute Collections, #642)*

Mafia Prototypes. Celeste Morello, author of *Before Bruno: The History of the Philadelphia Mafia* (two volumes), describes Mafiosi as individuals from western Sicily who followed a tradition of honor and service to family and community. Her great-grandfather Antonio Zummo, pictured here in 1942, came to America in 1883 from Monreale, Palermo. He settled in Norristown, Pennsylvania, but traveled back and forth to Sicily to visit his family and offer his services, for a fee, as an immigrant broker to people planning emigration. When they arrived at Ellis Island, he'd greet them and help them get settled and obtain jobs. He gained the respect of the immigrant community, helping newcomers navigate the maze of American laws and customs. Informed by the details of her great-grandfather's life and through further study, Morello suggests that the "true" Mafia offered protection to those threatened by Black Hand extortionists (Italian criminals who preyed on their own) and petty criminals and that they did not use violence and other illegal means to obtain profit. Morello traces the emergence in Philadelphia of Italian-American criminals as bootleggers and gambling entrepreneurs during Prohibition. These American-made criminals operated illegally and with violence to obtain money and power. Frank Viviano's book *Blood Washes Blood: A True Story of Love, Murder, and Redemption Under the Sicilian Sun* details a somewhat different historical trajectory in his own family chronicles. He notes a transition between the 1850 and 1860s Garibaldi era followed by the imposition of the new Cavour government land policies, which fostered the use of paid guards (often brigands) to maintain order on the newly acquired estates of absentee owners. *(Courtesy Celeste A. Morello)*

Strength in Unity. In 1915, a new Ku Klux Klan developed across the nation. Not only did the group persecute African Americans, but they also targeted Catholics, Jews, and immigrants. In addition, its members considered themselves defenders of morality and threatened those who manufactured alcoholic beverages for home consumption or violated Sunday restrictions against nonchurch activities. Immigrant children remembered crosses burning in front of Italian-Catholic homes and torchlight parades through the city streets of Louisville and Lafayette, Colorado. In fact, the first lodge of Sons of Italy in Colorado, pictured here, formed in 1924, in Salida, Colorado, mainly in reaction to Klan activity. Italians in the area of Birmingham, Alabama, told of Italian miners fleeing when Klansmen shot into their homes at night. An Italian grocer in Brighton, Alabama, received a threatening visit from Klansmen after she sold a customer a loaf of bread on Sunday. In 1922, in Carnegie, Pennsylvania (about seven miles from Pittsburgh), Klan members, who were Anglo neighbors of the Italian-immigrant Aldisert family, silently paraded round their home to show they were not welcome. *(Courtesy the Lionelle family)*

Ethnic Slurs. The headline for this 1925 article about boxer "Marine" Orlando Ranieri reads, "He's a Wop." While his professional name, Marine, derived from his early 1920s service in the Marine Corps, the term "wop" referred to his Italian heritage. His father, Davide, emigrated from Santa Maria del Giudice, Lucca, to Great Falls, Montana. The text of this article describes Marine as "this husky Italian . . . the deep-set black eyes in the olive complexion appearing like pools of ink." In the late nineteenth and early twentieth centuries, the media echoed popular stereotypical names given to different ethnic groups, such as "guinea," "wop," "hunky," or "greaser." Some trace the term "wop" to "working on Pacific," since so many Italians were railroad workers. Others say it meant "working without papers." It is interesting to note that in the 1920s, the derogatory names "limeys" or "micks" were no longer applied, in the press, to people of English or Irish descent. Newspapers in Louisiana in the early 1900s referred to Italians as "dagoes." Even today the word "wop" creates waves. In 2007, when The Blue Parrot restaurant in Louisville, Colorado, where Italians have lived since the 1890s, introduced a Wopburger, reactions were mixed. One Italian-American customer felt that "Wopburger" was offensive and an ethnic slur, but co-owner Joe Colacci replied that his dictionary said that "wop" came from *guappo*, meaning swagger or pimp. The majority of Joe's customers encouraged him to retain the name of what is now one of the most popular items on the menu. *(Courtesy Larry Ranieri)*

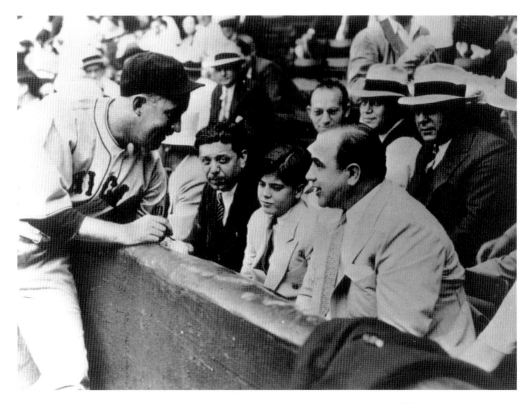

Crime Celebrities. Chicago Cubs player Gabby Hartnett autographs a baseball for Sonny Capone, who is sitting with his father, Al Capone, and his associates at a charity baseball game, c. 1931. The superstar of American crime, Alphonse Capone learned his "trade" on the streets of Brooklyn, New York's Red Hook section where he was born in 1899. His father had emigrated from Naples. Capone avoided the ethnic hostilities of neighborhood gangs; he applied his bulk and quick temper as a bouncer in Irish-operated brothels. His objective was to succeed as an entrepreneur by supplying alcohol and running gambling activities. The crime organization he established included men from many ethnic groups in New York and Chicago. Capone's political connections and influence during electoral campaigns and his generous charitable contributions gave him an aura of prominence. Luciano Iorizzo's *Al Capone: A Biography,* published in 2003, documents the reality of American organized crime as being multicultural and a product of American opportunity, not a practice imported from Italy. Other notorious crime figures, such as Lucky Luciano, a Sicilian, worked with Jewish Americans like Meyer Lansky and Bugsy Siegel, Neapolitans like Johnny Torrio, and people of many backgrounds. The Italians followed the examples of the Anglo, Irish, Germans, and Jewish crime figures who preceded them on the American scene. *(Courtesy Library of Congress, Prints and Photographs Division, reproduction # LC-USZ62-124508, collections of the 12858)*

Enforcing the Law. While Prohibition was in effect from 1919 to 1933, many Americans ignored or violated the law. Demand for alcohol increased, and some were willing to risk arrest for the money made from the sale and manufacture of liquor. Italians had brought to America a culture that linked moderate drinking, mainly wine, with daily life and they continued to make and drink wine. Some branched out into making and selling beer and whiskey to customers including judges and politicians. Officials attempted to enforce the law although some accepted bribes to look the other way. Here police dismantle a still in the predominately Italian Hill district of St. Louis, Missouri. *(Courtesy Gary Mormino)*

Mystery Writer. Lisa Scottoline speaks to the Continuing Legal Education meeting of the Women's Bar Association of western Pennsylvania at the Allegheny County Courthouse, April 13, 2007. Lisa grew up in an Italian family in Philadelphia, Pennsylvania. Her mother's family is Abruzzese, and her father emigrated from Teramo, also in the Abruzzo. Her best-seller mysteries feature Italian-American characters drawn from her personal family experience and informed by her training as a lawyer. She writes about "honest, hard-working professionals, not the mobsters so often portrayed." Her characters reflect the charm and tradition she attributes to her own extended family, "interesting, and sometimes quirky." For these reasons, Lisa has won the support of Italian-American organizations. Yet she was "a big *Sopranos* fan. I love the show for what it is intended to be, Hollywood entertainment. . . . Every nationality has its dark side, and I don't think you can do anything to stop the entertainment industry from capitalizing on it. The way you counteract it, is by producing products that project positive images of Italian Americans, and then supporting those products. . . . The answer to bad talk is good talk." Since all nine books in her Rosato and Associates series have been purchased by Fox TV Studio for development into a TV series, the public may soon see this "good talk" version of Italian-American life on their home screens. *(Courtesy Steve Bucci)*

Adjudicating the Law. Judge Leo Serini, president judge of the Delaware County Court of Common Pleas and Judge Alex Bonavitacola, president judge of the First Judicial District of Pennsylvania display the awards bestowed by Richard F. Furia (center), chancellor of the Justinian Society of Philadelphia, Pennsylvania, in 1997. The society granted the awards, the Justinian Eagles, to honor the judges' tenure and service. Founded in 1935, the Justinian Society of Philadelphia accepts only attorneys, judges, and law students of Italian ancestry and promotes honor and dignity in the legal profession, perform civic duties, administer justice, and promote the study of law. Thirty lawyers of Italian descent founded the Justinian Society of Advocates (later called the Justinian Society of Lawyers) in Chicago, Illinois, in 1921. While these are the only Justinian Societies in America, an International Italian American Bar Association serves the United States and Canada. *(Courtesy The Justinian Society of Philadelphia Archives)*

Fair Playing Field. In October 2006, a concerned parent, whose son attended the Rotolo Middle School in Batavia, Illinois, sent to the Order Sons of Italy in America national headquarters in Washington, D.C., a copy of the play *Fuggedaboudit: A Little Mobster Comedy,* which was to be performed by the Bada Bing Players. OSIA's Commission for Social Justice and its Illinois chapter contacted the school principal and the superintendent of schools, expressing their concerns about the play's stereotyping and requesting that performances be cancelled. The coalition claimed that the play, written by Matthew Myers, who teaches drama and communications at the school, featured mobsters with Italian last names who run an Italian restaurant while under surveillance by the FBI. At a press conference on November 14 in Geneva, Illinois, the coalition group, including (left to right) Marina Amoroso-Levato, the concerned parent; OSIA Grand Lodge President Tony Baratta; speaker Anthony Rago; and lawyer Joe Rago (behind and to the right of the speaker) declare their intention of suing the school district. The court refused to grant an injunction to cancel the play because of freedom of speech protections. The school eliminated the words "greaseball" and "friggin" from the script before performing it as scheduled in mid-November. The coalition gave Marina an award for her initiative and collected money for her son's tuition at a private school. (Fra Noi, *courtesy Jerry Daliege*)

Prominent Law Enforcers Under Siege. Giuliano Zaccardelli (left), COM (Commander of the Order of Merit of Police Forces), a former Royal Canadian Mounted Police (RCMP) officer and Commissioner of the RCMP from 2000 to 2006, is honored at a tribute dinner held at the *Famee Furlane* (Friulan family) hall in Vaughan, Ontario, February 2007. Zaccardelli emigrated from Prezza, L'Aquila, to Canada at age seven and grew up in the Montreal, Quebec, area. During his tenure, his agency faced two major cases of misconduct. Although Zaccardelli was not involved directly in either misconduct, he assumed full responsibility for the RCMP and resigned his commission, becoming the first person in the history of that agency to be forced out because of failures. Julian Fantino (right) COM, O.Ont (Order of Ontario), was appointed commissioner of the Ontario Provincial Police in 2006. He was born in the hamlet of Vendoglio, Treppo Grande, Udine, and immigrated with his family to Canada at age eleven. He began his career as a policeman in Toronto in 1969 and became the city's chief of police from 2000 to 2005. Diana Ricciutelli, a staff/volunteer at the Columbus Centre, stands in the middle. Funds raised at the dinner benefited two Italian-Canadian long-term care facilities, Villa Leonardo Gambin and Villa Colombo, both located in Vaughn. *(Courtesy Villa Charities, Toronto, Canada)*

CHAPTER 9

WHERE IS OUR HERITAGE?

While we can honor the past, we cannot re-create it. No longer are Little Italies the mecca of new arrivals. Some scholars use the term "ethnic theme parks" to describe what's left—businesses and churches but little residential concentration. A graphic account in Melania G. Mazzucco's novel *Vita* describes a tour of Manhattan's Little Italy as "not a particularly populated or lively neighborhood—more like a museum or theatre. It was depressing. Everything had been redone for the tourists: Italian flags; windows decorated in white, red, and green; restaurants with bogus Italian menus (the Neapolitan restaurant was serving Milanese-style cutlets and saffron rice) . . . this was not really Little Italy. There were no more Italians here—they had all gone away, disappeared, blended into, and cancelled out the America around them."

Still communities such as Hammonton, New Jersey, where fifty-three percent of the thirteen thousand residents are Italian American, welcomes visitors to its annual Our Lady of Mount Carmel celebration. Started in 1875, the celebration is believed to be the oldest Italian festival in the United States. Although third- and fourth-generation residents generate most of the *italianitá,* there are still strong traditions of foods and extended family relationships throughout the community. Gabriel J. Donio's pictorial history *Hammonton* illustrates this Italian orientation. According to the 2000 census, Hammonton has the highest percentage of Italian Americans of any municipality of more than one thousand people in the United States.

America changed in the twentieth century from an industrial to a post-industrial economy. Immigrants who arrive today encounter a sociopolitical structure very different from the one that existed in 1907. Italian Americans no longer dominate the labor force in certain occupations; they do not live in ethnic enclaves; they are part of the general culture. Have these shifts in lifestyles and worldview eradicated ethnic identity? Or has this identity adapted to the changing times?

The census shows that increasingly more Italian Americans claim a tie to their heritage. Italian festivals have experienced a renaissance. But as Sam Patti of Pittsburgh warns, "We've got to mean more to people than a yearly hot sausage sandwich. What these festivals mean, aside from the food, is a longing for a spiritual nourishment, a sense of place and proportion in our lives. That hunger increases the further we go from our family origins."

Maria Laurino expresses the view of a third-generation daughter in her book *Were You Always an Italian? Ancestors and Other Icons of Italian America* (published by W. W. Norton & Company): "Once many, many years ago, my grandparents escaped the abysmal poverty of southern Italy when they boarded ships for America. They tried to leave behind the sadness of their land, but this lachrymose history could not be erased, it was a part of them. They would bring the stories and traditions of this land; they would carry the effects of its deprivation and misery. I once refused to listen to these stories. I refused to enter the black-cloaked world of the peasants and discover my relationship to it. Now I can never fully enter or recover that world. But each time I denied its existence, embarrassed to stand out, monochrome in my neediness, I lost something irreplaceable, a texture of the soul."

How do we connect with our story, and which story do we acknowledge? Many descendants of immigrants know little of their past; even those who research their family's history often fail to place it in a larger context. What specifically motivated their ancestors to leave Italy? How did they adjust to life in America? Most descendants honor the nostalgic story, perpetuate family recipes, and keep in touch with relatives in America and in Italy.

Today many Italian Americans can reconnect with their Old World heritage by visiting Italy. The internal pride and sense of history they gain by walking the same streets and attending the same church as their ancestors can be expressed best in the heart. Elissa Ferraro Hosseinzadeh's account of her recent visit to her parents' birthplace in Agrigento adds another dimension. "What a wonderful experience . . . to see those people and places about which they spoke so lovingly. Visiting the house of my great grandfather, still in the family after almost two hundred years, was such an overwhelming moment for me. . . . We encountered so many Sicilian Americans who were visiting the towns of their forefathers for the first time. A wonderful guide in Siracusa [told] me how touched she was when she was able to help people find the location of a family home, and even in some cases find family members. She said many of her fellow guides have had the same experience and loved being able to facilitate these reconnections to the past."

This connection with place of origin often sparks an interest in learning more about our families and their individual journeys to America. While there is a wealth of published accounts describing many areas of settlement in America, the public has limited access to articles appearing in scholarly journals that are only found in university libraries. Often nostalgia substitutes for a full understanding of the experience. Most picture books, memoirs, and "memory pieces" in newspapers and newsletters entertain rather than provide accurate depictions of the immigrant reality.

Fiction writers often get closer to the bone of immigrant reality. Joseph Napoli's *A Dying Cadence: Memories of a Sicilian Childhood* has been described by Rudoph Vecoli as "one of the most vivid, evocative accounts of a childhood in an immigrant family I have ever read. Joseph Napoli is indeed a skillful writer. While he does not disguise the grim aspects of working-class immigrant life, the account is relieved by humor and affection."

Most Italian-American writers who rose to prominence during the 1980s, either as novelists, poets, or critics   for example, Robert Viscusi, Felix Stefanile, Tina De Rosa, Frank Lentricchia, Tony Ardizzone, Josephine Gattuso Hendin, and Fred L. Gardaphe—came from third-generation backgrounds. Writers Jay Parini (*The Patch Boys*) and Kenny Marotta (*A Piece of Earth*) set their novels in the period of migration. Thomas Ferraro's *Feeling Italian: The Art of Ethnicity in America*

examines some of the elements that contribute to Italian-American identity, discussing writers who seek examples from the past to inform the present. The Jimmy Durante role model of the good-natured working-class Italian set the standard for the characters of Tony Banta and Louie DePalma in the television series *Taxi*.

Most writers of Italian-American literature credit their family experience as a source for their fiction. Italian-American writers and artists benefit from closeness to their subject, as the last lines of Daniela Gioseffi's poem "Bicentennial Anti-Poem for Italian-American Women" illustrates:

remember Grandma, her olive face
wrinkled with resignation,
content just to survive
after giving birth to twenty children,
without orgasmic pleasures or anesthesia . . .
I remember
Grandma
got out of bed
in the middle of the night
to fetch her husband a glass of water
the day she died,
her body wearied
from giving and giving and giving
food and birth.

"Bicentennial Anti-Poem for Italian-American Women," by Daniela Gioseffi. Reprinted by permission of the author, © 1979, 2008, Daniela Gioseffi, from EGGS IN THE LAKE: Poems, Boa Editions; Rochester: NY. Also appeared in WORDS WOUNDS & WATER FLOWERS: Poems, VIA Folios/Bordighera Press: NY, 1995.

Rita Ciresi, the youngest daughter of an immigrant father and Italian-American mother, has written short stories and novels (e.g., *Pink Slip*) from the perspective she gained growing up in New Haven, Connecticut.

"Girls were trained to do the dishes without complaining. Sweep the floor without complaining. Sew their own clothes rather than buy them at Sears Roebuck (also without complaining). For a long time, I did not want to be that kind of girl—nor did I want to step into the sensible shoes of her natural successor, the good Italian housewife who mopped the floor every Saturday and made a big pot of spaghetti sauce every Sunday. I still hate to cook. I don't clean my house often enough. I rarely sew. But I still keep the habits of a *casalinga* each time I sit down at the computer to write a novel. I let my plots   instead of my pots   simmer. I make a mess on the page—and then carefully clean it up. My last drafts hopefully reveal that I know how to make a tight, even stitch with my words . . . So yes: I was raised as an Italian girl. For this I am grateful, and happy."

However, not all writers or artists of Italian heritage choose to use ethnic themes in their creations, such as writers Richard Russo and David Baldacci. On the other hand, some non-Italians have produced meaningful images of the immigrant experience. Winslow Homer's paintings of the Italian quarter in Gloucester, Massachusetts, and Tennessee Williams' play *The Rose Tattoo* give us insight into a lost era.

The innovative aspects of Italian-American expression remain a characteristic of the culture. The dynamics of a group that supported all shades of political philosophy, contributed to a wide range of popular entertainment and culture, and introduced a variety of foods, traditions, and lifestyles to America deserves our full attention. Paul Paolicelli has written, "Those of us privileged with memories of grandparents speaking in accents, wearing Old World clothes and attitudes, have come to realize how much they did for us. And that if we don't honor their memory and accomplishments, we'll lose them." We need to search closer to home, to the family archives, the correspondence, and the memories of the second and third generation to recapture the past and create a foundation to build towards a future.

In 1989, Dominic Candeloro urged the Italian-American community to focus on preserving its heritage. He described the scenario he envisioned for a usable past in his insightful piece *An Italian Ethnicity in the Year 2000: The Cultural Imperative to Organize Our Institutions for Creative Ethnicity*. He hoped for a partnership of the major Italian-American organizations, scholars of Italian America, and the community at large to present a more complete story of our experience. The year 2008 finds us still distant from this goal. Candeloro reminds us that as the third generation fades away, the documents of Italian America will vanish as the fourth generation discards family items they do not recognize nor understand.

The field of immigration history remains fertile for professional and community historians to explore. While much has been written, so much remains untold. We need more, not less. Not only do we need to read these scholarly books and articles, we need to encourage more publication with grants. And we need to help archival institutions with strong Italian-American collections manage their collections. Some large historical societies, major universities, as well as local libraries and museums, hold treasures that are not cataloged and improperly recorded and maintained. They lack the funds to implement their goals. What a wonderful opportunity for national organizations to support student internships, curatorial positions, and inaugurate public history projects throughout America. In order to tell the whole story, funders must grant freedom of information and freedom to choose all aspects of the immigrant experience. Too often students or family members are rewarded for telling the "nice" story with the "happy" ending. Essay contests request essays and short stories that "positively portray the Italian-American experience."

While many Italian-American organizations include as part of their mission statement the goal of preserving Italian heritage, they promote a partial picture. Instead of funding efforts to gather the documentation and family records, which are vital to understanding the past of Italians in America, they establish chairs in Italian language and Italian studies, and they develop K-12 curricula that focus on the Romans and the Renaissance—a recent one is entitled "The Universality of Italian Heritage." They stress the importance of regaining the language and with it, the culture of Italy, but they do not factor in the reality that most immigrants did not speak literary Italian, and most immigrants had little concept of a united Italy.

This does not diminish the general cultural value of studying the Italian language. In Pueblo, Colorado, the success of an informal program teaching Italian after school to elementary students led in the late 1970s to Italian being offered at the high-school level. Currently, all four high schools in Pueblo offer Italian language classes. Recently retired Italian teacher Rosalie Galasso Caputo, whose grandparents were from Monteu du Po, Torino, and Bovina, Agrigento, noted, "We have always had full classes and many non-Italians take the classes too. Most children, even if they are just one-eighth Italian, really want to learn the language and consider it their heritage." Many programs on the high-school as well as college level combine the study of Italian with exchange study opportunities in Italy.

This tendency of present-day Italian organizations to look to Italy to establish identity—cashing-in, so to speak, on modern Italy's leadership in fashion, cinema and as a travel destination—veers away from the reality of Italian-American heritage. These symbols cannot satisfy the hunger for a lost past, which was described by Maria Laurino. The teaching of Italian and the appreciation of Italian literature and music cannot replace the history of the immigrant journey that we have lost.

From other perspectives, many organizations, including the Italian-American press, often equate the socioeconomic success of individual Italian Americans as the full story—as if the sum of General Anthony Pace, Amedeo Giannini, and Mario Cuomo represented the entire spectrum of our heritage. Are Italian-American professionals or successful businessmen or politicians the sole keys to our past? Selective history that only documents positive images of a group distorts reality. Few Italian Americans attain the pre-eminence of Nancy Pelosi, Antonin Scalia, Gay Talese, or Danny DeVito. Whether achievement in certain fields, such as the arts and drama, reflects a cultural preference on the part of Italian Americans is again a difficult issue. Rosa Ponselle and Giancarlo Menotti may have been more inclined to follow their careers in opera and music because this tradition is a favored one for Italians. In areas such as sports, some say that the combination of street-wise gamesmanship and the attraction of professional careers intertwine so that talented Italian-American boxers, football players, and baseball players moved from their boyhood games into the major leagues.

However, there's no doubt that North America has been Italianized. Americans praise the healthy "Mediterranean diet" and stand in awe before a Leonardo DaVinci painting. America loves Italian wine and food, admires chefs who study in Italy, eagerly purchases Pucci and Gucci designs, and applauds singers, Cecilia Bartoli and Andrea Boccelli; film director Bernardo Bertolucci; and director/actor Roberto Benigni. Tourists flock to Italy to experience its variety of sights and history. While tourists return with wonderful memories, their trip does not inform them about the millions of Americans whose ancestors came from Italy.

In seeking a usable past, many choose to relate to a reality that did not exist for their ancestors. The present focus on Italian language summer camps, semesters abroad, and Italian art, fashion, and cinema does not speak to the pre-1960 immigrant experience. Such well-meaning attempts, which offer the grandeur of Rome and the bounty of Florence as the immigrant experience or select the most successful Italian Americans as the major accomplishment of an entire people, fail to preserve the immigrant heritage.

Fortunately for Italian America, the energy and perseverance of individuals, family, and community have stepped up to the plate. Academic institutions create Italian immigrant archives; community historians use innovative ways to document the immigrant experience; and governmental programs support the preservation of America's ethnic past and present. New York State's Department of Education issued a major study guide, "Italian Americans: Looking Backward Moving Forward," in 1994. New Jersey is the first state to create an Italian and Italian American Heritage Commission—Delaware is the second. Currently California's Assembly is considering a bill to include the role and contribution of Italian Americans to the economic, political, and social development of California and the United States of America in its K-12 curriculum. Local and regional museums, libraries, and historical societies collect materials from the public to record that area's past. Places like Stamford, Connecticut; Ossining, New York; Louisville, Colorado; Butte, Montana; Auburn, Washington; and Priest River and Kellogg, Idaho often contain a wealth

of photographs and information about their Italian residents. We need a "union catalog" that lists the locations and types of materials stored across North America.

Museums in Italian towns display the artifacts common to its residents at different periods. They also exhibit the evidence of emigration from Italy to other countries, which include pictures, letters, and artifacts sent by immigrants to their families remaining in the *paese*. The Italian government recently sponsored a major exhibit on immigration, "The Dream . . . *per non dimenticare.*"

The 2007-2008 exhibit "Italians of Denver", at the Colorado Historical Society, illustrates community energy and archival support. While this project can serve as a model for others, Nicholas Ciotola, curator of the Senator John Heinz History Center of Western Pennsylvania, writes, in his foreword to the exhibit catalog, "[S]imilar partnerships between Italian-American communities and museums have not been widely initiated [elsewhere]." He reminds us that "[i]n households and communities nationwide, there exists a wealth of artifacts, photographs, oral traditions, and other historical research materials, which, when archived following professional museum standards, become the tangible essence of a community's collective past."

Several institutions and organizations are revitalizing Italian-American history by organizing special events, exhibits, or lectures. In 2008-2009 the Western Regional Chapter of the American Italian Historical Association will be conducting a series of symposia, Immigrants and the Land: Italian Americans in California Agriculture. The State University of New York at Stony Brook announced its acquisition of Pietro Di Donato's papers. In New Castle, Delaware, the Friends of Bellanca Airfield are working to restore the service hangar that aircraft designer Giuseppe Mario Bellanca and Henry B. duPont built in 1935. The plant produced approximately three thousand aircraft before closing in 1954. As part of its program to sponsor forums and programs, which address many aspects of Italian-American immigrant/ethnic past and present, the John D. Calandra Italian American Institute, in April 2008, organized an international conference, Italians in the Americas, to examine the diasporic experience of Italian Americans of the Western Hemisphere. The institute plans a conference, The Land of Our Return: Diasporic Encounters with Italy, for April, 2009 Joseph Sciorra, Calandra's assistant director for Academic and Cultural Programs, registered the Lisanti Chapel at 740 East 215th Street in the Williamsbridge section of Bronx, New York, and also the Our Lady of Mount Carmel Grotto in Staten Island, on the New York State and National Register of Historic Places in July 2000.

Major historical agencies have acknowledged the importance of the Italian-American experience. From

October 1999 through February 2000, the New-York Historical Society sponsored an exhibit of the Italians in New York City; a collection of essays accompanied the exhibit. Alisa Zahller, associate curator of decorative and fine arts at the Colorado Historical Society, coordinated a five-year historical documentation project called The Italians of Denver. This grassroots project engaged Colorado's Italian-American community in collecting, identifying, and authenticating materials to portray the families, communities, history, and traditions that Italians brought to Colorado, with a focus on Denver. The exhibit closed in June 2008, but the materials collected and cataloged will provide a wealth of information for a fuller, documented history of the Italian presence in Colorado.

Publishing companies such as Arcadia Publishing's Images of America series use pictures to provide snapshot accounts of these communities over time. To date, the series contains thirty-two titles specifically focused on, or including, Italians in America. Other presses, such as SUNY Press (State University of New York), Macmillan Publishers Ltd, Fordham University Press, and the Center for Migration Studies, publish books for the public on the Italian-American experience.

Family historians continue to connect the heritage of their ancestors with the larger story of the immigrant experience, searching their roots—across oceans, across generations. Genealogy and family homage delves into the internal life of Italian America. This might reveal adultery, dishonesty, mental illness, domestic abuse, and other dysfunctions. Many family historians discover a sense of ambiguous loss in the immigrant experience, which cannot be soothed with the creation of a mythical past. They establish Web sites and communicate with researchers who also trace their roots to the same village, province, or region. Together they form online data banks of information.

However, in order to be fully productive, family efforts to document their history requires guidelines and training. Besides knowing how to access the Ellis Island passenger list records, it is important to know how to conduct oral history interviews. It is essential to learn not only about the history of the specific region of origin and the lives of the *contadini* or *artigiani* there, but also to know details about the place of settlement, its economy, political, and social structure. For without a framework, the little pieces of family life remain anecdotal and disconnected. Fortunately, organizations, museums, educational institutions, historical societies, and libraries offer resources.

Individuals and groups continue to find ways to connect to their heritage. Internal migration of Italian Americans to Florida and Arizona does not signal the twilight of ethnicity. In 2006, the Society of Fairfield (Iowa) Italian Americans (SOFIA) staged its second annual All Things Italian street festival at the First Fridays Art Walk on Fairfield Square. Sixty families from this town of ten thousand, located an hour south of Iowa City, belong to SOFIA. In fact, new chapters of established national organizations spring up quickly in the Sunbelt. Some local organizations develop extensive libraries, featuring books and other printed materials and DVDs relating to Italian and Italian American history, music, and literature. They invite speakers and sponsor panel and group discussions, dance and choral groups, language and conversation classes, and trips to different regions of Italy.

Old wine appears in new bottles as descendants of the immigrants work to restore traditions of *la cucina* and religious observances. Some of this activity attracts non-Italians too. Recently the *New York Times* printed a story about the Bacchus School of Wine, the first independent wine school in New Jersey. Started in 1997, the company has four schools in operation in New Jersey and one located in Staten Island. Bacchus is one of ten wine schools unattached to vineyards that guide their students from grapes to glass in about ten months. School administrators note that many of their students are Italian Americans in their thirties and forties, who have memories of the "basement wine" on their grandparents' tables.

What is an Italian American? Who are they? Since World War II, the majority of people in the United States who claim Italian heritage are third generation. Many have memories of grandparents who spoke little or no English, yet they see little in their daily lives that connects with those memories. The Canadian experience differs because of the thousands of Italian immigrants who immigrated there in the 1950s and 1960s. Canadian Italians still live their ethnicity. Fortunately, for them, the concept of multiculturalism was impacting government policy as they settled, and the pioneering efforts of Robert F. Harney, at the publicly funded Multicultural History Society of Ontario, established a base line for historical preservation. Even so, as the generational distance between first arrival and contemporary assimilated lifestyles increases, shall immigrant culture disappear?

The heritage of a people can continue in a variety of ways. There are the obvious visual elements of customs, dress, life choices (endogamy), and retention of language; the less obvious ones are culture, attitudes and beliefs, and preferences in lifestyles. Since most people do not analyze why they do things or think about things in certain ways, it is difficult for the majority of Italians to pinpoint any continuity in heritage. It is also difficult for the scholar—the social scientist who observes and measures behavior. Are Italian-American family attitudes different in degree from those of Polish Americans? Is the fact that some Italian Americans remain in blue-collar occupations (the thirty-six percent recorded in the 2000 census includes farmers, firefighters, and police officers), rather than in white-collar professions, a statement of lack of upward mobility, prejudice and discrimination, or perhaps a preference for the craft traditions that the third generation inherited from their fathers and grandfathers? The meaning of Italian-American identity and the persistence of ethnicity is fraught with the dangers of overgeneralization, vagueness in interpretation, and definition of terms.

Italian America looks towards the family as its most successful institution. Throughout the transition from immigrant to ethnic, from first to fourth generation, the family structure and its primacy has served Italians well in Italy and in America. Ethnic identity is closely intertwined with family; it persevered because of family, and will persist because of family.

Perhaps the answer lies within our memory of a generation of hard-working, ordinary people who settled North America. Most of us would agree with Paul Paolicelli's self-definition: "[I]f I had to say what part of me is Italian, I'd have to say my heart. For if I understand the sense of 'Italicity,' then it comes from the heart and from the values of our culture and heritage, which rest in the heart as much as, if not more than, the psyche."

An Italian Enclave. Many of the two hundred immigrant stonemasons recruited in the late 1890s to construct the Croton Dam settled in Ossining, New York, in an area of town called "the Hollow." Gennaro Fiores's shoe repair shop stood on North Highland Avenue, which was paved with yellow brick. In the 1920s, the brick building beyond Gennaro's shop became the Columbus Lodge of the Sons of Italy, still in operation. Each year Highland was blocked off for a weeklong Columbus celebration. Colangelo's meat market stood on the corner of Highland Avenue where it meets Denny Street and Yale Avenue, a sleepy dirt road. Once Route Nine became a main thoroughfare, the Italian enclave scattered. The area now has a large Hispanic population mostly from Ecuador. (*Courtesy Ossining Historical Society Museum*)

Home as Identity. Italian Americans, mostly from the Milan and Catania areas, first settled in the Hill section of St. Louis, Missouri, in the late nineteenth century. Many of the homes date from the 1920s, and were occupied by immigrants who labored in the area brickyards, foundries, and small businesses. After World War II, the younger more upwardly mobile families moved out. Urban renewal, which had already bulldozed the mostly Sicilian area of Little Italy in downtown St. Louis, also threatened the Hill. In the 1970s, a coalition including the politically savvy pastor of Saint Ambrose Catholic Church, St. Louis neighborhood organizations, and helpful national figures such as Secretary of Transportation John Volpe stopped urban renewal and preserved the ethnic flavor of the Hill. The subsequent influx of 150 newly arrived Italian immigrants rekindled a more contemporary *italianità*. (*Courtesy Jerry Krase*)

Neighborhood Networks. The Gonnella Bakery wagons deliver bread to Italian markets throughout Chicago, Illinois, each wagon making two hundred stops a day. Chicago had a number of Italian enclaves throughout the city, similar to a cluster of villages in Italy. Alessandro Gonnella opened a small Chicago storefront business on De Koven Street (near Taylor Street, settled mostly by Italians from Toscana) in 1886. By 1896, he and his wife, Marianna Marcucci, who had joined him from their hometown of Barga, Lucca, moved the business to a larger building on Sangamon Street near Ohio Street. This is the location in the photograph, which is in the Grand and Ogden neighborhood (also mostly Toscani until the 1930s when Sicilian immigrants settled there). The men sit on flour barrels in front of the bakery. A woman (member of the family) holding her baby can be seen looking out the window between the wagons. A few years later, Alessandro sent for his teenaged brothers-in-law, Lawrence, Nicholas, and Luigi Marcucci, to assist in his growing business. The Erie Street plant (in Chicago's near west section populated by Italian and Ukrainian immigrants), now the corporate headquarters, opened in 1915. In the mid-1970s, Gonnella started selling frozen dough, and in 1980, built a plant in Schaumburg, Illinois, dedicated exclusively to this product. The company, led by its corporate president Nick Marcucci, continues to serve Chicago and the upper Midwest area. *(Courtesy Dominic Candeloro)*

Anchored in Time. East Harlem once had the largest concentration of Italians in New York City (eighty thousand in 1930). Today, it is populated mainly by other ethnic groups. Remaining Italian landmarks include the 110-year-old Morrone Bakery, Patsy's and Rao's restaurants, two funeral homes, and Our Lady of Mount Carmel Roman Catholic Church. Claudio Caponigro still cuts hair in his barbershop at 116th Street, between First and Second Avenues. Born in 1931, in Salerno, into a family of barbers, Claudio experienced the Nazi occupation and bombing by American planes in 1943. At the end of World War II, when he was fourteen, he started his own barbershop. He arrived to a still vibrant Italian-American East Harlem in 1951, with two or three barbers on each street. Second- and third-generation Italians moved to the suburbs as crime and drugs increased on the streets. Although Claudio moved his family to the Bronx in 1969, he did not move his business. His customers are predominately Puerto Rican now. He maintains a steady business, still charging eight dollars a haircut and says the price is right for his customers, many with modest incomes. *(Courtesy Jerry Krase)*

Reinventing _Italianità_. The corner of College and Clinton Streets in Toronto, Ontario's historic Little Italy continues to be a magnet for tourists and locals who prefer the neighborhood's people-scale atmosphere. The café on the corner, Café Diplomatico, was one of the first in the city to have an outdoor patio. More than 250,000 Italian immigrants came to Toronto after World War II, transferring their brand of _italianità_. A three-block stretch of College Street, from Manning to Crawford Streets, became the center of their neighborhood. Today the area is home to a cross-section of Portuguese, South American, and Turkish immigrants. Many outdoor cafés retain an Italian façade but are no longer Italian owned or operated. Public transportation provides easy access to the area, located near the theatre and business sections in downtown Toronto, thus facilitating an Italian-like pedestrian lifestyle. CHIN radio, run by the third generation of founder Johnny Lombardi's family, remains the most visible symbol of a past era. The multicultural station broadcasts in over thirty languages. During the late 1980s and 1990s, many Italian Canadians moved to suburban Vaughan where they created a "New Italy." (© _Vincenzo Pietropaolo_)

Past Forward. At night crowds of locals and tourists fill Columbus Avenue in North Beach San Francisco, California. This area includes Fishermen's Wharf, Fugazy Hall, and SS. Peter and Paul Italian National Parish Church. Still dotted with Italian-owned and Italian-style businesses, North Beach combines the traditional with newer renditions of _italianità_. Molinari's Grocery (1896), Liguria and Vittoria bakeries share space with newcomers such as Café Sport and Il Pollaio, the latter founded by Italians from Argentina. Fior d'Italia Restaurant recently relocated to the first floor of the Hotel Remo and the original building became home to DiMaggios Italian Chophouse. Nearby Chinatown continues to receive emigrants from Hong Kong and mainland China. SS. Peter and Paul Church schedules a Chinese- and an Italian-language mass each Sunday. (_Courtesy Jerry Krase_)

Well-Worn Identity. The mural on Arthur Avenue, Little Italy in the Belmont area of the Bronx, New York, overlooks the locale used for the film *Marty* (1955), starring Ernest Borgnine (born Ermes Elforon Borgnino) and Betsy Blair. Paddy Chayefsky's story describes the life of Marty, a thirty-four-year-old butcher, whose Italian family is constantly after him to get married. Although most of the Italian immigrants and their children who lived on these streets have departed for the suburbs, this area still supports three butchers, two fishmongers, two cheese stores, two dedicated sausage makers, a fresh pasta shop, a coffee roaster, a well-stocked wine store, myriad delis and groceries, and eight bakeries—four for bread, four for Italian pastries. Most of the food stores, such as Biancardi's Butcher Shop, Madonia's Bakery, and Cosenza's and Randazzo's fish stores represent third-generation Italian-owned family businesses. Roberto Paciullo, who emigrated from Salerno to New York City in 1970, considers this neighborhood a small Italian town. His restaurant, Robertos, which he established in the late 1980s, combines old and new southern Italian *cucina.* With the help of an Italian, Albanian, and Mexican staff, Robertos received a Zagat rating as the second-best Italian restaurant in New York. In October 2007, Roberto opened a second restaurant, a trattoria, Zero Otto Nove, at 2357 Arthur Avenue near 187th Street. This restaurant features an imported wood-burning oven for baking Salernitana-style pizza. *(Courtesy Peter Rodda)*

Ongoing Presence, 1990s. This shrine belongs to Mola Bari, a local Italian club in Carroll Gardens, a section of Brooklyn, New York. Although the area has undergone gentrification, an Italian presence is still evident. On warm summer evenings, one can hear Italian spoken by neighbors sitting on their stoops. The movie *Moonstruck,* starring Nicolas Cage, used the Cammerei Brothers Bakery on Henry Street as the store in the film. Every Christmas and Easter residents decorate their front yards with elaborate displays. Many also participate in the Good Friday processional sponsored by St. Stephens Church, now combined with Sacred Heart parish. Cammerei Brothers closed its Henry Street business and now operates on Court Street jointly with Monte Leone's Pastry Shop. *(Courtesy Jerry Krase)*

Enhancing a Neighborhood. Tony DeSales, the "ambassador" of Baltimore, Maryland's Little Italy, captured the essence of this historical community in his drawings. He worked outside on the corner of Fawn and High Streets in Little Italy for over thirty-five years. Tony engaged the locals, tourists, and celebrities, such as Dustin Hoffman, Luciano Pavarotti, and Danny DeVito, who came to eat in Little Italy's restaurants. In *The Neighborhood: The Story of Baltimore's Little Italy* (1974), Gilbert Sandler describes a neighborhood changed by urban renewal in the 1950s but still retaining an ethnic identity up through the 1950s and 1960s. Several new restaurants opened in the 1970s, and they formed the Little Italy Restaurant Association. Residents renewed the traditional festivals for St. Gabriel and St. Anthony. In the summer of 2000, locals established the Little Italy Open Air Film Festival. It shows movies on the side of a building at the corner of High and Styles Streets, one block from Tony's corner. John Pente allowed them to convert his third-floor room-with-a-view into a projection booth. Films, such as *Roman Holiday* and *Cinema Paradiso,* were projected onto a plywood-covered brick wall. The event drew large crowds into the piazzalike setting. *(© 1992 Greg Pease)*

Italian Oasis. The Woodbridge section of Vaughan, Ontario, a suburb of Toronto, is home to 160,000 people. More than two-thirds of the population, who moved there in the 1970s, are of Italian heritage. Since most Italian Canadians are first-generation immigrants, they and their children speak Italian and English. These houses, located in the Kipling Road/Highway No. Seven area, were built mostly by Italian-Canadian contractors. They simulate villas or *palazzetti* and are large and showy with expensive interiors including marble and ceramic-tile floors. Today this "New Italy" contains six predominately Italian-Canadian Catholic parishes and over thirty large banquet halls for family celebrations and *feste* for Italian patron saints. Italian businesses joined the exodus from the urban Little Italy to Woodbridge. Stores have signs in Italian and English, with names such as Roma Optical and Venice Cleaners. In 2006, Tony Carella, councilor for Vaughan's Ward Two, noted that his constituents demand one-on-one interaction with their council member whom they know personally, rather than use the bureaucratic process that reminds them of the system in Italy. *(© Vincenzo Pietropaolo)*

Ninth Street Italian Market. Epifany "Pip" DiLuca has been president of the Italian Market Business-men's Association in Philadelphia, Pennsylvania, since 1992. He owns and manages the Villa Di Roma restaurant, an area landmark since the 1930s. The DiLuca family purchased the restaurant in the early 1960s. Pip's grandfather, Epifanio, came from Spadafora, Messina, to south Philadelphia, probably after the Messina earthquake of 1908. He sold fish and produce at the South Ninth Street Market to support his family of thirteen who lived nearby. Although the market now has a variety of ethnic businesses, the Italian flavor remains. On October 12, 2007, a historical marker commemorating the Ninth Street Curb Market was located on the sidewalk near Ninth and Christian Streets. The marker celebrates the market's ethnic diversity. Since 1993, historian Celeste Morello has offered tours of this unique Philadelphia neighborhood and has preserved some of its signature recipes in a cookbook, *The Philadelphia Italian Market Cookbook: The Tastes of South Ninth Street. (Courtesy Celeste A. Morello)*

ITALIAN AMERICANS VISIT ITALY

A Grandmother's Joy. Luigi Fioretti and Stella Milela Fioretti proudly take a *passeggiata* in the Piazza dell'Orologio of Carbonara, Bari, with their two-and-a-half-year-old grandson Gene Fioretti, who was visiting with his parents and his thirteen-month-old brother Joe in 1950 from Auburn, Washington. Luigi was still living in Auburn when Gene was born in 1947, but he returned "home" to retire in 1949 after having worked in Washington State for thirty-five years. Stella had never been to America and this was the first time she met her daughter-in-law, Antonetta, and her two young grandchildren. The reunited couple spent their remaining years together in Carbonara. Interestingly, many years after graduating from college, Gene stopped by to see his grandparents en route to an extended tour of Europe in June 1971. He stayed longer after meeting a lovely young woman, Anna Addante, whom he later married in September 1972. Gene continues to visit his ancestral home, now with his and Anna's sons. *(Courtesy Matt and Antonetta Fioretti)*

Paying Respects, 1998. Joe Gasperi visits the grave of his great aunt, Mary Gasperi Nones, in Sover, Trento, with his parents, Urban and Emily Gasperi. While Joe had previously met his Aunt Mary, this 1998 visit was his parents' first trip as well as their thirty-fifth wedding anniversary. Joe's grandfather, Tom, had come to the United States in 1921 and returned to visit his only sibling, Mary, fifty years later. Over time, the family had exchanged letters and pictures, and Tom had sent care packages to Sover to help during hard times. Joe recalls, "Meeting Aunt Mary on my first visit to Italy in 1987 was very difficult. I wasn't able to speak. All I could do was hold her hand and cry. I just felt all the pain of our family having been separated for so long and the joy of finally being together. It was such a powerful experience that even today it still brings back tears. Sometimes it feels as if you are feeling the pain of all families who have been separated through immigration. One can't imagine how difficult life must have been to break the bonds of family for a new life in a new country." *(Courtesy Rosa and Tom Gasperi)*

Family Ground, 1995. Irma Crocetti Carter and her brother, Chuck, visit their mother's (Maria Cella)1896 birthplace, a farm in Fiorenzuola D'Arda, Piacenza. The Cellas did not own the farm. They paid rent in money and produce to the owner, a count who lived nearby. Irma first visited the town in 1961 when traveling in Italy with a college friend. They inquired at the Stato Civile (town hall) for some information on the Cella family. The record clerk found Irma's mother's birth record and the home address of her parents—he then closed up the office and drove the young women to this house. Back in Framingham, Massachusetts, Irma showed the photos to her mother and Uncle Charlie, who instantly recognized the house. They said it had not changed since they left more than fifty years before. *(Courtesy Irma Crocetti Carter)*

Civilizations Past. Antoinette Scarpaci and her daughter, Vincenza, pose with their cousin, Rosario Ragona, and his coworker at the temple of Segesta near Calatafimi, Trapani, c. 1993. Antoinette and her husband, Frank, met Rosario in 1970 when they first located Rosario's mother, Caterina, Antoinette's first cousin. In 1970, Rosario and his wife had one child and Rosario drove a taxi. Now he supervises the security guards at the temple/theatre complex at Segesta. Antoinette told Rosario that her mother, Vincenza Gerardi, who settled in Brooklyn, New York, had wondered why foreigners would be interested in these "ruins" (Segesta) near Calatafimi. This outstanding example of the Greek heritage of Sicily, attracting thousands of tourists each year, was only a part of the landscape to the young woman growing up in its shadow. *(Author's collection)*

A Family Legacy of a Returning Great Grandson. Franca Terra washes clothes on the rock ledge alongside the stream in Belluno Veronese, Verona, with her American cousin, Sandro Kaiser, in July 1998. When her great uncle, Giuliano Emanuelli, a prosperous farmer from California's Imperial Valley, returned to his birthplace for a long visit, in the early 1950s, he observed women washing in the stream at a time when plumbing was primitive and availability of electricity scarce. He decided to contain the stream that originated in a hill behind his sister's home, an area called Il Molino—where the mill had once been. His hired crew raised the level of the stream by building a low rock and concrete wall and contained the sides of the stream with low rock walls. On one part of the wall, he placed a rock ledge sloping toward the stream, where the women could stand while using it as a washboard. Even in the 1990s, Franca used the rock ledge in nice weather, in preference to her washing machine, much to the delight of Sandro, Giuliano's great grandson. *(Courtesy Sharon K. Emanuelli)*

Pursuing a Dream. Robert Chaupette had longed to visit his parents' hometown of Salaparuta, Trapani. Accompanied by his wife, Cora, and his daughter, Bonnie, he set out from Alexandria, Louisiana, for Sicily in November 2004. From a hotel in Palermo, the family contacted Father Baldassare Graffagnino in Salaparuta to arrange a visit. When the Chaupettes arrived, Father Graffagnino introduced them to Rosario Drago (whose mother was a Chiapetta). Since neither of the two Italians spoke English, Father called Ninfa Ippolito, an English teacher, to help translate. With Ninfa's help, Father explained that the Belice earthquake of January 14-15, 1968, had destroyed the mother church (note its picture on the wall in the office) and much of the town. Father made around sixty trips to recover village and family histories from the rubble. That evening the Chaupettes (the name change from Chiapetta occurred in Louisiana) had dinner and drank the wine their cousin Rosario made from his grapes. The next day they returned to Palermo. *Left to right:* Rosario Drago, Bonnie Chauppette Michel, Robert A. Chauppette, Cora C. Chauppette, Ninfa Ippolito, Father Baldassare Graffagnino. *(Courtesy Cora C. Chauppette, Robert A. Chauppette, and Bonnie C. Michel)*

Searching for Clues. During a visit to the city of Cava de' Tirreni, Salerno, in January 1998, Bob Masullo of Sacramento, California, a third-generation Italian American, takes notes about his paternal grandparents and other relatives born in the city from official records in the Ufficio dello Stato Civile. His grandparents, Felice Masullo and Maria Santola D'Amore, emigrated from Cava de' Tirreni to New York City's East Harlem in the early 1900s. Over time, Bob's family had lost whatever contact they had with any relatives, so he did not attempt to check out over a hundred telephone listings of Masullo in Cava's phone book. But he could not help thinking, "How beautiful!" and "Why did they ever leave? Cava is a jewel, set on a small plain surrounded by jagged mountain peaks." Then Bob remembered a scene in Paul Paolicelli's book *Dances with Luigi: A Grandson's Search for His Italian Roots.* When Paul returned from the army, he told his grandfather how beautiful he found the Italy he'd seen near Naples. Paul asked, "How could anyone leave such a place?" His grandfather replied, "You saw it with a full stomach." *(Courtesy Eileen M. Masullo)*

Lest They Forget, 1997. Ray Martire had emigrated from Pedace, Cosenza, to Spokane, Washington, in 1949. He felt, "now that Italians are doing much . . . better economically, and do not need the help from their emigrant relatives, [it] comes easier to them to forget people who are far away. So I wanted to do something to remind them of the help received and the room we left for them." Ray wrote to as many Calabrese clubs as he could find in the world to invite Pedacese to participate in the dedication of a monument. He persuaded the architect Franco Scarcello to contribute his design pro bono. The mayor of Pedace provided the location, the money for the materials, and support for the inauguration. Ray, who maintained close connections with Pedace over the years, recruited free labor and wrote the inscription for the monument: *Ricordali è un dovere—Amarli è un bisogno—Incontrali è una gioia* (To remember them is a must—To love them is a necessity—To meet them is a joy). On September 14, 1997, sixty emigrants from Pedace, representing many countries and carrying their respective country's flags, attended. This photo records some of the emigrants gathered at the monument the day following the dedication. *(Courtesy Ray Martire)*

Reconnecting. Using letters and photographs her grandmother owned when she died in the 1960s, Andrea Mistretta Quaranta and her husband Perry, from Waldwick, New Jersey, left their 1999 organized tour of Sicily to visit Andrea's father's ancestral village of Mussomeli, Caltanissetta. First, they visited the Norman Castle on the hill and then the Church of Our Lady of Miracles (Chiesa Della Madonna Dei Miracoli), where Andrea's grandparents had worshipped. When they reached the address written on the old letters, they found that the house was empty. They asked a man strolling down the street if he knew of any Vullo family members in the village, and he immediately crossed the street and spoke to a woman sitting behind closed shutters. When the shutters opened, the now older face of Carmellina Vullo, Andrea's father's first cousin, resembled the face in a photograph carried from Waldwick. In turn, Carmellina showed them a letter Andrea's mother, Rose Mistretta, had sent in 1962 with a photo of her daughters Andrea and Janine. As a farewell gift, Carmellina gave Andrea (the two are pictured here) some *lentichie* (lentil) seeds to symbolize family roots. When she returned from Sicily, Andrea shared the precious seeds with all family members with ties to the hilltop village of Mussomeli. *(Courtesy Andrea Mistretta Quaranta)*

Returning to the Ancestral Font. Giuseppe De Maio and his wife, Ursula, traveled from San Francisco, California, to Sarno, Campania, for their newborn son Lorenzo Luigi DeMaio's baptism at S. Maria della Foce. Giuseppe's devoutly religious mother, Maria, had made it clear that she expected to witness her grandchild's baptism. And here, on May 15, 2005, Maria watched with pride as Giuseppe, Ursula, and Giuseppe's brother-in-law (Lorenzo's godfather) participated in the rites. *(Courtesy the DeMaio family)*

Instant Recognition. When Don Gesualdi visited Pisticci, Matera, in the fall of 2005, searching for the home of a friend's father who had immigrated to Toronto, Canada, in 1923 and never returned, the townspeople escorted him to the oldest lady on the Via Cristoforo Colombo to see if she remembered the family's house. This elderly woman turned out to be the sister of Don's aunt through marriage. Maria Viggiani's sister, Antonietta Viggiani, had married Don's father's younger brother, Antonio Gesualdi. Antonio, Antonietta, and Maria had not emigrated. Although Don and Maria had never met, when she heard Don speaking in dialect, she "immediately asked me who I was and quickly knew who I was. Here we bridged the generations, the cultures across two continents with a cell phone connecting to my mom back in Canada." *(Courtesy Julian Nawrocki)*

Wedding Abroad. Jennifer Gange of Chicago, Illinois, decided in 2005 to celebrate her wedding in Sicily, the ancestral home of her paternal grandparents, since the family now had "more relatives in Sicily than we do in Chicago." She had first visited Sicily with her American cousins, Diane and Dixon Gange Landers, in 2003. With the guidance of her Sicilian relatives, she reserved the Palazzo Butera in Palermo for June 3, 2006. Jennifer had met her fiancé, Alex Hafez—half English and half Afghani—in San Francisco. The couple chose a civil ceremony performed in Italian by a court official, assisted by a translator. The picture shows the couple and their bridesmaids, and, in the background on the far left, Jennifer's parents, Jim and Linda Gange. Approximately one hundred wedding guests, from America, Sicily, parts of Europe, and Afghanistan, attended the ceremony and savored traditional Sicilian foods at the meal that followed, including swordfish, calamari, and a cassata wedding cake. This trend of Italian Americans marrying in Italy is clearly popular. In August 2005, Jamie Prontera Carkonen married her fiancé, Michael Delapez, in Lecce, Italy, in the same church, San Antonio A. Flugenzio, where Jamie's Italian-American grandmother, Mary Vacca, had married Michele Prontera, a former Italian prisoner of war, in June 1946. *(Courtesy Diane Gange Landers; photographer Tony Castro)*

Military Emissary. Italian Americans of Cleveland, Ohio, welcome General Armando Diaz on an official visit, c. 1921. United States general Buckey and Italian consul Nicola Cerri accompany him. Italian Americans were proud when several leading American political writers, journalists, and politicians praised the economic success of Fascism during the 1920s and 1930s. During this visit, Diaz joined Lt. General Baron Jacques of Belgium, Admiral David Beatty of Great Britain, Marshal Ferdinand Foch of France, and General John J. Pershing in the groundbreaking ceremony for the Liberty Memorial in Kansas City, Missouri. During World War I, Diaz won acclaim for routing the Austrian army in the decisive battles of the Piave River and Vittorio Veneto. In 1935, bas-reliefs of Jacques, Foch, Diaz, and Pershing, by sculptor Walker Hancock, were added to the memorial. (*From* Columbus Revista Magazine)

Operatic Friends. Italian Americans welcomed Italian opera personalities to their homes. John Flandina (left), the son of successful milliners and opera buffs, stands in front of the family home in Rego Park, Queens, New York, in August 1948. Baritone Luigi Montesanto, who sang the role of Luigi in the 1918 world premiere of Puccini's *Il Tabarro* at New York's Metropolitan Opera, stands next to John. In later years, he taught and represented the operatic tenor Giuseppe Di Stefano (sitting behind the wheel), his most famous pupil. Born in Sicily, Di Stefano was well known in Europe before making his American debut in 1948 at age twenty-seven as the Duke in *Rigoletto* at the Metropolitan Opera. Giovanni Zenatello, a famous tenor during the first quarter of the twentieth century, who later became a voice teacher, stands next to Montesanto. In 1963, Luciano Pavarotti made his international debut when he filled in for Di Stefano at the Metropolitan Opera. (*Courtesy Luisa Granitto*)

Slow Food. This 2003 International Cheese Fair in Bra, Cuneo, organized by Slow Food International, showcases traditional, high-quality artisanal methods that respect biodiversity in food preparation. In 1986, Carlo Petrini introduced the Slow Food movement to challenge the industrialization of food production. Slow Food International was established in 1989 and headquartered in Bra. Twelve thousand of its eighty thousand members belong to Slow Food USA. Italian immigrant practices of raising food to feed the family and preserving regional traditions fit well with the Slow Food concept. Thus Italian-American food artisans—from the internationally known chef Mario Batali to Mazzi, an artisan baker at Hideaway Bakery in Eugene, Oregon—embrace these concepts. Sicilian immigrant Angelo Garro, an ornamental blacksmith who lives in San Francisco, California, exemplifies the traditional practice of foraging for food that he and his family followed in Siracusa. Michael Pollan describes Garro's approach to food in his book *The Omnivore's Dilemma: A Natural History of Four Meals* (2006). *(© Slow Food Archive, all rights reserved)*

Reverse Tourism. Ernesto Milani, founder of Lombardi del Mondo, introduces a group from Cuggiono, Milano, to the sites their ancestors settled in the United States. During this 2005 trip, the group visited the "Hill" district of St. Louis, Missouri, and Italian sections of Herrin, Illinois, and Rosati and Ironton, Missouri. Some discovered long-forgotten relatives or located the graves of their ancestors. The group stands on the steps of St. Anthony Church, which was built by immigrants who settled in Rosati. Milani notes that most Italians today know these areas only through references in immigrant letters or stories told by those who repatriated. For example, they look for the clay pits on the "Hill" where their ancestors made bricks. *(Courtesy Steve Zulpo)*

Simpatico. Italian President Francesco Cossiga wearing a bonnet, receives a ceremonial headdress from members of Chicago, Illinois's Native-American community, January 1992. The delegation wished to show its appreciation to the Italian government for its help in arranging the upcoming visit of Native Americans to Italy in April of that year. President Cossiga had traveled to Illinois to receive an honorary degree, Doctor of Humane Letters, from Loyola University. At a reception hosted by Governor Jim Edgar, President Cossiga presented the governor with a sixteenth-century map of Italy. In turn, the governor announced the creation of a fellowship in cartography at Chicago's Newberry Library for an Italian scholar of the president's choosing. *(Courtesy* Fra Noi*)*

Dramatic Tribute. The Italian Carabinieri Band participated in New York City's Columbus Day parade in 2000. Here they perform on Liberty Island in New York harbor. Italian musicians have played an important role in U.S. bands since the nation's beginning. In 1805, Thomas Jefferson recruited a group of Italian musicians to form the first U.S. Marine Band. Over the years the band had several Italian directors, the most famous being Francesco Scala, who led the band from 1855 to 1871. Under Scala's leadership, the Marine Band became the premier military band in the country. *(Courtesy* Italian Tribune*)*

Espresso Culture. Italian café culture now permeates North America although *baristi* in Italy produce a glass of steamed milk when American tourists simply order a "latte." Sam Patti, whose ancestors came from Milazzo, Messina, and Calabria, started La Prima Espresso Company in 1988 to sell espresso machines. His family had operated bars in the greater Pittsburgh, Pennsylvania, area. Sam located his company in an old building near the Pittsburgh Produce Terminal at Twentieth and Smallman. The hundred-year-old Pennsylvania Macaroni Company is still in operation down the block. Sam added an espresso bar and sells coffee roasted on the premises. He prides himself in serving authentic dark-roast Italian-style espresso. Some of Sam's employees are Italian-language majors at the University of Pittsburgh; they add to the café's *ambiente*. (*Courtesy Samuel J. Patti*)

An Italian Tribute. President Vincent Tummino of the New York City Fire Department's Columbian Association presents Italian president Carlo Ciampi with a helmet and title of honorary fire chief in 2003. Ciampi placed a wreath at the World Trade Center Ground Zero monument on November 16, 2003. The men on the right are firefighters and those on the left are from New York City's Police Department. The Columbian Association continues this tie with Italy and the commemoration of the September 2001 disaster in which 343 firefighters died while trying to save people trapped in the Twin Towers. On October 1, 2007, a team of gondoliers from Venice, Italy, and New York firefighters began a six-day trip on the Hudson River from Albany to the Ground Zero site. (*Courtesy Vincent Tummino, Ambassador, International Columbia Association*)

Italians Abroad. Renato Turano, an Italian senator, stands (second from right) at a reception in Saddle River, New Jersey. In November 2001, the Italian Senate passed a law allowing Italians abroad with valid Italian citizenship to vote in the national elections for a select group of twelve representatives and six senators. The elections took place on April 6-9, 2006, and the votes of Italians living abroad helped to elect Prime Minister Romano Prodi. Turano emigrated from Calabria with his family at age seven. He transformed a family-size *panetteria* (bakery) in Chicago, Illinois, into a multimillion-dollar business. His major role in establishing Chicago's Casa Italiana, which provides services to the Italian community, helped him gain the position of *senatore* for the regions of North and Central America. Some of these representatives of "Italians abroad" hold dual citizenship with their country of settlement. They vote and initiate laws in the Italian Parliament to benefit their constituency, such as the reacquisition of Italian citizenship, exemption from double taxation, health insurance while in Europe, and participation in the Italian old-age pension system. A recent attempt to develop an independent Italians Abroad Party did not succeed. Approximately two-thirds of these elected officials belong to Italian national parties on the left and one-third on the right. *(Courtesy Mary Ann Re, New Jersey Italian and Italian American Heritage Commission)*

Hero of Two Worlds. For the bicentennial anniversary of Giuseppe Garibaldi's birth in 2007, Ted Jacobsen, a member of the Harry S. Truman Masonic Lodge, designed and produced a personalized U.S. Postal Service stamp to honor the "defender of liberty" in South America and Italy. The Masonic Stamp Club of New York sponsored the stamp and special envelope (cachet). On July 4, the date of Garibaldi's birth, Judy Riley, the postmistress of Garibaldi, Oregon, the only town in North or Central America named for the hero, cancelled stamps mailed from the town that day. (Although the United States Postal Service does not distribute the stamp, it is recognized as a private issue by postal employees.) There are cities named after Garibaldi in Brazil and Uruguay. After the failed revolution of 1848-1849 and the death of his wife, Anita, who fought beside him against the Austrian and French troops near Ravenna, Italy, Garibaldi sought refuge in the home of the inventor Antonio Meucci in Rosebank, Staten Island. He earned his keep by making the smokeless candles Meucci had invented. Garibaldi left in 1853 to return to life at sea; he returned to Italy in 1854. Some historians claim that when the Civil War broke out in the U.S., Garibaldi offered his services to President Abraham Lincoln and was invited to serve as a major general in the Union army, but he withdrew his offer when Lincoln failed to name him commander of the Union army and to promise the abolition of slavery. *(Courtesy Theodore "Ted" H. Jacobsen, designer and producer of the bicentennial Giuseppe Garibaldi stamp)*

Refurbishing an Icon. In 1982, President Ronald Reagan asked Lee Iacocca (whose father came from San Marco, Campania), the chairman of Chrysler Corporation, to raise funds for the restoration and preservation of the Statue of Liberty and Ellis Island. He secured more than $500 million to repair, restore, and maintain these monuments. The state-of-the-art Ellis Island Immigration Museum opened in September 1990, in the space where millions of immigrants had passed during the entry process. Leading scholars of immigration, including specialists on Italian immigration, such as Rudolph Vecoli (whose parents came from Camaiore, Lucca) and Virginia Yans (her father, whose original name is Yaui, came from Malvito, Cosenza, and her mother's parents emigrated from Varese), worked with the National Park Service to develop the exhibits. Vecoli chaired the History Committee during the planning phase. Yans continues as a member of the History Committee, advising on exhibit additions and reconceptualizations in order to incorporate the experience of post-1960 immigrants. Descendants of thousands of immigrants have included their ancestors' names on the American Immigrant Wall of Honor located near the main museum building. (*Courtesy* Italian Tribune)

La Storia. Jerre Mangione presents high-school Italian-language-class students, in Lawrence Township, New Jersey, with copies of *La Storia: Five Centuries of the Italian American Experience,* a social history of Italian immigration to the United States that he and Ben Morreale wrote. The students had written winning essays describing, "What it means to be an Italian American," for a contest sponsored in 1993 by the Central Jersey Chapter of the American Italian Historical Association. Mangione's autobiographical novel *Mount Allegro* and his autobiography *An Ethnic at Large: A Memoir of America in the Thirties and Forties* have added to the wide range of literature documenting the Italian-immigrant experience. Many books and articles continue to widen our understanding of the experience through scholarly examination of specific areas of immigrant settlement or specific topics of interest. Among these are the journals *Italian Americana* and *VIA (Voices in Italian Americana)*; the book *Italian American Experience: An Encyclopedia,* by Salvatore Lagumina; and the annual proceedings of the American Italian Historical Association. (*Courtesy Robert B. Immordino*)

Birmingham Colossus. This statue of Vulcan has dominated the skyline of Birmingham, Alabama, since 1939. The Commercial Club of Birmingham commissioned Italian sculptor Giuseppe Moretti to create the piece for the 1904 World's Fair in St. Louis, Missouri. Club members decided that the statue, built locally and composed solely from Alabama minerals, would capture the spirit of their industrial city. Moretti portrayed Vulcan as a strong colossus renowned for his mythical role as architect, smith, armorer, chariot builder, and artist. The statue stood fifty-six feet from pedestal to spear tip and weighed about sixty tons—the largest statue made in the United States and the world's largest cast-iron statue. At the fair, Moretti received the grand prize for best exhibit in the mineral department. For the next three decades, Vulcan stood all but forgotten in Birmingham's fairgrounds until the city's Kiwanis Club and the state director for the Works Progress Administration joined the effort to move Vulcan to a new five-acre park on Red Mountain, donated by U.S. Steel, which had provided the ore for the statue. (This photo dates from 1965.) *(Courtesy Birmingham Public Library, Department of Archives and Manuscripts; catalog # 1556.32.34)*

Research Center. Rudolph Vecoli, director of the Immigration History Research Center (IHRC) at the University of Minnesota in Minneapolis, discusses the center's collections with Roger Winter, former director of Immigration and Refugee Services of America, c. 1990s. Established in the late 1960s, the center pioneered the preservation of materials related to emigrants from southern and eastern Europe. Vecoli's own articles, and his role as the first president of the American Italian Historical Association, encouraged scholarly research. Vecoli describes the IHRC's role in preserving, "Old paper (letters, documents, books, newspapers, etc.) . . . the raw materials of history . . . The IHRC's Italian American Collection today constitutes a vast [archive] upon which we can draw to write histories, novels, dramas, anthologies, and create films. It includes the archives of [major Italian American] national organizations and local societies, files of over five hundred Italian American newspapers, a library of several thousand volumes, and the letters, diaries, memoirs, and family histories of a multitude of Italian immigrants and their descendants. If the IHRC had not gathered these precious materials, much of our history would have been lost forever." Scholars from all over the world have used the center's extensive collections. *(Courtesy Immigration History Research Center, Photograph Collection, University of Minnesota)*

Community Histories. Grassroots projects that collect, record, and publish the history of their area have created valuable resources for future generations. Project organizers interview families and individuals to place their experience in the context of the larger community. For example, Rocchina Russitano of Canastota, New York, was inspired to research and record the history of her community in 1982. She formed a project committee and mounted displays at St. Agatha Church and in store windows to attract more participants. A group of teachers and a librarian helped to edit the family stories and the first book, *An American Journey-Our Italian Heritage,* was published in 1998. When retired Canastota schoolteacher Lynne Stagnitti Ahnert traveled to Linguaglossa, Catania, in 2000, she carried a copy to the town hall. The town clerk noticed the book and said, "Where are you going with this book? Do you realize that this is the only record we have of the people who left our villages years ago to immigrate to America? The stories in it are fantastic! I saw this in Florida and have been trying to obtain a copy." Lynne returned home and assisted in collecting material for a second volume, which was published in 2001. Two volumes of *Greenbush . . . Remembered,* by Catherine Tripalin Murray, detail the Greenbush neighborhood of Madison, Wisconsin, where immigrants from villages such as Palermo, Trapani, Bagheria, and Piana degli Albanesi had settled. Other published examples of local history projects are Pueblo, Colorado's, *100th Anniversary Celebration* (sponsored by the Sons of Italy for their anniversary and also for the centennial anniversary of Columbus Day as a Colorado state holiday), and retired New York City schoolteacher Mario Toglia's study of emigrants from Calitri, Avellino, *They Came By Ship: The Stories of the Calitrani Immigrants in America.* *(Courtesy Rocchina Russitano and Catherine Tripalin Murray)*

A Journey of Discovery. Paul Paolicelli, author of *Dances with Luigi: A Grandson's Search for His Italian Roots* and *Under the Southern Sun: Stories of the Real Italy and the Americans It Created,* looks over his laptop at his "new" Italian relative, cousin Angelo Rafael Buono (far right) in Miglionico, Matera. Paul's father, also Angelo Rafael, and this Italian cousin were named after the same grandfather. "There was the same picture of my grandmother and grandfather hanging on Angelo's wall that hung on our own wall back home. That was the truly emotional part for me. I didn't know that family existed until that afternoon in 1992." Paul used his journalistic skills to find the pieces of his family's story. His books use "legacy history," combining the historical research with his personal story, told from "a highly individualistic point of view." Paul encourages Italian Americans to tell "the little stories [based on memory as well as documentation] that overarch the much larger historical events and places, while offering a unique perspective on some very important pieces of the American puzzle." In *Under the Southern Sun*, Paolicelli explores "the theory of cultural subconscious . . . and the idea of a Southern Italian 'sensibility.'" He does it by using the physical and cultural terrain of this region to explain how "familial history" can influence the way emigrants from southern Italy developed their own "internal value system." *(Courtesy the Paolicelli & DePasquale families)*

ACCENT i

The Canadian Magazine with an Italian Accent

September / October 2003, Vol. 1, No. 4

Canada's Italian Heritage

A Celebration at the Canadian Museum of Civilization

$8.00

Also in this issue

The Valigia d'Oro Award Recognizes Our "Pioneers"
Pondering the Style and Substance of Marisa Minicucci's Creations
Home Winemaking: Reviving an Italian Tradition
Fiction: Long Espresso

Italian-Canadian Heritage. The September/October 2003 cover of *Accenti: The Canadian Magazine with an Italian Accent* spotlights the Canadian Museum of Civilization's 2003-2004 exhibit "Presenza: A New Look at Italian Canadian Heritage." The exhibit focused on the traditions, values, and skills that post-World War II Italian immigrants "brought in their suitcases" to Canada. The museum used artifacts and videotaped interviews with immigrants from Vancouver, Calgary, Winnipeg, Thunder Bay, Sarnia, Toronto, Ottawa, and Montreal to create an exhibit to show how often modest, everyday lives influenced the creation of an Italian-Canadian identity within the nation. (*Courtesy* Accenti Magazine)

Communiy-Wide Observance. Traditionally families observed the feast of St. Joseph with relatives and friends; however, modern-day celebrations often are more public and inclusive. This 2004 St. Joseph altar at Sacred Heart Church Hall, in Houston, Texas, was sponsored by the Ladies of Sacred Heart, the St. Joseph's Guild, and other Italians. The early settlers, mostly from Sicily, worked on the railroads and farmed; some owned grocery stores, vegetable markets, and saloons or restaurants. Since the 1950s, other Italians have migrated there from other parts of the country. In 1970, a federation of thirty-one clubs joined to form the Italian Cultural Society. The group purchased an old house with an attached auditorium from Rice University where they sponsor a St. Joseph Altar. Newcomer Vicki Tamburo Sengbusch, from Kenosha, Wisconsin, and Des Moines, Iowa, recounted how Houston's Italians blended the social aspects of feast preparation with a reverence for the tradition. (*Courtesy Vickie Tamburo Sengbusch*)

Book-of-the-Month Club Selection. Pietro di Donato speaks to members of the American Italian Historical Association's annual meeting at Rutgers University in 1979. His classic novel *Christ in Concrete* was published in 1939 and was praised as "the epithet of the twentieth century" and described as a blue-collar proletarian novel written by a proletarian. He was born in West Hoboken, New Jersey, to parents from the Abruzzo. His father's death in a construction accident on Good Friday 1923 dramatically changed the life of twelve-year-old Pietro. He became a construction worker to support the family and identified with the working-class throughout his life. *Christ in Concrete* was chosen over John Steinbeck's *The Grapes of Wrath* for a Book-of-the-Month Club selection bringing di Donato the financial success to support his writing career. It was adapted for film in 1949, with the title *Give Us This Day,* and directed by Edward Dmytryk, who was blacklisted by the Hollywood studios. The production was banned in the United States but won awards at film festivals in Europe. His later writings, *Christ in Plastic* and *Immigrant Saint: The Life of Mother Cabrini* also earned critical praise. Di Donato's example continues to inform artistic expression. The 1990 film *Wait Until Spring, Bandini,* based on the novel of the same name by John Fante, is another Italian-American classic made into a film, depicting the family's struggle through hard times in the 1920s in Colorado. Joe Mantegna plays the role of Svevo Bandini. *(Courtesy Frank Cavaioli)*

Recapturing the Past. Self-taught artist Alfonso DeCesaris draws upon his memory to illustrate Italian-immigrant women cooking down tomato sauce in Ossining, New York. He uses watercolors to paint scenes from the history of Ossining and its Italian community. He re-creates events from memory, e.g., the Columbus Day *feste,* everyday scenes of life and work, and construction of the Croton Dam. His paintings document a past that the younger generation and newcomers to Ossining do not know. Some of his paintings hang in police headquarters, the municipal building, and the public library. What started for Alfonso as a "means of expression, an outlet . . . later on became a means of giving something back to my community." Celebrated folk artist Ralph Fasinello also turned to painting at age thirty because he felt he was losing touch with his ethnic roots. He supported his family by working in the evenings at his brothers' Bronx gas station. In 1972, at age fifty-eight, the art world "discovered" his work and labeled it a treasure of "primitive" art. His subjects include social justice, family life, work, the role of religion, and urban landscapes. *(Courtesy Alfonso DeCesaris)*

National Leaders. Nancy Pelosi, daughter of Thomas D'Alessandro, Jr., and currently speaker of the U.S. House of Representatives, congratulates Catherine Balestrieri Burton for receiving the title *cavaliere* of the *Ordine della Stella della Solidarietà Italiana* (Knight of the Order of the Star of Italian Solidarity), at a ceremony at the St. Francis Yacht Club in San Francisco, California, January 7, 2005. Roberto Falaschi, the consul general of Italy, presented the award, conferred by the president of the Italian Republic to Italians living abroad and to foreigners who bring special contributions to the prestige and honor of the Italian Republic. Burton's award acknowledged her work promoting Italian language and culture by initiating and building a four-year Italian program at Tomales (California) High School, serving as coleader of an exchange program between Tomales High School and Italian schools, and speaking to other teachers of Italian. Her grandparents came to California from Sant' Elia, Palermo. The presence of Italian as a language in public schools has grown as Italian-American students and their parents advocate for its inclusion. *(Courtesy Spence F. Burton; http://spenceburton.com)*

Documenting the Past. Producer Peter Miller films an interview with Fernanda Sacco, Nicola Sacco's niece, in Torremaggiore, Foggia, January 2005, for his documentary *Sacco and Vanzetti*. He attempts to "bring to life the stories of people who have tried to create a better world. . . . In the wake of the 9/11 attacks, I started to notice parallels between the time of Sacco and Vanzetti and what I was seeing our government doing in the present . . . about the way in which our system of justice can be compromised during a time of crisis." Near the end of the documentary, scenes of the U.S. prison at Guantanamo Bay heighten this comparison. Miller recalls a college student who said, "that until she saw my film, she hadn't heard about Guantanamo, and now that she had, she was appalled about what her country was doing. I set out to make a film about an eighty-year-old legal case, and in the process got one student to learn something important about American justice today." The film raises several issues, among them the death penalty, which represents a major divergence between United States and Italy. No member of the European Union can subscribe to the death penalty. *(Courtesy Peter Miller; photograph by Amy Linton)*

Anchoring Tradition. For four generations, Orsi's Bakery, at 621 Pacific Street in Omaha, Nebraska, has made and sold bread. Founder Alfonso Orsi left St. Andrea Composto, Lucca, and found work on the Burlington Railroad. Since he could speak French, Greek, Italian, and English, he became a foreman. While working on the Chicago to Omaha stretch, he was injured on the Council Bluffs Bridge. Although he did not suffer permanent disability, he lost his job because he missed a few days of work. He got a job at a bakery owned by Pardini, a fellow *paesano.* In less than a year, Pardini returned to Italy, leaving Alfonso with the bills. He and his brother-in-law, Raffaelo, took over the business and prospered. All family members, including the women, started helping at age nine. Alfonso's son, Claudio, took over in 1945. Claudio and his Sicilian-born wife lived in an apartment in the bakery for forty-one years until their son, Bob, took over in 1982. In 1996, they added double-crust pizza—a Sicilian recipe that includes a choice of potato, spinach, broccoli with garlic, anchovy sauce, and cheese. Today twenty people staff the business. Most are family members. Bobby Orsi, Jr. is the fourth-generation partner/owner. *(Courtesy Omaha Photo Collection, Box 1 Folder 3, IM100034, Immigration History Research Center, University of Minnesota)*

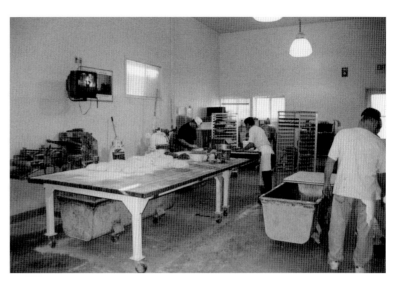

Italian-American Heritage at Harvard. Although Harvard University has fostered Italian studies for many years, interest in the Italian-American experience is a recent development. In fall 2005, a group of undergraduate students formed the Harvard College Italian American Association to promote events that connect students to their common heritage and to other Italian Americans in the Boston area. Members hope to acquaint the Harvard community with the legacy of Italian Americans and their accomplishments. Approximately fifty members participate in a variety of activities. On February 6, 2007, Italy's consul general Liborio Stellino spoke to the HIAA and members of the Italian-language department about "Challenges of European Unification." He discussed the history of unification, the pros and cons of the European Union, and the role played by the United States and Italian Americans. The HIAA plans to publish *The Harvard College Journal of Italian American History and Culture,* which will feature the culture, history, and contemporary issues of Italians in America. *(Courtesy Dominick and Antonio Pino)*

Cross Fertilization. In 1997, Brian Castine traced his great-grand-father, Luigi Cristoforo Castelvecchi, to his birthplace in Barga, Lucca, in 1860. Brian created a Web site with a Barga page and a message board for other Barga researchers. The Barga Genealogy Research Group (http://barga.homedns.org:81/) grew out of this exchange. Members with ancestors from Barga and neighboring villages foster an interest in that area of Tuscany. The group has seventy-two members in seven countries: Brazil, Canada, France, Germany, the United Kingdom, Italy, and the United States. BGRG has digitally photographed all of the church records from the seven parishes within the Barga *comune* (Albiano, Barga, Castelvecchio, Loppia, San Pietro, Sommocolonia, and Tiglio), including bap-tism, marriage, death, and *stato delle anime* (census). This process will help to preserve the original documents by reducing the need for researchers to handle them and will allow members to pursue research online. Many Italian Americans join organizations and attend workshops specifically dedicated to Italian genealogical re-search. *(Courtesy The Barga Genealogy Research Group)*

Community Connections. Lucia Galizia, accompanied by Marino Masolo, broadcasts *The Italian Hour* on KBOO-FM (a volunteer-run station) in Portland, Oregon. The program airs every other Sunday from nine to ten in the morning and includes Italian music and commentary in both Italian and English for a listening audience in the greater Portland and Vancouver, Washington areas. Lucia, born in Naples, and Marino, a more recent emigrant from Vicenza, announce events of interest and also interview a variety of guests, such as Metropolitan Opera tenor and Sicilian-born Marcello Gior-dani and, more recently, Sardinian Pasquale Madudu, who opened his Café Umbria in Portland in December 2007. An insurance salesman and immigrant, Agostino Potestio (from Grimaldi, Cosenza) pioneered the first Italian program in fall 1948. He broadcast, on a variety of Portland stations, for thirty-five years. Franco Albi succeeded Potestio for two years then asked Lucia to help him, promis-ing to teach her the technical broadcast skills she needed. She's been producing the program now for nine years. Sixteen years ago, she was one of the community leaders who responded to a request to inaugurate a *Festa Italiana* in Portland's Pioneer Courthouse Square. Lucia has served as president of the *Festa Italiana* Association, which organizes the weeklong late-August festival attracting close to sixty thousand Italophiles. *(Courtesy Lucia Galizia)*

Italian Tribune
The Premier Italian American Newspaper Since 1931
July 21, 2005   www.ItalianTribune.com   Price One Dollar

ITALIAN TRIBUNE CELEBRATES
UNION WITH CATANIA

BUDDY FORTUNATO, Publisher of *The Italian Tribune*, left, hosted the historic event at The Manor honoring Mayor Umberto Scapagnini of Catania, Sicily. Here, Mr. Fortunato presents Mayor Scapagnini with the bronze bust of Christopher Columbus, the same award given to President Ronald Reagan in 1988.

NJ CONGRESSMAN William J. Pascrell, left, presented Mayor Umberto Scapagnini of Catania, second from left, with an American flag that flew over the Capitol building in Washington, D.C. From left holding the flag are members of the Sicilian delegation that accompanied Mayor Scapagnini to the United States: Dr. Innocenzo Leontini, Minister of Agriculture in Sicily and Salvatore D'Urso, City Manager of Catania; and Honorable Antonio Bandini, Consul General of Italy in New York.

WEST ORANGE, NJ - In an unprecedented event celebrating the newly formed bond between *The Italian Tribune* and Sicily, Publisher A.J. Buddy Fortunato recently honored Mayor Umberto Scapagnini of Catania, Sicily, at a reception commemorating Sicilian culture and heritage at The Manor in West Orange.

Mayor Scapagnini's recent reelection to office propels him to the position of a principal leader in Italian politics. The mayor was accompanied at the event by a prestigious Sicilian delegation, with the purpose of increasing American knowledge and interest in the Catania region of Sicily. The group included City Manager Salvatore D'Urso and Dr. Innocenzo Leontini, Minister of Agriculture of Sicily.

The Italian Tribune spearheaded the creation of a Sister City relationship between Catania and Bayonne, NJ, as a means of societal exchanges between representatives of both cities. The relationship will help to develop a strong cultural understand of the very similar cities, located on opposite sides of the Atlantic.

"I am so proud that *The Italian Tribune* was recognized as the conduit of a relationship between Bayonne and Catania, and that we were selected to host such a prestigious group of Italian leaders," said Publisher Buddy Fortunato. "The recognition from both Mayor Scapagnini and NJ State Senator and Mayor Joseph Doria of Bayonne, along with

the rest of the guests at the event, implies that Sicilian and Sicilian Americans truly value the contributions of *The Italian Tribune* in preserving and promoting our collective heritage."

At the event, Mr. Fortunato presented Mayor Scapagnini with a bronze bust of Christopher Columbus, the same award given to President Ronald Reagan in 1988. New Jersey Congressman William J. Pascrell was also on hand to honor the mayor, awarding him with an American flag that once flew over the Capitol building in Washington, DC. Passaic attorney Anthony Fusco represented the New Jersey Fraternal Order of Police in offering Mayor Scapagnini a plaque on the organization's behalf. Hon. Antonio Bandini, Consul General of Italy, also took time out to honor Mayor Scapagnini at the historic event.

Leading Italian television network RAI International covered the event, along with other notable media outlets from the United States and Europe. In attendance were prominent representatives from the international spheres of government, education, and business, and major constituents of the travel/tourism, food, and cultural industries.

"It was wonderful to bring so many Italian and American leaders together for the common purpose of honoring a great man," said Buddy Fortunato. "We at *The Italian Tribune* will continue to seek avenues in which to forge new relationships and promote acquaintance between our two communities."

THE ITALIAN TRIBUNE announced the creation of a Sister City relationship between Bayonne, New Jersey and Catania, Sicily at a recent reception held at The Manor in West Orange, New Jersey. Catania Mayor Umberto Scapagnini, right, accepts the Key to the City of Bayonne from New Jersey State Senator and Bayonne Mayor Joseph Doria. In return, Mayor Doria received the Symbol of Catania from the Mayor.

All photos pertaining to the event by Vito Catalano & Bill Gregorio.

LOOK INSIDE TO FIND......
Italian Lesson #13?.....3
Tempo Italiano......18
Spotlight on Pizza.....25
Italian American Serenade......30

INSIDE !!! Special Photo Pages
CELEBRATING CATANIA
Pages 19 - 22

NEW YORK
NEWS & PHOTOS
pages 9 - 17

Facilitating Connections. Since 1931, the *Italian Tribune* has covered events of interest to Italian Americans in the area of northern New Jersey. Founding editor Ace Alagna used his skills as a photographer to secure images of nationally known Italian Americans and pictorial records of Italian-American activity in the greater metropolitan area. Seton Hall University has offered to house Alagna's photograph collection in a room dedicated to him at the university library. Current publisher Buddy Fortunato actively promotes friendship and cultural exchange between Italy and the United States. In 2005, the *Tribune* initiated the union of Bayonne, New Jersey, with Catania as sister cities. Mayor Umberto Scapagnini of Catania, joined Mayor Joseph Doria of Bayonne to endorse this special relationship and to "promote our collective heritage." *(Courtesy* Italian Tribune*)*

A Place to Gather. The *bambini* dancers of the Italian Cultural Society of Sacramento perform at the annual *Festa Italiana*, October 2004. The society was founded in 1981 by William Cerruti. From the beginning, it included a wide range of activities. In particular, it featured presentations by authors of memoirs and fiction, and scholarly studies of the Italian experience in America. It also scheduled an Italian film series, language classes for all ages, and guided trips to Tuscany and Sicily. This community group also coordinated two major exhibits—"The Italians of Sacramento, California" and the "Italian Legacy of the Mother Lode" (California's Gold Country). Both exhibits displayed artifacts, photos, and family records. In the fall of 2007, the society dedicated its own center in Carmichael, a suburb of Sacramento, where a large portion of the Italian population resides. When fully operational, the six thousand-square-foot center will cost a total of two million dollars, mostly from public grants and private donations. It includes a nursery, a large multipurpose room, a lending library, office, and conference room. In Milwaukee, Wisconsin, the history of the Italian Community Center somewhat parallels Sacramento's. *Festa* organizers purchased a small storefront office in 1978. Using proceeds from the *Festa* (considered the largest in the United States), members purchased a larger facility in 1980, and, in September 1990, dedicated a new building on a 15.7-acre site in the heart of the historic Third Ward, where many of the Italian Cultural Center's current members and their ancestors were raised. *(Courtesy Italian Cultural Society)*

Musical Tradition. Musicians Enzo Fina and Roberto Catalan perform as Musicàntica for students, faculty, and guests at California State University, Long Beach, sponsored by the Italian department. The musicians often play at coffee houses in the Los Angeles area. Enzo Fina, from Salice Salentino, Lecce, and Roberto Catalano, from Catania, Sicily, formed Musicàntica (www.musicantica.org) in 1994. Their goal is to present "songs of the oral tradition of our southern land . . . No more songs like, "O Sole Mio" or "Funiculì Funiculà," but just the power of the *pizzica*, the poetry, and the love drama of the Neapolitan *villanelle* (a poetic form), the intriguing sound of the cane clarinets from Sardinia, the passion of Sicilian cart driver songs, and a heavy dose of sound experimentation with the sounds of our native Mediterranean area." Their performances are a mix of ethnomusicology and the musical expression of the common folk. *(© 2008 Kayte Deioma, all rights reserved)*

Italian-American Literature. Since the late 1960s, the voices of Italian-American women writers have enriched the literature of the immigrant experience. Helen Barolini's first book, the novel *Umbertina,* was followed in 1986 by *The Dream Book: An Anthology of Writings by Italian American Women,* which provided a woman's perspective, and won the American Book Award for literary achievement by people of various ethnic backgrounds. The anthology celebrated earlier writers whose works merited rediscovery and brought together a host of younger writers. It also inspired a group of feminist filmmakers, writers, teachers, musicians, artists, dancers, historians, photographers, and community activists to form Malìa: A Collective of Italian American Women (Malìa means a spell or charm). Barolini's life and work bridges the Italy of her ancestors and the country they adopted. She has lived in Italy and in the U.S. with her Italian author/journalist husband, Antonio Barolini. *(Courtesy Helen Barolini)*

Access to Language. Roberto Alvarez has developed an enjoyable way to learn a language. He learned both Italian and Spanish from his parents. His father, Giuseppe, was born in Spain of Sicilian heritage, and his mother, Emma, came from Naples. His parents met in Naples during World War II, married and moved to Chicago, Illinois. Roberto studied Italian at Indiana University and at the *Università di Bologna*. After a nineteen-year stint as a sports broadcaster for network television, he moved to Tampa, Florida, and decided to tutor Italian. In 2002, he combined the linguistic with the culinary by introducing the program "Eat Italian and Learn Italian." He works with restaurateurs and deli/café owners to offer classes in Italian for traveler and conversational Italian, both of which include a "taste" of Italy. The courses run for four or five weeks. Approximately seventy percent of his fifty-plus students each month are Italian American, and most of them plan a trip to Italy. Many of his students hope to meet or locate relatives and to converse with them on some level of competence. His former students send him e-mails describing how they were able to communicate with their relatives and navigate the back roads of their ancestors' village. One couple decided to bring Roberto with them to Italy to assist in gathering genealogical information and to help with their efforts to discuss family history with their relatives. *(Courtesy www.learnitalian.us)*

Witnessing Heritage. Sponsored by the Order Sons of Italy in America, this group of young Italian Americans visited Washington, D.C. in 2003. They stand on the staircase in the entry hall of the Library of Congress to view its Italianate architectural design. Italian stonemasons helped to construct the library and many other buildings in the nation's capital. The group also toured the Capitol to see the work of Italian artists and sculptors, such as Constantine Brumidi, Giuseppe Franzoni, and Giovanni Andrei. OSIA and NIAF (National Italian American Foundation) have developed programs to acquaint younger Italian Americans with their heritage and to introduce them to role models in the professions of communications and public policy. Italian-American youth have also taken the initiative to connect with their heritage. In 1984, a group of young Italian Americans in the Belmont area of Bronx, New York, founded FIERI, the plural form of *fiero*, Italian for proud. FIERI includes people from the ages of eighteen to thirty-nine, and fosters the study of the Italian language and the Italian-American experience; promotes educational and personal achievement, including the study of Italian; provides career opportunities and networking relationships for young professionals; and supports a positive image of Italian Americans in the mass media and in popular culture. Currently FIERI has thirteen chapters throughout North America. *(Courtesy Dona DeSanctis, for the OSIA)*

Capturing the Essence. This center portion of *D'Amore Triptych: Family Stories* (wood, tin, photo, mixed media, family artifacts; 41" x 36" x 10") was part of the "Life Line"—*filo della vita* (thread of life)—exhibit displayed at Ellis Island Immigration Museum during 2000-2001. B. Amore conceived and created the exhibit, which included artifacts from her families' (D'Amore and De Iorio from Avellino) immigrant experience. Amore integrated materials from museum archives of oral histories with artifacts, sculpture, family writings, and videotaped interviews she conducted. The *filo della vita,* a red thread, ran across the panels to symbolize the ties of continuity across oceans and between generations. Creating the exhibit allowed Amore to "home in" on her past. She discovered that her "search into family had as much to do with what was not said, what was not divulged in addition to all that was told." To understand the "truth" of the family story the artist discussed the shadow side of her family's past. Her maturity and wisdom to recognize the necessity of recounting the entire story of the immigrant/ethnic experience illustrates how a clearer, honest view of the past helps the present generation to understand and appreciate their ancestors and themselves. A full account of the exhibit, photos of the displays, and essays written by individuals representing various disciplines can be found in Amore's book *An Italian American Odyssey, Life line—filo della vita: Through Ellis Island and Beyond. (Courtesy B. Amore, artist)*

The Journey Continues. Tourists and locals gather to view the statue of an Italian-immigrant family arriving on the levee in New Orleans, Louisiana. In 1995, the Italian American Marching Club engaged the sculptor Franco Alessandrini, from Sansepolcro, Arezzo, to create the piece in recognition of the Crescent City's role as a port of entry for Italian immigrants from the early 1800s until the 1930s. The U.S. census of 1850 showed New Orleans had the largest numbers of Italians in the country. The statue demonstrates how an understanding of the past illuminates the present. Standing on the threshold to America, the newcomers experience the ongoing dynamic interplay of the immigrant heritage within the broad range of American society. Although the immigrants "become American," their descendants acknowledge elements from their heritage when they identify as Italian Americans or Italian Canadians. Today many belong to multiethnic and multiracial families, adding important new variables into the mix, like new wine in old bottles. A significant increase (seven percent—about one million) of Americans claiming Italian heritage occurred between the 1990 and 2000 census. During that same decade, the percentage of other European-American groups declaring affiliation with their ethnic ancestry declined. *Quo vadis?* As more scholars, communities, and families preserve and research the Italian experience, future generations will gain an appreciation for how their ancestors' journeys in North America continue to shape their lives. *(Courtesy Greg Chaupette)*

INDEX

A

Abatangelo, Frank, 208
Abbaticcio, Ed "Batti", 115
Abruzzo, Italy, 85, 107
Accolti, Michael, 11
Acunto, Stephen, 244
Adami, Emma, 213
Adams, Frances (Adamo, Francesca), 109
Agostini, Bob, 236
Ahnert, Lynne Stagnitti, 298
Aiello Calabro, Cosenza, 145
Airaudi, Claudio, 205
Airaudi, Domenico, 205
Alaimo, Palma, 149
Albanesi, Piana degli, 298
Albano di Lucania, Potenza, 179
Albertini, Maria Dellama, 118
Albertini, Emma Elisa, 118
Albi, Franco, 303
Albi, Tony, 220
Albuquerque, New Mexico, 48, 59, 79, 106, 246, 262
Alburtus, William, 10
Aldisert, John S., 237
Alessandrini, Franco, 307
Alfano, Alessandro, 150
Alfino, Frank, 54
Alia, Palermo, 91
Alito, Justice Samuel, Jr., 245
Alpi, Angelo Pietro, 94
Alvarez, Roberto, 306
Amalfi, Salerno, 110
Amarone, Carmelina, 222
Amato, Marina, 161
Amato, Salvatore, 93
Amendola, Carolina Lucibello, 99
Amendola, Joe, 110
Amicarella, John, 107
Amore, B., 307
Amoroso-Levato, Marina, 272
Ancona, Italy, 105
Andrei, Giovanni, 11
Andretti, Mario Gabrielle, 123
Andrighetti, Albano

Andrighetti, Julio, 29
Anselmo, Fortunato, 60
Antioch, California, 124
Antonini, Luigi, 173
Antonio, John, 239
Antrosio, Delfino, 250
Ardizzone, Tony, 274
Ariano Villanuova, Benevento, 231
Arnone, Vincenzo, 48
Arona, Novara, 103
Arpino, Frosionone, 90
Ascota, Pennsylvania, 241
Asti, Italy, 105
Atena Lucana, Salerno, 219
Atrani, Salerno, 75, 222
Auburn, Washington, 276, 285
Auriana, Larry, 244
Avella, Pennsylvania, 212
Avellino, Italy, 307

B

Bacchi, Pietro, 10
Backus, Billy, 225
Bagheria, Palermo, 298
Baia e Latina, Caserta, 228
Balangero, Torino, 205
Baldacci, David, 274
Baldini, Mary, 63
Baldwin, New York, 232
Baltimore, Maryland, 129, 133, 151, 158, 173-74,199, 239-40, 247, 283
Bambace, Angela, 240, 261
Bandini, Father Pietro, 55
Barasa, Judge Bernardo, 186
Baratta, Tony, 272
Barbanti, Tullia, 64
Barca, Baptista, 178
Barca, Vincenza, 178
Barecca, Anthony Joseph, 203
Barecca, Joseph Anthony, 203
Barecca, Rosa Venterella, 203
Barga, Lucca, 114, 116, 176, 222, 303
Barolini, Antonio, 305
Barolini, Helen, 305
Baroni, Geno, 23, 241, 261

Barsetti, Ed, 205
Bartoli, Cecilia, 276
Basile, John X., 238
Basilio, Carmine, 225
Bassiano, Latina, 80
Bassotti, Carlo, 95
Batali, Mario, 292
Batavia, Illinois, 272
Bayonne, New Jersey, 304
Beard, James, 250
Bellanca, Giuseppe, 106, 276
Belluno Veronese, Verona, 143, 287
Beltrami, Giacomo Constantino, 10
Benigni, Roberto, 276
Bennett, Christine, 229
Bennett, Tony, 80
Berkeley Heights, New Jersey, 245
Bernardi, Robert, 102
Bernardo, Tony, 145
Berra, Lawrence Peter "Yogi", 130
Bertolucci, Bernardo, 276
Bertucci, Angelo, 50
Bertucci, Maria Basile, 50
Bessemer, Alabama, 239
Bevier, Missouri, 215
Bevilacqua, Anthony (Bevi), 153
Bevilacqua, Julia, 153
Bibbiano, Reggio-Emilia, 229
Bingham Canyon, Utah, 145
Birmingham, Alabama, 114, 163, 193, 254, 269, 297
Bisaccia, Avellino, 242
Bisaquino, Palermo, 91, 121
Blairmore, Alberta, 87
Blundi, Angelo, 221
Blundi, Letizia, 221
Blundi, Rita, 221
Blundi, Vincenzo, 132, 221
Boccelli, Andrea, 276
Bodio, Peter, 87
Boldini, Andrea, 139
Bomba, Chieti, 104
Bonapace, Davide, 37
Bonaparte, Charles, 258
Bonassisa, Raffaele, 54

Bonavita, Rose, 204
Bonavitacola, Alex, 271
Boncarbo, Colorado, 91
Bonino, Gene (Jenny), 205
Borgnine, Ernest (Borgnino, Ermes Elforon), 282
Borrelli, Vincenza DiNucci, 69
Boston, Massachusetts, 116, 188, 212, 217, 247, 253
Botto, Eva, 249
Botto, Maria, 210
Botto, Pietro, 210
Bovina, Agrigento, 275
Bovino, Puglia, 38, 54
Bowers, Nancy, 100
Bra, Cuneo, 292
Bracco, Lorraine, 259
Branca, Angelo, 196
Bridgeport, Connecticut, 215
Brighton, Alabama, 269
Brioschi, Carlo, 264
Brocato, Angelo, Jr., 97
Brocato, Angelo, Sr., 97
Brocato, Joe, 97
Brocato, Michelina, 97
Brocato, Roy, 97
Broccoli, Albert R. "Cubby", 81
Brockton, Massachusetts, 125
Bronx, New York, 147, 209, 256, 276, 282, 306
Brooke, Edward W., 253
Brooke, Remigia Ferrari-Scacco, 253
Brooklyn, New York, 54, 84, 96, 147, 149, 170, 173, 176-77, 184, 187, 205, 208, 224, 228, 234, 243, 247, 270, 282, 286
Brueckman, William, 210
Brumidi, Constantino, 80, 82
Bryan, Texas, 57, 159, 249
Buccellato family, 198
Buccellato, Nick, 198
Buccellato, Rocco, 198
Buffalo, New York, 147
Buffo, Matteo, 94
Buffo, Umberto, 94
Bugni, Domenico, 70
Bugni, Guido, 92
Buono, Angelo Rafael, 298
Burien, Washington, 219
Burton, Catherine Balestrieri, 301
Buscate, Milano, 137
Butera, Sam, 124
Butler, Pennsylvania, 166

Butte, Montana, 92, 100, 183, 191, 218
Butterfield Canyon, Utah, 145

C
Cabot, John (Caboto, Giovanni), 10, 264
Cabrini, Mother Frances, 157-58, 169
Caccavale, Phil, 170
Cacicia, August, 159
Cacicia, Charles, 159
Cacicia, Joseph, 161
Cacicia, Mary Amato, 161
Cadrezzate, Varese, 87, 192
Cage, Nicolas, 81, 282
Cairo, Frank, 220
Calabria, Italy, 294-95
Calatafimi, Trapani, 132, 147, 286
Calcagno, John, 141
Calcagno, Julia, 141
Calcagno, Louis, 141
Calcagno, Mary, 141
Calgary, Canada, 299
Calitri, Avellino, 158, 187, 197, 207
Calore, Avellino, 133, 219, 227
Cameron, Evelyn, 57
Camerota, Antoinette, 219
Camp Custer, Michigan, 179
Campigo, Treviso, 37, 44, 53
Campobasso, Italy, 38, 69
Campobello de Mazzara, Trapani, 73
Campofranco, Caltanissetta, 30
Canastota, New York, 50, 105, 139, 141, 225, 230
Cancassi, Mike, 194
Candelora, Carmelina Amarone, 222
Candelora, Salvatore (Cannelloro), 222
Candeloro, Dominic, 258, 261, 275
Canepa, Father John B., 163
Canischio, Torino, 177
Cannizzaro, Gregg, 171
Cannon, Delaware, 134
Canolo di Corregio, Reggio-Emilia, 229
Canonsburg, Pennsylvania, 135
Cantoria, Mike, 71
Capecchi, Mario R., 66
Caperna, Ron, 121
Capillo, John, 238
Capone, Alphonse, 270
Caponigro, Claudio, 280
Capra, Frank, 81

Caproni, Grant, 192
Caproni, Pietro Paolo, 116
Caputo, Louis, 163
Caputo, Lucio, 244
Caputo, Nick, 242
Caputo, Rosalie Galasso, 275
Carabetta, Jerry (Corbetta), 211
Carbonara, Bari, 49, 76, 89, 202, 285
Carbondale, Pennsylvania, 70
Cardello, Al, 205
Cardetti, Richard, 152
Cardinalli family, 198
Carella, Tony, 283
Carkonen, Jamie Prontera, 290
Carlini, Lucrezia, 35
Carlo Tresca, 211
Carmichael, California, 304
Carnevale, Peppina, 69
Carola, Charles, 267
Carolina, West Virginia, 77
Carrier, Joseph D., 80
Carrington, Nancy Gerardi, 232
Carrington, Nicole, 232
Carrington, Mike, 232
Carro, Andenito, 134
Carter, Irma Crocetti, 286
Caruso, Enrico, 80, 118
Casabona, Cortone, 47
Casalvelino, Napoli, 138
Casandrino, Napoli, 245
Casapulla, Al, 99
Casapulla, Luigi, 99
Caserta, Rose, 176
Cassettari, Rosa, 32
Castelamare del Golfo, Trapani, 147
Castelbuono, Palermo, 203
Castellano, Gaetano, 176
Castellano, Rosa Caserta, 176
Casteltermini, Agrigento, 30
Castelvecchi, Luigi Cristoforo, 303
Castiglione, Catania, 139
Castiglione, Laura, 140
Castiglione de Carovilli, Isernia, 75
Castiglioni, Luigi, 10
Castine, Brian, 303
Castle Gate, Utah, 60
Castrofilippi, Agrigento, 149
Catalano, Roberto, 305
Cataldo, Joseph, 11
Catanese, Rosaria (Sarah), 159
Catania, Josephine, 162
Catania, Sicily, 304-5
Catanzaro, Grace, 147

Catanzaro, Joseph, 147
Catanzaro, Mary, 147
Cataudella, Giorgio, 98
Cava de' Tirreni, Salerno, 288
Cavalli, Ben, Jr., 143
Cavalli, Benevento, 143
Cavalli, Francesco, 143
Cavriago, Reggio Calabria, 72
Cefalú, Palermo, 97, 151
Celico, Cosenza, 48, 188
Cella, Desiderio, 71
Cella, Ermina, 236
Ceracchi, Giuseppe, 11
Cerri, Nicola, 291
Cerruti, William, 304
Cesnola, Luigi Palma di, 80
Chapel, Lisanti, 276
Chauppette, Anthony, 154
Chauppette, Gaetano (Chiapetta), 154
Chaupette, Cora C., 287
Chaupette, Robert, 287
Chestnut Hill, Pennsylvania, 234
Chianese, Dominic, 259
Chiarani, Carlo, 37
Chicago, Illinois, 61, 131, 144, 164,
    175, 186, 190, 192, 203, 220, 264-
    65, 271, 280, 290, 293, 306
Chiloquin, Oregon, 52, 76, 88, 197,
    250
Chiordi, Ciro, 79
Chippari, Giuseppe, 32
Chippo, Calogera "Callia", 162
Christopher, Illinois, 137
Ciarlo, Maria Pizano, 178
Ciarlo, Vincenzo, 178
Ciccone, Louise, 80
Cimino, Sam, 187
Ciotola, Nicholas, 276
Cipolato, Alfredo, 63, 197
Cipolato, Pietro, 56
Cipriani, Leonetto, 11
Cirelli, Charles, 85
Ciresi, Rita, 274
Cirillo, Carlo, 245
Cirillo, Angelina, 215
Cirillo, Antonio, 215
Cirillo, Cesaria, 215
Cirillo, Francesca, 215
Cirillo, Michael, 215
Cittanova, Reggio Calabria, 19, 33
Civita di Boiano, Campobasso, 230
Clearwater, Florida, 100
Cles, Trento, 164

Cleveland, Ohio, 267, 291
Cocozza, Alfredo Arnold.
    See Lanza, Mario
Codella, Anthony, 207
Codella, Domenic, Jr., 207
Colacci, Joe, 269
Colma, California, 179
Colombo, Cristoforo, 10
Colombo, Joseph, 214
Colucci, Robert, 252
Columbia, South Carolina, 81
Columbus, Montana, 59, 144
Columbus, Ohio, 72, 229
Commellini, Leda, 146
Como, Jack, 259
Como, Perry (Pierino Ronald), 125
Contursi Terme, Salerno, 54, 100
Coppola, Anton, 128
Coppola, Carmine, 81, 128
Coppola, Francis Ford, 81, 128
Coppola, Sophia, 81
Cordasco, Francesco, 261
Corigliano, John, 80
Corleone, Palermo, 159
Cornuda, Treviso, 76, 197
Correggio, Canolo di, 229
Cosentino, Dominic, 149
Cosentino, Isabelle, 149
Cosentino, Philip, 149
Cosenza, Italy, 153
Cossiga, Francesco, 293
Cossombrato, Asti, 140
Costello, Lou (Cristillo, Louis
    Francis), 119
Cottini, Alberto, 262
Crisconi, Madeline Lucia, 107
Crisconi, Rocco, 107
Crocetti, Dino Paul, 125
Crosetti, Frank, 260
Croton-on-Hudson, New York, 84
Cuggiono, Milano, 32, 292
Cuomo, Mario, 275
Curcio, Caterina Venneri
    d'Ambrosio, 186
Curcio, Joe, 186
Curilo, Raffaele, 86
Cusimano, Filippo, 138
Cusimano, Giuseppina, 138
Cusimano, Mary, 138

D
D'Alessandro, Thomas, Jr., 173,
    240, 301

D'Ambrosio, Antonio, 227
D'Ambrosio, Francesco, 186
D'Ambrosio, Tony, 186
D'Amore, Maria Santola, 288
D'Andrea, Carlo, 148
D'Andrea, Lucia Tonti, 148
D'Antoni, Salvatore, 80
D'Arrigo, Andrea, 133
D'Arrigo, Stefano, 133
D'Elia, Felice, 54, 100
D'Orazi, Ann, 197
DaPonte, Lorenzo, 10
Dardano, Sister Prisca, 169
Dawson, New Mexico, 71, 233
DeBortoli, Angelina, 76
DeBortoli, Guglielmo, 76, 197
DeCesaris, Alfonso, 300
DeFelice, Fileno, 107
DeFelice, Joe, 107
DeFelice, Vincent, 107
DeGrandis, Onelia Baggio and
    family, 37, 44, 53
DeGregorio, Giusippina, 138
Deiro, Count Guido, 116, 174, 224
Delapez, Michael, 290
Delligatti, Jim, 112
DeLuca, Dora, 36
DeLuca, Leonard, 53
Deluca, Anna, 152
Deluca, Rose, 152
DelZotto, Jack, 112
DeMaio, Giuseppe, 171, 289
DeMarco, Joe, 152
DeNiro, Robert, 81, 260
deNiza, Marcos, 10
Denver, Colorado, 109, 211, 258,
    266, 277
DePasquale, Pietro "Pete", 51
DePompa, Angelo, 38, 54
DePompa, Renato (Ron), 38, 54
DeRosa, Tina, 274
DeSales, Tony, 129, 283
DeSanctis, Dona, 258-59
DeSanguine, Antonio, 52
Desimone, Giuseppe (Joe), 136, 185
Des Moines, Iowa, 146, 299
desPlanches, Edmondo Mayor, 55
DeVito, Danny, 275, 283
Diaz, General Armando, 59, 291
diCesnola, Luigi Palma, 258
DiDonato, Pietro, 276, 300
DiFrisco, Dominic, 258, 265
DiGiorgio, Giuseppe (Joe), 151

DiGiorgio, Robert, 151
DiGiorgio, Salvatore, 133
DiGirolamo, Pietro, 84
DiGregorio, Frank, 146
DiLuca, Epifany "Pip", 284
DiLuzio, Bill, 107
DiLuzio, Tom, 107
DiMaggio, Dom, 120
DiMaggio, Joe, 120, 260-61
DiMaggio, Vince, 120
DiMeo, Anthony III, 155
DiMeo, Anthony, Sr., 155
DiMeo, Michael, 155
Dindia, Salvatore, A.J. "Gus", 154
Dindia, Don, 154
DiNino, Senator Consiglio, 244
DiNucci, Catarina, 69
DiNucci, Lena Vellani, 229
DiRienzo, Felice, 204
DiRienzo, Felix, 204
DiSanto, Nicola, 104
DiSanto, Pulcheria, 104
Discepola, Nick, 243
Dishman, Washington, 146
DiSilvestri, Pietro 103
DiStasi, Lawrence, 259
DiStasi, Rev. Anthony, 161
DiStefano, Giuseppe, 291
DiVito, Joe, 76
DiVito, Nina, 76
Domenico, Don, 62
Dominis, John Owen, 10
Donati, Emilio, 215
Donio, Gabriel J., 273
Doria, Joseph, 304
Drago, Rosario, 287
Drusacco, Torino, 190
Duluth, Minnesota, 158
Dunmore, Pennsylvania, 120, 227
Du Quoin, Illinois, 137
Durante, Jimmy, 123, 274

E

East Harlem, New York, 118, 150, 280
East Lake, Alabama, 163
Elisa, Emma, 118
Elk Park, Montana, 70
Ellis Island, 43, 117, 196-97, 296
Emanuelli, Brian, 143
Emanuelli, Donald, 143
Emanuelli, Giuliano, 143, 287
Emanuelli, Scott, 143

Emanuelli, Steve, 143
Ensley, Alabama, 158, 163
Erie, Pennsylvania, 83, 133, 153, 166
Esposito, Antonio, 75
Esposito, Phil, 127
Esposito, Raffaela, 75
Ettor, Joseph, 211
Eugene, Oregon, 292
Eula, Rev. John, 165
Eveleth, Minnesota, 158

F

Facciponti, Carmelo, 149
Facciponti, Palma Alaimo, 149
Faggio, Frankie, 99
Faietta, Remo, 102
Falaschi, Roberto, 301
Falsetto, Henry, 220
Fante, John, 300
Fantino, Julien, 272
Fara San Martino, Chieti, 107
Farfaglia, Santo, 139
Farfariello (Eduardo Migliaccio), 97
Fasi, Lidia, 54
Fasinello, Ralph, 300
Fassino, Joe, 177
Fassino, John, 177
Federici, Gaetano, 119
Fergus County, Montana, 132
Ferla, Siracusa, 235
Ferlita, Castenzio, 150
Ferrara, Pasquale, 170
Ferraro, Geraldine, 173
Ferraro, Thomas, 274
Fife, Washington, 60
Figgins, Gary, 155
Figgins, Rusty, 155
Filice, Gennaro, 153
Filipi, Maria, 162
Fina, Enzo, 305
Fiorenzuola D'Arda, Piacenza, 286
Fiores, Gennaro, 279
Fioretti, Gene, 76, 285
Fioretti, Luigi, 49, 76, 285
Fioretti, Stella Milela, 49, 76, 285
Fioretti, Matteo (Matt), 89, 202
Fiumalbo, Modena, 215
Flandina, Giovanni (John), 109, 291
Flynn, Elizabeth Gurley, 210, 249
Fontana, Marc, 221
Forato, Maria, 52
Forges, Frank (Francesco), 52, 213
Forli del Sannio, Isernia, 148

Formia, Latina, 228
Fort Missoula, Montana, 196
Fortunato, Buddy, 304
Fossombrone, Pesaro, 64
Framingham, Massachusetts, 71, 236, 286
Frances, Connie (Franconero, Concetta Rosa Maria), 80
Franchini, Ettore, 48
Franchini, Fanny, 79
Franchini, Ovidio, 48
Frankfort, New York, 32
Franzoni, Giuseppe, 11
Frazzini, Benilda Albina Victoria, 35
Frazzini, Emiliano, 35
Freeh, Louis, 260
Freilino, Secondo, 105
Frinzi, Dominic, 244
Fubini, Alessandria, 216
Fugazi, John, 170
Furia, Richard F., 271

G

Gaeta, Giovanni, 194
Gaeta, Latina, 10
Gagliano, Anthony, 101
Gagliano, Bonnie, 101
Gagliano, Josephine, 101
Gagliano, Vincenzo, 101
Galgano, Vito, 187
Galizia, Ann, 207
Galizia, Lucia, 207, 303
Gallina-Santangelo, Rosemarie, 244
Gallo, Ernest, 155
Gallo, Joseph, 152
Gallo, Mary, 249
Gamberale, Chieti, 51
Gambero, Giuseppe, 137
Gange, Jennifer, 290
Garbarino, Arturo, 142
Garbarino, Giuseppe, 68
Gardaphe, Fred L., 258, 274
Garibaldi, Giuseppe, 11, 295
Garibaldi, Oregon, 295
Garre, Giuseppe, 60
Garro, Angelo, 128, 292
Gasperi, Emily, 285
Gasperi, Joe, 285
Gasperi, Urban, 285
Gatto, Rose 161
Gazzara, Biagio Anthony (Ben), 130
Gentile, Giovanni, 104
Gentile, Nicolantonio, 104

Gentilini, Dave, 98
Genzale, Angelina, 133, 219
Genzale, Antonette Camerota, 133, 219
Genzale, Francesco, 133, 219
Genzale, Frank, 133, 219
Genzale, Tony, 133, 219
Geraci, Palermo, 108
Geraldi, Mike, 108
Gerardi, Antonina, 4
Gerardi, Jane, 232
Gerardi, Joseph, 232
Gerardi, Joseph (Giuseppe), 147
Gerardi, Josephine, 232
Gerardi, Nicola, 94, 132
Gerardi, Rosario (Sardi), 232
Gerardi, Vincenza, 173, 286
Germantown, Pennsylvania, 193
Gesso, Messina, 138
Gesualdi, Don, 290
Gesuiti, Cosenza, 220
Ghilani, Alice, 236
Giaccono, Francis X., 238
Giampietri, Sam, 107
Giannini, Amedeo, 275
Gibellina, Trapani, 90
Gilroy, California, 153
Gioiosa Jonica, Reggio Calabria, 167
Giordina, Marcello, 303
Giorgio, Ciro, 185
Giorno, Luigi, 193
Gioseffi, Daniela, 274
Giovannitti, Arthur, 211
Giuliani, Rudolph, 243, 260
Giulianova, Teramo, 187
Giustina family, 30
Gonnella, Alessandro, 280
Graffagnino, Father Baldassare, 287
Granata, Pietro, 188
Granato, Biaggio, 140
Granato, Vincenza Troppea, 140
Grand Forks, North Dakota, 231
Grande, Francesca, 53
Grandis, Onelia Baggio De, 44
Granieri, Al, 205
Granitto, Joe, 224
Granitto, Nicholas, 205
Granzella, Richard, 88
Grasseschi, Al, 223
Grasseschi, Alfred, 223
Grasseschi, Maurice, 223
Grasseschi, Romeo, 223
Grasseschi, Rudy, 223

Grassi, Giovanni, 11
Graziano, Agostino, 156
Graziano, AJ, 156
Graziano, Joseph, 156
Great Falls, Montana, 31, 74, 89, 265, 269
Greco, Antonietta, 168
Greco, Michael, 168
Gregori, Emily, 251
Grimaldi, Cosenza, 109
Grittani, Ralph, 243
Gromo, Ernesto, 135
Gromo, Maria Picetti, 135
Groppi, James (Father James), 23, 254
Grossi, Francesco, 10
Grossi, Giovanni, 10
Grosso family, 36
Gualdo, Giovanni, 10
Guaragna, Salvatore Anthony, 268
Guardiani, Antonio, 87, 202
Guardiani, Cesidia Sticca, 51
Guardiani, Eustacchio Antonio, 51, 202
Guardiani, Mary, 202
Gubbio, Perugia, 164
Gulotta, Andrew, 73
Gurisatti, Fr., 163

H
Haledon, New Jersey, 210, 249
Hamilton, Ontario, 165
Hamilton Township, New Jersey, 110
Hammonton, New Jersey, 138, 155, 166, 182, 198, 252, 273
Harris, Franco, 129
Harris, Gina Parenti, 129
Harrison, Idaho, 148
Hayward, California, 223
Haywood, "Big Bill", 210
Hazelton, Pennsylvania, 222
Hendin, Josephine Gattuso, 274
Herrin, Illinois, 236, 292
Hibbing, Minnesota, 158, 211
Higbee, Missouri, 215
Hine, Lewis, 68
Hosseinzadeh, Elissa Ferraro, 274
Humphrey, Washington, 76
Houston, Texas, 299
Hyde Park, New York, 110

I
Iacino, Joe F. 109

Iacocca, Lee, 296
Ianni, Francis A. (Francesco), 184, 208
Iannidinardo, Angelo, 195, 226
Iannidinardo, Claurinda Giannantonia, 195, 226
Iannidinardo, Sister Barbarina (Ambrosina), 38
Iannidinardo, Tony, 195, 226
Imana, Carolina, 164
Inga, Charles (Chuck), 205
Innocenzi, Nick, 110
Iorio, John, 245
Iorio, Mayor Pam, 245
Iorizzo, Giovanni, 231
Iorizzo, John, 231
Iorizzo, Luciano, 231, 270
Iorizzo, Marilee, 231
Iron Mountain, Michigan, 31
Iron Town, Missouri, 292
Isernio, Frank, 113
Isola delle Femmine, Palermo, 169
Iuppa, Barney, 108
Izzo, Anna, 184

J
Jablonski, Ernest, 147
Jacobs, Mike (Jacobucci), 144
Jansen, Colorado, 187
Jessup, Pennsylvania, 164
Julian, Carmen, 107

K
Kaiser, Sandro, 287
Kalispell, Montana, 31
Kananakis, Alberta, 195
Kansas City, Missouri, 291
Kellogg, Idaho, 91, 148
Kenosha, Wisconsin, 299
King City, Ontario, 230
Kino, Eusebio, 10
Knobview, Missouri. See Rosati, Missouri
Kozen, Ima, 251
Krase, Jerry, 261
Krebs, Indian Territory (Oklahoma), 94, 177

L
LaBella, Angela, 62
LaRocca, Accurrio, 108
LaRocca, James Dominick "Nick", 80

Lago, Cosenza, 78
LaGuardia, Fiorello, 23, 130, 173, 239, 261
Lambert, Alabama, 67
Lammari, Lucca, 106, 246
Lancilotti, Rose, 213
Lanni, Bill, 205
Lanza, Mario, 123
Lapolla, Garibaldi M., 83
Latina, Lazio, 44
Latrobe, Pennsylvania, 115
Latuda, Carlo (Charles), 137
Latuda, Francesco, 71, 233
Latuda, Rose Scampini, 137
Laurella, Vincenzo, 35
Lauretta, Constantine, 20
Laurino, Maria, 273, 275
Lavagetto, Lorenzo, 134
Laverock, Pennsylvania, 234
Lawrence, Massachusetts, 211
Lawrence, New Jersey, 10
Lazzeri, Tony, 120, 260
Leahy, Patrick, 173
Lecce, Italy, 290
Lentini, Jack (Concetto), 193
Lentini, Siracusa, 193
Lentricchia, Frank, 274
Leonetti, Frank, 155
Leonetti, George, 155
Leonetti, Rose, 155
Leonetti, William, 155
Lester, Washington, 89, 202
Levaggi, G. B., 55, 170
Libretti, Mary Costellano, 176
Libretti, Vincent, 176
Ligato, Concetta Fonti, 33
Ligato, Rosa, 33
Liguria, Italy, 88, 233
Lindenhurst, New York, 149
Linguaglossa, Catania, 50, 298
Lipari, Leonardo, 90
Lloyd, Susan Caperna, 174
LoBianco, Tony, 130
Locati, Giuseppe, 144
Locati, Tony, 160
Lodi, California, 85
Loiacano, Concetta Morrone, 72, 178
Loiacano, Domenick, 72, 178
Lombardi, Johnny, 281
Lombardi, Vince, 81
Lonate Pozzolo, Varese, 29, 144, 160
Lopardo, Frank, 80
Loranzana, Campobasso, 59

Lorenzo, Tony, 220
Los Angeles, California, 158, 171, 224
Louisville, Colorado, 210, 269
Lucca Sicula, Agrigento, 101
Lucca, Italy, 55
Luciano, Lucky, 270
Lucibello, Frank, 99
Luisetti, Angelo Enrico, 119
Luisetti, Hank, 119
Lungo, Mike, 86
Lutterotti, Vladimiro, 118
Luzzi, Cosenza, 193
Lynnbrook, New York, 199

M
Machi, Rosa, 167
Machi, Vito, 167
Madison, Wisconsin, 62, 81, 172
Madonna (Ciccone, Louise), 80
Madonna de Campiglio, Val Rendena, Trento, 37
Madudu, Pasquale, 303
Maestri, Angele, 223
Maestri, Francis, 223
Maestri, Robert, 173, 223
Maffucci, Barney, Jr., 199
Maffucci, Bernardino, 199
Maggio, Catherine, 216
Maggio, Donato, 160, 216
Maggio, Gaetana Petrone, 160, 216
Maggio, Maria, 160, 216
Maggio, Phillip, 216
Maglione, Rose, 42
Magna, Utah, 145
Magnago, Milano, 71, 233
Maierato, Vibo Valencia, 128
Malfitano, Catherine, 80
Mallozzi, Phil, 205
Maltese, Rose, 62
Mancini, Henry, 80
Mancuso, Charles, 147
Manetti, Ernesto, 187
Manetti, Rose, 187
Mangione, Jerre, 226, 260, 296
Mantegna, Joe, 131, 300
Marano, C. Antonio, 231
Marano, Luke, Jr., 231
Marano, Luke, Sr., 231
Marano, Pat, 205
Marano Principato, Cosenza, 150
Marcantonio, Vito, 24, 173, 261
Marchetti, Gino John, 124

Marchi, John J., 242
Marchi, Lena Donati, 152
Marciano, Rocky (Marchegiano, Rocco Francis), 125
Marcozzi, Carlo, 187
Marcozzi, Mary, 187
Marcucci, Lawrence, 280
Marcucci, Luigi, 280
Marcucci, Marianna, 280
Marcucci, Nicholas, 280
Marino, Mike, 171
Marnell, Thomas, 87
Marotta, Kenny, 274
Marsilii, William J., 200
Martin, Dean (Crocetti, Dino Paul), 125
Martini, Louis, 152
Martire, Ray, 255, 288
Martorano, Mike, 91
Martorano, Sal, 91
Marzano Di Nola, 199
Mascagni, Pietro, 56
Mascarino, Pierrino, 131
Maschito, Potenza, 40
Masciola, Rev. Louis, 165
Masio, Flora, 113
Masolo, Marino, 303
Massa Carrara, Toscano, 81
Massapequa, New York, 170
Massaro, Judge Dominic, 244
Mastracchio, Antonio, 223
Mastracchio, Giovanni, 223
Masullo, Bob, 288
Masullo, Felice, 288
Matteucci, Alessandro, 246
Matteucci, Amedeo, 246
Matteucci, Joseph, 74
Matteucci, Josephine, 74
Matteucci, Nelli Quirolleo, 74
Matteucci, Pompilio, 106
Matteucci, Rose, 74
Mazzarise, Giuseppa, 91
Mazzei, Philip, 10, 258
Mazzeo, Al, 153
Mazzeo, Jess, 153
Mazzi, 292
Mazzoni, Maria Carmela, 43
Mazzucco, Melania G., 273
McAlester, Oklahoma, 58, 94
McCann, Marilyn Locati, 144
McCloud, California, 209
Medford, Oregon, 121
Melito di Napoli, 215

Memoli, Philip, 114
Mengarini, Gregorio, 10
Menotti, Gian Carlo, 80, 275
Mercante, Nicholas, 107
Merli, Gino, 206
Merli, Mary, 206
Merlino, Angelo, 85
Messa, Robert A., 244
Messina, Italy, 95, 186
Meucci, Antonio, 295
Mezzanares, Tommaso, 162
Miceli, Marcello, 44
Michel, Bonnie Chauppette, 287
Miglionico, Nina, 254
Milani, Ernesto, 292
Millay, Edna St. Vincent, 188
Miller, Peter, 301
Milwaukee, Wisconsin, 47, 54, 58, 181, 218, 254
Minato, Alfeo, 250
Minato, Anselmo, 52, 88
Minelli, Liza, 80
Minelli, Vincent, 81
Mineola, New York, 106
Minori, Salerno, 75
Missoula, Montana, 197
Mistretta, Rose, 225, 289
Mobile, Alabama, 20
Modica, Ragusa, 77, 98
Moffo, Anna, 80
Monangah, West Virginia, 71, 117, 167
Mondavi, Caesar, 85
Mondavi, Robert, 152
Monessen, Pennsylvania, 145, 172
Monreale, Palermo, 208
Montecalvo, Giustina, 54
Montecucco, Giuseppe, 49
Montecucco, Paul, 64, 252, 255
Monteleone di Spoleto, Perugia, 110
Montella, Avellino, 231
Monterey, California, 169
Montesanto, Luigi, 291
Monteu du Po, Torino, 275
Montona (now Croatia), 123
Montreal, Quebec, 121, 272
Morello, Celeste, 268, 284
Moretti, Giuseppe, 117, 297
Mormino, Gary, 259
Morreale, Ben, 296
Moscia, Francesco, 78
Mosellie, Anthony, 251
Mt. Holly, New Jersey, 129
Mundelein, Illinois, 168

Muro Lucano, Potenza, 117
Murray, Catherine Tripalin, 298
Musmanno, Michael, 205
Mussolini, Benito, 95, 173, 189
Mussomeli, Caltanissetta, 289

N
Naccarato, Angelo, 220
Naccarato, Charlie, 220
Naccarato, George, 220
Naccarato, Joe, 220
Naccarato, Tony, 220
Naples, Italy, 33-34, 62, 171, 181, 185, 242, 303
Napoli, Joseph, 274
Napolitano, Anne, 173
Napolitano, Janet, 244
Nazareth, Pennsylvania, 123
Nemoitin, Dr. J., 248
New Castle, Delaware, 62-63, 166, 208, 276
New Castle, Pennsylvania, 181
New Haven, Connecticut, 75, 110, 162, 175, 222, 274
New Orleans, Louisiana, 67, 80, 97, 122, 124, 154, 158, 173, 175, 222-23, 247, 255, 267, 307
New York City, New York, 20, 63, 68-69, 82, 84, 94-95, 97-98, 103, 109, 115, 117-18, 122-23, 127, 130, 132, 147, 149-50, 158, 172-73, 176, 190, 194, 199, 209, 211, 213-14, 216, 223, 231, 234, 238-39, 242-43, 256, 260-61, 267, 282
Newark, Delaware, 184
Newark, New Jersey, 2, 180, 199, 207, 242
Nicholetti, Louis, 145
Nincheri, Guido, 121, 189
Nobili, Giovanni, 11
Nocera Inferiore, Salerno, 31
Nocera, Umbria, 120
Nola, Napoli, 111, 170, 225
Norristown, Pennsylvania, 268
North Bay, Ontario, 264
North Boston, New York, 147
North Haven, Connecticut, 140
North Tarrytown, New York, 204
North York, Ontario, 214

O
Oakley, California, 198
Obici, Amedeo, 80

Oderzo, Treviso, 80
Olevano, Salerno, 107
Oliva, Giacoma, 62
Oriolo, Cosenza, 32
Orsi, Alfonso, 302
Orsi, Amelia, 146
Orsi, Bobby, Jr., 302
Orsi, Frank, 146
Ossining, New York, 73, 84, 164, 223, 279
Ottato, Rosa, 150

P
Paca, William, 258
Pace, Anthony, 275
Pacelli, Dominick (Dionisio), 209
Pacino, Al, 81
Paciullo, Roberto, 282
Padula, Salerno, 267
Paglieri, Vincenza (Rosetta), 41
Pagnano de Asolo, Treviso, 52
Paietta, Charles, 246
Pajarola, Marietta, 70
Palazzo Adriano, Palermo, 187
Palazzo Butera, Palermo, 290
Palermo, Italy, 80, 109, 122, 124, 129, 169, 267
Palma, Napoli, 170
Palmisano, Vincent, 239
Panepinto, Florence, 142
Panepinto, John, 140, 142
Pantone, Margaret, 139
Paolicelli, Paul, 275, 288, 298
Parigi, Nazzareno, 145
Parini, Jay, 274
Parion, Ann, 134
Parkersburg, West Virginia, 69
Parodi, Dominic "Mingo", 88
Partanna, Trapani, 90
Pasqualicchio, Leonard H., 191
Pasqualini, Alice, 195
Pasqualini, Lina, 195
Pasqualini, Lino, 195
Pasqualini, Santo, 195
Passo di Mirabella, Avellino, 136
Pastore, John Orlando, 240
Patchogue, New York, 100
Paterno, Joe, 81
Paterson, New Jersey, 119, 122, 210, 249
Patranella, Bonnie, 137,
Patranella, Francesco Paolo, 137, 249
Patranella, John, 137

Patranella, Luke, 137
Patterelli, Michael, 139
Patti, Adelina, 80
Patti, Sam, 273, 294
Pavarotti, Luciano, 283, 291
Peckville, Pennsylvania, 206
Pedace, Cosenza, 36, 53, 72, 178, 186, 288
Pelaia, Domenico, 96
Pellicore, Albert, 203
Pellicore, Edward, 203
Pellicore, George, 203
Pellicore, Henry, 168, 203
Pellicore, Joseph, 203
Pellicore, Philip, 203
Pellicore, Raymond, 203
Pellicore, William, 203
Pelosi, Nancy, 275, 301
Pente, John, 283
Perini, Louis R., 80
Perone, Giovanni, 105
Perosa Canavese, Torino, 36
Perrelli, Joseph, 153
Perri, Brigidia Maria, 138
Pesaro, Italy, 205
Petonito, Sal, 99
Petosa, Maria, 144
Petosa, Pasquale "Pete", 59, 144
Petrini, Carlo, 292
Petrini, Remo, 120
Petromilli, Antonio, 116
Petromilli, Pasquale, 116
Petrosino, Giuseppe (Joe), 267
Philadelphia, Pennsylvania, 10, 123, 134, 172, 184, 221, 231, 241
Phillips, Albert, 153
Phillips, Marion, 153
Piacenza, Emilia-Romagna, 71
Piana, Libero Della, 24
Pianella, Abuzzo, 102
Piatanese, Finan, 116
Piatanesi, Colombo, 116
Piazza, Marguerite, 122
Piazza, Martina, 152
Piazzola, Rosina Dalpaz, 135
Piazzola, Trento, 135
Picatti, Giuseppe (Joe), 111
Piccirilli, Giuseppe, 81
Pietropaolo, Vincenzo, 128
Pignola, Potenza, 160
Pinti, Annetta Smarrelli, Eustacchio, 39
Pinza, Ezio, 196

Pinzola, Trento, 114
Piro, Gene, 86
Pisa, Italy, 115
Pisani, Nunziata, 54, 100
Piscitello, Calogera, 47
Pisticci, Matera, 80, 290
Pittsburg, California, 198
Pittsburgh, Pennsylvania, 51, 103, 112, 126, 129, 161, 168
Pizzarelli, John "Bucky", 122
Pizzoferrato, Chieti, 126
Plana degli Albanesi, Palermo, 138, 162
Poggioreale, Corelone, 137, 159
Point Richmond, California, 74
Poletti, Charles, 205
Poli, Sebastiani, 80
Ponselle, Rosa, 80, 275
Ponte Buggianese, Pistoia, 146
Ponte San Antonio, Chieti, 104
Pope, Generoso, 95
Popolizio, Al, 205
Port Jervis, New Jersey, 51, 87
Portland, Oregon, 49, 64, 93, 133, 141-42, 151, 154, 156, 159, 161, 188, 201, 217, 250, 252, 255
Porto Empedocle, Agrigento, 30
Pratiglione, Torino, 94
Prato, Italy, 121
Pratola Peligna, L'Aqulia, 244
Pregno, Camillo, 133
Prelee, Joe (Prili), 228
Prelee, Mary Rose, 228
Prelee, Mike, 228
Prescott, Arizona, 68
Prezza, L'Aquila, 272
Priest River, Idaho, 220
Prima, Gia, 124
Prima, Louis, 80, 124
Principe, Alberto, 178
Procaccino, Mario, 242
Prodi, Romano, 295
Prontera, Michele, 290
Prontera, Mike, 202
Providence, Rhode Island, 185, 240
Pueblo, Colorado, 140, 142, 275
Pugliano, Theresa, 70
Pugliano, Violet, 70
Pullo, Frank, 251
Pullo, Philomena "Mamie" (Mosellie), 251
Puzo, Mario, 18, 81, 216

Q
Quaranta, Andrea Mistretta, 225, 289
Quarata, Arezzo, 145
Quebec, Canada, 176

R
Rafella, Stefano, 108
Rafella, Vincenzo, 108
Rago, Anthony, 272
Rago, Joe, 272
Ragona, Rosario, 286
Ragosta, Andreana, 225
Raine, Sam, Sr., 239
Raino, Raffaella, 206
Ranieri, Davide, 31,132
Ranieri, "Marine" Orlando, 269
Ranieri, Olie (Elondo), 89
Ranieri, Romeo, 74, 89
Rathdrum, Idaho, 53
Raton, New Mexico, 90
Ravizza, Luigi, 216
Recoaro Terme, Vicenza, 136
Redwood City, California, 205
Rego Park, Queens, 291
Reina, Salvatore, 150
Rende, Cosenza, 203
Renzetti, Joseph, 200
Riccardi, John, 80
Ricci, Barney, 252
Riccio, Anthony, 175
Ricciutelli, Diana, 272
Richmond, California, 153, 204, 221
Rigali, Michele, 176
Riggi, Stephen J., 113, 227
Riggi, Vincent II, 113, 227
Riggi, Vincent J., 113, 227
Riggi, Vincent S., 113, 227
Riggio, Joe, 187
Riggio, Mary, 187
Riolo, Annie, 162
Ripalimosani, Campobasso, 195, 226
Riva del Gardo, Trento, 118
Rizzo, Frank, 220
Rizzo, Mayor Frank, 241
Rizzotte, Tony, 138, 182
Rizzuto, Phil "Scooter", 120, 260
Robbinsville, New Jersey, 101
Robotti, Maria, 216
Rocca, Salvatore, 209
Rocca Canavese, Torino, 13
Roccabernarda, Crotone, 102
Roccapalumba, Palermo, 146

Rochester, New York, 195, 226
Rock Springs, Wyoming, 164
Rodin, Paul, 104
Rodino, Peter Wallace, 242
Romano, Tony, 205
Rome, Italy, 169
Roppolo, Torino, 104
Rosati, Bishop Joseph, 136
Rosati, Missouri, 98, 136, 152, 215
Roseto, Pennsylvania, 251
Roseto Val Fortore, Foggia, 251
Roslyn, Washington, 111
Rossi, Aldo, 142, 255
Rossi, Angelo, 173, 261
Rossi, Artillio, 216
Rossi, Joe, 142
Rovere, Umberto, 224
Rozwadowski, Antonio Ladislao, 56
Ruisi, Joseph, 205
Russitano, Alfred, 230
Russitano, Anthony, 230
Russitano, Dominick, 230
Russitano, Rocchina, 230, 298
Russitano, Tony, 230
Russo, Anna Izzo, 184
Russo, Antonio, 184
Russo, Emilia, 184
Russo, Richard, 274
Russo, William, 184

S
Sabella, Antonio, 108
Sabino, Helen Vellani, 229
Sacco, Fernanda, 301
Sacco, Francesco Rosario, 47
Sacco, Nicola, 22, 173, 188, 212, 301
Sacramento, California, 81, 162,
    226, 235
Salaparuta, Trapani, 134, 154, 287
Salerno, Emily, 200
Salerno, Frank, 200
Salerno, Tony, 200
Salerno, Italy, 123, 176, 193, 280, 282
Salida, Colorado, 269
Salto Canavese, Torino, 116
Sammartino, Bruno, 126
San Basile, Cosenza, 146
San Cataldo, Caltanisetta, 113, 227
San Fili, Cosenza, 200
San Francisco, California, 11, 50, 52,
    56, 108, 116, 119-21, 167, 170-71,
    173-74, 190, 204, 213, 233, 251,
    261, 281, 292

San Giovanni Rotondo, Foggia,
    77, 225
San Joaquin Valley, California,
    151, 154
San Jose, California, 133, 149, 174
San Marco, Foggia, 112
San Martino al Tagliamento, Porde-
    none, 91, 148
San Massimo, Molise, 35
San Pietro Arvellana, Molise, 35
San Sebastiano al Vesuvio, Napoli, 209
San Valentino Torio, Salerno, 238
San Vito da Capo, Palermo, 169
San Vito di Cadore, Veneto, 30
Sanfillipo, Larry, 140
Sansepolcro, Arezzo, 307
Sant'Angelo Lodigiano, Lodi, 158
Sant'Elia, Palermo 167
Sant'Olcese, Liguria, 60
Santa Maria, Benevento, 84
Santa Maria del Giudice, Lucca, 31,
    74, 223, 269
Santo Stefano di Camastra, Messina, 47
Sarno, Campania, 171, 289
Sartori, Verna, 236
Sartorio, Brigida, 192
Sartorio, Chiarina, 192
Sartorio, Giacomo, 192
Sartorio, Pio, 192
Sartoris, Charles, 87
Sartoris, Peter, 87
Sassinoro, Benevento, 223
Saudino, Domenico, 190
Sault Ste. Marie, Ontario, 127
Savaglio, Ben (Benedetto Domenico
    Luigi Alfano), 190
Savaiore, Lombardia, 139
Savarino, Giorgio, 77
Savarino, Rosaria, 77
Savona, Liguria, 41
Scala, Francesco, 293
Scalia, Justice Antonin, 245, 275
Scanno, Giovanna Zari, 183
Scapagnini, Umberto, 304
Scarcello, Angelo, 53
Scarcello, Franco, 288
Scarpaci, Antoinette, 286
Scarpaci, Francesco, 4
Scarpaci, Tommaso, 96
Scarpelli, Antonio, 201
Scarpelli, Louise, 201
Scarpelli, Salvatore, 201
Scarpitti, Rev. Fortunato, 166

Schettini, Fabio, 242
Sciacca, Agrigento, 30, 106
Sciara, Palermo, 194
Sciorra, Anna, 228
Sciorra, Enrico, 228
Sciorra, John, 228
Sciorra, Joseph, 228, 276
Sciorra, Nicholas, 228
Scoca, John, 187
Scorci, Olinto, 105
Scorsese, Martin, 260
Scorsone, Vito, 247
Scottoline, Lisa, 271
Scranton, Pennsylvania, 113, 120,
    163, 204, 262
Seattle, Washington, 41, 85, 113,
    133, 136, 185, 202, 219, 227
Sebastiani, Samuele, 83, 152
Sellaro, Vincenzo, 234
Sengbusch, Vicki Tamburo, 299
Serene, Colorado, 212
Serini, Leo, 271
Serra Pedace, Cosenza, 155
Sestri Levante, Liguria, 135
Sharon, Pennsylvania, 228
Sheepsgulch, Montana, 135
Shire, Talia, 81, 128
Sienna, Italy, 117
Sinatra, Frank, 125
Sinclair, Upton, 210
Siracusa, Sicily, 169, 292
Sirey, Aileen, 244
Sirica, Judge John Joseph, 242
Sisson, Allen, 142
Sola, Fred, 108, 139
Sola, Roco, 139
Sonazzaro, Louis, 140
Sonazzaro, Romano, 140
Sonoma, California, 83
Soria, Regina, 80
Sorrenti, Caterina Ligato, 33
Sover, Trento, 285
Spadafora, Messina, 284
Spera, Casimiro, 80
Spezzano Albanese, Cosenza, 132
Spezzano della Grande, Cosenza, 140
Spinola, Francis, 20, 258
Spitelli, Nardy, 200
Spizzirri, Billy, 203
Spizzirri, Marion, 168
Spizzirri, Rev. Leo, 168
Spizzirri, Susan, 168
Spizzirri, William, 168

Spokane, Washington, 11, 53, 64, 107, 146, 231, 255
Springsteen, Bruce, 80
St. Louis, Missouri, 130, 203, 270, 279
St. Paul, Minnesota, 218, 264
Stagnitti, Amalia (Mary), 141
Stagnitti, Concetto, 50, 139, 141
Stagnitti, Giuseppe, 50
Stagno, Tony, 129
Stamford, Connecticut, 61, 181, 248
Stagno, Bologna, 98
Staten Island, New York, 51, 276
Stefanile, Felix, 274
Stella, Joseph 117
Stellino, Liborio, 302
Steubenville, Ohio, 125
Stevens, Connie (Concetta Ann Ingolia), 126
Stone Park, Illinois, 174
Strollo, Joanne L., 175
Succivo, Caserta, 215
Suffolk, Virginia, 80
Sulmona, L'Aquila, 155
Syracuse, New York, 39

T
Tachi, Antonia, 160
Tachi, Joseph, 160
Taggi, Rosalie, 204
Talese, Gay, 275
Tamburo, Concetta Annaloro, 146
Tamburo, Pietro, 146
Tampa, Florida, 150, 245, 263
Tangipahoa Parish, Louisiana, 152
Tanner, Marisa, 208
Tarantino, Salvatore, 108
Teitel, Jacob, 256
Teitel, Morris, 256
Teramo, Abruzzo, 187, 271
Termini Imerese, Palermo, 149, 154, 156, 161, 239
Terra, Franca, 287
Tesca, Carlo, 249
Tiberti, Jelindo, 139
Timmins, Ontario, 29
Tocca Casauria, Pescara, 39, 51, 87, 202
Toffoli, Vickie, 221
Toglia, Mario, 298
Toluca, Illinois, 226
Tom, Hoy, 246
Tonti, Dominic, 148
Tonti, Enrico (Henry) de, 10, 55

Tonti, Josephine, 148
Tontitown, Arkansas, 55
Torbole sul Garda, Trento, 37
Torchiati, Avellino, 184
Toronto, Ontario, 10, 35, 78, 80, 85, 112, 121, 128, 148, 175, 218, 243, 253, 281, 290
Torricella Peligna, Chieti, 75
Torricella Sicura, Teramo, 78
Tortorento Alto, Teramo, 184, 208
Toscanini, Arturo, 213
Totta, Andreana Ragosta, 111, 225
Totta, Luigi, 77, 225
Trail, British Columbia, 37, 44, 53, 237
Trani, Bari, 52
Trasolini, Elmo, 206
Trasolini, Luigi, 206
Travena, Fr. D., 162
Trebezzano, Salerno, 242
Trenton, New Jersey, 101, 110, 157, 189, 245
Tresca, Carlo, 196, 210-11, 249
Trevignano, Veneto, 29
Tribuani, Alfredo, 99
Tricarico, Matera, 43, 168
Trinidad, Colorado, 90, 108, 137-39, 210
Tropea, Antonio, 167
Truant, Mary D'Andrea, 148
Truant, Natale (Ned), 91, 148
Tua, Giovanni Battista, 58
Tummino, Vincent, 294
Tuono, Giulio, 165
Turano, Renato, 295
Turbigo, Milano, 196
Turida, Friuli-Venezia Giulia, 195

U
Ustica, Palermo, 50, 124
Utica, New York, 160, 169, 216
Uzzano, Pistoia, 48

V
Vacca, Mary, 202, 290
Vacca, Amalia, 227
Vacca, Giuseppe, 227
Vacca, Giuseppina, 227
Vacca, Madeline, 227
Vacca, Prisco, 227
Vacca, Salvatore, 227
Vacca, Vincenzo, 227
Vaccaro, Felix, 80
Vaccaro, Joseph, 80

Vaccaro, Lucca, 80
Val di Ledro, Trento, 118
Valenti, Girolamo, 201
Valentino, Rudolph, 80
Valerio, Alessandro Mastro, 67
Valle, Domenico, 78
Valli, Frankie, 80
Vallucci, Vincenzo, 90
Valstagna, Vicenza, 143
Vancouver, British Columbia, 178, 195, 206, 211
Vancouver, Washington, 64
Vanzetti, Bartolomeo, 22, 173, 188, 212
Varazze, Liguria, 141
Vardaro, Saverio, 218
Varese Ligure, La Spezia, 135
Varischetti, Andrew, 135
Vastola, Anthony P., M.D., 238
Vaughan, Ontario, 272, 283
Vecchiano, Danny, 170
Vecoli, Rudolph, 259, 261, 274, 296-97
Vellani, Emma, 72
Vellani, Helen, 72
Vellani, Leonida, 72
Vellani, Virginia, 72
Velleggia, Enrico, 129
Vendoglio, Treppo Grande, Udine, 272
Venice, California, 56
Venice, Italy, 56, 221
Venneri, Frank, 72, 178, 186
Venneri, Josephina, 72, 178
Ventura, Frank, 220
Ventura, Joe, 220
Ventura, Maria Cairo, 220
Ventura, Raffaella, 220
Venturi, Ken, 121
Verna, Ted, 107
Veroli, Frosinone, 121
Verrazzano, Giovanni da, 10
Versi, Lorsica, 68
Vespucci, Amerigo, 10
Vicenza, Italy, 54, 303
Viggiani, Antonietta, 290
Vignole Borbera, Alessandria, 64
Vignole Serrivale Scrivia, Alessandria, 134
Villafrati, Palermo, 152
Villamaina, Avellino, 204
Villella, Edward, 127
Villoni, Domenico, 193
Vinchiaturo, Campobasso, 144
Virginia, Minnesota, 158

Viscusi, Robert, 274
Visintainer, Adolfo, 164
Vitale, Constantino, 181
Vivaldi, Antonio, 85
Viviano, Frank, 268
Volino, Vito, 179
Volpe, Edmond, 183
Volpe, John, 279
Vullo, Carmellina, 289

W
Waldwick, New Jersey, 77, 111, 225, 289
Walla Walla, Washington, 57, 64, 72, 95, 143-44, 155, 160, 178, 186, 246, 263
Warren, Harry (Salvatore Anthony Guaragna), 268

Washington, D.C., 191, 244
Waterbury, Connecticut, 238
Wayne, Pennsylvania, 78
Welby, Colorado, 75
West Duluth, Minnesota, 158
Westbury, Connecticut, 242
White Castle, Delaware, 187
White Castle, Louisiana, 158
Wilkes-Barre, Pennsylvania, 80
Willowbrook, New York, 183
Wilmington, Delaware, 96, 99, 180, 182, 235
Woodbridge, Ontario, 229
Woonsocket, Rhode Island, 121

Y
Yakima, Washington, 73, 111
Ybor City (Tampa), Florida, 248

Youngstown, Ohio, 149

Z
Zaccardelli, Giuliano, 272
Zahller, Alisa, 277
Zambelli, Antonio, 181
Zambelli, George, 181
Zanco di Villadeati, Alessandria, 216
Zari, Angelo Bartolomeo, 115, 183
Zarrilli, John, 158
Zenatello, Giovanni, 291
Zulpo, Louis, 136
Zummo, Antonio, 268